A circular approach to architecture
ZHAW IKE

From the construction and real estate sectors

[Fig. 34] External view.
[Fig. 35] Central hallway with staircase.
[Fig. 36] Bedroom with exposed stone.
[Fig. 37] Plan of upper floor.
[Fig. 38] Axonometry.

[Fig. 1]   Granby Four Streets is an ongoing community-led project to rebuild Granby, a once lively multicultural area of Liverpool that had, after decades of failed regeneration efforts, almost been left to ruin. Working with the community land trust set up by residents in 2011, Assemble succeeded in renovating ten terraced houses on Cairns Street, establishing the Granby Workshop, which provides training for locals, and developing a public indoor garden for the use of residents.

[Fig. 2]   To compensate for the lack of practical experience in courses, a group of Parisian architecture students established an annual full-scale building festival in 2006, during which several hundred participants designed, built, and inhabited a temporary settlement over the course of four days. Today, the Bellastock team organizes reuse projects on various scales. Pictured here: the temporary kitchen at the 2015 Playmobile Festival.

[Figs. 3, 4]   Proposal for the reuse of an environmental catch basin watershed unit from Duteurtre's group into the skeleton of the abandoned San Cristoforo station of Milan, via a 5 × 5 m grid of lightweight residential modules. A full-size model of the proposed design was presented at the Venice Biennale in 2008.

'We ask an awful lot of our buildings these days … The costs — in particular the environmental costs — of such luxury are now just much too high.'

Reuse
in Construction

A Compendium
of Circular
Architecture

 PARK BOOKS

The concept of reuse can be compared with the practice of cross-referencing in typography: different pieces of content that reference each other, which usually takes place in the margins.

Throughout the main part of this book, the margin columns are defined vertically and horizontally by chapter and are colour coded.

The different layers of the content thus expand on and complement each other, so comparisons can be drawn and connections made—in short, they can be 'reused' for a maximized, comprehensive and multifaceted understanding of the topic of reuse.

Contents

↗ p. 5		Oya Atalay Franck	Foreword
↗ p. 7		Marc Angst, Guido Brandi, Eva Stricker	Introduction
↗ p. 11		Barbara Buser	Reuse!
↗ p. 17		Ákos Moravánszky	Circular materiality—key concepts in ecological construction

↗ p. 33 K.118 reportage Michel Massmünster

Hunting and gathering	↗ p. 35
Designing and joining	↗ p. 39
Testing and planning	↗ p. 42
Constructing and coordinating	↗ p. 46
Adapting, repairing, reinstalling	↗ p. 51

↗ p. 57 Essays

Eva Stricker	Reusers	↗ p. 59
Deborah Fehlmann	Where there's a will ...	↗ p. 79
François Renaud	Out of scarcity	↗ p. 95
Patric Fischli-Boson	Circular load-bearing structures	↗ p. 111
Guido Brandi	A circular approach to architecture	↗ p. 129

↗ p. 149 Discussion

Guido Brandi, Michaël Ghyoot, Pascal Hentschel, Arne Vande Capelle	New generalists, new specialists: Rotor and the practice of reuse in Belgium	↗ p. 151
Marc Angst, Kerstin Müller, Katrin Pfäffli, Michael Pöll, Eva Stricker	New paths toward net zero? Potentials for climate protection	↗ p. 165
Guido Brandi, Michael Eidenbenz, Nathanea Elte, Christian Kohler, Tina Puffert, Barbara Rentsch, Andreas Sonderegger, Cyrille Veron, Barbara Zeleny	Values and processes: Reuse from a developer perspective	↗ p. 177
Andreas Abegg, Marc Angst, Meinrad Huser, Eva Stricker	Uncharted legal territory: Reuse under Swiss law	↗ p. 189
Guido Brandi, Marc Loeliger, Alexis Ringli, Andreas Sonderegger, Eva Stricker	From part to whole and back again: Teaching reuse in architecture	↗ p. 197

↗ p. 213 K.118 case study

Component map	↗ p. 214
Component catalogue	↗ p. 216
Design and construction	↗ p. 233
Construction organization	↗ p. 238
Costs	↗ p. 248
Greenhouse gas emissions	↗ p. 256

↗ p. 265	Marc Angst, Guido Brandi, Barbara Buser, Marc Loeliger, Andreas Oefner, Alexis Ringli, Andreas Sonderegger, Eva Stricker	Eight theses
↗ p. 283	Andreas Sonderegger	Reuse in construction—a look ahead

Documentation

Creating K.118	↗ p. 289
K.118 plan set	↗ p. 313
ZHAW IKE: Teaching	↗ p. 323

Appendix

Circular construction—terminology	↗ p. 341
Biographies	↗ p. 342

Foreword

The Department of Architecture, Design and Civil Engineering at ZHAW, the Zurich University of Applied Sciences, sees itself as a driving force for future-oriented building design, using teaching and research to foster progressive thinking against the backdrop of a constantly changing building industry. Together with partners from professional practice, the department seeks to address and investigate various issues of great contemporary relevance. In the development of our Circular Construction research project, Andreas Sonderegger, Eva Stricker (project manager), and Guido Brandi of ZHAW's Institute of Constructive Design IKE worked closely with Barbara Buser, Marc Angst, and Michel Massmünster of baubüro in situ. This partnership came about thanks to the commission of Stiftung Abendrot, a Swiss pension fund, for an academic analysis of its 'K.118' redevelopment project. That evaluation, carried out in collaboration with an interdisciplinary group of experts, constitutes a major part of this book.

Our involvement is further proof of the department's commitment to exploring issues affecting not only the building sector but society as a whole, and to initiating forward-looking processes. In particular, we aim to teach our students methodological knowledge to meet tomorrow's challenges in the fields of building design, structural engineering, and construction economics, giving them the skills they need to contribute in a meaningful way. Students had the opportunity to engage with the K.118 project in different modules. Insights from these endeavours are also presented on the following pages, alongside individual essays by team members of IKE. *Reuse in Construction* makes an important contribution to the exploration of architectural and constructional aspects of reuse. My sincere thanks go to everyone who helped make it a success.

Oya Atalay Franck
Director Department of Architecture, Design and Civil Engineering, ZHAW

Marc Angst, Guido Brandi, Eva Stricker

Introduction

When the first tenants moved into the newly added upper storeys of the K.118 building on Winterthur's Lagerplatz in March 2021, it marked not just the culmination of an almost four-year planning and construction process but also the completion of a pilot project—largely set in motion by Barbara Buser—the likes of which had never been seen before in Switzerland. Commissioned by Stiftung Abendrot, baubüro in situ had set out to construct a building that would use reclaimed components wherever possible, a goal they pursued with unprecedented rigour.

At the client's request, the K.118 project was evaluated by the Institute of Constructive Design at ZHAW, the Zurich University of Applied Sciences. Under the umbrella of the institute's Circular Construction research project, Eva Stricker and Guido Brandi analysed the entire planning and construction process, liaising closely with Marc Angst and the baubüro in situ team. This evaluation, overseen by Andreas Sonderegger in his capacity as the institute's co-director, sought to address such questions as these: how can the reuse of building components, something once practised as a matter of course, be implemented in the context of our domestic construction industry? What constraints will it come up against? And what opportunities does it offer? With the aid of interdisciplinary experts, these questions were explored in four dossiers compiled between 2018 and 2021. Aided by ZHAW's Building Sector Platform, the work identified specific process requirements related to building component reuse and examined what consequences these had for how the project was organized, while ZHAW's Centre for Public Commercial Law was brought

Marc Angst, Guido Brandi, Eva Stricker

on board to help with legal issues. A detailed cost analysis, based on the cost accounting for the K.118 project, was drawn up with the aid of ZHAW's Building Sector Platform. Finally, the key question of potential savings in the amounts of energy used and greenhouse gas emissions produced in the course of the project was addressed in conjunction with the City of Zurich's Office for Sustainable Construction and the sustainability expert Katrin Pfäffli, whose study 'Graue Energie und Treibhausgasemissionen von wiederverwendeten Bauteilen' is based on this analysis. Obviously, these in-depth explorations of a single test case are no substitute for broad-based, empirical research. But until enough built examples exist for such research to take place, the K.118 building, an experimental pilot project completed under real-world conditions, remains exceptionally valuable. Firstly, it offers direct insights into the specific processes required for, and problems encountered in, component reuse and thus allows us to examine the potential consequences for future developments in construction. Secondly, it can help us to swiftly gain a realistic picture of how building component reuse might contribute to the climate action we so urgently require.

From our evaluation, it's clear that, even with the situation as it is, component reuse can indeed make a contribution to climate protection, and a significant one at that. The K.118 project offers further evidence that dramatically extending the service life of building elements, either via preservation of the existing fabric or via reuse elsewhere, is absolutely key. This, though, is not the end of our architectural learning process but the beginning. For high-quality, forward-looking architecture to be created from reused components under current conditions, we not only require solutions to technical and procedural problems, we also need a thorough examination of the constructional and architectural aspects of such reuse. While K.118 was taking shape on Lagerplatz, a rethink in architectural education was taking place next door at ZHAW's Institute of Constructive Design. Since then, the institute has, alongside its well-established work with existing buildings, also been focusing increasingly on the reuse of building components, addressing questions such as these: to what extent can component reuse serve as an urban renewal strategy? What spatial opportunities are opened up by components designed for other building types? What kind of architectural expressions result when materials and components at differing life-cycle stages are combined in meaningful, reparable ways? Since 2018, the institute has run a series of design courses, led by Andreas Sonderegger, Marc Loeliger, Alain Roserens, and Alexis Ringli, with support from Eva Stricker and Guido Brandi, exploring the architectural and constructional potential of building component reuse.

In addition to research findings and coursework, this book also features a range of individual author contributions, among them an essay on the historical context by guest author Ákos Moravánszky, which delves into the background of building component reuse through time. This is followed by the main body of the book, whose colour-coded chapters explore the subject of reuse from four different angles. First, the K.118 reportage ↗ **p. 33** offers an inside view of the project's development, cultural anthropologist and urban researcher Michel Massmünster having accompanied those directly involved and provided a journalistic record of his observations. Then comes a series of Essays ↗ **p. 57** in which members of ZHAW's Department of Architecture, Design and Civil Engineering consider specific architectural and constructional facets of, and strategies for, component reuse and circular construction in general, looking beyond just the single example of K.118. These are accompanied by project profiles that not only document the featured examples but also bring together useful points of reference. The subsequent Discussion ↗ **p. 149** section is a record of conversations focusing on key aspects of component reuse. Participants included reuse practitioners, developers, and architecture teachers, as well as the experts in their field who contributed to the K.118 project's academic evaluation and thus to ZHAW's Circular Construction research. The results of that evaluation are documented in the chapter K.118 case study ↗ **p. 213** in the form of diagrammatic double-page spreads—

a useful tool for others intending to plan and build projects involving reclaimed components.

These different sections were developed successively and created in parallel with the planning and construction of the K.118 project. Taken together, they underline the breadth of ways in which building component reuse affects architectural practice and emphasize that, in all areas of the building sector, measures need to be taken to foster the integration of reuse. Despite the diversity of the issues raised and perspectives represented in the various texts, it is striking how often they connect with and loop back to each other. In the coloured margins of the main body of text, we have therefore included cross references to related aspects in other chapters—so that you can practice circular thinking already while reading this book.

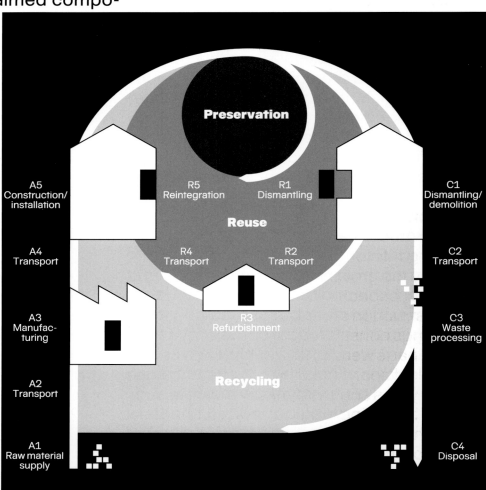

Circular construction

Circular construction means giving new usage cycles to the fabric of buildings, thereby allowing their actual lifespan to be exploited to the full. In the model shown here, the smaller the cycles become, the lower the loss of environmental, economic, and cultural assets, and the more circularity and architecture become intertwined. Recycling building waste into new material such as recycled concrete or steel is primarily a question of processing that has only peripheral relevance to design and planning. By contrast, the reuse and reusability of entire building components, like the repair, repurposing, and extension of existing buildings and parts of buildings, are genuine architectural challenges in which every aspect of sustainability needs to be considered. In this book, we have used the umbrella terms 'preservation', 'reuse', and 'recycling' for those three cycles, though each of these terms can be differentiated depending on their different contexts (i.e. with regard to environmental impact, economics, cultural significance, etc.). The above diagram also shows how the various phases of reuse (R1, R2, R3, R4, R5) fit into this life cycle model, which is based on the SN EN 15804+A1/SIA 490.052+A1 norms and underpins the environmental footprint assessment of Swiss buildings.
• Preservation ('Erhalt'): the in situ retention of the fabric of buildings or parts of buildings in order to extend their usage.
• Reuse ('Wiederverwendung'): the reutilization of building components irrespective of any divergence in quality standards between their original and new usage contexts (these may be dismantled and reclaimed or surplus items, processed or unprocessed, and either repurposed or used as per their original function).
• Recycling ('Verwertung'): the conversion of building material into new materials or products via processes in which their original form is broken down (such as shredding or melting).
↗ **p. 341** Circular construction–terminology

Barbara Buser
Reuse!

After working for ten years as a development expert in Africa, I returned to Switzerland in 1991. Following this long absence, I was especially struck by the growing throwaway mentality in all realms, especially in my area of expertise, the construction sector: increasing numbers of buildings constructed of high-quality materials and parts were being demolished, and the materials discarded or carted off to landfills. Salvage yards and material storehouses such as those belonging to the firms Musfeld in Basel, Abbruch Honegger in Zurich, or Kappeler in Berne no longer existed. Only Martin Hiltbrunner, a demolition and dismantling contractor in Riedtwil, had retained his large storage yard in the countryside. Instead, a new phenomenon was on everyone's lips: the internet.

Building component exchanges in Switzerland

In Africa I had learned that one person's waste can be valuable raw material for others. To make that possible, supply and demand must be brought together via a platform with broad reach. What could be more fitting than to use the new medium of the internet to do so? After all, the period between deciding to demolish a building and carrying out the actual demolition could be used as 'storage time'. This eliminates storage costs, and the building parts only need to be handled and transported once—they can be transferred from the demolition site directly to their new place of use without intermediate storage.

Therefore, together with Klara Kläusler, I founded the component exchange Buser & Kläusler in 1995 and, in 1996, Bauteilbörse Basel as well as the corresponding umbrella organi-

A sign reads 'All windows to give away ... plus brand-new shutters for sale!' while building marker poles signal imminent construction work.

zation, Bauteilnetz Schweiz. We developed a database to enable us to offer building components via the internet, just like eBay, tutti, and Salza did later. The idea of the Bauteilbörse (Building Component Exchange) was to use the new medium to broker components—but not to dismantle, store, or transport them ourselves.

Even though the idea was well received, it was far from able to cover its costs. All the telephone enquiries meant we could hardly get any work done. Basel's Office for Environment and Energy provided us with unemployed specialists who were able to answer the phone and provide information.

With this type of building component procurement, we succeeded in finding a new use for about 10 per cent of the parts offered. However, given the outlay involved, this amount was too meagre. We realized that it is not enough to offer building parts virtually. Those looking for building parts wanted to see them for themselves, measure them, touch them, and preferably take them straight away.

We therefore coupled the idea of building component reuse with one of the nascent job creation programmes for the unemployed, and this combination developed into a successful business concept: with the allotted personnel, we were able to dismantle, store, clean, inspect, and resell components ourselves. Over the years that followed, more than 24 building component exchanges, shops, and markets—all non-profit organizations that make building parts available for reuse—were established in Switzerland based on this model, and the umbrella organization Bauteilnetz Schweiz continues to develop and operate the internet platform www.useagain.ch for distribution purposes.

Building component reuse in Europe

Architects all over Europe also came up with similar ideas. Be it in Bremen, Berlin, Paris, Rotterdam, Brussels, Copenhagen, London, or Vienna, young specialists everywhere were thinking about what and how to build with discarded building materials and elements. Internet platforms, warehouses, and department stores emerged, along with spectacular

[Figs. 2, 3]   Bauteilbörse Basel

examples of building with used parts of buildings. Architects everywhere take inspiration from empty factories and attempt to rescue existing buildings by finding new uses for the old walls. Beneath the map of Europe, a selection is provided—albeit incomplete—of players sorted according to their specific offerings.

Building component reuse in Switzerland

In Switzerland, too, the idea of reuse has been pushed further. In 2012, Daniel Glauser launched the platform www.useagain.ch for brokering individual parts of entire properties designated for demolition, and in 2016, on behalf of the Federal Office for the Environment (FOEN), Olivier de Perrot created www.salza.ch, a new platform for the reuse of building components. In 2020, the non-profit association Bauteilnetz was renamed Cirkla; in the future it will represent the interests of all players involved in component reuse.

All these initiatives have the stated goal of producing less waste, protecting resources, and saving CO_2, and they revolve around reuse as part of the circular economy.

In contrast to the Swiss building component exchanges, however, most organizations elsewhere in Europe do not simply broker used building parts one for one, but instead create new things from the old parts and materials, which they combine to create unexpected building elements; they devise means of processing, design buildings, and plan cities. Thus, they outperform Switzerland's staid component exchanges. Today, it is no longer enough to salvage building components and simply reuse them in the same form and function. The fit is too poor for that. The available materials have to be carefully dismantled, transformed, reinstalled, and placed in a different context. This gives rise to a new language of architecture: an architecture of reuse; an architecture that creates the new from the existing, that reassembles and reinterprets things. In the future, the sources of

European region
• As early as 1993, Emanuele Almagioni, Giacomo Borella, and Francesca Riva founded Studio Albori in Milan, a combination of architectural practice and workshop that engages in preservation, repair, and reuse. ↗ **pp. 130, 143**
• In the German cities of Bremen, Berlin, Hanover, Gronau, Cologne, Herzogenrath, Augsburg, and elsewhere, various building component exchanges based on the Swiss model have been established since 2002. The Bundesverband Bauteilnetz Deutschland e.V. was founded in 2010.
• In Rotterdam as early as 2005, Superuse Studios developed an internet platform and their 'Harvest Map' to promote the reuse of building materials. In 2017, Superuse converted a former indoor pool into the BlueCity offices, with space for roughly 100 desk workers.
• Since 2005, the collective Rotor has been working in Brussels with salvaged building components. In addition to interior fit-out work, architectural consulting, and developing the online network Opalis, Rotor Deconstruction's portfolio has also included the dismantling and sale of used building parts since its founding in 2016. ↗ **p. 151**
• In 2010, the Bellastock association, whose members regard waste as a resource and are concerned with circularity in the building sector, was founded in Paris. They seek to establish synergistic ties between demolition and new-build projects in a region. ↗ **p. 131** [fig. 2]
• Also in Paris, the architectural collective Encore Heureux conceived the exhibition Matière grise (Grey Matter) in 2014; it was also shown in Switzerland from 2017 on.
• In London, a group of young professionals joined forces to form Studio Assemble, a multidisciplinary collective that unites architecture, design, and art with reuse and do-it-yourself construction. ↗ **p. 131** [fig. 1]
• In Copenhagen, the Lendager Group, with its UP (Upcycling Product Development) and TCW (The Circular Way), has become the leading Danish architectural practice when it comes to reuse and waste minimization.
• In Vienna, Materialnomaden have been assisting building owners since 2016 to identify reuse potential and make components available in the re:store.
• In Berlin, the CRCLR House opened in 2016 as a centre for the circular economy.
• In Amsterdam, Thomas Rau established the Madaster Foundation in 2017 with the aim of thwarting waste in the building sector by registering and documenting products and materials (material passport).
• Since 2020, Concular UG of Stuttgart has been offering diverse services for circular construction.

building materials will no longer be standardized catalogues offering components from all over the world; instead, every demolition site will be an urban mine.

baubüro in situ and K.118

In 1998, together with Eric Honegger, I founded baubüro mitte for the purpose of converting the former Volksbank into Unternehmen Mitte, a lively urban meeting place in the heart of Basel. Later, in line with our agenda, we renamed the firm baubüro in situ. Since then, instead of designing new buildings, we have concentrated on renovations, interior fit-outs, rooftop additions, alterations, and conversions. For example, we took the idea of reuse to the next level, transferring it from individual components to entire buildings and sites—such as Gundeldinger Feld in Basel, Walzwerk in Münchenstein, and Lagerplatz in Winterthur.

The fact that this preservation and adaptive reuse also makes economic sense, or at least covers its costs, is demonstrated by the conversion of the former Gundeldinger Feld industrial site. The success of this project encouraged the Abendrot Foundation to purchase the Lagerplatz site in Winterthur. Again, the project's development follows the principle of preserving as much of the fabric of the buildings as possible, repurposing and continuing to use them instead of constructing new ones, and the commissioned architects are urged to reuse existing building components. A good example of this is the architect Valérie Waibel's fit-out of the porter's lodge, backpacker hostel, and studios in Building 190.

[Figs. 5, 6]   Gundeldinger Feld, Basel

As the Lagerplatz project's 11-year-long development process drew to a close, we decided as project managers to exploit the potentials for reuse as fully as possible in the last major conversion. As a prominent showcase project, the end portion of Hall 118 was to be built entirely from reused components—a huge challenge that baubüro in situ embraced in full awareness of the complexity of the undertaking. The Abendrot Foundation granted an advance of 500,000 Swiss francs to procure salvaged materials—on condition that the new building constructed out of second-hand materials would not be more expensive than a conventional new build. Another condition was that the project needed to be accompanied by academic research, which ultimately provided the stimulus for this book!

For the reuse community in Switzerland, the K.118 pilot project is of great importance. The plans and the first salvaged building parts were immediately shown in an exhibition at the Swiss Architecture Museum (S AM). Both Radio SRF and Swiss Television reported on the project before the building permit application was even submitted. Multiple articles and interviews appeared in various newspapers and professional journals.

During the search for components and the planning and construction of the K.118 project, we came to realize that reuse actually needs to be the focus of specific technical planning. Traditional architecture firms are unable to cope with the additional tasks posed by reuse. Thus, in 2020, baubüro in situ founded Zirkular GmbH, which, in the spirit of an open-source policy, passes on the experience and knowledge gained to all those interested, gives guidance to architects and clients, conducts lectures and presentations, and also serves on juries as an advocate for reuse.

Hardly anyone has enough expertise to be able to professionally dismantle, refurbish, and examine all types of building components. Only when efficient processes of reuse have been developed and tested for the widest range of building materials and trades can reuse become mainstream.

It's necessary to rethink

The Swiss construction sector currently produces 17 million tonnes of waste per year. The landfills are filling up rapidly. At the same time, we have been overexploiting our natural material resources for decades: as improbable as it sounds, even sand has fallen into short supply. The utilization of building materials through recycling can offset resource consumption and the volumes of waste entering landfills to a certain extent, but it does not address another fundamental problem of our construction sector: the massive consumption of energy and emission of greenhouse gases to manufacture new building components. If we want to emerge from this one-way street, we have to transform the linear processes into cycles. And this will only succeed if everyone involved in the construction sector—from building owners to banks to architects and construction companies—rethinks things. Right now!

It is not enough to build today in a way that enables buildings to be reused in 50 or 100 years.

It is not enough from now on just to combine homogeneous materials in such a way that they can be separated from each other again without destroying them.

It is not enough to record the materials used in a property register so that in 50 or 100 years they can serve as a repository of reusable material.

These are all valuable investments in the future, but they do not change the fact that we need forceful and effective measures right now:

Right now, we must stop replacing existing buildings with new ones.

Right now, we must pay attention to the grey energy in our buildings.

Right now, we must stop constructing new buildings with nothing but new building materials.

Right now, we must employ all our inventiveness and all our creative energy to ending the present squandering of raw materials and to drastically reduce the volumes of waste entering landfills!

Since the introduction of the Energy Act in 1984, we have focused all our efforts on reducing the operating energy of new buildings. And we have been so successful at it that we can build passive houses that no longer need additional energy to operate them. Now we need the same revolution in the construction of new buildings, and we need it in half the time. The construction of K.118 has proven that reuse is a path that can quickly lead to this goal.

Ákos Moravánszky

Circular materiality—key concepts in ecological construction

'Most works of man are at some point modified and transformed, be they insignificant trifles or "immortal" works of art. A woman might alter her old dresses, and even literature gets revised, dramatized, and set to music,' wrote Konstanty Gutschow and Hermann Zippel in the introduction to their 1932 book *Umbau*.[1] 'A conversion is more interesting than a new build—because, really, everything is conversion,' Hermann Czech added some 40 years later.[2] Although both Gutschow and Czech refer to the ubiquity of rebuilding, they also distance themselves from a modernism that is merely about 'expressing an external need to design'.[3] With its linear concept of time, its exclusive focus on the new, on the future, modernism sees 'the old' as being at best fit for the museum. Gutschow's comments on the works of man, on the other hand, point to a circular reading of time, especially when it comes to working with what's already there—and that includes reusing building components in new structures. It is, then, about more than just what is 'interesting': if everything is a form of conversion, as Czech says, then a new build could simply be a more interesting conversion. When architects make conversion their central focus, however, their aim is to address not just a physical structure but a process too: here, the built work is a place where materials, be they geological or technological in origin, intersect with images that, in turn, have their origins in art or architectural history, in films, or in literature. Everything is in a process of constant transformation or conversion—structures, cities, spaces, images, identities. Not only could appreciating the full implication of what that means give rise to interesting new solutions, it could also allow us to rethink architecture, to make it an integral part of what the Rhenish architect-mystic Rudolf Schwarz called 'the built Earth'.[4]

Expropriation: loot and spolia

In art history, building components that have been removed from their original setting and reused in a new structure are known as spolia. Originally the Latin word *spolia* referred to military spoils, primarily to weaponry seized from the enemy. This was not private plunder but trophies of war intended for public display. Similarly, spoliation, the removal of goods or parts of buildings from an earlier built setting, was a symbol of domination and subjugation used to demonstrate the victor's military and cultural superiority.

By the Middle Ages, the term spolia had come to incorporate not just plundered artworks and building fragments but reused building components as well. It was, in those days, almost impossible to get quality building stone in Rome, as all the ancient quarries had been abandoned. As a result, the Colosseum itself became a quarry, its stone being highly valued for its enduring quality and usable format, which saved time and labour.

Many of the buildings built in Rome in late antiquity were made almost entirely from spolia, among them the Santa Costanza church [fig. 1]. Where columns were salvaged from different sources, plinths of new stone were used to balance variations in height, while spolia were also often turned around, with uprights serving as horizontals and architraves as side supports. In those days, this pragmatic approach to valuable materials was ubiquitous:

Ákos Moravánszky

ivory panels were re-carved, and parchment sheets scraped clean to be written on anew. In such cases, greater value was attached to the material than to the art.

When discussing such spoliation, we need to distinguish between a pragmatic, material-driven approach and an ideological, meaning-based one. Examples of the former include medieval city walls in former Roman colonies, structures that were often built with stones taken from old cemeteries or temples. Here, spoliation was driven by a desire to save labour—aesthetic considerations were secondary at best. The rapid pace of development in medieval cities, meanwhile, could only be maintained by reusing timber. Likewise, the expansion and large-scale remodelling of European cities that took place in the 19th century depended on the reclamation of existing building material.

The ideological, meaning-based approach relies on the recognition of an object's commemorative values, to borrow art historian Alois Riegl's term: its art value, its historic value, and the sensory value of its material and workmanship. The aim was to harness these values and the original iconography within the new cultural and architectural setting. St Mark's Basilica in Venice is a common reference point for such an approach: its façade features columns and reliefs looted from Constantinople during the Fourth Crusade (1204), including the elaborately carved Pilastri Acritani [fig. 2], described by Ruskin as 'the two most noble pillars in Venice', and the porphyry sculpture group *Portrait of the Four Tetrarchs*. Probably the best-known example of medieval spolia, the latter was repurposed as a cornerstone of the basilica's façade, thereby underlining Venice's supremacy over Constantinople.[5] The public display of objects belonging to another place—and another era or culture— may be the bread and butter of today's museums and galleries, but back then it necessitated a great deal of effort; the objects in question were thus much admired by local citizens and their erection or installation accompanied by public rituals. The primary function of the tetrarch sculpture, then, isn't to serve as a cornerstone of the basilica or to present military spoils but to contribute to identity-building within the city.

The line between the pragmatic and the ideological, however, is fluid. Is the use of attractively worked stone, such as fluted antique column drums, in substructures and supporting walls, as seen in the Church of St Donatus in Zadar, Croatia, or in the Frankish fortress of Parikia [fig. 3] on the island of Paros, always a deliberate act of degradation, or can it, in fact, be an act of historic preservation? Created by architectural practice KARO and completed in 2009, Magdeburg's Lesezeichen Salbke [fig.4] is similarly ambiguous. With its façade featuring distinctive pressed aluminium panels salvaged from the demolished Horten department store in Hamm, Westphalia, this open-air library makes you wonder whether locals saw any irony in material from a temple to West German consumerism being transferred to a shrinking city in the once Communist East.

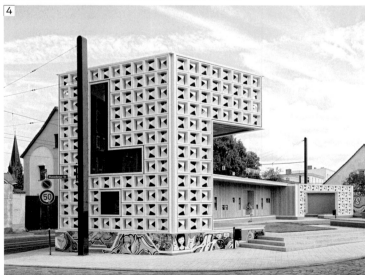

The looting of parts of old buildings is rarely a spontaneous act: in most cases, spoliation was something either permitted or proscribed by local leaders. Revolutions and wars have always been the chief creators of spolia. The French Revolution brought new impetus to the international trade in art from destroyed buildings. At its centre was the city of Rouen, from where glass windows, wooden carvings, and stone fragments from cathedrals were frequently sold via cloth trade networks to England's landed gentry.[6] Stone taken from monasteries in southern France, meanwhile, went into the construction of the courtyards from which the Cloisters, home to the medieval collection of New York's Metropolitan Museum of Art, takes its name; spolia from monasteries dismantled after the Revolution were bought by art collector George Grey Barnard around 1910, then shipped to America and in 1925 sold on to John D. Rockefeller, the patron behind the museum's new building. As recently as 1971, stones from the old London Bridge of 1836 were used to clad a concrete bridge over a channel leading to Lake Havasu, a reservoir in Arizona. Today, even examples of Americana such as distinctive building components or billboards and promotional mascots are salvaged from demolition sites and put into storage. [fig.5]

As the American economy boomed, a huge market for European spolia developed in the US. Even well-known architects such as Stanford White got involved, acting as advisers and sometimes as dealers too. Between 1919 and 1940, newspaper tycoon William Randolph Hearst, the biggest media mogul of his day and the real-life inspiration for Orson Welles's classic film *Citizen Kane*, had architect Julia Morgan build him a fairy-tale palace—La Cuesta Encantada—in San Simeon, California. [fig.6] Hearst's agents, who nicknamed him the Great Accumulator, bought him European cloisters, patios, building ornaments, and coffered ceilings—primarily from Spain and Italy—which were then integrated into Hearst Castle.[7] The incorporation of Spanish spolia brought Iberian flair to the vast estate, Iberian culture being something that then loomed large in the Californian imagination. Ensconced beneath his mighty Spanish coffered ceiling, Hearst must have felt like he was at the epicentre of power, the sensationalist reporting in his newspapers having whipped up public sentiment for the war against Spain (1898).

Small wonder, then, that an American newspaper felt moved to festoon its own seat with spolia: embedded into the base of Tribune Tower [fig.7], built for the *Chicago Tribune* by John Mead Howells and Raymond Hood (1923–1925), are around 150 fragments of famous buildings that the *Tribune*'s correspondents collected from across the globe. Today, the spolia also include a piece of steel from the destroyed World Trade Center, a reminder of the consequences of war, destruction, and expropriation. Although the looting of archaeological sites is now forbidden, destruction and spoliation still figure among the tragic consequences of demonstrations of power, be it in Iraq, Afghanistan, or Syria. The artworks and fragments thus plundered cannot be shown in public, meaning they often vanish into private collectors' safes.

Appropriation: Constructing identities

Spoliation, though, is not just expropriation but appropriation too, with new owners seeking to harness the illustrious lineage of their spoils. Appropriators of stone from the Roman Empire thus sought to associate themselves with imperial glory, while Christian conquerors who broke up heathen idols and removed them from their original context did so both to rid them of their power and to harness their beauty for their own religious purposes. Ancient sarcophagus lids featuring heathen cult imagery, for instance, were incorporated into church walls, providing an apparent incongruity with the Christian setting while also demonstrating Christian culture's capacity for assimilation.

A particularly notable example of appropriation is when an entire structure is subsumed into a later one, the old building becoming a constituent part of the new. Rome's Theatre of Marcellus from 13 BC [fig.8], for instance, was transformed into a medieval fortress and later converted into a palazzo for the Savelli family in the 16th century. Built around AD 300, the Palace of Diocletian became the town of Split in the Middle Ages and still forms the heart of the Croatian coastal city today, while the Baths of Diocletian in Rome were turned into the Basilica of St Mary of the Angels by Michelangelo and Vanvitelli. In 16th-century Córdoba, a new cathedral [fig.9] was inserted into the old Umayyad mosque, a building that itself already contained numerous even older spolia. Rimini's Tempio Malatestiano [fig.10], created by Leon Battista Alberti between 1450 and 1460 as a mausoleum for Sigismondo Malatesta and his lover, was built around a Gothic church from the 13th century. And Frank Gehry's 1977/78 conversion of his Santa Monica residence [fig.11] extends and surrounds a detached house from the 1920s. Gehry, however, also opened up the original house with a brutality that calls to mind the 'splittings' of Gordon Matta Clark, while additions made of chain-link fencing and corrugated steel were viewed as similarly aggressive interventions by the architect's neighbours. Architecture critics interpreted the house as an architectural psychogram, calling it 'the house that built Gehry'.[8]

Even more noteworthy are spolia that serve not to enhance personal mythologies but rather to root a new building in local and national architectural history. Built between 1911 and 1923, Ragnar Östberg's Stockholm City Hall [fig.12] is a key example of Scandinavia's National Romantic style. In 1912, the planning committee asked the architect to salvage components and objects from condemned buildings that would capture the aspect and history of the city.[9] The wood from which the entrance was carved thus came from a 17th-century Swedish battleship that had recently been recovered from the fjord, while other spolia such as wall fountains, baroque portals, and wooden ceilings documented different phases in the city's development.

For his pathways on Philopappos Hill opposite the Acropolis (1951–1957), Greek architect Dimitris Pikionis devised an imagined archaeological site comprising 'established' landscape elements, ancient fragments, and newly built structures, though he often let his craftsmen decide on the detail execution. Pikionis also built a small church dedicated to Saint Demetrius Loumbardiaris, incorporating stone from a neoclassical school building and the remains of a chapel. The overall effect was to create a rich tapestry of artefacts spanning antiquity and the present day. [figs.13, 14]

After the Second World War, East and West Germany pursued differing strategies when it came to dealing with the rubble of their bombed-out cities. Their approaches, however, were similarly pragmatic: serviceable girders, beams, and bricks were salvaged and incorporated into new buildings; the rest was used to fill in cellars or piled up in parks, with now mostly landscaped 'rubble hills' [fig.16] created in major cities from Dresden to West Berlin. Where the 'ideological' utilization of spolia in the GDR—as with the integration of the former Royal Palace's 'Liebknecht portal' [fig.17] into the governing State Council's headquarters in Berlin—was a good fit with the regime's Socialist Realism doctrine and its commitment to national and local building traditions, West Germany favoured a clean break with the past and therefore opted for pragmatic modernization. It's true that Hans Döllgast incorporated bricks from war debris when rebuilding a bomb-damaged wall at Munich's Alte Pinakothek, but his renovation also used concrete and steel in place of stone pillars and capstones.

At Gibellina Nuova in Sicily, spolia even helped to shape the identity of a whole new town. After the original town of Gibellina was razed by an earthquake in 1968, Italian artist Alberto Burri covered the ruins with a crust of white cement (1984–1989), while architect Francesco Venezia gave the new town an exhibition space (1980–1987) in which the remains of a stone façade from Palazzo di Lorenzo are embedded within a concrete body. [fig.15]

Post-reunification Germany's veneration of spolia is, therefore, somewhat paradoxical. There were calls for the rebuilt palace's façade to get its 'Liebknecht portal' back (like a copy of a Roman marble bust gaining the original nose), to thus give the reconstruction a stamp of authenticity—though the very name Liebknecht connects it to the GDR era. In a similar desire for authentication, original stone was incorporated into the reconstruction of both the Church of Our Lady in Dresden and the rebuilt façade of Braunschweig Castle, which had been demolished in 1960, while spolia have also been used to lend credibility to the reconstruction of Frankfurt's Old Town. It was important for the identity of a city, claimed architect Christoph Mäckler, that 'surviving original façade elements, so-called spolia, are reintegrated so as to reveal something of the history of the place'.[10] The city's urban planning department subsequently set up a website to catalogue existing Old Town spolia for use in this act of 'urban rehabilitation'.

Assemblage, bricolage, adhocism

The appropriation of building components for use in another setting requires a methodology based on what is to hand, one that thus has to embrace spontaneity and chance. This alternative creative method differs from the modern-day planning model, which aims to leave nothing to chance. In his 1962 book *La Pensée Sauvage* (published in English as *The Savage Mind* in 1966), French anthropologist and ethnologist Claude Lévi-Strauss described the principle of bricolage as the opposite of an engineer's 'domesticated' mode of thought;[11] rather than following some precisely formulated plan, a bricoleur improvises on the basis of the available resources, drawing on a diverse range of materials, objects, debris, and fragments. This idea was at the core of Charles Jencks and Nathan Silver's 1972 Adhocism manifesto [fig. 18], which set out a pluralist, non-determinist, and anti-elitist vision of architecture and design.[12]

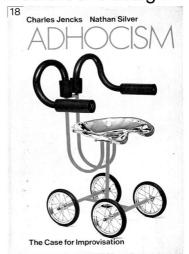

The idea of an architecture that incorporates chance into the design process had already been postulated by Austro-Swedish architect Josef Frank in his 1958 treatise 'Accidentism': 'Every place in which we feel comfortable—rooms, streets, and cities—has originated by chance,' he declared.[13] In the essay, Frank offers a trenchant critique of how dogmatic modernism has become. There were, however, still modernist architects applying bricolage principles.

Best known for his 1931 Maison de Verre in Paris, which he designed for the doctor Jean Dalsace, Pierre Chareau also built a 1946 studio [fig. 19] in East Hampton, Long Island, for the American avant-garde painter Robert Motherwell, using military shelters, known as Quonset huts, that were available at low cost from the army. The shelters were made of semicircular steel supports clad in corrugated metal sheets; Chareau had sections of the metal sheets cut away, fitting industrial greenhouse windows that acted as skylights.[14]

With his Casa Garelli in Champoluc, meanwhile, Carlo Mollino built what architectural historian Sergio Pace described as a 'ready-made assemblage'.[15] The structure was created between 1963 and 1965 using wood from a dismantled *rascard*, a traditional local grain store, that had stood on the opposite side of the Aosta Valley. ↗ **pp. 61, 74**

The economic slump of the 1970s and, in particular, the oil crisis of 1973 gave new impetus to the search for architectural alternatives to society's throwaway culture. Around 1978, one-third of North American architects' income was coming from adaptive reuse, i.e. from the conversion of old buildings using their serviceable components, as creatives followed Andy Warhol's lead and moved into abandoned factories.[16] Publications such as Steve Baer and Lloyd Kahn's *Shelter* or the *Whole Earth Catalog* spread the bricolage principle around the world. Creative recycling became the watchword for architects such as Michael Reynolds, who used metal canisters, tyres, glass bottles, or car body parts as building materials [fig. 20]. In 1973, British magazine *Architectural Design* dedicated its December issue [fig. 21] to the subject of 'garbage housing', publishing a long article by Martin Pawley, for whom the key to social and ecological housing lay not in individual-scale bricolage, but in the development of a technically advanced usage of consumer waste: 'In the developed countries of the West, housing can only achieve the universality which has so long eluded it, by moving its resource base from that which is scarce and costly to that which is not only plentiful and cheap, but ubiquitous and valueless.'[17] This alternative architecture not only aimed to make housing more socially and environmentally responsible, it also combined pragmatic solutions for waste reuse with the pursuit of an appropriate aesthetic.

Today, the aims of the alternative architecture movement of the 1970s are being pursued by groups such as Rural Studio. Founded by Samuel Mockbee in 1992 in Hale County, a deprived area of Alabama, it mostly consisted of students from the Auburn University, who each spent one semester there. Run by Andrew Freear since Mockbee's death in 2001, the studio rebuilds houses using materials such as hay, car tyres, and windscreens; its 2002 design for Lucy's House [fig. 22] even has walls made of 72,000 carpet tiles.

The subversiveness that avant-garde artists' loft apartments once represented lives on in the attitudes of many eco-activists, though it also increasingly shapes the kind of brownfield projects where investment potential lies.[18] Crumbling plasterwork, an aura of degradation, what Riegl would call age-value, these things can be an attractive selling point. Architects such as Rem Koolhaas have demonstrated, however, that adaptive reuse does not have to retain an air of ruin: instead, their successful transformations show that, via intelligent interventions, former industrial sites can provide new, attractive, and easily accessible urban spaces—see, for instance, Milan's Fondazione Prada [fig. 23].

In socialist states, adhocism was a necessity: their state-run construction industries didn't get involved in the building of single-family houses and so self-build was commonplace. Alongside new supplies, whose availability was limited, self-builders also utilized material from demolitions. The heavy prefab components favoured by the construction industry, on the other hand, rarely featured, as machinery would have been required to install them; there were nonetheless cases of small properties being built with prefab concrete panels—panels that were manufactured for housing estates but also found their way into private hands.

State socialism's debris, meanwhile, provided the building material for Alexander Brodsky's poetic structures. His Pavilion for Vodka Ceremonies (2004) consisted solely of 83 windows from a demolished factory [fig. 24], while his Rotunda was made out of old doors (2009). 'It was an experiment in space and an attempt to save some beautiful things',[19] the architect explains. ↗ **pp. 68, 77**

Simulacra, virtual spolia

The ability of spolia to provide historical associations has led architects from the Renaissance on to use virtual spolia. Architecture historians disagree as to whether the granite columns of Bramante's Tempietto in Rome are ancient spolia that were reworked at a later date or whether the architect used granite from various quarries in order to give the work a deeper historical dimension.

Rome is the city for spolia both real and virtual. Piranesi's fantastical designs combined fragments retrieved from the Pontanello marshes with details from other eras of imperial art, all of which he transferred onto *piccole architetture* such as fireplaces. Despite their modest size, these bricolages invoke the magnificence of ancient Rome. Luigi Moretti (1907–1973) also realized major projects in Milan, but his Casa Girasole (1947–1950) could only be in Rome, the radically split façade, which affords glimpses of the building's interior, expressing the presence and potency of the Eternal City's past. The tragically fragmented body and travertine base displaying fragments reminiscent of archaeological finds [fig. 25] can only be understood in connection with the still recent experience of the Second World War.

25

The town hall that Dutch architect F. P. J. Peutz built in Heerlen from 1936 to 1942 [fig. 26] also exhibits virtual spolia. A concrete structure with brick infill, its pale limestone-clad exterior is largely unornamented, but there are echoes of spolia in the main façade's heavy ceremonial balcony, which bears darker stone and a moulded edge, and in the two free-standing columns connected to the side wall by architraves. Peutz lectured in the history of classical architecture in Maastricht and also worked in heritage conservation—he led the reconstruction of the city's Roman baths in the 1940s.[20]

Often, building components are re-used for reasons of economy, in order to conserve scarce resources. Sometimes, though, salvage is about glut rather than scarcity, with the many salvaged objects not merely being preserved but also displayed so that the new building resembles a kind of museum of building components. This is reflected in the work of Alison and Peter Smithson. In the post-war period, their 'As Found' philosophy offered 'a new perspective on the commonplace, an openness towards the way entirely prosaic things can reinvigorate our powers of invention'.[21] In the 1990s, the Smithsons designed buildings for clients who had to live with a glut of assembled objects, calling their new concept of creating flexible homes whose elements, doors, and windows can be relocated 'conglomerate ordering'. Their Put-Away House [fig. 27], built between 1993 and 2000, and their Hexenhaus, designed for furniture manufacturer Axel Bruchhäuser, both date from this period. ↗ **pp. 63, 75**

26

27

Durability, obsolescence, sustainability, circularity

Architecture is an expression of humankind's pursuit of immortality. Buildings outlast people; not subject to the boundaries of human mortality, they symbolize permanence. The veins of marble indicate geological time, the grouting of brickwork suggests the rhythmic action of bricklaying, the bolt heads of an iron girder hint at the staccato action of machinery. Architecture is a combination of time and material—time both in terms of historic era and of its ability to endure. Our understanding of durability is indivisible from our understanding of time and material. Indeed, the word endure comes from the Latin *durare*, which originally meant harden (from *durus* for hard) and later came to mean last or persist.

But while hardness is a measurable quantity, durability is a relative concept. For the Slovenian architect Jože Plečnik, *architectura perennis* was a question of form: it is thus the continuity of classicism's visual language and of its rural vernacular transformations that imbues architecture with meaningful function, even if the material traditions of its constituent parts may vary. For his part, Plečnik used concrete sewer pipes as supports in his Church of St Michael [fig. 28] in the Ljubljana Marshes (built 1937/38 and fitted out in 1940), thereby showing that, with the right treatment and usage, even the most profane object can be made sacred. A later example of the reuse of material sourced from infrastructure is the communal residence at the Seitogakushi School [fig. 29], which was designed by Japanese architect Shin Takasuga and completed in 1980. Built by the school's students on the small island of Miyake, it was constructed entirely from around 5,000 wooden railway sleepers; the repurposed sleepers forming not only the supporting walls but also the roof truss and internal fixtures.[22] Be it sewer pipes or railway sleepers, here we find humble materials, infrastructure components that had played no prior part in architecture, being turned into enduring built works.

By the 19th century, the pursuit of durability was coming into conflict with the interests of industrial capitalism. Chicago's Marshall Field Wholesale Store [fig. 30], built by Henry Hobson Richardson in 1886 and a fixture of architectural chronicles of the modern age, is regarded as the epitome of enduring architecture: the surviving photographs seem to show a building that is both durable in its actual materials and enduring in its architecture. The solid brick walls clad in red Missouri granite; the stark façade with its structure reminiscent of Florentine Renaissance palaces or Roman viaducts; the huge size, and the rough, almost geological appearance of its granite blocks—all this was much admired at the time. And yet, ten years after its completion, the building had already become obsolete, both in its function as an inner-city wholesale outlet and in its construction, the combination of vast bulk and weak foundations quickly leading to uneven settlement. The store was soon pulled down, and those much-admired granite blocks were recycled as fill for the levelling of a new parking lot.

Ákos Moravánszky

As a booming centre of trade and commerce, Chicago was seeing accelerating production and consumption cycles. Hardly surprising, then, that it was here, in around 1900, that obsolescence, the phenomenon of products becoming outdated or redundant, first drew the attention of researchers and theoreticians. It was experiences such as this that led to the coining of the term 'creative destruction', which economist Joseph Schumpeter identified in 1942 as an essential fact of modern capitalism.[23] By the late 1950s, the criticism of obsolescence as a feature of America's throwaway society was growing louder.[24] As a consequence, preservationism took on a greater significance, leading to buildings that were deemed historically important being rescued and restored, then equipped with museum shops and opened to the public. Of perhaps greater significance was the opposition that came from the counter-culture movement, which took its cue from the vernacular tradition presented in Bernard Rudofsky's successful 1964 exhibition *Architecture Without Architects* at New York's MoMA. While 1970s alternative architecture was mentioned earlier in conjunction with adhocism and bricolage, of greater relevance today are those practitioners who took their cue more from minimal or conceptual art, who were interested not in tinkering but in painstakingly developing sustainable solutions.

The motto of Peter Zumthor's competition project for the Swiss pavilion [fig. 31] at EXPO 2000 in Hanover was 'Battery', though the completed structure became known as the 'Sound Box'. For Joseph Beuys, the battery epitomized the potential for energy to be stored— something he visualized via the combination of copper and felt and via his dense layering of cloth. As the book *Swiss Sound Box* notes: 'The word battery is used to illustrate the charged and synergetic interaction of materials.'[25]

Tasked with creating a national exhibition pavilion and thus with conveying a sense of identity, Zumthor responded not merely with images and symbols. For the pavilion's construction, 1,500 trees were cut down from woodland across 85 municipalities in 13 Swiss cantons, then sawn into timbers. These were held together with steel cables connected via spring tie rods, enabling them to be separated after the exhibition and reused elsewhere. In this case, identity and place are embodied by a representation of the commercial and ecological cycle of a commodity, namely of the energy source that is wood, which, in this temporary assemblage, is imbued with cultural value for the duration of the exhibition.

Of particular interest are the few cases where building components have been reused in an urban planning context. In 1938, Székesfehérvár, once the royal seat of the Kingdom of Hungary, hosted festivities to mark the International Eucharistic Congress, in preparation for which architect Iván Kotsis was charged with giving its historic Old Town a more harmonious overall look. Kotsis, an advocate of the moderate modernism associated with the Stuttgart School, interpreted his task as 'the knitting together of treasured old buildings within a coherent framework, via an ordering of the setting and an aesthetic overhaul'. He thus had wings of the town hall complex [fig.32] either demolished or extended via a new-build section; the closed bays of the demolished wing were relocated; while a nearby art nouveau façade, deemed too showy, was given a simpler look. The result was a delightful urban ensemble in which open and intimate courtyards are connected via external staircases.[26]

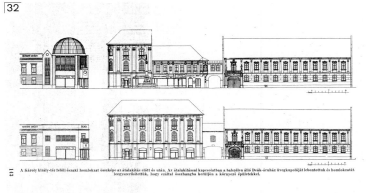

In the light of such projects, we need to rethink previous attitudes to identity of place. For Kevin Lynch, urban identity was primarily a consequence of clear orientation within a city, of the ability to comprehend its structure, i.e. to have a mental map,[27] while Christian Norberg-Schulz associated the genius loci with sensory perception.[28] The identity of Székesfehérvár as we know it today is indivisibly linked with the decisions taken by Kotsis. Here, rather than a strict preservationist approach that places existing buildings under a bell jar, we see a dynamic interpretation of enduringness characterized not by stasis or obsolescence but by ongoing metamorphosis, construction, and deconstruction. Such interventions demonstrate a 'curatorial' approach to the urban realm, in which things are picked out, juxtaposed with others, and appropriately orchestrated: the identity of a place is thus constructed via a deliberate and subjective selecting of materials and forms. It is, however, also possible for those forms and materials to break free from the curator's control so that unintended associations begin to develop, much as a painting in a gallery can interact with a hygrometer or a red fire extinguisher. Equally, meaningful connections can and do develop—often unintentionally—when architectural elements from different places and epochs are brought together in one place.

Such an orchestration of diverse things and eras can be seen at the house known as Dado, designed by Rudolf and Valerio Olgiati. Rudolf Olgiati collected spolia throughout his lifetime. In his polemic *Architekt*, he writes: 'I started systematically collecting cultural objects at the age of 20 in my home district of Flims, with the intention of returning each thing to its original place—something that, over the course of half a century, I have not succeeded in doing.'[29] In order to keep everything safe, to 'preserve it through bad times', he cleaned and catalogued these objects and stored them in a barn [fig.33].[30] The bulk of the collection later moved to Museum Olgiati in Flims, while Dado passed to Rudolf Olgiati's son Valerio, who established his architectural practice there. With its mix of spolia assembled and integrated by Olgiati senior and more recent fixtures and objects, the house can be seen as another example of the Smithsons' 'conglomerate ordering'. Rudolf himself highlighted the connections between Greek architecture, local vernacular traditions, and Le Corbusier's aesthetic—now Valerio has added another historical layer, as the monograph *Dado* makes abundantly clear.[31]

Both in Europe and Japan, the wholesale destruction experienced during the Second World War and the challenge of post-war reconstruction led architects to think about large-scale urban rebuilding. Japan's Metabolist movement perceived the city not as a finished entity but as a living organism that was undergoing constant metamorphosis. Rudolf Schwarz's book *Von der Bebauung der Erde* also dates from the last years of the war. It describes how natural and built landscapes merge, how the fabric of the Earth is transformed into building material. His Church of St Anna [fig. 34] in Düren (1951–1956) was built on the site of a Gothic church that had been destroyed during the war. When Schwarz visited the ruin, 'the old stone was still piled up there; we decided to reuse it for the brickwork of the new building so that the sacred stone could provide material for a new work, and the old be resurrected in the new.'[32]

This approach, albeit in a less explicitly religious form, was also adopted by Wang Shu for his museum in the Chinese city of Ningbo, which the architect built from the rubble of the surrounding villages [fig. 35]: 'The site chosen was typical for contemporary China: the original villages had all been torn down, the rice fields had been evened out, and the closest buildings were more than 200 metres away. There was no clue to follow. How to recall people's memories and spirits? I decided to design a hill.'[33] Rather than presenting identifiable symbols of the past, his design allows the visitor to connect with the villages' former inhabitants by touching the stone of their old homes: 'I decided to collect the materials from the ruins and use them to build this new museum so that the vanished memory, the haptic feeling, and the time past would be collected and preserved.'[34]

Today, the way we build upon the Earth needs to aid the regeneration of the Earth, and that requires a new appreciation of the way our planet's systems are interconnected. In the case of spolia, the reuse of stone, ornaments, or entire sections of buildings was, first and foremost, a symbolic act. Similarly, today's circular materiality, the reuse of building components, is not just a pragmatic choice, it is also integral to sustainable cultural practice.

1   Konstanty Gutschow and Hermann Zippel, *Umbau* (Stuttgart: Julius Hoffmann, 1932).
2   Hermann Czech, 'Zur Abwechslung' (1973), in id., *Zur Abwechslung: Ausgewählte Schriften zur Architektur*, rev. edn. (Vienna: Löcker, 1996), 76–79, here: 78.
3   Gutschow and Zippel, op.cit., 10.
4   Rudolf Schwarz, *Von der Bebaung der Erde* (Heidelberg: Lambert Schneider, 1949).
5   John Ruskin, *The Stones of Venice* (London: Smith, Elder & Co., 1953).
6   See Antón M. Pazos (ed.), *Nineteenth-Century European Pilgrimages: A New Golden Age* (Abingdon: Routledge, 2020).
7   Sara Holmes Boutelle, *Julia Morgan, Architect*, 2nd edn. (New York: Abbeville Press, 1995), 169–215.
8   Beatriz Colomina, 'The House That Built Gehry', in J. Fiona Ragheb (ed.), *Frank Gehry, Architect* (New York: Guggenheim Museum, 2001), 300–321.
9   Ann Katrin Pihl Atmer, *Stockholm Town Hall and Its Architect Ragnar Östberg* (Stockholm: Natur & Kultur, 2011), 537.
10 Nike Breyer, 'Flachdach ist spießig', interview with Christoph Mäckler, *taz*, 22 April 2006, 1001–1003.
11 Claude Lévi-Strauss, *The Savage Mind* (Chicago: University of Chicago Press, 1966).
12 Charles Jencks and Nathan Silver, *Adhocism: The Case for Improvisation* (Garden City, NY: Doubleday, 1972; rev. edn., Cambridge, Mass.: The MIT Press, 2013).
13 Josef Frank, 'Apostle and Apostate: Josef Frank's Modernist Vision', *Places Journal* (February 2018), accessed 25 Nov. 2021. https://doi.org/10.22269/180206
14 The studio was demolished in 1985 for want of potential buyers—the nominal sale price was $1.
15 Laura Milan, Sergio Pace, and Carlo Mollino, *L'arte di costruire in montagna: Casa Garelli, Champoluc* (Milan: Mondadori Electa, 2018), 30f.
16 Sharon Zhukin, *Loft Living: Culture and Capital in Urban Change* (Baltimore: Johns Hopkins University Press, 1982).
17 Martin Pawley, 'Garbage housing', *Architectural Design* 43, no. 12 (1973), 764–784, here: 775.
18 See Martina Baum and Kees Christiaanse (eds.), *City as Loft: Adaptive Reuse as a Resource for Sustainable Urban Development* (Zurich: gta Verlag, 2012).

19   Edwin Heathcote, 'Alexander Brodsky builds the impossible', *Financial Times*, 13 Mar. 2015, feldmangallery.com/assets/pdfs/Brodsky_Selected-Press.pdf.
20   Wiel Arets, Wim van den Bergh and William Gratama, *FPJ Peutz Architekt 1916–1966*, exh. cat. Technische Hogeschool Eindhoven (1981).
21   Alison and Peter Smithson, 'The "As Found" and the "Found"', in David Robbins (ed.), *The Independent Group: Postwar Britain and the Aesthetics of Plenty* (Cambridge, Mass.: The MIT Press, 1990), 201–202.
22   Reyner Banham and Hiroyuki Suzuki, *Contemporary Architecture of Japan* (New York: Rizzoli, 1985), 108–109; Urs Meister, 'Die Fäden des Netzes', *tec21*, 21 (2001), 17–27.
23   Joseph A. Schumpeter, *Capitalism, Socialism, and Democracy* (New York: Harper Perennial, 1942).
24   Vance Packard, *The Waste Makers* (New York, NY: David McKay, 1960).
25   Roderick Hönig (ed.), *Swiss Sound Box* (Basel: Birkhäuser, 2000), 24.
26   Iván Kotsis, *Épületek és tervek* (Budapest: Pósa Károly, 1945), 141–164.
27   Kevin Lynch, *The Image of the City* (Cambridge, Mass.: The MIT Press, 1960).
28   Christian Norberg-Schulz, *Genius loci: Towards a Phenomenology of Architecture* (New York: Rizzoli, 1979).
29   Rudolf Olgiati, *Architekt: Eine Streitschrift* (Stuttgart: Magazin und Buch, 1994; 2nd edn., Stuttgart: Judith M. Grieshaber and Manfred Kröplien, 2002), 40.
30   Ursula Riederer and Rudolf Olgiati, *Bauen mit den Sinnen* (Chur: HTW Chur Verlag, 2004), 81–82.
31   Selina Walder (ed.), *Dado—Gebaut und bewohnt von Rudolf Olgiati und Valerio Olgiati* (Basel: Birkhäuser, 2010).
32   Rudolf Schwarz, *Kirchenbau: Welt vor der Schwelle* (Heidelberg: F. H. Kerle Verlag, 1960), 223.
33   Wang Shu, *Imagining the House* (Zurich: Lars Müller, 2012), n.p.
34   Ibid.

K.118 reportage

Michel Massmünster

Hunting and gathering

First comes the hunt, then the construction: if you want to reuse building components, you first have to assemble them. This not only changes the usual processes and job descriptions but also alters our view of the city.

Pascal, the project manager of baubüro in situ, rides his bike down Hohlstrasse and then turns onto Duttweiler Bridge. The bridge takes him high above the tracks that lead to the main railway station. He looks down at the cranes and scaffolds that can be found all across the city. In between construction and demolition sites, there are those areas that are less interesting to him—where concrete and steel, bricks and glass, wood and aluminium slowly join together over some years to form a house. When he rides down Förrlibuckstrasse on the other side of the tracks, Pascal notices the batter boards that indicate a new building project at the site of the two Orion office buildings. At home, he does some research to find out what is going on. He discovers a newspaper article that baffles him: it describes the demolition of the two buildings, which seem to be intact and are only 26 and 27 years old. Why, then, he asks himself, would they be torn down? Pascal also finds the contact information of the owners and, in an email, introduces them to the project Head-End Hall 118 (K.118): a three-storey vertical extension on the premises of the Lagerplatz site in Winterthur that utilizes reused materials. Pascal is looking for used building components.

The city as mine

After many phone calls and emails, he is invited on a tour of the building together with the owners. There, he also meets the people from the demolition company. Somebody has already been awarded the demolition job. That means Pascal is almost too late: experience shows that it is easier to simply negotiate with the owners. 'That way, the owners can put in a good word for our project with the demolition company or we can even come to a contractual agreement.'

During the tour of the building, Pascal is trying to identify which parts might be used for K.118. There are many possibilities: apart from knowing that the vertical extension is supposed to have three floors and span the length of the existing building, its design is still up in the air. As a result, the steel fire escape, the façade slabs, various types of windows, and other items, such as handrails, plasterboard, radiators, and sinks will eventually find their way to Winterthur.

Finding these types of components is essential for K.118. The architects from baubüro in situ know that their search has to start in their personal surroundings because there is a lack of tools and information for a

When the 20-storey Gillender Building by architects Charles I. Berg and Edward H. Clark opened its doors in the financial district of New York City in 1897, it was one of the city's tallest buildings. After just 13 years, it had to make way for the Bankers Trust Building, which was nearly twice as tall.

methodical search. They would love to have a map with planned demolition projects. Unfortunately, that doesn't exist. When it comes to building with reused components, there is no infrastructure—and hardly any experience. A lot has changed since 1910, when, for the first time, a developer in Manhattan had to pay for the disposal of the remnants of the Gillender Building instead of getting paid. What was new at the time was the realization that the quick construction of a new building was more lucrative than storing the old construction materials on-site until everything had been sold.

When real estate prices are as high as they are in modern cities, time is money and a demolition is more profitable, which is why the building sector is geared toward the use of new building components. Reuse is hardly ever intended. This means that the search for components for the K.118 team is also a search for ways in which such a house can be built in the first place. While the architects design, plan, and construct the building, they are always also developing the techniques, tools, and methods that are required for the project. The tools they use to contact the responsible parties once the architects become aware of a planned demolition have now been automated. There is a standard email and a project portfolio that the team uses to contact the owners.

For Pascal, the search for building components has become routine. Just like on the Duttweiler Bridge, he is looking for evidence that economic shifts are taking another building out of service. That happens frequently, because what is deemed to be an optimal spatial solution changes rapidly at the pace of reinvestments, which means that buildings and their components are no longer needed long before the end of their life cycles. The city becomes a mine for reusable materials. Time and again, the K.118 team makes a discovery—seemingly by chance. But luck favours the prepared: while studying in the Netherlands, Pascal completed an internship in an office that works with recycled materials.[1] Since then, reuse has become a major aspect of his work. Marc, the co-project manager, has been aware of the importance of repurposing existing materials since the days of his

↗ p.218
K.118 case study
Component catalogue:
Lysbüchel load-bearing
steel structure

2 ↗ p.234
K.118 case study
Design and construction:
Process

3 ↗ p.240
K.118 case study
Construction organization:
Services and processes

Michel Massmünster

advocacy for activist do-it-yourself construction in the temporary use and DIY scenes. And Ben, the design architect, is no stranger to circular building either. So it was a no-brainer that they would be involved in the K.118 project.

Nobody will wait for you

Since the start of the millennium, the steel construction at Basel's Lysbüchel plot has held together the distribution centre of a major wholesaler. From a colleague in the Basel office, the team learns that the building will be demolished as the entire site is to be repurposed. This means that Pascal and Marc are taking a trip to the site. The steel structure could solve the problem of what should form the constructional basis for the vertical extension of the K.118 project. They measure the beams to get an idea of their stability. Back in their office, they draw the supporting structure. It gives them lots to consider: what possibilities does this structure offer? What does it require? What compromises may be possible? And how can it be placed atop the existing hall?

The search for suitable components and the planning process take place concurrently. They depend on each other: the components they find determine their planning process, but it's the plans that decide whether it was a find in the first place or a futile hunt. The time frame in which these decisions have to be made is limited. The date of the demolition has generally been set before the team can reach out to the demolition company. 'Nobody will wait until we have decided what we need and until we are ready to dismantle these components. In retrospect, we reckon that if we had already thought about the floors instead of just the steel construction, then we would have taken those as well. It would have been a perfect fit. It's best to reuse the entire system. After all, what we build will likely be similar. But we just didn't have time in that moment.'

Together with the steel contractor, the team of K.118 calculates how the beams can be combined, bundled, and placed on pallets to ensure that the packages can be moved easily. Once the beams have been removed, something does go wrong in spite of the logistical planning: differently sized beams got bundled together, which means that the packages are nearly impossible to handle. And that, in turn, drives transportation costs way up. Planning for these potential interfaces

[Fig. 2] Component logistics requires expertise: in order to store the steel structure until it is installed, it is taken apart and placed on pallets ready for transport. However, once the job is completed, it turns out that the steel beams are partially standing instead of lying on the pallets and they are not wedged together correctly, which makes the bundles unstable. When they arrive at the storage facility of the Pratteln distribution centre, they are 'de-bundled' and re-sorted. This requires the rental of a crane for two days. Now they are placed correctly.

[Fig. 3] During the dismantling process on the top floor of the distribution centre, the substrate of the flat roof falls through openings in the roof and forms impressive piles below the steel beams. What could be a part of a piece of art is actually just a pragmatic way of making the material easier to transport.

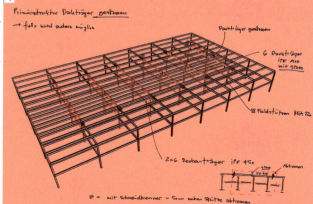

Getting hold of the old permit drawings makes it easier for the architects to test the steel structure even if the detailed planning has disappeared. The steel beams do not fit perfectly into the existing building yet, but they can be adapted. The red section in the

is important when handling old building components. And there are a great many such interfaces, precisely because the project has an oblique trajectory that intersects the institutions and professions that have been developed by the construction industry over the past century. The team assumes roles that are usually filled by experts. The steel contractor knows how elements have to be stored so that they can be used. This means that the disassembly should ideally be carried out by the company that later uses the components again.

Now that it is clear that the basic structure of the vertical extension will consist of steel beams, this will help define what happens next. It determines the height of the floors, as well as the shape and type of construction.[2] Each find dictates a new direction and other options are rejected. While it happens that such a decision is reversed or a better component is added, it still holds true that each decision makes the design of the project more precise and, as a result, the search for the next components has to be more specific. In the course of this search, it becomes clear that each solution leads to new challenges on the next level that call for more new solutions. That turns the hunt for components into its own area of responsibility.

The hunt for building components:
A new occupational field

Geraldine walks through the former bank building with the large window fronts. She measures the safety glass, notes its dimensions, takes pictures from a distance and up close: the corners, the mounting, and the seals. Geraldine is a building component hunter.

The K.118 team soon realized the importance of the search for components, the assessment of the finds, and the evaluation of whether they will fit, as well as the logistics involved in the processes of dismantling, transportation, and storage. They announced an internship focused on the hunt for components. Geraldine is already the third architecture student filling this role for the construction office. The internship offers her a new view of architecture. The work is very diverse; behind the complex system of lists, drawings, and filing systems that keep getting refined, there are a number of tasks that are usually associated with other positions within the architecture office.[3]

When the component hunter finds out about a demolition, she first organizes a tour. She notifies the owners, the architects managing the project, the demolition companies,

4 ↗ p. 252	5 ↗ p. 214	6 ↖ p. 11
K.118 case study	K.118 case study	Reuse!
Costs: Comparison per component	Component map	

'In Africa I had learned that one person's waste can be raw material for others. To make that possible, supply and demand must be brought together via a platform with broad reach. What could be more fitting than to use the new medium of the internet to do so?'

Hunting and gathering

and all the other stakeholders. On the premises, she takes pictures of all the components from different angles and creates an inventory list of all the potentially useful parts. It contains a hand-drawn sketch for each object, photos, the approximate dimensions, and information on any peculiarities, the manufacturer, and the year it was made. Using this list, the team will then select the potential components in their office. The information contained in the list should be as specific as possible. With windows, for example, their insulating capabilities can be estimated on the basis of the year in which they were built and their manufacturer. With the manufacturers, they have to check if spare parts are still available for the object. With other components, such as railings or doors, a decision is made on the basis of the way they were mounted or whether they can actually be dismantled and reinstalled. Geraldine's experience has taught her which part to pay special attention to. However, since each situation is unique and each component requires its own evaluation, she often has to visit a building a second or third time to get more specific information on the state of things.

The component hunter retraces the remaining objects in the inventory list on her computer. Ben, the designer, and Michèle, the drafter, then add the drawings to the design plan. This will illustrate if and how the components fit together with the existing materials. 'If everything fits, we'll organize the disassembly.' It is only at this point that the component receives a part number and a 'component passport' with specific details. Once the inventory list has been cleaned up, it is submitted to the demolition company as a 'shopping list'.

However, the inventory list not only includes what is needed for K.118 but also components that colleagues in the office are looking for or those that are always in demand, such as bicycle racks or letter boxes. 'Somebody always needs a letter box. They are expensive to buy, but the disassembly is cheap and easy and always pays off.'[4] Geraldine, the component hunter, distributes the list of items not intended for K.118 via email or the Salza platform. She takes on the role of a broker—even though that isn't her goal or job description. By making up for the lack of infrastructure for circular construction, her role in the team also makes her a key figure for others.

In the beginning, components for K.118 were collected very liberally because the design was not very specific at that point. Now the hunt is much more targeted. The 'wish list' primarily contains windows and doors with approximate dimensions.

centre of the overall structure can only be supported if it is offset a little from the walls of the existing hall, which means the added floors will protrude slightly above the building. However, that gives it a special shape.

At the demolition site, each component gets a red sticker that marks it for reuse and calls for special care. The QR code references the component pass, which compiles all of the documentation related to this component via the in-house component shop. The code also refers to those plans to which the components have been assigned unequivocally. In the storage facility, each component gets a label, the yellow storage pass on which the location, pallet number, and component number are documented. The first storage facility the office rented for the duration of the project on behalf of the building owners was established in Tössallmend Neftenbach in June 2017. After two years, it is nearly full. The other storage facilities are also filling up. In Pratteln, in addition to the outdoor storage for the steel structure, there is also an indoor warehouse. Another one is located near the in situ office in the SBB workshops in Zurich—primarily for the items that are dismantled on the site itself. The most recent is a former bus depot in Winterthur, and another small one can be found in Hall 181—right next to K.118.[5]

Additional lists contain the contact information as well as the costs of each element compared with its estimated price if it were purchased new. Once the component is in storage, it is added to the in-house 'component shop', which makes important information on the items easily available to all participants.

A hunt in different stamping grounds

There have been component exchanges in Switzerland since the 1990s, and they have been connected via the Swiss component network since 1996. The first of them was the Basel building component exchange—Bauteilbörse Basel.[6] It was founded by Barbara Buser, who would later become the managing director of baubüro in situ, and Klara Kläusler, who became a project manager of the Abendrot Foundation. Similar to a second-hand shop, Bauteilbörse Basel offers used components. It mainly stocks items with standard dimensions that always come in handy. Kitchenettes, sinks, and wooden doors with minimal dimensional differences are arranged next to each other in high racks. That's not enough if you want to add a few floors to a factory building though.

A second possible way to acquire components—as with the steel construction—is to contact the demolition companies that have already been hired. The Salza platform, which puts those looking for components in touch with the owners of buildings that are to be demolished, is an important resource in this regard. The wood sandwich panels that are used for the roof construction of K.118, on the other hand, were acquired from a company that not only does demolitions but also tests for harmful substances and is involved in recycling and reselling. Back in 1936, the grandfather of the current co-managing director Martin Hiltbrunner founded Hiltbrunner AG to get a foot in the door of the scrap material trade. Since then, the company has repeatedly had to adapt to changing market conditions. In the 1980s, for example, it purchased a shredder plant to invest in the wood recycling of horse pens and wood combustion. Now, the family-owned business also operates a recycling centre for private customers in the industrial sector as well as the online shop wiederverwendung.ch. 'Nowadays, everybody talks about sustainability, but our recycling-related turnover is declining. The reason is hardware stores: the prices they charge for sanitary ware do not even cover the disassembly of used equipment, which is why we now primarily sell special construction materials, such as wooden panels and steel beams, sheeting for façades, doors and windows, and more rustic components—for example, for the renovation of old chalets,' Hiltbrunner explains. The wood sandwich panels for the roof construction

7 ↗ p.138
A circular approach to architecture

8 ↗ p.254
K.118 case study
Costs: Construction costs and financing

↗ p.229
K.118 case study
Component catalogue: Zellweger interior door

Michel Massmünster

of K.118 sat in an exterior storage area for a long time until they found a taker. 'They were uninstalled from the makeshift railway station back in 2010. The panels had to be exposed step by step. Then the elements had to have holes drilled in them so they could be lifted off and transported to our warehouse. But it is unusual that they stayed in the warehouse for so long. Generally, we would move them on much more quickly. However, we cannot calculate supply and demand like in the retail trade.' Hiltbrunner AG used some of these panels itself, for the roof of the recycling centre on its premises. Hiltbrunner doubts that it will be possible any time soon to set up a trading network for reusable building components that demolition companies can use to offer materials even before they are dismantling them. As useful as this would be in order to reduce storage costs, his experience tells him that it is almost impossible to predict ahead of time whether materials can be dismantled without damage and without unreasonable costs. To do so, a new mode of construction would first have to be established that anticipates and simplifies the future demolition of a building.**7**

The third stamping ground of component hunters are demolitions that the team organizes itself. In this endeavour, it is supported by specialized craftspeople. Geraldine also researches the relevant online portals for used items and keeps calling demolition companies and construction companies to ask whether they are planning any demolitions. In some cases, somebody contacts her directly—and no longer just people from her own office. Thanks to its stature as a pilot initiative, the project has been covered in many media reports. As a result, other architecture offices, which know of an upcoming demolition or are also looking for used materials, are now reaching out to the team.

Wherever the market or the way of doing business has not yet been established, one moment is of the utmost importance: the deal. The economics are not always so obviously in favour of reuse as was the case with the steel structure. When Pascal and Marc meet with the owners and the demolition company for the first time, they ask up front what they can take. Sometimes, they are told that they can take whatever they want. In many cases, however, there is a meticulous accounting of the items. Frequently, things seem to be going very well at first, but the price goes up once the demolition company realizes that there is a real demand. Knowing that demolition companies otherwise have to pay disposal fees is beneficial for the team. The Abendrot Foundation, which is the owner of K.118, has paid an advance to fund the hunt for components. That is important because it amounts to about 10–15 per cent of the total costs.**8** The ultimate goal is to ensure that,

Hunting and gathering

[Fig. 6] Steel sections in the high-bay warehouse of the Zellweger textile machine factory. 'It would have taken forever to remove them individually. However, there was a rail system in place that had been used to supply the warehouse. We put a small wagon onto these tracks that could be pushed or pulled with a rope. At the end, there was a kind of slide we could use to push the beams onto the transporter.'

[Fig. 7] The architects wanted to pick up doors at the Uster textile machine factory. That was another learning experience: when they got there, there was just a hole where the door handle and lock had been. The doors looked like they'd suffered an arson attack, with the high-quality fixtures dynamited and destroyed. It turns out that, over the weekend, a police exercise had been held in the building, during which explosives had been put in the doors. Based on this experience, a new communication tool was developed that has become a vital part of the hunt for components: bright-red stickers that say, 'Components in situ—handle with care. Component will be reused!'

at the end of the construction, no materials remain in storage, which is why some are always sold to other projects.

**Careful!:
The demolition**
'Obviously, the demolition companies have better tools. But when we are working with our craftspeople, then we often build auxiliary constructions. This is not something we plan for but it happens on-site simply because solutions are needed. It helps that there is always a lot of material in the building. This is a dismantling process involving the existing building fabric, but it is about specific solutions, and things always have to happen quickly,' Pascal explains. 'In some cases, we spend half a day building an auxiliary construction that then allows us to complete the rest of the work much more quickly.'

While the K.118 team started out by simply walking into the buildings and beginning the dismantling process, after nearly a year of demolition experience, everything is now more organized. Everyone involved receives a list with clear instructions, including those related to safety. On this basis, people evidently enjoy the demolition process. 'It's not just "harvesting" but more like prospecting for gold, with the idea that you can recover something valuable. And then, when you can find the easiest way to dismantle something and you're making quick progress, that's extremely motivating. You are excited about your technical finesse.' Sometimes, however, there is no gold digger's euphoria. In the bank with the large window fronts made of safety glass, a kitchen worktop and a power distributor look promising. In addition, a few high-quality doors and the large panes of safety glass seem like a good fit for the design plan. However, when the dismantling process begins, it becomes clear that this would be too expensive. The dismantling of the glass panes would be extremely costly because it would require suction cups and other specific equipment. In the case of the heavy safety glass used in a bank, this would have resulted in costs that would be higher than the price of a new window. The hunt continues.

1 ↗ p.280 Eight theses 8 Sampling and serendipity
2 ↗ p.197 From part to whole and back again Teaching reuse in architecture
↗ p.224 K.118 case study Component catalogue: Ziegler façade metal cladding
3 ↗ p.254 K.118 case study Costs: Construction costs and financing
4 ↗ p.234 K.118 case study Design and construction: Process

Designing and joining

Reusing materials means designing incrementally: new material finds continuously call design decisions into question. The art of being able to respond, combine, and fit things together relies on flexible design principles—and an aptitude for sampling.[1]

Ben chooses a darker red and clicks on the upper part of the façade siding. He also colours and shades the other diamond shapes: pink, claret, brown, teal, ochre, beige. The façade of the vertical extension takes on colour. His design draws inspiration from the Yardhouse, which the architecture, design, and art collective Assemble built as a studio in Stratford in London. In Ben's imagination, the diamonds could consist of different residual materials. The height of the floors and windows will be determined by the components they have already collected. The existing building determines the position of the openings. The new façade is supposed to adopt the existing rhythm. That limits the design options. Using Photoshop, Ben has also sketched two other façade options: one consisting of waste wood and the other of the plaster remnants that form a type of camouflage pattern with different shades of grey. The sketches allow the team to explore different approaches further and specify the direction to take in the search for materials.

Designing—out and back again[2]

At the Ziegler print shop in Oberwinterthur, the team found red aluminium trapezoidal sheeting a few weeks later. 'In retrospect, it almost seems logical that we work with trapezoidal sheeting. It is often available in industrial areas where reconstruction is taking place. And it is a very protective and durable material for façades.'

Finding the material and the decision to use the metal sheeting come at an important time, making it possible to have the design of the façade ready for the planning application submission.[3] The exterior appearance of the building will not change much once the basic shape, the façades, and the exterior staircase have been put in place. However, with regard to the details, the design of the building will keep developing as components are added. Until the start of construction, many decisions have yet to be made, which will lead to other options being discarded.[4] In their design, the architects move from large to small—from the load-bearing structure, the façades, and the floors to the kitchens and, finally, all the way to the door handles.

What happened during the sketching of the façade designs will impact the entire design process. Different, highly detailed versions of the design are created in the office and the availability of materials often lags behind them. Although it is not yet clear which components can be used to implement the design, the team needs to at least have an idea of their role in order to be prepared for possible finds during the hunt for components. At the same time, the component hunters will also be open to making unexpected finds. This means that detailed pre-planning will usually end up with the design having to be reworked following each find. 'In this design process, we can't just say, "Let's not worry about this detail now, we will define it later," because there are always other areas that are connected, where we already know and have defined the details. If, for example, we already have the windows and know how they are supposed to be attached and how much space there should be between them, then the instructions for the search team are very specific with regard to what can be used around the windows. But that is something we only find in rare cases. This means that, when we have found the next piece, we have to look at how we can adapt the arrangement of the windows as necessary.'

The process is characterized by constantly having to backtrack, or rather by continuous circling. From an idea that arises during a design and that is, in most cases, already based on an existing material or an ideal, the process moves to the find and then to testing the material and reworking the design, which then results in new ideas for what else is needed. It is a constant compilation of a hypothetical image that remains abstract at first and is only specified once that material has been found, but may also be revised if necessary.

In many cases, the discrepancies between design and material cannot easily be resolved. The team then reaches out to the relevant expert from its network to talk about different options. 'This is a type of construction that is usually not able to adopt standard solutions but is guided by conventional processes, which is why people and their connections are very important. This will reveal the people we can experiment and find solutions with.' Experimenting, revising, and discarding are all key methods. The project takes shape on the basis of decisions that in retrospect turn out to be suboptimal and then through a process of revision. There are idle periods that are always also times of learning:

1 The trapezoidal sheeting for the façades comes from the Ziegler print shop in Winterthur. They have different profiles and shades of red depending on the part of the building they originate from, the year of construction, and their exposure to sunlight.

↗ p.224
K.118 case study
Component catalogue:
Ziegler façade metal
cladding

5 ↗ p.237
K.118 case study
Design and construction:
Glossary

↗ p.227
K.118 case study
Component catalogue:
Orion window

↗ p.218
K.118 case study
Component catalogue:
Lysbüchel load-bearing
steel structure

6 ↗ p.237
K.118 case study
Design and construction:
Glossary

Michel Massmünster

the experience will be beneficial next time around. The team uses an exploratory approach to develop its strategies for circular designing.

Overlaps, joints, latitude

Having decided in favour of the red trapezoidal sheeting, Ben makes additions to the design drawing and specifies it. Since the component hunter had already drawn the metal sheets  in the catalogue after finding them, he merely has to import them into his drawing and adapt them. However, when dismantling them, the team soon notices that not all the metal cladding has the same profile, since the print shop was built in different phases. While the profiles all have the same depth, they do not share the same width. This has to be taken into account in the drawing. These types of changes involving a design-relevant component can be corrected directly in the drawing in the component catalogue, which automatically adapts the elements in the design drawing. The metal sheets with the different profiles cannot be placed inside each other in order to be joined. This means that the corrections have consequences.

The solution is to choose one profile for each floor to ensure there are enough of each. However, the profile of the top floor can no longer be directly joined to that of the one below it. The claddings on the different floors thus overlap by 6cm throughout. Five for the profiled sheet metal and one more to allow for additional play. The building becomes bigger toward the top. The brick façade of the existing building and the aluminium façade of the additional floors are designed according to the same principle. These types of overlap turn out to be an important principle for the design. They create play between the two elements. Without these tolerances⁵, the design would keep having gaps between two components that had already been collected. Additionally, it would have been unlikely to find a part that fitted perfectly in those gaps later on.

The design process requires not only some play between the reused elements but also some tolerance when it comes to the implementation. This searching, cautious approach, and a development process without any particular result in mind, only work because the owner does not have overly specific demands. 'It is very helpful that the Abendrot Foundation allows us a relatively free rein when it comes to making planning decisions regarding the building and the materials.' Because time is often short and there can be sudden pressure to make decisions, flexibility is required to be able to implement new ideas and adapt quickly.

Chains of effect, separating functions

The solution of the joints and the overlaps between the different façade slabs and the different floors creates hiding places for insects in undesirable places in the protruding areas. This is something that happens frequently: when joining the available components, the design changes in a way that creates challenges elsewhere. Because the components are joined, the building serves as a place where chains of effect come together. These chains of effect must be regularly tracked and itemized during the design process. 'If we have to make a small change because of a newly discovered component, we always have to ask ourselves: is that still going to work elsewhere? For example, we found out that the steel beams from the Lysbüchel site featured two different lengths, which had not been properly documented during the dismantling process. That means we had to change the drawing once the steel constructor noticed this. As a result, the position of an entire wall changed because we obviously had to insert the walls in line with the beams of the steel frame. And, as a result, it is possible that many other things will shift as well until we get to the façade. That is why we are now debating whether it would be better to simply give up on our initial principle of ensuring that the walls are always in line with the beams instead of adapting everything.'

The design is a chain reaction, so it pays to precisely document the dimensions of key elements from the start. In order to limit the chains of effect in combination with the constant updates as much as possible, the team isolates the functions and works toward a system separation⁶ of the different structures. If everything that a building is supposed to do happens in the same location, then one change has much greater consequences. However, if the functions are separated, then they can be adapted on a modular basis. For example, the load-bearing structure of K.118 functions independently of the window grid. And the window grid is independent of the façade cladding. And so on. That is also why the decision was made to build the staircase externally. The stairs and the steel structure feature different floor heights. Using special sheets, the height of the steel structure is roughly adjusted, the external staircase creates play that can be levelled with door sills—and it even creates more rental space in the building. The lift, on the other hand, is located inside the building and accesses each floor seamlessly.

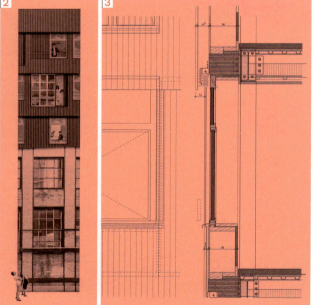

[Figs. 2, 3]   The sheet metal cladding of the façade overlaps from one floor to the next. This offsets any colour and profile differences between the metal sheets. The windows from the Orion office buildings in Zurich are also a little bit too big to maintain the required parapet height and to fit below the ceiling. As a result, the frame will slide in front of the ceiling front at the top. From the outside, it is hidden by the sheet metal cladding of the floor above, which covers the sun blinds that were harvested at the same time.

7 ↗ p. 266	8 ↗ p. 280	↗ p. 227	9 ↗ p. 236	10 ↗ p. 237
Eight theses	Eight theses	K.118 case study	K.118 case study	K.118 case study
		Component catalogue: Orion window 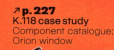	Design and construction: Glossary 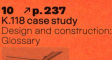	Design and construction: Glossary
Challenging the demands	Sampling and serendipity			

Designing and joining

Separating functions and chains of effect also tallies with another proven strategy used by baubüro in situ, which they refer to as 'Ready-Made': if possible, adopt the original construction of the components or of entire combinations of components. They work according to the following principle: revise and adapt as little as possible by installing items the way they were used in the previous building. This saves a lot of effort in adapting the components. It also means that the components remain reversible and can be dismantled more easily later on.

Reusing parts without significant changes is also in line with the concept of 'untreated' rooms. The functions of rooms remain undefined and conventional standards of comfort and aesthetics are intentionally not met.[7] No finish is required to hide signs of use or coarse materials since the owners are looking for tenants who will design the rooms according to their own wishes anyway. The process of designing and joining goes beyond constructed spaces and allows versatile uses. The house remains in motion.

Sampling: Assembly strategies[8]

To ensure that the components do not get in each other's way when they are being assembled, it is important that the design includes tolerance ranges from the start. In addition to working with overlaps and separating functions, the team has two additional options. The one that makes the most sense is to find a component that fits perfectly. However, in most cases, this would mean that this piece would first have to be built from scratch. Still, the team makes use of this option when new casement windows have to be added to used casements for the false edge of the windows of the existing building. In order not to have to rely on new pieces that fit, the proven strategy of filling the gaps between fixed components with malleable materials is used. As a result, the façades and windows are insulated with clay and straw: a wooden screen is constructed around the windows that is filled with straw and rendered with clay, ensuring that the wall surrounding the windows remains variable. In addition, the straw has good insulating properties and there is lots of clay from the excavated material of construction sites.

This means that a key aspect of the design process is to determine what happens in between the components. As a result, the materials sometimes dictate the design. In this regard, the team talks about the principle of 'form follows availability'. In this context, 'designing' means selecting components and figuring out the transitions between them. The planners are like DJs who do not invent new music out of thin air but rather take suitable passages of existing songs, analyse them, understand the impact they have, and turn their finds into a new composition.[9] This means that some elements are placed above one another so that a casual observer would not notice that they did not belong together at one time. In some cases, however, they are also set apart with a prominent discontinuity between the different components. The transitions play a central role when sampling the elements. They form the basis for the special aesthetic and the appeal of this type of construction.

There is something else the planners share with DJs: the joy to be found in a transfer[10], which can sometimes be explicit but often also involves implied or incidental references. These references are not limited to using the materials of the former buildings, such as the Ziegler print shop or the Orion office buildings. They also refer to the industrial cityscape of the Sulzer site. The red metal cladding determines the base colour of the vertical extension. The aluminium sheets are given a stove-enamelled finish for the construction of the print shop, which means the colour is 'baked' into it in the furnace. To remove this high-quality coating for K.118 would take a lot of effort and the sheets would have to be sand-blasted. Both from an environmental and a financial perspective, it would make more sense to take the components as they are and put one's own desires as a designer second. Fortunately, the red colour fits in well with the wide range of red colour shades at the Lagerplatz site—from red bricks and rusty iron to ruby-coloured fibre-cement shingles. 'This means that the colour was dictated but, luckily, it was a perfect fit for the colour range of the Sulzer site. Even better, it is the same shade of red as that of the logo of the building owner, the Abendrot Foundation.' The different components and references turn into a remix of this industrial landscape.

[4] 'Ready-Made' strategy: adopting the original design from the Orion office buildings in Zurich means bringing in not just the individual windows but also the corresponding blinds, coupling profiles, and cover plates.

[Fig. 5] 'We said that if we add a new element, then it should also be identifiable as new. That means we won't paint it like the used materials in order to hide the fact that we also used something new.' For example, the steel structure of the existing buildings, which needed to be painted for fire protection reasons, was given a new coat of paint. The light blue references other metal parts on the site, such as the rails in the halls. And the back of the red metal cladding from the Ziegler print shop is also light blue.

[Fig. 6] Used windows, fitted into the new façade elements: the form and function of the Orion windows are predefined. The new construction that surrounds them is adjusted to suit: the wooden substructure is tailor-made, while the straw insulation fills the cavity and can be flexibly formed. The same applies to the clay plaster that is applied following the installation of the elements.

↗ p.219　　　　　↗ p.220　　　　　↗ p.225　　　　　1　↗ p.234
K.118 case study　K.118 case study　K.118 case study　K.118 case study
Component catalogue:　Component catalogue:　Component catalogue:　Design and construction:
Zellweger steel section　Orion external staircase　Orion cladding slab　Process

Testing and planning

Planning with used components requires an in-depth knowledge of materials. Testing the suitability of the components is just one of the challenges. Another is to establish the right criteria.

Marc, the project co-manager, is going over his metal cladding notes at his standing desk, which is made of wine boxes, when the phone rings.

'baubüro in situ, this is Marc.'

'Hey, it's Pascal.'

'Hey, Pascal, how are things going in Uster?'

'Good, we're still dismantling things. And now we've discovered a gigantic high-bay warehouse consisting of several identical steel sections right here in the building. We could use it to build the external stairs and the balconies. What do you think?'

'Yes, that sounds great. How many are there?'

'Definitely more than we'll ever need—there are hundreds. There are dozens of hallways with about 15 shelves stacked on top of each other. We could start with the two bottom shelves because we can access them easily. The supports are just hooked in. Two people can easily disassemble them. It's almost too easy. And we'll be able to use them in any case. If not for the balcony, then elsewhere.'

Marc turns to Ben, who is sitting behind him: 'Ben, they found a high-bay warehouse with hundreds of steel sections in the Zellweger textile machine factory.' Ben asks about the dimensions.

'What do the supports measure?'

'They're about 120mm high and 60mm wide. The ones at the top measure 361cm, and the ones at the bottom 350cm, sometimes 355.'

'I'll take a look in the steel construction table to see if I can find the profile. … That's an IPE 120, geometric.'

Ben: 'Great.'

Marc (speaking into the phone): 'Yes, that sounds good. When do we have to get them out by?'

'The demolition excavators will be here in three days.'

'OK, I'll call the structural engineer to ask what he thinks about these dimensions. I'll be in touch.'

Marc hangs up and calls the structural engineer: 'Hey, Pascal's just made a nice discovery. IPE 120 steel beams. What do you think we can use them for? We were thinking the balconies. You know, we want there to be balconies for the external stairs on each floor. And then obviously the rails of the stairs. We've already got the large granite slabs for the floor.'

'Yes, with that cross section, you can definitely build balconies.'

'Do we have to send them to the lab to measure the quality of the steel? We would have to dismantle them in the next three days.'

'Haha! Wait, I'm just looking at the steel construction table. So, even if I assume the worst steel quality, a framework with these dimensions will be stable enough. And if you found the supports in a high-bay warehouse, then it will probably be standard structural steel. That performs even better. The corrosion protection may be an issue. But three days is not enough time to check that. Please send me the drawing. Then I'll do a detailed structural analysis.'

'OK. Thanks.'

Marc hangs up and turns to Ben and Michèle, the drafter and designer. 'Does one of you have time to draw this?'

'Yes, we are on it.'

'Great. Here are the dimensions and please send them to the structural engineer right away. And let me know how many pieces we'll need based on your design. Then I can use the daily scrap metal price to calculate whether that makes sense economically.'

When Marc gets back from lunch later on, Michèle looks up from the drawing and tells him how many beams are needed. Marc researches the sales price of new supports of this kind and compares the two. He calls Pascal: 'It's me. I did a back-of-the-envelope calculation of the costs. Dismantling and reassembling them is definitely a bit cheaper than new supports. On the other hand, they are a bit too big, which isn't the most efficient solution. But it is worth it if there are so many that are so easily accessible. Can you dismantle them in time? And what about transporting them? Do you have enough space on the trailer?'

'Yes, we've already organized a second vehicle. We'll get it done.'

Planning with the unknown

In the case of the steel supports from the high-bay warehouse, the idea of using them for K.118 was prompted by their availability. They were in the building where Pascal was already dismantling other materials. In addition, they were very easy to dismantle.

[Fig.1] Prior to demolition, countless steel sections are waiting to be harvested in the high-bay warehouse of the Zellweger textile machine factory. They are predestined to be used again in different ways: versatile, standardized components, which are available in large numbers and have a uniform shape and can be easily accessed and disassembled.

[Fig.2] Sometimes things have to happen quickly: the high-bay warehouse is already being disassembled a few days after the component hunters bagged their haul.

2 ↗ **p. 240**	**3** ↗ **p. 244**	**4** ↗ **p. 189**
K.118 case study	K.118 case study	Uncharted legal territory
Construction organization:	Construction organization:	Reuse under Swiss law
Services and processes	A legal vademecum	

And there was another factor that favoured their reuse: there were lots of identical parts. Only then did the team ask itself, 'What can we use that for?' To answer that question, the planners should always have a rough idea of their needs. And they knew they still needed a framework for the balconies. That means they were thinking of a function and not a specific material.

An assessment[2] of the components requires precise testing. While it's usually planners who draw a design that is then submitted to the structural engineering office so that they can find the best material to execute the design as drawn, the process in this case is the reverse. Once the components have been found, planning ideas are developed that will then be submitted to the experts (together with initial material data) for them to calculate. Since time is short, different checks are conducted simultaneously, and their results could impact each other. The person that coordinates the flow of information has to compare and double-check it and make sure that the right people are up to date on the other assessments. This person also needs to know which information is required in the first place and where it comes from. It is a dialogue between specialists—such as steelwork companies, plumbers, carpenters, and metalworking shops—involving laws and regulations, the demolition conditions, the costs, and a design that is slowly taking shape. These checks branch out into increasingly detailed questions. And if a decision is made in one place, this will generally affect other decisions that had been made previously. Marc calls this a 'decision dilemma'. The team constantly has to make decisions, even though they usually still have imperfect knowledge of whether something truly fits. However, not considering the use of a component because there is incomplete information about it is also no solution. Not taking a component because of a lack of information is also a decision—one that stops a vertical extension to a factory hall being built.

That is why the planning process is also circular. Testing and planning depend on each other and take place incrementally. Once a planning idea is in place, this gives rise to questions relating to testing, which will help advance the planning process, often revealing new uncertainties regarding usability. In this case, new questions about the material are raised. The goal is to eliminate all unknown variables as quickly as possible. And all according to a central principle: from a planning perspective, the key is to coordinate the intersections between conventional fields of activity in the construction sector, since these are especially delicate areas. Accordingly, the relevant information is needed up front. For example, if a demolition company hands on a window to a transportation company, then who bears the risk and

More than a year and a half after the spontaneous decision to use the Zellweger steel sections, they are reassembled in a new configuration. They now provide the structural support of the balcony and support the granite slabs that previously clad the façade of the Orion office buildings in Zurich.

liability?[3] Is this reused material a product or waste? Does product law apply or waste law?[4] When it comes to these uncertainties, legal questions often need to have a plan-based and not a law-based solution. This means that the team generally plans with a worst-case scenario in mind if the legal answers are not yet available. Better safe than sorry.

When the steel supports for the balconies are already sitting in the storage, the unknown variable, which the structural engineer referenced on the phone and which could not be resolved in the three days between discovery and demolition of the high-bay warehouse, comes up again. The weldability and the surface treatment, i.e. the corrosion protection, are still unknown. Especially in the case of older steel, it is unclear whether it can be welded conventionally and, as a result, whether the design can be implemented. Using an angle grinder, the groundsman cuts off a piece of a steel support and sends it to the materials testing lab. It turns out that the weldability is no problem. However, the laboratory says that the supports were only painted or sprayed with a zinc dust primer but not galvanized. This minimal corrosion protection was sufficient in the warehouses at the old location. However, as part of outdoor balconies, the supports will be fully exposed to the weather. That means they have to be sandblasted in order to remove the old coating and then dipped in a zinc bath. 'But at the entire site, all of the steel sections of the existing buildings are covered with surface rust. And it is a conscious decision to not sand and re-galvanize the existing materials. That's why we asked ourselves why this balcony should feature better corrosion protection than the existing building. And, because the supports are somewhat oversized, they will remain stable in the long term even with a bit of rust.' The building owners, the engineers, and the architecture office discuss the anti-corrosion recommendations of SIA and other professional organizations and agree to not fully implement these. They agree that they will not sue each other, which is what they had also agreed to with regard to the existing building on the plot. A pragmatic attitude on the part of everyone involved, and realistic risk assessment, are a great help when building with reused components. And that is only possible on a basis of trust.

Testing means redesigning

Different materials offer different challenges not only for the demolition process but also when it comes to assessing them. In the case of slabs, these are different from

↗ **p.225**
K.118 case study
Component catalogue:
Orion cladding slab

↗ **p.227**
K.118 case study
Component catalogue:
Orion window

↗ **p.226**
K.118 case study
Component catalogue:
Werk 1 window

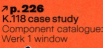

Michel Massmünster

those posed by steel supports. The dismantled Orion office buildings featured a cladding with massive, 3 cm thick façade slabs consisting of grey and pink granite. At a size of more than 1 m² they are relatively large and heavy. The pink slabs were not considered as an option because their edges were rounded. The grey slabs, on the other hand, featured a more neutral colour and their shape also allowed them to be used more universally. Any item that is neutral in terms of colour and functionality is often worth storing even if it is not yet exactly clear how it can be used. 'However, we didn't consider the slabs for the façade because it would have been too ostentatious. That would not have been a good fit. But natural stone is perfect for the floors,' said Marc in explaining the decision in favour of the slabs. An initial test had already been performed when it became clear that the grey slabs were an option. This assessment always begins relatively automatically as soon as the planners discover something: can we use that? The initial idea was to use the granite slabs for all the floors. However, they are extremely heavy, which is why they were only used for the wet rooms and the exterior, where wooden floors would have been a bad choice because of the moisture. Material properties, such as weight, which are not even consciously examined but rather registered subconsciously, often lead to changes to the plan.

In addition to their weight, the size of the slabs also became a challenge. However, the disassembly went smoothly and, just as in the case of the high bays, the component hunters were able to remove easily accessible slabs from around the building with little effort. The considerable slab size of more than 90 × 130 cm turned out to be an additional challenge. 'Even when we just stacked six of them on a palette, they weighed half a ton.' The options for storage and handling were very limited. In this case, smaller sizes that could be moved by one person would have been more efficient.

No matter how massive, the granite first needs to be checked to determine whether it will work as a floor slab. The team has got hold of the technical data sheets of the slabs from the caretaker at the old location. The granite came from a quarry in central Italy. Using this data, the engineers were able to calculate whether the slabs were stable enough. Just to be sure, a piece was sent to a materials testing laboratory in order to measure the breaking load. Here, using a standardized process, the granite was subjected to pressure until it cracked. The value determined in the laboratory corresponded with that from the data sheet. Then, when the floor plan had to be drawn, one of the slabs sat next to the desk in the office as a sample—on two pieces of wood so it could be picked up and put down again. During a coffee break, somebody jumped onto the slab and it broke. That was quite a surprise: the data sheet and laboratory report had promised greater stability. 'Our explanation for the fracture was that the sawn natural stone was not homogeneous. Obviously, that results in weak spots everywhere and you should actually test everything individually. However, if your entire balcony consists of that stone, as is often the case in Italy, then it will last because it was cleaved out of a rock as a whole piece. Whatever survives that will also hold as a balcony. Our granite slabs were sawn, however, but as part of a façade they didn't have to be so stable.' Accordingly, the steel supports of the balconies were placed closer to each other in order to reduce the span of the slabs. So it was good that Pascal grabbed a few more when the supports were being dismantled. In addition, as is usually the case with natural stone, the granite rests on a sheet metal membrane. While a stonemason would typically supply a stone that is durable, there's a gradual process when utilizing reused stone of facing up to new questions as they arise. The tests don't just happen during the selection process and prior to choosing a component but all the time—even during a coffee break.

Testing criteria

'The challenge of testing is learning to identify what needs to be tested in the first place.'

This is another area in which the planners keep learning. One type of component in all its variants raises many different questions. For example, it quickly became clear that not only did the insulation value and impermeability of the windows need to be checked but also how up to date the locking system is. A window fitter who took part in an inspection of the Orion office buildings stated, 'All the windows on the left-hand side of the building are unsuitable. The fittings are too old. There are no longer any spare parts for them and you would have to take many additional windows to have extra fittings.' This challenge prompted Marc to look for other solutions: 'Missing spare parts might be reproduced with 3D printers in the future.'

In the case of the small, glazed industrial windows from the Sulzer Werk 1, which is located across from Hall 118, different questions arose. 'We only noticed during the dismantling process that the frames

[Fig. 4]   Thanks to their neutral colour, the grey granite plates are better suited than the pink ones. The size of the slabs initially seemed to be an opportunity. However, their weight turned out to be a challenge and a cost factor.

[Fig. 5]   At the Orion office buildings in Zurich, only the most easily accessible bottom row of façade slabs was 'skimmed off', which was a difficult enough task because each of them weighed close to 80 kg!

5 ↗ p. 236
K.118 case study
Design and construction: Glossary

6 ↗ p. 236
K.118 case study
Design and construction: Glossary

7 ↗ p. 170
New paths toward net zero?
Potentials for climate protection

'If we want to use older windows with poor insulating properties, then we have to offset that somehow—by compensating in the system verification process or by turning the openings into box-type windows.'

8 ↗ p. 270
Eight theses

Inherited identity

Testing and planning

were not separated thermally.' Because aluminium is very conductive, a lot of energy escapes through the frame, which is why modern aluminium frames consist of two parts that are separated thermally via plastic in the centre. When using building materials from a time before these regulations came into effect, it is a challenge to meet the standards of energy-efficient building that are specified in the heat insulation guidelines of the cantonal energy law. 'We had to make a decision: what is the value of these windows if they don't insulate well? In the case of other such windows, we would have said that if the frames were not thermally separated, then we wouldn't take them. Here, however, we said to ourselves that since they came from across the street and from another Sulzer building, then we'd still take them. It's all about continuity**5**: These windows have a sentimental value—and they also helped define the look of the industrial ensemble on this plot.' Once again, a redesign was needed. After speaking with Kerstin, the office's energy expert, the team chose box-type windows. They could place one window behind another to create quadruple glazing, while the air gap serves as buffering**6**—this would offset the poor insulation values of the frames.**7** The building physicist confirmed that the detailed energy values support this decision.

Just as there was an overlap here between the thermal insulation and sentimental value of the windows, different testing criteria have to be taken into account for most decisions. First of all, there is the question of the components' dimensions. In the case of standardized components, these can often be determined on the basis of technical data. Statically and structurally, it is all about whether something will last and how it can be combined with other elements. From a regulatory perspective, it is important to check whether a component and the manner of construction comply with current laws. At a functional level the question is, can the components be used for this or that purpose? It is also necessary to check whether the costs are economically viable or if the expense involved in dismantling, transporting, and storing the items exceeds the cost of a new product.

During the construction of K.118, these economical assessments remained vague. It is not always extra costs that have to be added to the planned budget. In many cases, the reverse is true and the team finds out

Window from the Sulzer Werk 1

A crane had to be used for the dismantling of the steel stairs. It lifted them above the building to the side facing the street. This sounds elaborate, but since the demolition was progressing well, the costs were lower than anticipated.

that some tasks can be completed in a way that is easier and costs less. 'We can only truly know how expensive a reuse is and compare it to the purchase price of a new product by trying it out in each case. That is why we are always taking a bit of a risk. If something appears to be just fractionally more expensive, then we'll try it nevertheless. Only the specific actual costs matter.' The tests themselves are another economic factor: each of them costs money and takes time. It would make sense to have a duty of declaration to facilitate reuse, e.g. a QR code on the components that provides information on the type of material, the year of manufacture, coating, dimensions, density, etc.—similar to windscreens.

Just as in the case of the windows from Werk 1, the design and narrative aspects also matter. Owing to the limited selection of parts, it is impossible, when reusing components, to precisely control classic design elements like colour, shape, and surface finish. Their availability dictates a lot of that. However, the origin of the components could have a sentimental or symbolic importance**8** that allows the new building to fit into its surroundings: is the component a good fit for an urban industrial landscape, the kind of setting, that is, that characterizes K.118? This question is important to the team: 'For historic city centres and other protected landscapes, there is always a range of colours that may be used. The building commission first has to approve the effect of the new building on the existing ensemble. We did not need this analysis because our material had previously already been a part of this landscape. We are just recombining it.' For example, the red metal cladding, which gives the new building its iconic look, comes from another of Winterthur's industrial sites.

1 ↗ p. 237	2 ↗ p. 170
K.118 case study Design and construction: Glossary	New paths toward net zero? Potentials for climate protection

'The next step could be to replace the concrete that is used for fire protection with clay. However, we don't yet have the documentation and tests to substantiate this.'

Constructing and coordinating

The construction management and the companies involved on the building site and in the workshop each face a challenge when used components are repurposed. The key is to coordinate the areas in which the human actors, the components, and the work steps intersect.

The wood doesn't fit yet. It is too large and cannot be clamped into the corner of the steel structure. It was supposed to form a tight mould for the mortar that protects the metal from heat in case of fire. In order for the supports to be screwed together, the mortar now also has to fill those areas of the concrete-filled steel supports that were initially left empty. The mason loosens the clamp once again and pulls out the piece of wood. The sunlight hits his face in between the steel supports. He straightens up and walks with the piece of wood across the frame to the other side and one floor down to where the saw is. The floor here, in the place where the roof of the existing building stood just seven weeks previously, has already been re-concreted. Today, the mason is working on the bracing for the level above so that the floor can be built there as well in the following days. The piece of wood is quickly cut to size.

On the construction site

Once the mason has fitted it into place, back on the other side of the building, Pascal makes his way up the stairs of the scaffolding. The meeting with the engineer and the master builder has just finished. Pascal's phone rings. It is the timber construction specialist who currently has the windows in his workshop. With the steel structure now erected in recent weeks, he can work on a concrete design for implementing the façade. It will be completed later with clay and straw here on the construction site. Since the clay takes a long time to dry, this would block the hall of his workshop for too long. When the concrete for all the floors has been poured, the completed façade elements can be mounted. Now, the timber construction specialist has a question about fitting the windows. About 10 metres ahead of Pascal, the crane is lifting six wooden beams that serve as makeshift footbridges between the steel beams, onto the next level. On this Wednesday morning in May, there is a blue sky above the Lagerplatz site, which makes the grey beams appear like shadows when you look up. 'Yes, that's exactly how I envisioned it. Perfect, if it works out like that. I'll come to the shop and we'll take a look. Great.' When Pascal hangs up, the mason has already placed the wood, and the mould is ready for the mortar. Just like the mortar, Pascal, as the construction manager, holds everything together: the different sub-plans, the preparation of the components and their assembly, the deliveries and logistics processes, the work on the construction site, everybody who is involved and all the elements that, with their different specifics, tend to diverge rather than come together. Coordinating them is especially important in those cases when they don't fit together as intended.

'Adding the floors with reused components is similar to building in existing structures. While everything fits together according to plan in a new building and there are few surprises—as long as the plan is good—this was a classic example of building in an existing building. You never know what is going to happen and you often have to come up with a solution on the spot. We obviously want to protect the existing building and do it justice, ensure that it remains visible and preserve its appearance. And that's exactly how things continue when we are adding the floors. Each part we use is an existing material. And we only find out if it truly fits once it is actually here and has to be joined with the other components. In order to plan all that, it is important to study and record the construction when the component is dismantled. And then these parts have to be measured again and again by different people during the planning process. In many cases, though, things don't end up as planned.' However, thanks to the solutions developed on-site, the components come together in the end after all. That is why one of Pascal's main tasks is to familiarize the construction companies with the components and their peculiarities and to advise them to take a close look at each of them and then measure them again. Precise documentation is the central foundation. Two to three times per week Pascal visits the construction site or the companies' facilities and the storage spaces. Architect Valérie Waibel assumed the responsibility for strengthening the existing building on-site. Her office has been located on the Lagerplatz site since the repurposing process began. She has already implemented other projects

[Fig. 1] The edge beams were filled with concrete encasement. This retrofitting[1] was required by fire protection regulations. However, the mounting of the support remains visible and accessible so that the cast beams can also be separated again.[2]

[Fig. 2] Here, different notions of beauty and the perfect surface meet. 'All the concrete surfaces are very beautiful and smooth. When we announced the competition, we had emphasized that we would also be satisfied with less high-quality formwork. After all, it was about the beauty in something that was rough and raw. However, the site foreman did not want any surfaces that did not meet his standards and professional ethics.'

3 ↗ p. 292	↗ p. 219	4 ↗ p. 199	↗ p. 231	↗ p. 230	↗ p. 218
Creating K.118 [fig. 5]	K.118 case study Component catalogue: Zellweger steel section	From part to whole and back again Teaching reuse in architecture	K.118 case study Component catalogue: Eventbau marquee floor panel	K.118 case study Component catalogue: Vogelsang floorboards	K.118 case study Component catalogue: Lysbüchel load-bearing steel structure

on this site using reused materials, such as the Skills Park, the Depot 195 hostel, and the café Portier.

Strengthening the existing building

The façade scaffolding on the eastern side, where the vertical extension towers above the existing building, is doubled up. When the construction barricades are open, this is the way to access the building through the old hall doorway. For the vertical extension, the structure first had to be strengthened. The floors remained for the most part, which is why the locations of the old scales of the Sulzer AG pattern shop are still clearly visible in the floor. Since they were already incomplete (the scale pans were missing), they were covered with concrete and became an accessible yet visible part of the floor. The thermal isolation was important in this area, which is why only the edge of the workshop floor was cut out and re-insulated. 'Fortunately, the perimeter insulation at the edges was sufficient and the centre didn't require any additional insulation. If we had been forced to dig there, we would certainly have found all kinds of old foundations and lines.' And the wooden gallery that forms a mezzanine in the hall is also to remain. However, it will be narrowed to allow more daylight to reach the rear part of the hall through the windows—most of which are located above the gallery.

Four earthquake-proof braces were poured in concrete as reinforcement. One of them also doubles as a lift shaft. Apart from that, the vertical extension can be stabilized by means of the existing lattice stanchions: wherever they form a cavity, they have been filled with concrete encasement—primarily as a fire protection tool.

The large, former industrial windows had to be doubled in order to meet current insulation standards. Only the putty of the windows was removed since it was contaminated with pollutants. Unfortunately, some of the windowpanes broke. The beautiful, old opaque glass of the other windows prohibits a clear view but does allow light to enter. Throughout the different life stages of the building, individual panes had been replaced. As a result, they feature different degrees of opacity and do not form a homogeneous window surface, creating a vibrant mosaic effect.

The beech parquet flooring of the gallery will also be retained. Visually, the room is characterized by the new light-blue fire protection paint of the steel beams on the ceiling of the hall.**3** Two-part walls

On the ground floor, old and new bricks are combined with glass bricks found on-site and, together with the door lintel consisting of the steel sections from Zellweger, they form an unconventional collage.

consisting of new sand-lime brick as well as cement stones in a lighter grey tone, of which there were remainders on the storage yard, form the core of the gallery's sanitary facilities. The wet rooms are also provided with translucent glass bricks. Steel beams from the storage yard were sawn into shape to form the door frames, and two pieces were used as lintels. It turned out that it would not have been logistically and financially sensible to find used sand-lime brick: while it used to be possible to dismantle brick walls and then reuse the bricks, quick-drying, high-performance cement mortar has increasingly been used since the 1970s. That has made it nearly impossible to dismantle a brick wall. This was confirmed during an attempt to recover sand-lime brick from the dismantling of a swimming pool building.**4**

Access to the scaffolding from the gallery of the existing building is via a stepladder through the side window. One floor up, you can get back inside at the same spot. There is a stack of marquee floor panels covered with plastic. These will be turned into interior walls later. 'They had already been lifted inside. Because once the upper floor has been installed, it would be difficult to get them up there. This will be the same procedure on every floor: once the floor is in place, the crane operator lifts the material inside.' The new floor serves as a storage place not only for the future interior fittings but also for the machines and building materials needed for the vertical extension. For example, there are three pallets with sand-lime bricks on the side, and bags of mortar are resting against the wooden walls. Through the scaffold covering in front of the large window front, red light reaches a few iron beams, loose wood, an empty bottle, and a piece of balled-up plastic film. The existing brick façade is braced with slats and stabilized, for now, with steel supports that protrude into the room horizontally.

Instead of the dismantled roof of the existing building, there is now a composite slab consisting of concrete and sheet metal and supported by steel beams, which were once used to cover a roof. Together with the beams, the sheet metal is very stable, which is why the concrete layer can be thin. Here, too, it primarily serves to enhance the building's acoustics and offer fire protection, while also combining connective and load-bearing functions. Later on, an impact sound insulation and the strip wood flooring will be installed on top of it. This is also the last floor to feature the concrete discs used for earthquake-proof reinforcement. They form the base for the steel structure of the added floors.

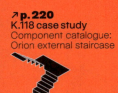 ↗ p.220
K.118 case study
Component catalogue:
Orion external staircase

 5 ↖ p.45
K.118 reportage
Testing and planning
[fig. 7]

↗ p. 218
K.118 case study
Component catalogue:
Lysbüchel load-bearing
steel structure

Michel Massmünster

Erecting the steel structure

Wetter AG took charge of the steel construction for the vertical extension. The company has been associated with the project for over two years. Back then they disassembled the steel stairs from the Orion office buildings.5 Since the stairs had to be moved with a crane from the other side of the building, the K.118 team contracted this job out at the time. Since then, Sven Tiemann, who manages the project at Wetter, has been consulted as an adviser on steel construction issues, so it was clear to him that Wetter would also be involved in the construction. However, their regular process was turned on its head. 'This approach was also new to us. We first had to get an idea of how that could work. Where we usually have a plan on the basis of which the steel is ordered, and tailored parts have already been drilled, welded together with other components, and coated, we now have a pallet of used beams with different profiles from three different locations. And that posed the question of how we could turn them into a new and different framework and do so in such a way that we, as planners, would not have privileged knowledge of how it should work—the fitters and others in the workshop would also know what to do.' The pieces need to be assigned to the new structure and numbered accordingly: that means taking the pieces of an old puzzle and putting them together to form a new one.

Once it was calculated how the new steel framework could be built with the old components, the planners created two workshop plans for each beam: one showing the beam in its former state with the existing mounting parts and indicating what had to be cut off; and another showing the intended state of the beam—i.e. in its newly cut shape—and indicating where a plate (to which a crossbeam is to be screwed later) needs to be welded to it. The two plans cross-reference each other so that it is clear in each case what happens to a component.

'On these plans, we have assigned different numbers. One for plates that are already attached and another for those that still need to be welded to it. However, because these plans are very confusing, we also marked the spots on the beams themselves where new plates would be attached. And we were constantly talking to the people on site because we were only planning things in theory. But when a 16 m steel beam is sitting in front of you, you need to lift it with a crane every time you have to move it.' In some cases, they also turned an old beam into two smaller ones. This was especially challenging in terms of storage and transportation when the two pieces were not installed on the same floor.

Most of this preparation is done entirely in the plant because this is where the machines are set up and the conditions are familiar and unvarying. Each beam usually goes through a standardized sequence for each unit: from the lorry, they are taken to the sandblasting plant, then to the metalworking and welding operations, and from the coating plant back to the lorry, which then takes each unit to the construction site. The reused beams had already been coated and only had to be trimmed. The drilling was done by hand. Wherever plates had to be welded on, the paint had to be sanded off—burning it off was not possible because of hazardous fumes. The plates, shear studs, and other attachment parts were then welded on. And all of that then received a protective coating. From that point on, the process for the steel constructors was standard: the steel beams were driven to the construction site, with four lorryloads per floor.

Only one mistake was made in the process of turning the old beams into new ones: the positioning of one of the installed slabs was 10 cm off. However, when this was noticed on the construction site, the problem could be corrected quickly and easily. New lateral bracing and screws were ordered. During the assembly process and as a result of the movement of the building, these elements were put under so much stress that they could not be used again. In addition, the holes of this stabilizing bracing were so worn out that they could not hold screws again.

On the construction site, the builder lined the edge beams with concrete. This concrete encasement would not have been required for structural purposes, but it was useful for fire protection. Essentially, the beams lined with concrete form a frame. In case of fire, regular steel beams will bend. However, the edge beams lined with concrete can withstand it. And because the composite floor is interlocked with them via shear studs, the membrane ceiling will bend in a fire, but it will not fall for at least the legally required 60 minutes. The K.118 team would have loved to have found a fire protection solution without concrete. Research and development are still needed in this area.

That's another way to build!

All the way at the top, the sandwich panels, which came from a makeshift railway station in Aarau, will be installed as roof elements in two weeks. This means that the

[Fig. 4] Handling tolerances: the steel structure of the vertical extension on each floor was too low in relation to the platform spacing of the external staircase. As a result, jack rafters were used for the bearings of the support until the dimensions were right: 'The fitter added one shim after another, like slices of ham, until the height was right.'
[Fig. 5] Corbels are screwed to the outer beams of the steel structure and will later be used as supports for the façade. These sections of shortened beams are also reused components.

↗ p. 221	↗ p. 220	↗ p. 225	↗ p. 231	6 ↗ p. 243
K.118 case study Component catalogue: Siemens photovoltaic system	K.118 case study Component catalogue: Orion external staircase	K.118 case study Component catalogue: Orion cladding slab 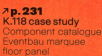	K.118 case study Component catalogue: Eventbau marquee floor panel	K.118 case study Construction organization: Component organigram

Constructing and coordinating

roof's entire edge will then consist of wood, on top of which a railing will be placed. In addition, a 20-year-old photovoltaic system from the Siemens site in Zurich-Albisrieden will be installed and operated on the roof. The sole purpose of a used balcony rail, which almost seems too high-quality for this task, is to secure the support of this solar array. 'But it would have been even less satisfactory if we had simply discarded it.' The façade is then assembled. And once the additional floors are in place, the balcony and the steel stairs will be built on the western side, i.e. on the opposite side of the cantilever. Wetter had painstakingly documented the stairs while they were being dismantled and reinstalled them accordingly, whereby the flights remained in one piece anyway. The rails and the connections had to be adapted because the stairs had been installed transversely to the previous building but longitudinally to this one. The balcony was designed according to the same principle as the large steel structure. Correspondingly, it was set up with additional cross connections to stabilize the relatively heavy granite slabs.

Wetter invested a lot of time in the process of planning all their work so that everything only had to be put together on the construction site. 'That is just like putting together a cabinet: if one piece is missing, you're lost. But if the numbers of the parts are correct and all of them are accounted for, then it becomes a kit with instructions. We only had about nine working days in which to add the new floors. Then the screws had to be tightened. And just like that, the steel construction was completed in three weeks. However, we had been planning it for more than a year.'

'In hindsight', Tiemann said, 'you're always smarter. It was also a pilot project for us. Looking back, we should have created a plan right at the beginning with all the data for each individual beam. We only took possession of the beams after the detailed planning was done. We shouldn't have done it like that—we should have had them here earlier and measured and assigned them. Because picking out the individual beams takes a lot of time. It would have been even easier if we had had the plans from the previous construction. Since the halls the steel came from were already old, these implementation plans no longer existed. When we are building these days, we list all the data and values for each beam in a table along with the associated plan. The existence of these plans would simplify the reuse of the components tremendously. In the future, digitization will likely allow this to happen.'

In Pascal's experience, the changes to the usual processes and approaches were reason enough for other construction companies to not bid for this project. 'Many of them say that this isn't for them. Not because they can't do it but because it interferes with their processes and capacity utilization. Most importantly, the production process is eliminated because the material already exists. However, the assembly is more extensive because of the adaptations that have been made, for example. When their order books are already full, then it is simply not worth it for some companies.'

Wetter was very interested in the project. But here, too, the communication within the team posed a challenge. Not all the team members initially thought it made sense to not simply melt down the beams and mill new ones. However, over time, the enthusiasm in the plant and among suppliers and their network kept growing. The project had a signalling effect and the attention has shifted toward reuse: 'Oh, that's another way to build!' For example, Wetter began receiving emails with tips about materials that could be reused.

At the intersections

While the steel structure was being erected, Michael Wick planed wooden panels in the shelter on Lagerplatz opposite K.118 and polished them with a floor sander. These panels will later turn into interior walls. One of the sections of this shelter serves as a trading centre for the components on-site, and the other serves as a workshop for these types of preparatory tasks. The 3-ply panels came from a company that does event construction: they were used as flooring tiles and panels for different major events, such as gymnastics and wrestling meets or trade fairs, and then discarded at some point. Once the sides that will later be visible as walls are sanded and polished, the high-quality panels are as good as new.

Since 2016, Michael has been working with the in situ team intermittently—to the point where he is a part of it: he assumes tasks in those areas that are not envisaged at all in a conventional building operation.6 Michael studied energy and environmental technology—and the sustainable handling of resources was a central topic. Because he had worked as a metalworker and gate fitter prior to his studies, and often worked with waste wood, he started to connect these aspects more consciously. Together with two friends, he founded an association which they used to support a workshop. They started selling waste wood in order to fund the workshop. After a year, they were able to pay rent from their sales and they also started getting other jobs. This

The shelter next to Hall 118 is used as a workshop for processing materials. Four discarded 3-ply boards are placed against the rear wall. It turned out during planing that their condition was too bad to be reused.

7 ↗ p.246
K.118 case study
Construction organization:
Circular models

↗ p.231
K.118 case study
Component catalogue:
Eventbau marquee
floor panel

Michel Massmünster

Constructing and coordinating

soon left them with hardly any time to make their own things. 'That's when we said that we should found our own limited liability company and pay ourselves salaries.' In addition to the work from baubüro in situ they also received a lot of smaller jobs—often from private individuals. Michael views the cooperation with K.118 as a boon: it is often uncomplicated, informal and, in some cases, he has found waste wood for his workshop at the demolition sites. 'At the same time, we are doing things that others won't. We view our work in its entirety. We do everything ourselves. From the walk-through to the dismantling and transporting—including packing and securing the materials—and sometimes also the inventory, cutting, assembling, and processing. During the demolition for K.118, everything always had to happen very quickly and we were on standby too. The assembly and the processing can now be planned better.'

The complete service offered by Wick Upcycling GmbH allows circular construction to take place in an environment where there is no applicable industry. Working in these intersecting areas requires a combination of hard manual labour, a talent for organization, and expert knowledge of materials and environmental protection. A multilayered scope of operations of the kind Michael foresees for the future of circular construction is still rare these days: serial production has led to the automation of logistics and processing. That is why Michael's versatile skills and expertise—also relative to the handling of the components—play a key role when it comes to reusing materials for K.118.⁷

Processing the wood flooring panels from the event construction company was one such task in these intersecting spaces. For Michael, this took a lot of effort, which is why he wanted to work with an industrial sawmill or a large joinery that could have simply run the panels through a belt sander. However, all of them declined. If there were any screws in the wood, the sanding sheet would have to be replaced and the machine taken apart to do so. That is not efficient. 'That is why we bought this large carpenter's plane. However, after 20 panels, it has become clear that you can only plane an average of two panels before the blades are shot. That means it is also expensive, time-consuming, and physically demanding. While the end result is panels that are as good as new, they unfortunately also cost nearly as much. However, the main objective is to not just throw everything away and then buy new things.'

The 'wiederverwerkle' warehouse and workshop at Wick Upcycling GmbH: the wealth of material inspires visitors to start their own projects with the leftover wood.

↗ **p.230**
K.118 case study
Component catalogue:
Vogelsang floorboards

↗ **p.222**
K.118 case study
Component catalogue:
Vogelsang radiator

Adapting, repairing, reinstalling

K.118 continues the story of the Lagerplatz site's careful transformation into a diverse, vibrant urban space. The Abendrot Foundation's development strategy, which is based on participation and sufficiency, is again proving its worth as a pioneering force in sustainable building.

Michael lifts the crowbar below the wood slat, pushes down on it and lifts the ridge of the parquet board out of the groove. With one twist, he places the board  with the others. They are tied together in bundles of four and then lifted out of the window down to the transport vehicle. There is no time to remove all the nails and clean the grooves so that they can later be interlocked with the ridges. They've been given only a one-day time window to dismantle the entire apartment building. A complicating factor is that asbestos remediation measures are also being carried out today, which is why the room from which the floors are being removed has to be vacated from time to time. An old couple walks up Vogelsangstrasse. They stop in front of the house and watch the activity. After a while, the woman says, 'Too bad that all of this will be thrown out. I played on this floor as a child. I grew up here.' 'We won't throw this floor in the rubbish. We're going to reinstall it, and the radiators as well. Over there, on the Lagerplatz site on the other side of the tracks.'

Whenever Michael talks about the dismantling of the parquet floor, this meeting with the woman who grew up in that apartment building becomes the turning point of the story. For him, all the hard work pays off in this moment. It is another story that doesn't end. Instead, it is revived with the reuse of the building components. First, the pieces of stripwood are taken to the component storage facility at the old bus depot, where any nails and dirt are removed. That facility is a bit further away from the dismantling location than the Lagerplatz site where they will be installed later.

The Lagerplatz

The Abendrot Foundation purchased the Lagerplatz site in 2009 and has since been continually investing in the renovation and restoration of the existing buildings on the former premises of Sulzer AG. In the late 1980s, the spaces in the area were rented out as a temporary solution after they were no longer being used for industrial purposes. While the other parts of the factory site were gradually put to new uses, the Lagerplatz located in its southern section fulfilled a temporary function for longer than anticipated and during that time turned into a vibrant city quarter. In order to preserve the Lagerplatz for tenants and to protect it against being resold, a dedicated association was formed which persuaded the Abendrot Foundation to invest in the site's future as a new urban nexus for the neighbourhood.

In accordance with the foundation's sustainability objectives, it was clear that the existing building would be retained and its current uses refined to make them fit for long-term use. This not only established a link to the building but also to the existing social networks and local businesses. In order to begin this process with and on behalf of the users, the consulting company denkstatt sàrl, which specializes in the transformation of such sites, was tasked with the project management. The process at the Lagerplatz began with a two-day workshop with the participation of residents and tenants. The question of who wants what in regards to the site was hotly debated. Stakeholder meetings of the project management team with the association representing the Lagerplatz site have been continually taking place on a regular basis since then. As the renovations would also have an effect on rent in the neighbourhood, this was discussed with the tenants in each case. What do you want, what do you need, what can you do without? One striking example of this participatory process is the staircase in the lift shaft of Building 165 right next to Hall 118. The lift no longer met safety standards and needed to be replaced. The tenants decided that they would rather pay less rent than have the comfort of a lift. Therefore, a reused industrial staircase was installed in the shaft instead of a new lift.

Since the 1980s, industrial production has been gradually moving out of the cities of central Europe. Hardly anything is manufactured in urban areas anymore and, initially, these sites were in danger of becoming entirely useless stretches of land. Urban planning was no longer focused on accommodating the industrial sector. Instead, the idea was for residents, tourists, service providers, as well as corporate headquarters to move into the cities to ensure that new jobs would be created and taxes collected even without the presence of manufacturing companies.

[Fig. 1]   Extraordinary solutions thanks to participatory planning: the staircase in the lift shaft at Lagerplatz 165 offers a surprise to anybody who unwittingly opens the lift doors.

[Fig. 2]   Since the staircase was too narrow, the room-width floorboards had to be lifted out of the window at Vogelsangstrasse. Therefore, the dismantling process was limited to the bottom floors. Here, too, the selection of components depended on which of them could feasibly be dismantled.

1 ↖ p. 11
Reuse!

'Therefore, together with Klara Kläusler, I founded the component exchange Buser & Kläusler in 1995 and, in 1996, Bauteilbörse Basel as well as the corresponding umbrella organization, Bauteilnetz Schweiz.'

2 ↗ p. 195
Uncharted legal territory
Reuse under Swiss law

'Older components can legally remain installed without problems, despite changes in the standards. But once they have been removed, they must usually be adapted to current standards.'

Michel Massmünster

Thus, priorities in urban planning had shifted. The creative city of today seeks to be vibrant and attractive. This works when fashionable small businesses, event sites, and restaurants revive the vacant plots of land left behind by the industrial sector. At the same time, it is to be expected that the way in which business is conducted, and therefore the requirements people have of these spaces, will keep changing. For this reason, it makes sense for any design undertaking not to go down the path of a fixed approach to planning and implementing the buildings, the sites, and their uses; rather, it should provide different options and maintain a provisional aspect that facilitates continuous development for future uses and demands. Instead of sourcing materials remotely and bringing them in from the places the production companies have relocated to, the local economy should be relied upon. The space for something new emerges from what is left behind and supposedly no longer needed. As a result, the Lagerplatz is now an extremely vibrant urban quarter: each day at noon, students meet in front of a whole array of food trucks to have lunch. Further along, in the Skills Park, children are bouncing on trampolines and shooting down skate ramps. In the offices and studios now located on the site, people are working on projects in the areas of design, research, and development. Type is set, lunches are served, hotel rooms are cleaned, and backs and limbs are stretched in the local yoga studio. This seemingly useless industrial site has been turned into the showpiece quarter of the post-industrial city.

Klara Kläusler, who was in charge of real estate for the Abendrot Foundation until October 2018, tells the story: 'When we took over the site, it was obvious that renovations were needed. From the start, we said that we would do that with and for the people who would use these spaces: this allows the tenants to identify with the place. They care and stay. Still, due to the renovations and the corresponding rent increases, there was some turnover throughout the years. K.118 is the last building that still needs to be renovated. It had no thermal insulation, no heat, and the roof was leaking. Most of the time, it was unoccupied and only had some short-term tenants—including a laboratory for water treatment. That raised the question: what are we to do with this last property, which still needs to be worked on but has not been used the whole time like the other buildings? And, unlike in the other cases, we were not able to renovate it with an eye

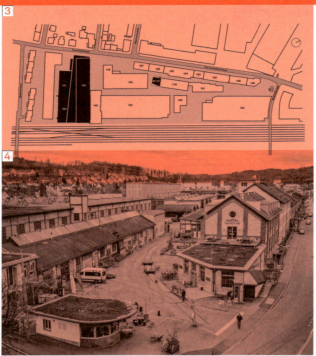

[Fig. 3] The Lagerplatz in the former Sulzer site: the location of the ZHAW School of Architecture, Design and Civil Engineering (large) and that of K.118 (small) are marked in black.
[Fig. 4] The Lagerplatz brings together provisional and existing materials.

Playing with the available spaces: in 1990/91, the former boiler shop was the first hall of the Lagerplatz site to be repurposed and has since served the ZHAW's School of Architecture, Design and Civil Engineering as a teaching and research facility.

toward a specific use. That is why we had the idea of focusing our attention on the goals of the Abendrot Foundation and asking, what does sustainable building mean today? How can we take the reuse of materials to another level? Reused materials have often been utilized for construction, but it's something new for an investment property.'

The reuse of materials was a key focus for Klara Kläusler even before she came to work at the Abendrot Foundation. Back then, the foundation was in charge of renovating a number of houses located at the corner of Inselstrasse and Gärtnerstrasse in Basel while at the same time aiming to keep rent at a reasonable level. The foundation had taken over these buildings when the owner declared bankruptcy. If this had been a case of a 'normal' renovation, the tenants would have had to move out and thus experience a significant disturbance in their daily lives. This resulted in the idea of conducting the renovation with used materials and enlisting the help of the tenants. Since Klara Kläusler and Barbara Buser, as architects and founders of Bauteilbörse Basel,[1] were already familiar with such approaches, they were given the job of overseeing this project. For the two founders of the building component exchange, it was a good opportunity to reuse old gas ovens, toilet bowls, and boilers in the renovation.

Even with the renovation of the last building, K.118, the work on the Lagerplatz will not be at an end and the result won't be perfect. It will keep changing—together with the people who use it and with shifts in society and the economy. And, most of all, with the different uses that are adapting to the existing buildings.

Raw and comprehensible

K.118 not only blends into its environment visually. It also adopts the principle of the Lagerplatz in terms of circularity. The goal is not a completed, perfect building constructed for a specific use. The careful transformation adapts to the possibilities of the existing buildings. With the use of the components on-site, the flow of materials and the energy consumption are reduced. While the legal regulation for old houses stipulates that existing buildings do not have to meet all current regulations, those components taken from elsewhere for the purposes of reuse do.[2] The components are therefore included in the utilization planning. In this way, an open-ended process of use, adaptation, repair, replacement, and dismantling arises from existing resources. Just like the Lagerplatz itself, the house is raw and variable. Both consist of diverse layers and

3 ↗ p.236	4 ↗ p.237	↗ p.221	5 ↗ p.247	6 ↗ p.256	8 ↗ p.266
K.118 case study	K.118 case study	K.118 case study	K.118 case study	K.118 case study	Eight theses
Design and construction: Glossary	Design and construction: Glossary	Component catalogue: Siemens photovoltaic system	Construction organization: Circular models	Greenhouse gas emissions	
				7 ↗ p.165	
				New paths toward net zero?	
				Potentials for climate protection	Challenging the demands

Adapting, repairing, reinstalling

stories. Based on the potential of the materials and the imagination of the users, the building will continue to develop even after its construction is complete.

The plan is that on every floor the rental units will each feature three rooms that connect to a common area. This common area consists of a terrace, the lift, and two wet rooms as well as a common room that connects to the three studios. With the flooring recovered from Vogelsangstrasse and the freshly planed 3-ply boards from the event and trade fair company, which now function as walls, the interior design is fairly 'raw'. The idea is for tenants to adapt the rooms to their respective needs and continue working on them. The walls consisting of the 4×1m panels can be painted or papered. It is easy to drill and screw into them, and any holes that are created can be filled again later. With a thickness of 30 mm, the panels are also very robust compared with conventional office partitions. They can be sanded time and again, and they are wear resistant and durable. Additional walls can be installed or, if at some point a future tenant requires an entire floor, they can also be removed and later reinstalled. This allows the rooms to be designed for all types of requirements, which has advantages for a studio apartment building. The raw interior design also keeps costs low.

'The parquet tiles, which now measure 20mm, are 3mm thinner than they were when they were installed during the construction of the houses on Vogelsangstrasse. That means we can sand them any number of times.' Spare parts are no concern when it comes to the floors and the wooden walls. It's like a pencil that is being sharpened: renewal by planing. Other components, such as toilet bowls or the hinges of windows, however, follow the principle of a refill pencil: the problematic part can be replaced. That is why the construction remains simple, visible, and accessible. Preferably screwed or clamped rather than bonded or held in place with mortar. Preferably made of wood or steel and not concrete. The support structure, technical equipment, and building circulation don't feature any cladding. The goal is to ensure the legibility **3** of the components and their construction. When the design logistics are visible, then existing materials can be more easily replaced, repaired, and adapted. The building is constructed in layers and components are joined with tolerance **4** ranges. This allows a separation of functions to be maintained and ensures the components are accessible. As a result, not all components have to last as long as the building itself: for example, the exterior blinds, which were

dismantled together with the windows, were used again following a revision and can be replaced if needed.

The photovoltaic system  that was installed on the roof will also not last forever. It was not added to the component storage of K.118 but rather remains in the possession of Alteno Solar AG, which will continue to operate it for the rest of its service life since it could not remain at its previous location. This means that the roof will be rented out by the operator of the system. Not all components have to be bought and sold. A circular adaptation of the building can also benefit from the borrowing of material or the renting out of spaces. **5**

Setting priorities, redefining values

'K.118 does not have to be able to do it all. Above all, we are seeking perfection in the process of combining things and not just in the result. That is our priority. If the steel beams had needed to be newly sandblasted and coated, they would not have been able to compete financially with new steel beams, given current labour costs. But now they can. They haven't been recoated—but, on the other hand, we are reducing our CO_2 emissions and are excited about the patina. There really is beauty in the imperfection of the existing building. It is about setting priorities and asking what is in short supply—and that is energy in this case. The way we build offers an opportunity to greatly reduce our domestic CO_2 output.' **6, 7** Out of necessity, the team working on K.118 does not need to worry about conventional quality and beauty standards because the modern concept of the perfect house results in a lot of wear and does not meet the changing needs of users. The team's experience with the use of steel structures has also shown that it is simply not possible to build for the same cost while following the same ideal of beauty and aiming to be environmentally friendly at the same time. It was necessary to set the right priorities, which meant that sacrifices had to be made. Sufficiency is not just a question of using as little energy and as few raw materials as possible: how much space, how much money and how much energy is someone entitled to? It is also a question of one's own standards: what can and what should a building achieve—aesthetically, qualitatively, and technically, and with regard to construction standards and energy costs? **8**

This is how old standards are questioned and new ones are established. What can be considered as construction resources

[Fig. 6] Almost done: the partitions have already been covered with the sanded marquee floor panels while the wooden floorboards are still being installed.
[Fig. 7] From a discussion with the joinery that made the doors, it transpires that the quality is higher than expected. Their anti-theft and sound insulation properties exceed the technical requirements.

Michel Massmünster

and what is to be declared waste? That is a question currently being redefined. What we today commonly view as waste is the result of a long-established societal construct of value and worthlessness. The good news is: it doesn't have to be this way. Circular building rethinks the interplay between scarcity and excess. Because what is available today is what there is plenty of after the era of industrial cities has come to an end. However, the resources of this type of industrial building and thinking have become scarce. That is why the leftovers of this industrial use have become resources that can be used to create something new.

As a pilot project, K.118 symbolizes a process of learning that explores what is possible in the process of planning the future development of cities. The associated labour itself is also undergoing a process of rethinking. It is no longer the labour of industrial mass production but rather the kind that turns waste into resources. That also makes labour a part of local networks.

The doors with wooden frames and a glass insert, which the K.118 team was able to acquire from the temporary solution of the Volkiland shopping centre, have also become a valuable resource. The team bought the doors from a recycling company that dismantles components and sells them on via the online platform Ricardo. The doors still feature the markings from the carpenter's workshop that made them. Marc contacts the workshop to hopefully be able to find out the insulation value and climatic class of the doors. The answer he gets illustrates yet another one of their benefits: 'Good that the doors will be used again. These are very valuable interior and exterior doors that were manufactured and coated with great care in our workshop! These are not ready-made doors.' That is why Marc also views reusing components as a process of honouring the energy and labour invested in them and benefiting from their appeal, their robustness, and the clever workmanship that went into making them.[9]

Reusing ideas

To Klara Kläusler, one of the keys to visionary projects, such as the Lagerplatz in 2009 and K.118 today, is to involve people from the start. Financial backers, public authorities, users, residents, construction companies, craftspeople, and the individual workers have to be won over and/or motivated by the project. At the same time, it is important that these projects are developed not only on the basis of but by making use of the knowledge and perception of these people, and that they are designed together in a collaborative process. After all, the end result is not set in stone right from the beginning. And this is precisely the challenge in terms of communication. 'When it comes to this kind of project, if you do everything behind closed doors and then come out and say, "Here is the finished building," then you've got to expect problems. Which is why it is important to get people excited from the start, to make sure the process is transparent and developed together. And there was another question: will we even be able to convince these financial backers, the building authorities, the Office for Urban Planning of this idea up front if we don't know what it will look like in the end? And it's not as though it was just at the very beginning that we didn't have this information to present them with. It's something that remained uncertain for a long period of time. In the beginning, there was merely the idea of adding the floors by using as many reused components as possible, but liquid funds still had to be available.[10] Even before the hunting and gathering began, the main job for the entire team was to get people to imagine a different future of construction.'

The *Transform* exhibition at the Swiss Architecture Museum in autumn of 2018 signified an important moment that drew attention to the project and the topic as a whole. Since then, the team at baubüro in situ have clearly demonstrated their enthusiasm for reusing materials in a number of presentations in which Barbara, Ben, Kerstin, Marc, and Pascal have put across their exploratory approach to implementing a different type of building. As a result, sustainability is no longer an abstract goal but rather something that can be experienced through the attitude of the team. This gives this alternative type of building a performative character: relatively rigid patterns are broken up and contrasted with sustainable building. This enthusiasm is often infectious.

As a result, communicating the ideas not only gets decision-makers on board, it also becomes an aspect inherent to circular construction: developing existing buildings also means understanding them. The dismantling and reinstalling of components becomes much easier when the documentation detailing the type of construction and the components can be consulted. That is another reason why it is so important for the team to document its ideas and processes in a transparent manner: the reuse of components benefits from the reuse and adaptation of ideas. The building remains its own beta version, which can be maintained and refined by its users.

[Fig. 8] A museum-like storage facility for components: the *Transform* exhibition at the Swiss Architecture Museum in Basel in the autumn of 2018.
[Fig. 9] Transparent and reversible: the façade of K.118 as a 1:1 model in the *Component Recycling* exhibition at the ZHAW's School of Architecture, Design and Civil Engineering in 2019. The model was used to discuss façade design principles with the Office for Urban Planning during the building permit application process.

Adapting, repairing, reinstalling

However, the entire process should not only be transparent, it should also be changeable. After all, the goal of the pilot project is that this type of construction will be developed further in the future and catch on as a valid construction process for a wide array of uses. Therefore, it is important to the Abendrot Foundation that the project also has a scientific vision. The insights and the authorship are shared in order to benefit from each other and to exemplify the ideal of a creative, vibrant, and open city at the Lagerplatz as a kind of laboratory in which other people's innovations and experiments can be refined. Accordingly, in the case of K.118, it was not just the components that became resources for creating something new but also the social network, collective knowledge, and communication involved in its evolution. The exploration and detours, the temporary failures, and the process of learning by doing—which are all part of developing new approaches—become a design principle that, when it is communicated to the outside world, ideally gets others thinking along similar lines and makes them want to participate in similar projects. In the case of K.118, this is why the different stakeholders and components not only derive mutual benefit but also get the most out of each other.

Essays

Eva Stricker

Reusers

In 20th- and 21st-century Europe, influential architects have devoted themselves to working with surplus or reclaimed building components. Five examples illustrate their thoughts and approaches.

Where should we begin when looking for ways to deal with the reuse of building components in architecture? Modernism is regarded as a drastic turning point: not only did the industrialization of construction and the replacement of craft conventions with architectural details developed far from the building site reduce the economic legitimacy of reuse, but since then the clear division of labour between design and construction has in a way also undermined the implicit understanding that materials should be used economically. Reuse went from being a ubiquitous real-world practice to a conscious intellectual choice, be it in the centuries-old idea of incorporating richly historic spolia or in the activist anti-architecture of the 1960s and 1970s à la Drop City. There, dwellings collaged from the detritus of civilization were elevated to an expression of fundamental social criticism and thus went on the offensive to break with all the architectural conventions and structural achievements their time had to offer. In this case, reuse developed from a self-evident feature to a premise to a provocative end in itself for architecture. So what can we build on as we seek a new implicitness in reuse that infiltrates the architectural practice of our time? Do we really have to resort to pre-modern references?

Since 1950, despite the rationalization of construction and an increasingly theoretical approach to planning, numerous architects throughout Europe have, with various motives and in a more or less critical confrontation with the (long-term) consequences of two world wars and the achievements of modernism, reused building components or anticipated their future reuse—not as an end in itself for their architecture but as a relevant part of it. These include well-known figures whose practical and theoretical work we have long appreciated for entirely different reasons. Some of these figures are presented again in this essay—this time as 'reusers'.

Eva Stricker

↗ p. 73
Maison Prouvé

Crisis as incentive

Was Jean Prouvé (1901–1984) a reuser? The brilliant designer is commonly known as a visionary pioneer who preferred to look ahead instead of relying on what already existed: innovations in construction and materials that stemmed from aircraft and automobile production were his model for starting on the path to the building technology of the future. Even when helping to rebuild France after two world wars, he did not want to dwell on how to make use of the ruins. 'We need factory-built houses'[1] was his clear response to the challenges of the time. Prefabricated building kits of lightweight precision components optimized for design and building physics would alleviate the housing shortage caused by the war. In his plea for innovative lightweight construction systems, even considerations regarding the expenditure of energy in construction, which we now identify as 'grey energy', played a role alongside advanced thermal insulation.[2] His numerous experiments and inventions for portable pavilions and buildings that can be taken apart again also appear visionary in the context of today's discussions on circular structures.

When Prouvé finally decided to build a house for himself and his family (1952–1954), the circumstances were rather unfavourable: the plot of land on a former vineyard in the north of Nancy was idyllically overgrown, very sunny, and had a beautiful view, but the steep terrain made it impossible to use construction machinery and the bearing capacity of the soil was also poor. Moreover, even before construction began, Prouvé was forced out of the management position at his workshops in Maxéville—which he had successfully built up in the preceding years—by the new majority owner, Aluminium française. This not only deprived him of access to professional production facilities but also made financial resources scarcer. Under these adverse circumstances, Prouvé demonstrated his talent for improvisation: he built the new house himself, with help from his friends and family but without the use of heavy equipment. His wife's off-road vehicle served to transport material and people. He abandoned the original plan for a custom-fabricated composite shell roof and instead adapted the design to make use of available finished products and remnants from past production series. The roof consists of so-called Rousseau panels, industrial cross-laminated plywood boards in a standardized format, which rest on the steel structure. The south façade consists of elements that were developed or produced for other building projects. For example, wooden panels with retractable windows, like those in the Croismare school (1949), are lined up next to panels with fixed glazing. Still others are made of aluminium and feature the characteristic round porthole windows. In the struggle between the constraints of given standardized components and the specific requirements of a design task that could not be more individual, spaces with an unusual,

1   'Wir brauchen fabrikfertige Häuser' [We need factory-built houses], lecture on 16 Feb. 1946 in Nancy, in Vegesack 2006, 176–185.

2   Translated from ibid.: 'In Saarland, where buildings can be built of steel, we break down the proportional material costs. We found that 4.5 tons of coal are consumed to produce the building material needed for a small house, including [production of] the briquettes, heating equipment, glass, etc. … while in the same region, at least 29 tons of coal are consumed to build a traditional house with 30 cm thick brick walls, plus the heating fuel in addition.'

cheerful lightness emerged, which was only made possible through the transfer[1] of mundane industrial components into the world of habitation.

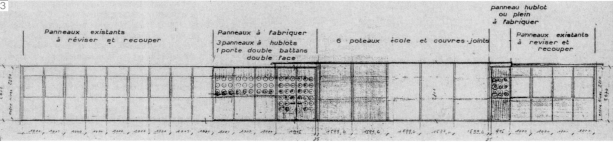

[Figs. 1, 2]   Maison Prouvé construction site.
[Fig. 3]   Sketch indicating the sources of the façade panels.

1 ↗ **p. 237**
K.118 case study
Design and construction: Glossary

In the balance

'Classic modernism' was just beginning to pass its zenith when Carlo Mollino (1905–1973), who was only a few years younger than Prouvé, began his architectural career in his father's studio in Turin. Countless bizarre anecdotes surround his reputation as a colourful enfant terrible. Besides his well-known passions for aviation, skiing, fast cars, and beautiful women, early on the photographer, designer, art historian, and architect developed a penchant for rural construction. While still a student, he meticulously surveyed and documented utilitarian farm buildings of the Aosta Valley and their construction principles. Although the planned reference book on the topic remained unwritten, Mollino has been associated ever since with the archaic farmhouses and granaries of the region, known locally as 'rascards'. Thus, the motif of a simple alpine hut repeatedly surfaces in his work—as part of sometimes adventurous alliances.

Casa Capriata, for example—his proposed contribution to the Triennale X in Milan in 1954—unites elements of traditional timber structures with bold cantilevers, industrial prefabrication, and innovations in energy and materials technology. The iconic triangular wooden hut appeared in antecedent forms years earlier in other unrealized projects, such as the Dusio (1946) and Cranda (1947) villas, and as a ski club on the roof of the imposing Centro sportivo Quota 2600. For the Vetroflex Domus

↗ **p. 74**
Casa Garelli

competition of 1951, the same idea was developed constructively in greater depth. In 2014, Casa Capriata was ultimately built posthumously in Gressoney-Saint-Jean, with scholarly support from Politecnico di Torino.

Whereas Casa Capriata was only relocated in theory, the move was real in Champoluc: in 1962 Felice Garelli, a surveyor and producer of cement-based building products, bought the almost 300-year-old Taleuc rascard in the Aosta Valley. It was a traditional granary built of solid timbers resting on mushroom-shaped piers, called 'boléri', above a quarry-stone base. He commissioned his friend Carlo Mollino to relocate the historic wooden structure to the other side of the valley and convert it into a holiday home. A new base was built, again of stones instead of concrete as initially planned. Ten boléri of grey granite, each 50 cm high and Mollino's own interpretation of the traditional prototype,[3] support the log structure—which, with its new balconies, cantilevers acentrically far beyond the base. A wrap-around band of windows in the joint above the base admits light to the ground floor. The carpenter meticulously catalogued the timbers of the upper storeys to facilitate disassembly and reassembly. Yet what emerged at the new location was a new house: additional openings and covered balconies alter the façades, a central staircase gives access to the interior rooms, and green glazed tiles clad the new stove. The new elements remain recognizable in places, but elsewhere they optically merge with what has been reused. The result is neither a 'correct' conservational reconstruction nor a didactically legible addition of old and new. Preserved and retrofitted, unifying and contrasting parts interweave to form a multivalent whole that embodies both the rural tradition of its antecedent and the modern elegance of a structure fragilely hanging in the balance. A futuristic exterior stair underscores the ambivalence of the composition. Against the rural alpine backdrop, it seems utterly exotic: its dynamically cantilevered reinforced-concrete mono stringer with slender larch treads and white-painted railing was custom-made for this house but could well have come from a fashionable coastal resort—or from Mollino's famous sled-lift station on Lago Nero.

3 See Reichlin 1991, 12–14.

[Figs. 4, 5] Taleuc rascard on its original site (left); Casa Garelli at its new site (right).

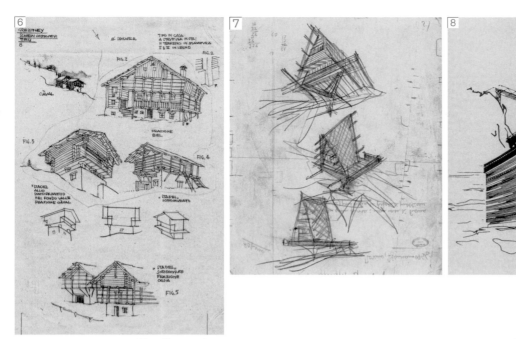

[Fig. 6] Documentation of traditional building methods in the Aosta Valley (c.1930).
[Figs. 7, 8] Precursors to Casa Capriata: sketches for a holiday home (c.1940) and a sports centre with ski club on the roof (1945–1947).

As found

'Setting ourselves the task of rethinking architecture in the early 1950s, we meant by the "as found" not only adjacent buildings but all those marks that constitute remembrancers in a place and that are to be read through finding out how the existing built fabric of the place had come to be as it was … Thus the "as found" was a new seeing of the ordinary, an openness as to how prosaic "things" could re-energize our inventive activity.'[4]

In their late work, Alison (1928–1993) and Peter (1923–2003) Smithson's critical exploration of the guiding principles of modernism led them to a scrupulous, reactive approach to the found. Otherwise, a place like the Bad Karlshafen residence of Axel Bruchhäuser, owner of the furniture manufacturer Tecta, would have been almost inconceivable. When Alison Smithson first visited the 'Hexenhaus' in the summer of 1984, the story of its sustained transformation had already begun long before: in 1978, the artist, architect, and designer Stefan Wewerka (1928–2013) and his client Bruchhäuser were pursuing a daring project nearby. On an artificial plateau on the north bank of the Weser near Bad Karlshafen, a modernist icon was brought back to life. A building permit application was posthumously submitted in Mies van der Rohe's name for his 'Fifty by Fifty Feet House', an archetypal residential pavilion made of steel and glass, which had previously existed only on paper. Although the building authorities rejected the request, the square travertine slabs for the floor had already been delivered.

4 Alison and Peter Smithson, 'The "As Found" and the "Found"', in Robbins 1990, 201.

↗ p. 75
Hexenhaus

Eva Stricker

While studying potential alternatives, Axel Bruchhäuser stumbled upon the vacant house on the neighbouring property. After war's end, a retired captain had built an archetypal gabled cottage as a retreat for himself in the enchanted woods. It had a stone base, half-timbering on the upper floor, and a pointed gable roof, and was known in the neighbourhood as the 'Hexenhaus', or 'Witch House'. The decision to purchase it ushered in a shift from an ideal project on a levelled base to a process of delving beneath the leafy canopy of the woods and contriving something new from what they found. After their interim use in a trade-fair stand, the available stone slabs were laid on the ground floor of the Hexenhaus, while, on the upper floor, Wewerka designed large-scale imagery for the floors using lacquered woods, river pebbles, and marble tiles.[5] Four of the floor panels featured reused black horsehair coverings by Peter Keler.[6]

    Yet Bruchhäuser wanted even more light and to share in the beauty of the forest, so he consulted Alison and Peter Smithson, with whom he was already collaborating at Tecta, thanks to a referral from their Team X colleague Wewerka. The formal enquiry about collaboration on the Hexenhaus was sent on 2 May 1984 in a letter on behalf of 'Sir Karl', Bruchhäuser's cat. Three weeks later, a pawprint-signed written reply from his British counterpart, 'Snuff Smithson', arrived with initial sketches, and that was the basis for years of friendship and collaboration. In the ensuing nine years, the Smithsons, having succumbed to the fairy-tale magic of the place, were regular guests at the Hexenhaus for architectural interventions both large and small: inward and outward openings, new seating areas, footbridges, and lookouts for the master of the house and his cat have since linked the house and the landscape into a 'conglomerate ordering'.[7] In the beginning there was 'Axel's Porch'. On the western gable wall, an earlier entrance with a glass door had not achieved the desired sense of openness to the landscape. Alison Smithson had the double-leaf door removed and, in its stead, added a spatial windowed enclosure that extends out polygonally into the woods. Its individual facets are framed with Douglas fir wood, and the organic divisions resemble the branches of the trees. The two used door leaves were saved, cut to size, and carefully fitted into the new construction. 'As found is a small affair: it's about being careful.'[8]

    Since this process began almost forty years ago, there have been continual selective interventions that, starting from the found, have established new vistas, spatial relationships, and places of retreat in the house and garden. At first, Alison Smithson was in charge. After her death it was Peter, and today their son Simon and his wife continue to work with Bruchhäuser on the house: an iterative, interpretative, and dialogical process that neither seeks nor finds completion.

5   *Strawinsky Boogie Woogie*, Stefan Wewerka, 1983.
6   The Bauhaus architect and designer Peter Keler (1898–1982) had previously contributed an original Gropius handle for the Hexenhaus in 1981. Despite showing traces of use, it was fitted to the entrance door.

7   Smithson 2001, 161.

8   Peter Smithson, in: Lichtenstein and Schregenberger 2001, 198.

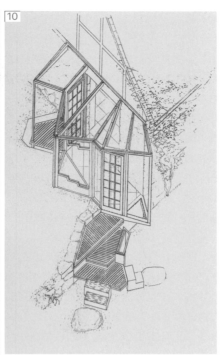

[Fig. 9]   Hexenhaus prior to the Smithsons' first interventions.
[Fig. 10]   'Axel's Porch', 1984–1986.
[Fig. 11]   From left to right: Peter Smithson, Axel Bruchhäuser, and Alison Smithson working on 'Axel's Porch'.

Precision and foresight

Iterative can also be used to describe some of the works of Hermann Czech (born 1936), who has for decades persistently advocated giving recognition to the results of architectural design with the found as 'fully valid work',[9] especially in renovations. In both his practical work and his writing, he emphasizes it as 'a theme of importance to architectural theory; maybe the most central one of all—because, in essence, everything is transformation'.[10] On the one hand, this is based on the recognition that cities consist of systems of different scales and lifespans—think traffic patterns and property divisions, buildings, and uses—and that preservation and urban renewal therefore naturally take place simultaneously. But it also has to do with the nature of architectural design itself: 'When one recognizes that every design process consists of a series of decisions, and that later decisions are determined by earlier ones, it will make no essential difference whether the earlier decisions were one's own or someone else's.'[11]

Czech's 'Kleines Café' in Vienna shows that this applies not only to immovable property but also to the reuse of building components. Unlike the customary practice at the time, the existing Franziskanerplatz entrance was retained and reused in the 1973–74 expansion. But used components from elsewhere were also integrated: the paired pillars dividing the mirrored wall surfaces, for example, are pieced together from marble slabs of varied colours taken from demolition sites. [figs. 15, 17] The mitred slabs have veining that continues around the corners,

9   Hermann Czech, 'Der Umbau', in Czech 1996, 125–127, here: 126.

10   Czech 1998, 6.

11   Czech 1996, 127.

↗ p. 76
Haus S

suggesting solid stone, and the absent half of each rear pillar is completed in the mirror.[fig.13] Cut into suitable squares and sorted by colour, the slab remnants, together with used tiles, complement the existing flooring. [fig.14] When the floor in the older part of the café was replaced a few years later, Czech was inspired by the artist Karl Prantl's provocative proposal to pave Stephansplatz with discarded gravestones from Viennese cemeteries. Transposed to the café, Czech had gravestones cut into slices and laid according to their tapered geometry to create a pattern, as he sketched in August 1977, whose 'fields of association' could hardly be more multifaceted.[figs.18,19] They illustrate his conviction: 'All the parts of a building have something to say; to begin with, they belong to a world of thought or an epoch that we respond to; as a result and through similarities, they trigger conscious or unconscious personal memories. They communicate how and why they came to be; the structural, economic, and social conditions are inherent in every architectural form.'[12] Besides the inherent origin story of found components, deliberate acts of architectural refinement and defamiliarization are decisive factors in their recoding[2] in a new context. The inscribed 'outer faces' of the gravestones, for example, were not used in the Kleines Café. Where the intrinsically 'unreproducible characteristic of age'[13] is lacking as a vehicle for associations, Czech sometimes uses pseudo-aged components as a 'short cut'. The inviting gesture of the ostensibly centuries-old trodden granite threshold in front of the Hummel Gallery in Vienna, for example, is a well-calculated design concept from the late 1970s, and the fragments of 'Gothic' ribs in the vaulting of the Wunder-Bar are only a few years older.

In Haus S on Vienna's Seemüllergasse (1980–1983), by contrast, Czech employs wooden columns that are actually reused. He had personally commissioned them in 1980 for the Forum Design exhibition in Linz, where they surrounded the central room of the exhibition. The costly handcrafted work was only conceivable and affordable for short-term deployment because reuse of the columns was planned from the outset, with five of them in Haus S and four in the bathroom of a private Viennese apartment. This illustrates an additional level in the above-mentioned system of differing lifespans: given that the relatively transitory nature of uses contrasts with the potential longevity of built substance, the logical consequence is not only transformation but also reuse—especially if one also takes into account the ideal and artisanal value of carefully designed and produced building components. Czech also takes this into account in his most recent projects: lighting fixtures from Vienna's Hotel Messe and from his interior for the MAK Café (sadly destroyed) are now being used a second time in the lobby of the Sigmund Freud Museum, which reopened in 2020, and in the currently ongoing renovation of the Josephinum.[14]

12 Kuß 2018, 228.

13 'Wohnbau und Althaus', in Czech 1996, 106–109, here: 107.

Reusers

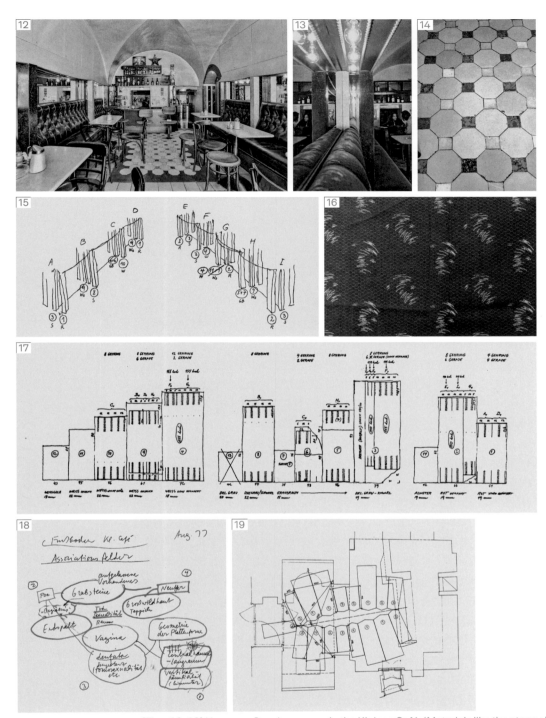

[Figs. 12–19] Hermann Czech on reuse in the Kleines Café: 'Materials like the stone slabs and tiles (the latter were octagonal, practically worthless without the squares) were often available at scrapyards after the war and into the 1970s, along with stone slabs and cast-iron feet for tables, bentwood chairs of all kinds, etc.—all usually much cheaper than new material, making it easy to convince the client. I remember that in 1973–74 the slabs for the pillars cost ATS 2,000; the stonemason who installed them (and recognized some of them from their previous use, such as the grey-brown ones from the former Café Goethe at the corner of Mariahilferstraße and Schweighofergasse) about ATS 4,000; the mitre-cutting, which had to be done on machines in a factory, about ATS 7,000. The pillars were arranged in an alternating pattern of light and dark, with the red ones in the corners of the room. The professional stonemasonry work done with new materials in 1985 to insert the entrance to the WC between the new pillars E and F cost about ATS 100,000. The use of old material in a rather demanding architectural context was, however, primarily a conceptual step that also worked selectively with a kind of 'stylistic' distance in time: for example, in the upholstery that was originally covered with fabric. This fabric [fig. 16] was a stock item from 20 years earlier, which was perceptible at the time even to a layman as having a weird 'out of time' impact—until leather was finally used in the first of the later renovations. This is also when Karl Prantl pointed out the disused Gründerzeit gravestones stockpiled in a large storage yard belonging to the municipality of Vienna, which he proposed using as pavement for the Stephansplatz pedestrian zone then under discussion. Here—as with the fabric (and the parquet panels in Haus S)—the specific found material was essential to the design decisions. However the use of available older material in general is an essential design idea.'[14]

14 Hermann Czech to the editors on 17 June 2021

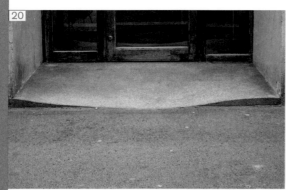
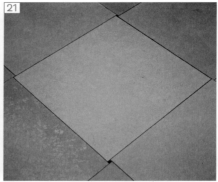

[Fig. 20] Galerie Hummel: 'trodden' doorstep.
[Fig. 21] Antiquariat Löcker: stone floor slabs measuring 50 × 51 cm laid in an intentionally irregular pattern.

Wondrous transformations

'Watching the sculptor work was fascinating—the way they had to keep the clay wet the whole time so that they could model it, and how they kept recycling the clay. … After I worked with it myself I thought of all the other things it had once been— the nose of Lenin or Stalin's moustache, Khrushchev's ear or maybe even Mayakovsky's boot.'[15]

Lively imagination and narrative elements full of irony and soulful melancholy characterize the life and work of Alexander Brodsky (born 1955), who routinely crosses the border between art and architecture.[16] His architectural training at the Moscow Architectural Institute (MARKHI) in the 1970s opened up an abundance of eclectic influences: grey-haired constructivists taught how to precisely draw antique columns, while enterprising classmates and alumni brought contemporary Western architecture and international competition procedures into the conversation through conspiratorial lectures. In the stagnation of the Brezhnev years, Brodsky, like other young Russian architects of his generation, used this platform to make incisive contributions in the form of imaginary designs that gained international regard as 'paper architecture'. This was also the beginning of the well-known etchings created in a long-lasting collaboration with his childhood friend Ilya Utkin. One of the recurring themes in this work is Brodsky's concern about the gradual disappearance of his beloved native city of Moscow, which he perceives as 'huge, but somehow … incredibly cosy'[17] and whose historical legacy and unique character as a 'city of fragments'[18] he sees falling victim to a misguided faith in progress. In the *Museum of Disappearing Buildings* from 1984, for example, accompanied by a quotation from Chekhov's 'The Old House: A Story Told by a Houseowner', previously demolished Moscow buildings are neatly archived in colossal shelving units; we see a gigantic ossuary, as in Rossi's San Cataldo cemetery, but inscribed within the competition perimeter inside a Moscow city block. The same subject—with an admonitory wrecking ball in the middle—is repeated in 1989/90

↗ **p. 77**
Villa PO-2

15 Weaver and Brodsky 2016, 145.

16 'It took more than twenty years before I began to respond to the question of my profession as "architect,"' Brodsky says in an interview with the architecture journal *Project Russia* (no. 41, 3/2006), quoted in *Hintergrund* 50/51, 2011, 112.

17 Weaver and Brodsky 2016, 144.
18 Ibid.

in *Columbarium Habitabile*, complemented by the words: 'A house dies twice—the first time when people leave it[;] then it can be saved if they return. The second time finally when it[']s destroyed.' It does not end with the literary intellectual appreciation, however. In his works of virtual architecture, too, Brodsky begins to actually reuse obsolete building materials. Instead of using paper, he sometimes makes his graphics on old roofing felt—what Daria Paramonova describes as the omnipresent 'building material of Soviet favelas'.[19] Another of his preferred materials, as previously mentioned, is unfired clay, which can be reused again and again.

Brodsky's architectural works also draw from the trove of used building parts. In the Pirogovo resort, an idyllic landscape of forests and lakes north-east of Moscow, he has been carrying out various architectural interventions since 2000, including the *Pavilion for Vodka Ceremonies* for the Art-Klyazma contemporary art festival in 2003: the roof and walls are a collage of windows from the razed Butikov factory (19th century) in Moscow's Ostozhenka district—today an exclusive residential area. The frames and glass panes, painted white from the outside, create intimacy for the drinking revelry celebrated inside and bathe the protagonists and their conversations in mild light. Rotunda I is the name of a work for the 2009 edition of the Archstoyanie art festival held south of Moscow. The two-storey elliptical pavilion in the middle of a field opens all around with doors taken from abandoned houses in the surrounding villages. A modified version for the Perm Museum of Contemporary Art, Rotunda II, was temporarily also on view in the Tuileries Garden in Paris. Thanks to a precise form and well-balanced proportions, worn-out doors and windows combine here under their superficial coat of white paint to form a disconcertingly elegant garden pavilion. The pictoriality[3] of a carefully composed form also distinguishes Villa PO-2, built in 2018. Beneath a deeply cantilevered wooden cornice, discarded concrete elements of the PO-2 industrial fence system that was prevalent throughout the former Soviet territory coalesce into a miniature of a dignified Renaissance palazzo. In their new context, the characteristic relief of the elements—once chosen to repel dirt and refract sound—evokes the proud defensiveness of a Palazzo dei Diamanti (Ferrara, 1492–1567). Vladimir Nabokov had previously found words that aptly describe Brodsky's wondrous ability for imaginary refinement: It is the 'trash of life which by means of a momentary alchemic distillation—the "royal experiment"—is turned into something valuable and eternal.'[20]

---

19 Daria Paramonova, 'Alexander Brodsky: Techniques and Impact', in Tchoban Foundation 2015, 15.

20 Vladimir Nabokov, *The Gift*, trans. Michael Scammell and Dmitri Nabokov [1938], London 2012, 161; quoted in Alexei Muratov, 'Man on the Frontier', in *Hintergrund* 50/51, 2011, 15.

3 ↗ p. 236
K.118 case study
Design and construction: Glossary

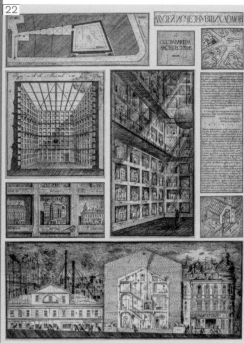
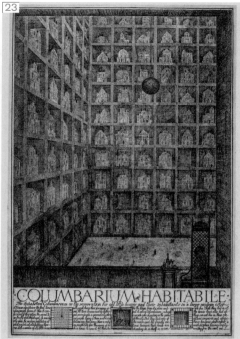

[Fig. 22] *Museum of Disappearing Buildings*, Alexander Brodsky and Ilya Utkin.
[Fig. 23] *Columbarium Habitabile*, Alexander Brodsky and Ilya Utkin.
[Figs. 24, 25] Rotunda I (left) and Rotunda II in Paris (right).
[Fig. 26] Pavilion for Vodka Ceremonies.

What to draw upon?

These examples demonstrate that 'reusers' do not fit into a niche any more than the houses they build. They do not inevitably groan under the historical significance of their parts, nor do they, out of necessity, break with all conventions as provocative bricolage. Diverse and complex are the architectural ideas and opportunities that can arise from the simple fact that building fabric often lasts longer than the acute demands placed on it at the time of construction. The question remains:

What can we draw upon? When it comes to reuse, direct references are hard to find—design and construction decisions are, after all, closely tied to the individual building components. Nonetheless, the works examined here stimulate ideas that could also be of interest to future 'reusers'.

Jean Prouvé's buildings, for example, which were designed to be dismantled, unquestionably make him a pioneer of so-called design for disassembly.[4] Despite all due admiration, however, we must note that even he was unable to think 50 to 70 years ahead about the technical aspects of the elements used in his buildings. Disassembly and reassembly proved to be difficult under real conditions, and adaptations to the hybrid façade elements—which were thermally advanced when built—to meet today's energy standards also pose technical and heritage conservation challenges.[21] It is not the anticipated technical potential that ultimately compels us to preserve and reuse his works today. It is the underlying clarity of thought and the beauty of the resulting structures.

By contrast, back in 1944 Carlo Mollino thought it 'easy to predict what total eclecticism we are heading towards and what authentic works will emerge from it'.[22] His visionary spirit and his ability and passion to appropriate design ideas and building components of widely differing types and origins and to bring them into a suspenseful imbalance are what distinguish him. Who else would design a staircase worthy of a spaceship for a house assembled from centuries-old timber? Walking a tightrope between sustainable construction techniques and salvaged building components can lead to previously unknown aesthetics—provided we dare to let our thinking and viewing habits become unbalanced at the right moment.

The Smithsons' work on the 'Hexenhaus' also challenges habitual ways of thinking. It is one of the last joint projects by the prominent architect couple and is especially fascinating for how it came into being, which anticipates thinking about circularity: their interventions are part of a continual series of localized interventions that for decades have been constantly re-evaluating, reframing, and recalibrating the existing ... A totally ordinary house in the woods thus evolves—from the site, its own fabric, and added and found parts—into an architectural work without an actual master and without any claim to finality.

In his work, Hermann Czech dispels a latent prejudice: no one could be clearer in dispelling the suspicion that 'reuse' in architecture is inevitably synonymous with 'bricolage'. The precisely staged illusion of the pieced together and reflected marble pillars in the Kleines Café proves the opposite. Coincidences, such as the shapes of the gravestones on the floor, are not simply 'allowed' or 'accepted' with a shrug of the shoulders; they are assimilated and instrumentalized to arouse associations and to enrich the work with layers of meaning.

21 See *Restaurer les objets techniques: L'œuvre de Jean Prouvé*, colloquium on 21 September 2018 at the École Polytechnique Fédérale de Lausanne, under the direction of Franz Graf and Giulia Marino.
22 Carlo Mollino, 'Disegno di una casa sull'altura', in *Stile* 40, April 1944, 2–11.

4 ↗ p. 138
A circular approach to architecture

Where 'real' coincidence is lacking, it is helped along: in the case of the nearly square floor tiles inside Antiquariat Löcker [fig. 21], for example, calculated imperfection attains perfection.

In Alexander Brodsky's buildings, the simplicity, even shabbiness, of the materials and means often stands in disarming contrast to the carefully composed and staged beauty of the work. It is not the material itself but the creative devotion bestowed upon it that determines its value and impact. Use and its traces are not a flaw; they have the wonderful power to enrich the banal with meaning and the new with history.

One could also identify the challenge by quoting Le Corbusier, as the Smithsons did in 1964: 'Viz: "Architecture is the masterly, correct and magnificent play of masses brought together in light." That the architecture of the next step is in pursuit of the ordinary and banal does not mean that it has lost sight of its objective. Ordinariness and banality are the art-source of the new situation.'[23]

23 Alison and Peter Smithson, 'The Ordinary and the Banal', in Lichtenstein and Schregenberger 2001, 141.

Literature:

Crisis as incentive
- Archieri, Jean François, and Jean Pierre Levasseur (1990), *Prouvé: Cours du CNAM 1957–1970; Essai de reconstitution du cours à partir des archives Jean Prouvé*, Liège: Mardaga.
- Costa, Isabella da (1984), 'Histoire d'une maison: Le dernier entretien avec Jean Prouvé', *AMC Revue d'architecture*, June 1984.
- Sulzer, Peter, and Jean Prouvé (2008), *Œuvre complete / Complete Works*, vol. 4: *1954–1984*, Basel: Birkhäuser.
- Vegesack, Alexander von (2006) (ed.), *Jean Prouvé: Die Poetik des technischen Objekts*, Weil am Rhein: Vitra Design Museum.

Up in the air
- Brino, Giovanni (1987), *Carlo Mollino*. Munich: Bangert.
- Dercon, Chris, and Stiftung Haus der Kunst München GmbH (2012) (eds.), *Carlo Mollino: Maniera moderna*. exh. cat., Cologne: Walther König.
- Milan, Laura, and Sergio Pace (2018), *Carlo Mollino: L'arte di costruire in montagna; Casa Garelli, Champoluc*, Milan: Electa.
- Reichlin, Bruno (1991), 'Mollino in Bau und Schrift', in (ed.), *Carlo Mollino baut in den Bergen*, exh. cat., Basel: Architekturmuseum.

As found
- Conversation with Axel Bruchhäuser in the 'Hexenhaus', 14 September 2020.
- Kuehn, Wilfried (2002), 'Mies à Bad Karlshafen', *L'Architecture d'Aujourd'hui* 343, 58–65.
- Lichtenstein, Claude, and Thomas Schregenberger (2001) (eds.), *As Found: The Discovery of the Ordinary*, Zurich: Lars Müller.
- Robbins, David (1990) (ed.), *The Independent Group: Postwar Britain and the Aesthetics of Plenty*, Cambridge, MA: MIT Press.

- Smithson, Alison and Peter (2017), *The Space Between*, ed. Max Risselada, Cologne: Walther König.
- Smithson, Alison and Peter (2001), *The Charged Void: Architecture*, New York: Monacelli Press.
- Smithson, Alison and Peter (2020) (eds.), *Alison & Peter Smithson: Hexenhaus; A House for a Man and a Cat*, Cologne: Walther König, 2020.

Precision and foresight
- Czech, Hermann (1998), 'Alles ist Umbau', *werk, bauen + wohnen 85*, March 1998, 4–11.
- Czech, Hermann (1996), *Zur Abwechslung: Ausgewählte Schriften zur Architektur*, Vienna: Löcker.
- Kuß, Eva (2018), *Hermann Czech: Architekt in Wien*, Zurich: Park Books.

Wondrous transformations
- Lecture by Alexander Brodsky as part of the 'Blue Monday' lecture series on building component recycling at the ZHAW School of Architecture, Design and Civil Engineering, 2 December 2019.
- Architekturzentrum Wien (2011) (ed.), 'Alexander Brodsky. It still amazes me that I became an Architect', *Hintergrund* 50/51, June 2011.
- Tchoban Foundation, Museum for Architectural Drawing (2015), *Alexander Brodsky: Works*, exh. cat., Berlin.
- Weaver, Thomas, and Alexander Brodsky (2016), 'Alexander Brodsky in conversation with Thomas Weaver', *AA Files* 72, 134–151.
- Hönes, Jiří (2020), 'Der PO-2, eine russische Legende', *moderneREGIONAL* 20/2, <moderne-regional.de/fachbeitrag-betonzaun-po-2/>

Project profiles

Maison Prouvé   Nancy, 1954 • Client: Prouvé family • Architecture and engineering: Jean Prouvé (1901–1984) • Construction: self-build

To build his own home, Jean Prouvé relied on standardized products and surplus material. In the summer of 1954, on a steep hillside site in the north of Nancy, he worked with friends and family to assemble a steel framework of sheet metal and IPN profiles to support the floor and form a 27 m long backbone for the house, filled along its entire length with wall cabinets. Opposite it, tiny bedrooms and a relatively huge living hall line the south façade, which opens to the view and consists of various panels—some of which are surplus products from his company while others are specially made. For the single-pitch roof, Prouvé used 40 mm thick plywood 'Rousseau'-type panels for the first time, clad with aluminium.

[Fig. 27]   Exterior view around 1954/1955.
[Fig. 28]   Jean Prouvé in the large space dubbed 'salle de réunion'.
[Fig. 29]   Axonometric view.
[Figs. 30, 31]   Roof details of 'Rousseau' panels and steel structure.

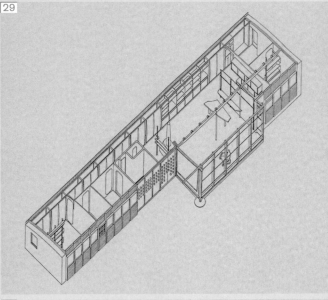

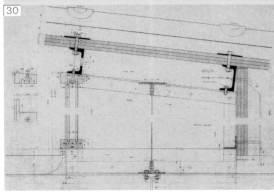

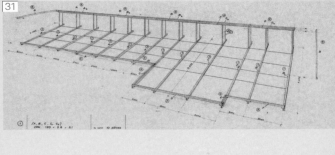

Project profiles

Casa Garelli

Champoluc, 1965 • Client: Garelli family • Architecture: Carlo Mollino (1905–1973) • Contractor for timber structure and carpentry: Luigi Tesio

For the translocation and conversion of a 300-year-old granary into a holiday home in the Aosta Valley in northern Italy, Carlo Mollino benefited from log construction's long-established and frequently used capacity for damage-free disassembly and reassembly. His project pays tribute to the historic substance and construction, while updating it in stylized form with a new stone base and reinterpreted mushroom-shaped supports for the timber structure. By the same token, structural changes to façades and interior spaces, as well as contrasting additions such as the new exterior stair, pose a challenge to the existing structure. The archaic log cabin is showcased on the outside, but on the inside it is clad. The rooms are furnished with furniture by Mollino.

[Fig. 32]   Exterior view from the south.
[Fig. 33]   One of the new 'boléri'.
[Fig. 34]   First-floor plan.
[Fig. 35]   West elevation with new balconies.

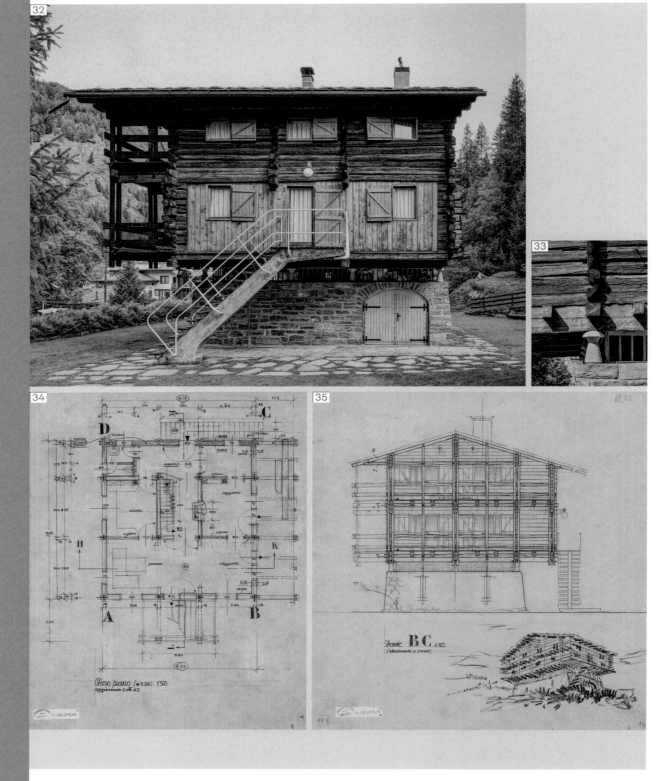

Reusers

Hexenhaus   Bad Karlshafen, since 1980 • Client: Axel Bruchhäuser • Architecture: 1980–83, Stefan Wewerka; 1984–1993, Alison and Peter Smithson; 1993–2003, Peter Smithson; since 2014, Simon Smithson and María Prieto

Axel Bruchhäuser's home in the Hessian town of Bad Karlshafen has been continually transformed since the 1980s. After initial interventions by Stefan Wewerka, Alison and Peter Smithson worked from 1984 until their deaths on a total of 26 smaller and larger measures to open up the house inwardly and outwardly. Like Wewerka, the Smithsons made consistent use of salvaged and surplus building components. In addition to new openings and new window niches, wooden footbridges connect the house to various seating areas and places of retreat that integrate the house into the landscape.

[Fig. 36]   View from the west.
[Fig. 37]   Sleeping room on the upper level with floor designs by Stefan Wewerka. When Peter Smithson designed the en suite bathroom in 1996/97, he integrated the existing bathtub.
[Fig. 38]   The 'Hexenbesenraum' (1996) is entered through a wooden door with lenticular cross section that was left over from another building project. Alison Smithson had designed it according to one of Jean Prouvé's construction principles.
[Figs. 39–42] From house to conglomerate order: the Hexenhaus in 1985, 1986, 1997, and 2001.

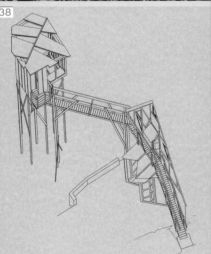

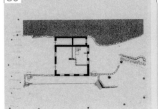
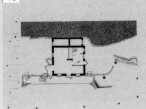
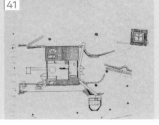
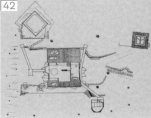

Project profiles

Haus S

Vienna, 1983 • Client: Private • Architecture: Hermann Czech (born 1936)

A round tower functions as a hinge between the two parts of the single-family house that stand askew to each other. It links the storeys and accommodates the library. The wings were originally planned to be at an angle of 28° to each other which was only changed to 22.5° when the clients found parquet flooring for the upper levels that had been salvaged from a demolished building and had a pattern of eight-pointed stars. The five wooden columns surrounding the central open space on the first floor are also reused. Variously sized pedestals compensate for their different heights, and they are topped off on the storey above by a bookcase at balustrade height.

[Fig. 43] Exterior view with library tower.
[Figs. 44, 47] With a row of books as a frieze above, the open space between the columns seems like a temple-shaped pavilion.
[Fig. 45] Section through the library tower.
[Fig. 46] First-floor plan.
[Figs. 48, 49] Nine columns were made for the exhibition Forum Design in Linz, 1980 (left). Five were reused in Haus S, and the other four in the bathroom of the Monika Pöschl apartment (right).

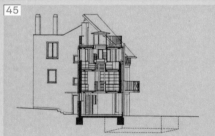

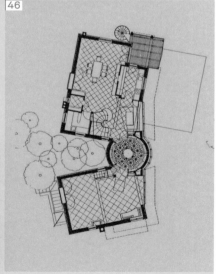

Villa PO-2

Nikola-Lenivets, 2018 • Client: Archstoyanie Festival 2018 • Architecture: Alexander Brodsky (born 1955), Anthony Timofeev

Villa PO-2, both an exhibit and a guest house, was designed for the 2018 Archstoyanie Festival. Inside is a wood structure, while the outside is a shell made of discarded precast concrete units of the PO-2 industrial fence system that is ubiquitous in the former Soviet territory. The size and shape of the elements determine the houses' dimensions. The inner structure is only 2.4 metres wide, but elongated and has two storeys. A large skylight illuminates the long dining table on the ground floor, and the upstairs gallery offers space for up to ten people to sleep. In contrast to the wooden structure, the wire-reinforced concrete panels with their characteristic relief, now put to a new use, are reminiscent of diamond-point rustication.

[Fig. 50] Exterior view.
[Fig. 51] Interior with dining table.
[Fig. 52] Sketch by Alexander Brodsky.
[Fig. 53] The PO-2 industrial fence system was developed in the 1970s under the direction of the Russian architect and engineer Boris Lachmann at the Moscow engineering and design office Mosgorstroimaterialy.

Deborah Fehlmann

Where there's a will …

In contemporary Swiss architecture, the reuse of building components is a fringe activity. This tour of five very different projects—by Flury + Furrer Architekten, MOKA, N11, Christian Jelk, and baubüro in situ—gives us hope, however, that this might soon change.

Designing buildings in Switzerland is probably now more complex than ever. Fire safety standards, noise control, listed building regulations, flood protection, energy efficiency: all this and more has to be considered, while budgets and time frames are often tight. At the same time, technology and prosperity mean today's planners and clients have the luxury of being able to specify components in almost any shape and material—and have them delivered on time to the building site. The load-bearing capacity, insulation properties, and pliability of our materials is constantly being improved, enabling us to achieve whatever form we desire, yet still satisfy almost endless sets of requirements. And if something is not available on the domestic market, it can always be ordered from abroad.

All the same, some architects and clients are still voluntarily sacrificing that luxury and instead tackling the challenges of building with reclaimed components. Doing so mostly doesn't cut their costs or require less labour, and it definitely doesn't save time. So what motivates them to grapple with dented façade panels, old bathtubs, and discarded wood? Spread across different locations around the country, the five examples in this essay show that their reasons for adopting such an approach are as varied as the resulting buildings.

Poetic pragmatism

Our first stop is Sittertal in St. Gallen, a place that hums with creative activity. In 1994, Kunstgiesserei St. Gallen began renting a single space at Sittertal's converted dye works, an industrial building nestled in a verdant river valley. Today, the foundry's workshops occupy a large part of the site, employing 60-odd professionals who cast, cut, grind, and weld sculptures for artists, galleries, and exhibitions all over the world. Working with the firm's founder, Felix Lehner, architects Christoph Flury and Lukas Furrer have continuously adapted the built structures to their occupants' changing needs, often incorporating objects found on-site or salvaged from demolitions, in keeping with their appreciation of quality materials. Over the years, the trio have honed their eye for choice finds and perfected the art of architectural assemblage, as Felix Lehner and Katalin Deér's studio home from 2008 shows.

The story begins with Hans Josephsohn, a sculptor who, in the years before his death in 2012, enjoyed a highly productive period at the dye works' former boiler house, cherishing its

↗ p. 89
Transformation of Sittertal dye works: Deér-Lehner residence

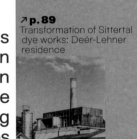

excellent light. From 2003 on, its large main space served as a warehouse and gallery for Josephsohn's many sculptures, while Lehner and Deér lived in the building's narrow annex. Soon, though, the boiler house was bursting at the seams, so the couple set about looking for a new place. Having envisaged something temporary, they came across a listing in *Tierwelt* magazine, in which a steel restaurant pavilion was being advertised for sale. It turned out to be the pavilion that had housed the Rigihof cafeteria at the Museum of Transport in Lucerne—a design by architects Gigon/Guyer.

Gigon/Guyer provided Flury + Furrer with original plans for the structure, which comprised steel sections clad in hot-galvanized steel panels and had been painted frog green inside. A suitable location for the couple's future home was soon found: the rooftop of the old boiler house. Thanks to its particular dimensions and its metal envelope, the pavilion looks as though it was purpose-built for the site. For access, the architects installed a staircase inside a disused water tower adjacent to the boiler house façade.

Client and architects organized the dismantling and transportation of the pavilion themselves, carefully inventorying all the parts and noting details of their connections to aid reconstruction. Following relocation, internal walls were inserted, insulation was added to the inside of the envelope, and storage space created beneath the wooden floor of what is now the studio. The bright-green colour scheme gave way to a carefully coordinated palette of virgin-white gypsum plaster walls and anhydrite floors treated with shellac and linseed oil. Both the existing large opening at the front and the newly created openings were furnished with oiled oak windows; these let in ample light and afford fantastic views of the landscape.

In the living area, the star attraction is a light-grey wooden unit with black handles. So taken were the client and architects with the piece, which was sourced from a property in Zurich, that it provided the inspiration for the new fitted units.

Today, the one-time Sittertal AG dye works are home to the Kesselhaus Josephsohn sculpture gallery and the Sitterwerk Foundation, which has established an art library, material archive, and studios on the site. Over a period of around 20 years, Flury + Furrer Architekten have helped to renew parts of the complex from the inside out, regularly using reclaimed components in the process. Hans Jörg Schmid, the complex's owner and the foundation's co-founder, was receptive to such a practice from the start.

Where there's a will ...

[Fig. 2] In the library, the gallery's steel structure and tension rods were assembled from the foundry's own trove of materials. The shelving and drawer units were previously used for storage at the former Saurer AG factory in Arbon.
[Fig. 3] In 2015, a meeting room for project managers was created within Kunstgiesserei St. Gallen's office spaces; the partitions for the new space consist of windows salvaged from a demolished factory in St. Gallen.
[Figs. 4, 5] New and old combine seamlessly in the architects' latest project, the conversion of a former farmhouse (left), which gained an additional storey and now serves as the studio of photographer and sculptor Katalin Deér (right).
[Fig. 6] Kesselhaus Josephsohn.
[Fig. 7] Small ad in the magazine *Tierwelt*.

Next generation

In the renovation of an office building on Winterthur's Römerstrasse, fitted units played a starring role. In 2017, the property's owner invited tenders for a general contract for the refurbishment of this elongated slab-and-column structure, which boasts a glass-walled ground floor and a striking façade of cast aluminium panels. Designed by Edwin

↗ **p. 90**
Renovation and refurbishment, Römerstrasse office building

Deborah Fehlmann

[1] ↗ p. 179
Values and processes
Reuse from a developer perspective

'It would have been simply criminal to dispose of the existing solid-wood fixtures and replace them with new and less durable wood-veneered board.'

Bosshardt in the early 1960s, it was added to the local authority's listed building register in 2013—a rare distinction for a post-war office block.

With its smooth granite floors, sculptural spiral staircase, and slate-clad lifts, the open-plan ground floor still exudes refinement today. By contrast, the upper floors, which had rows of identical office cubicles arranged along corridors, looked somewhat outdated, while the encasing of the spiral staircase in the 1990s for fire safety reasons had further added to the claustrophobic feel. The task therefore was to completely strip out the upper storeys in order to create open-plan spaces.

That could easily have resulted in a key element of Bosshardt's design being lost, namely his ingenious partition system: columns between the office cubicles and corridors served to alternately support door units and—instead of simple partitions—elm-wood cabinets that opened in both directions. The latter had glazed lighting strips above and below that made them look as though they were hovering in mid-air.

In the end, though, the high-quality cabinetry survived: the winning tender, submitted by general contractor Losinger Marazzi together with MOKA Architekten, proposed reusing the fitted units. To open up the layouts, they moved the cabinets to the central core, which contains the toilets, technical services, and emergency stairs. Together with new elm-wood fittings, the old cabinets now form a multifunctional central zone featuring lockers, coat-hanging areas, printer alcoves, and ample storage space. Even old doors were reused wherever fire safety regulations allowed.

First, though, the architects had to show the cost-conscious clients and occupants that investing in such an update of existing furnishings made financial sense. That they were able to do so was in part thanks to the versatility of their central zone, which meant less additional furniture would be required, allowing part of the furniture budget to be allocated to joinery work. It also helped the architects' case that, while they could have got new furniture for the same money, these would undoubtedly have been inferior to the originals in terms of materials and craftsmanship.[1]

To guarantee quality and longevity, the general contractor insisted suppliers provided a sample and a transportation plan when tendering for the joinery. The winning tender came from the very firm that built the original fixtures in the 1960s, with the son of its then director leading the work to give them a new lease of life.

[Figs. 8–10]   Too good to discard: the salvaged cabinetry.

Actions not words

A life cycle approach is also evident in the work of engineer Regula Trachsel and architect Sascha Schär. Their maiden project in Zweisimmen in the Bernese Oberland region is a clarion call for resource-efficient architecture. The duo planned this residential and commercial building along cradle-to-cradle lines so that, should the building one day be dismantled, as much material as possible could be returned to the natural resource cycle or reused in another project.

Dating from 2014, their polygonal creation is in many ways a modest building, but it stands out despite—or perhaps because of—that fact. For starters, it has an extremely modest footprint but its five storeys and peaked roof mean it compensates with height, towering over the surrounding low-slung, space-hungry warehouses and providing a blueprint for how densification can be achieved in industrial zones. The two lower floors are rented out, the remaining upper floors form the couple's own home. Its energy use is similarly modest, requiring no heating or mechanical ventilation. Hot water comes courtesy of a heat pump powered by electricity from a rooftop solar array. Composite wood-and-concrete ceilings and rammed earth floors add thermal mass, while floor plans and windows took their cue from the relative position of the sun. This gives the building outstanding operational energy efficiency and means that, other than water and waste-water rates, there are virtually no running costs.

In the building's construction, Trachsel and Schär emphasized natural materials and reuse: the 30 cm thick external wall sections, which are made of dowelled, cross-laminated timber, can be completely taken apart to facilitate dismantling and subsequently reassembled to make new sections. No adhesive was used and additional insulation layers were also not required. The façade is clad in strips of untreated live-edge wood, a waste product from timber processing, while the sanitaryware and kitchen furniture were all sourced from salvage outlets and

↗ **p. 91**
Residential and office building, Zweisimmen

Deborah Fehlmann

second-hand stores. Finding the right parts and tailoring the design to incorporate a particular find require time and patience, but these were things that Trachsel and Schär also enjoyed. Their unconventional planning process was aided by the fact that they were their own clients. However, some educational input was required at times, as some of the tradespeople were unaccustomed to working with pre-used parts. As a result, Sascha Schär is convinced that it's critical to communicate to all those involved just what reuse means when it comes to planning and construction. Specific know-how is not required to work with reclaimed components, he argues, just the will to do so.

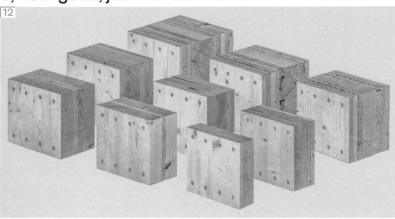

[Fig. 11]   Undressed live-edge timber for the façade.
[Figs. 12, 13] In the Holz100 construction system, solid timber boards are cross-laminated and connected using dowels rather than glue.

↗ p. 92
DomaHabitare cohousing project

Built with conviction

Daniel Béguin would surely concur. The rural engineer and translator's current home—located in the small town of Sainte-Croix in the canton of Vaud—is the third he has worked on himself. Environmentalism had long been important to him, but the apartment building he realized in 2017 as a member of the DomaHabitare cooperative went one step further. This time, the aim was not just to show you can maintain a modest environmental footprint when building and using housing, but also to offer a template for living in intentional communities. Alongside the ten apartments, the complex thus also boasts a shared space and a communal vegetable plot for which the residents themselves produce fertilizer—via compost toilets in their homes. The community is largely independent of the water and electricity networks: a pair of cisterns store 40 m³ of rainwater for showering, washing, and drinking, while photovoltaic panels and thermal collectors generate power and hot water.

The look of the building is even more unusual than the way it is used: designed by local architect Christian Jelk, it has a basement level that's partly built into the slope, above which are four floors of living space and a barrel-vault roof. The east elevation has traditional shingling, but the three other aspects boast double-skinned façades: the outer layer comprises a bricolage of transparent corrugated plastic, solar panels, and assorted new and used windows, through which the posts and beams of the wooden primary structure can be made out, while new triple-glazed windows and straw-filled wooden sections ensure the inner skin is well insulated. The area between these two layers serves as a thermal buffering[2] zone, as well as providing access areas and adding semi-private extensions to the accommodation. The building has no central heating, though every apartment boasts a wood burner.

Made of laminated Swiss timber, the hefty structural frame was prefabricated by a carpenter and then assembled on site. The composite timber-and-concrete ceilings are load-bearing, but the façades and internal walls are not. For the latter, the members of the cooperative carried out much of the work themselves, drawing up floor plans on site according to their own needs and creating dividing walls out of 23,000 adobe bricks they compressed themselves. For the sake of flexibility, electrical installations were left exposed. Residents were also free to fit out the spaces as they desired: Béguin and his wife opted for second-hand sanitaryware and doors, though others chose new products.

In this far-from-straightforward construction process, Jelk saw himself more as a mediator than as a designer with absolute control. Having previously been ready to walk away from the profession, the architect found himself reinvigorated by this alternative approach. He and Béguin are convinced that their design meets the requirements of the SNBS, the Swiss standard for sustainable construction, though they have not yet provided the data to back this up.

[2] ↗ p. 236
K.118 case study
Design and construction: Glossary

[Fig. 14] The buffer zone.
[Fig. 15] New use for a familiar technique: shingles have been protecting façades for centuries, so why not bathroom walls?
[Fig. 16] Having compressed the raw material themselves, the future residents lay adobe bricks to create dividing walls.

Deborah Fehlmann

↗ p. 93
ELYS culture and business hub

3 ↗ p. 237
K.118 case study
Design and construction: Glossary

Budgets and values

It's one thing for self-builders to do without certification or technical verification. For investors or public sector clients, however, the picture is rather different; here, value is determined to a large extent by usage concepts, returns on investment, warranties, and certifications. Such things are not designed to accommodate reuse. In their conversion of a food production and distribution centre into a mixed commercial and cultural hub for the Canton of Basel-Stadt, baubüro in situ nonetheless succeeded in incorporating two façades made of reclaimed materials and rejected components. To allow daylight to penetrate deep into the 86 × 88 m former industrial building, which is situated on Basel's Lysbüchel site, the architects cut an internal courtyard into the concrete structure. In addition, they trimmed 14 m off the outside of the building, the entire breadth of which had previously adjoined a pair of neighbouring properties, thereby allowing in even more light. This trimming generated a large amount of waste material, which, the architects thought, could surely be used to create façades for the newly opened-up building. Despite their municipal client's initial reservations regarding design, construction time, costs, and technical feasibility, the proposal was given the green light.

It soon proved impossible, however, to only use material from the site, with many of the required items not available in sufficient quantity or quality or at the right time. Nonetheless, 1,500 m² of old trapezoidal metal sheeting was used to create façade sections that lend rhythmization[3] to the exterior, while hot-galvanized metal grilles from the distribution centre roof were turned into safety barriers.

Beyond that, the architects had to widen their search radius. Working with a timber construction firm, they developed timber frames for prefabrication that were 2.85 m wide and up to 9.1 m high. These were filled with insulation and enclosed with board on each side. Forty per cent of the wood came from old purlins, cut into slats and glued to create sections that were virtually good as new. For the remainder, the firm resorted to virgin Swiss wood. The insulation is made of rockwool, the firm Flumroc providing surplus material which would have otherwise been melted down at high temperatures and recycled. Where energy was saved in one area, however, labour was added in another, with the timber construction firm having to insert the rockwool by hand into the frames.

Windows were sourced from manufacturers within a radius of some 100 kilometres, the architects acquiring more than 200, at an average cost of just 285 francs, within two weeks. Neither pre-used nor defective, they were merely products that had been rejected as a result of misplaced orders or incorrect painting. There was a catch, though: none of the manufacturers wanted to provide a warranty for their rejects. Consequently, the savings made in purchasing surplus windows were set aside in a repair fund—an unconventional solution that nonetheless gained the client's approval.[4]

Compared with a conventional construction process, this kind of sourcing and the associated logistics meant a lot more work for the architects; on the other hand, it also allowed them to gain valuable experience for future projects. Together with their clients, they proved that, with creative thinking and mutual goodwill, unconventional solutions can be realized within a set time frame and budget.

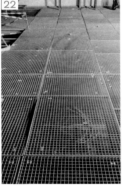

[Fig. 17] Establishment of a new access lane alongside the existing building, which has been stripped back to the load-bearing structure.
[Figs. 18–22] Reclaimed components: trapezoidal metal sheeting found on-site, rejected windows, used purlins for the façade's frame, rockwool offcuts for insulation, heavy-duty grilles for safety barriers.
[Fig. 23] Windows of varying shapes and sizes being inserted into the façade's wooden sections at the workshop. The frames were filled with rockwool offcut and cavities sealed using rockwool flakes.[5]

Opportunities for tomorrow's architecture

In the context of contemporary Swiss architecture, the five buildings presented here would appear to be outliers or audacious experiments. That's perplexing really; after all, the Sainte-Croix and Zweisimmen examples demonstrate that reuse can, in conjunction with recycling, renewable materials, and intelligently installed technical services, help to reduce construction's resource use across the board. With their projects in Winterthur and Basel respectively, MOKA Architekten and baubüro in situ have even shown that it's possible to utilize reclaimed components while working within predefined budgets and established organizational structures.

---

4 ↗ **p. 184**
Values and processes
Reuse from a developer perspective

'Of course, you then have to bear the risk for any flaws in the material yourself. This is something we resolved via a reserve fund, a budget item in the tender that's ring-fenced for any repairs.'

5 ↗ **p. 171**
New paths toward net zero?
Potentials for climate protection

'To ensure that there would be no cavities, we then sealed them with granulate. That means we always used relatively new, high-quality materials. However, for the thermal insulation certificate, we still had to calculate it as a "non-monitored" building material according to the SIA standard.'

6 ↗ **p. 248**
K.118 case study
Costs

7 ↗ **p. 238**
K.118 case study
Construction
organization

8 ↗ **p. 189**
Uncharted legal territory
Reuse under Swiss law

Flury + Furrer, meanwhile, have spent over two decades teasing out and enhancing the existing qualities of one particular site, thereby creating a uniquely atmospheric and organic whole. There is, then, no shortage of good reasons for reusing building components. Those wishing to do so, however, still face numerous obstacles.

Firstly, planning for and building with reclaimed or rejected components require a lot of time and initiative on the part of clients and architects. In Switzerland, the trade in such parts has yet to establish itself as a viable business model; would-be reusers thus have to organize the sourcing, disassembly, transportation, and storage of components themselves. Often, the desired items are not available in the required quantities or at the right time, meaning many aspects of planning go unresolved for longer and possible changes of direction have to be factored in. And, of course, the extra work involved is also reflected in increased costs. On the other hand, this could soon change as digital trading platforms and specialist deconstruction firms emerge.[6,7]

Secondly, using alternatives to new products means having to overcome legal hurdles and find approval-related workarounds. Reclaimed building components are generally not covered by existing statutory regulation—especially when it comes to meeting fire safety, structural stability, or energy efficiency requirements. There is thus a need to develop the laws and approval processes that would allow reuse to become more broadly established within the Swiss construction industry.[8]

And finally, working with reclaimed components means prioritizing subtle qualities such as the fine craftsmanship or rich heritage of a component over the flawlessness of new equivalents. Here, the onus is particularly on architects—not only to recognize such qualities and convey them to their clients, but also to relinquish a little of their usual control over every detail and to instead be open to alternative design strategies.

Project profiles

Transformation of Sittertal dye works: Deér-Lehner residence

Sittertal, St. Gallen, 2009 • Clients: private • Architects: Flury + Furrer Architekten, Zurich • Civil engineers: Schnetzer Puskas Ingenieure, Zurich • Contractor for metalwork: Ammann & Thürlemann, Zuzwil

Up until 2008, this pavilion by Gigon/Guyer stood outside the Lucerne Museum of Transport, where it housed a cafeteria. Flury + Furrer Architekten had it broken down into its component parts and translocated to the Sittertal dye works in St. Gallen, specifically to the roof of the converted boiler house. There, the reassembled and refitted structure now serves as a private residence and studio. The project is just one aspect of the architects' approximately 20-year involvement at the dye works, during which time reclaimed components from the site and elsewhere have been used as a matter of course.

[Fig. 24] Now: studio and home atop the old boiler house in Sittertal.
[Fig. 25] Then: restaurant pavilion outside the Lucerne Museum of Transport.
[Fig. 26] North elevation.
[Fig. 27] Floor plan.
[Fig. 28] Section.

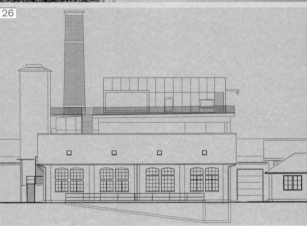
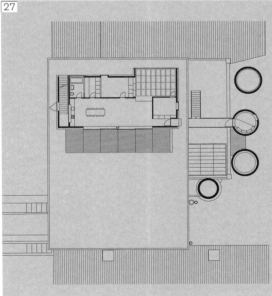
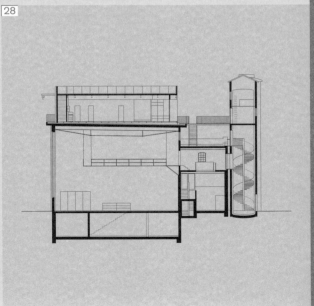

Project profiles

Renovation and refurbishment, Römerstrasse office building

Winterthur, 2020 • Client: AXA Lebensversicherung, Winterthur • Architects: MOKA Architekten, Zurich • General contractor: Losinger Marazzi, Berne • Joinery: Schreinerei Hugener, Winterthur

This office building on Winterthur's Römerstrasse is listed on the local authority's heritage register. In their renovation, MOKA Architekten were keen to preserve and emphasize the interior's specific qualities and ambience. A new usage concept for the upper storeys, however, meant the triple-loaded layout had to be overhauled, but by reconfiguring and reusing the spaces' finely crafted solid-wood fixtures, the architects were nonetheless able to partially preserve their original character.

[Fig. 29]   External view showing cast aluminium cladding.
[Fig. 30]   Plan of upper floor before refurbishment.
[Fig. 31]   Before: finely crafted fitted cabinets separate the cubicles from the corridor.
[Fig. 32]   Plan of upper floor after refurbishment.
[Fig. 33]   After: open-plan layout with reused cabinetry around the central zone.

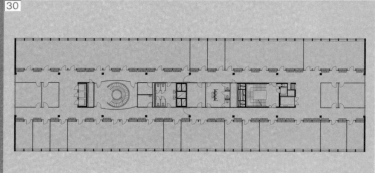

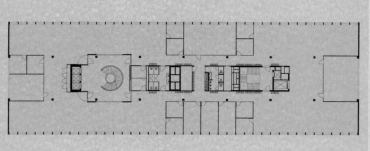

Residential and office building, Zweisimmen

Zweisimmen, 2014 • Clients: Regula Trachsel, Sascha Schär • Architects: N11 Architekten, Zweisimmen / Consultants: Pfleger + Stöckli Architekten, Chur • Civil engineers: N11 Bauingenieure, Zweisimmen / Consultants: Hunger Ingenieure, Chur • Energy consultants: Hanimann Energie- und Gebäudetechnik, Zweisimmen • Timber construction: Kunz Zimmerei, Zweisimmen

With their tower-like 'Haus ohne Heizung' (House without Heating) in Zweisimmen's industrial zone, N11 Architekten und Bauingenieure present their take on how to minimize the spatial and environmental footprint of rural new builds. Built using the Holz100 dowel-laminated timber system, it aims to conserve energy and resources across the board and conform to circular design principles. Pared-down installations, untreated materials, and separable assemblies thus feature alongside waste-wood cladding for the façade and reclaimed sanitaryware.

[Fig. 34]   North-east elevation.
[Fig. 35]   Cross section.
[Fig. 36]   From bottom to top: plans of the ground floor, third upper floor, and fourth upper floor.
[Fig. 37]   Living space with exposed solid-wood walls and rammed earth floor.

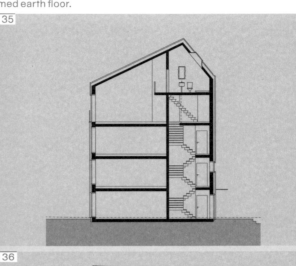
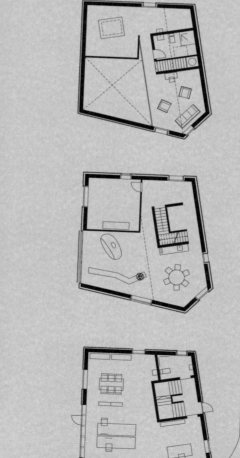

Project profiles

DomaHabitare cohousing project

Sainte-Croix, 2017 • Clients: DomaHabitare cooperative / Daniel Béguin, Sainte-Croix • Architects: Christian Jelk, Sainte-Croix • Timber construction: JPF-Ducret, Orges

Situated on the quiet outskirts of Sainte-Croix village, the DomaHabitare new build embodies its creators' vision of sustainable construction and cohousing. The prefabricated wooden frame is wrapped in a double-skinned façade, inside which is an intermediate zone that provides additional living space and acts as a thermal buffer. There are plans for a second-phase development that would connect with the access on the west-facing end wall, though, for now, that space is occupied by the vegetable plot, which is ultimately destined for the roof. The imaginative design also extends to the façades, where traditional shingles combine with a colourful collage of second-hand windows and corrugated greenhouse panels.

[Fig. 38]　　View of garden-facing aspect.
[Fig. 39]　　View from Avenue des Gittaz.
[Fig. 40]　　Apartment interior.
[Fig. 41]　　Plan of living space.
[Fig. 42]　　Cross section.

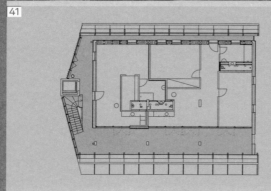

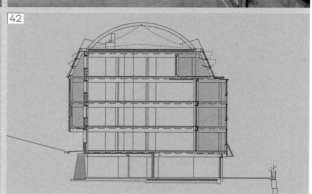

Where there's a will …

ELYS culture and business hub

Lysbüchel site, Basel, 2021 • Clients: Immobilien Basel-Stadt • Architects: baubüro in situ, Basel/Zurich • Timber construction: Husner AG, Basel • Window suppliers: Erne AG Holzbau, Schwald Fenster AG, EgoKiefer AG, René Schweizer AG, Biene Fenster AG, Gawo Gasser, Wenger Fenster AG, Gautschi Fensterbau AG, Blumer Techno Fenster AG

Basel's Lysbüchel site is being reborn, as old buildings are demolished or converted across the site. The one-time Co-op distribution centre is among those that have been transformed—in this case, into the ELYS culture and business hub. Wherever possible, the architects wanted to utilize material reclaimed from the various demolition and conversion projects, to thus renew the area using its own resources. The most eye-catching rescued items, though, came from elsewhere: around 200 reject windows from incorrect orders or surplus production were acquired and subsequently arranged in the manner of a 'salon-style' picture wall, an installation made possible by the building's generous ceiling heights.

[Fig. 43]   High-ceilinged office space.
[Fig. 44]   Mock-up of the new façade.
[Fig. 45]   Detail of façade design.

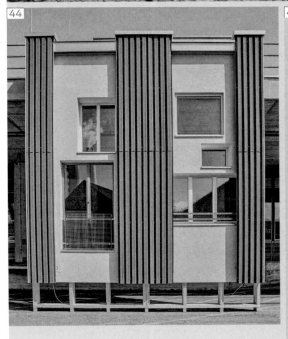

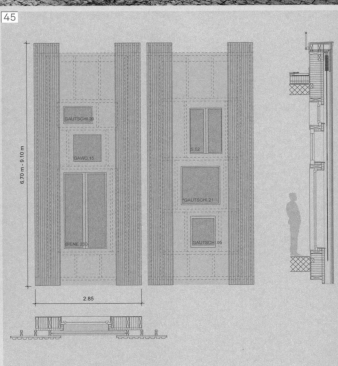

François Renaud

Out of scarcity

Four examples from the history of construction demonstrate that load-bearing structures conceived with circular principles are not unique to our time. Scarcity of materials and means has always been a powerful driving force behind innovative strategies that succeed by combining locally available materials, leftover pieces, and used parts into structurally and spatially potent constructions that can also be taken apart again.

In 1775, on the southern edge of the large forests of Chaux (Franche-Comté), the architect Claude-Nicolas Ledoux (1736–1806) began constructing replacement buildings for the Royal Saltworks, which had previously been based in present-day Salins-les-Bains. The reasoning behind the move was that it would be easier to supply brine to the new saltworks via a 15-kilometre-long aqueduct than to transport the large quantities of timber needed from the 'Forêt de Chaux' to the old site, where the forests had been cut down for miles around.

Scarcity, of whatever kind, has been an important driver of innovation and invention for centuries, indeed millennia, and for hundreds of years the scarcity of timber had a lasting impact on large areas of Europe. In the 16th and 17th centuries, European forest stands were seriously threatened by mining, iron, glass, and brick production, and shipbuilding, as well as by expanding towns and villages. The increasing demand for timber had to contend with a dwindling supply.

The scarcity of timber meant energy was also scarce. Attempts to replace rare and expensive charcoal with bituminous coal, which was available at no cost, met with little success until the early 18th century. It was not until the 1730s that Abraham Darby II, building on his father's efforts, succeeded in operating the blast furnace with coke, obtained from bituminous coal, instead of charcoal. The first fossil energy source was thus exploited, and this led to an unforeseen increase in the energy supply. In Switzerland, however, the blast furnaces of the Von Roll ironworks in Choindez were still operated with charcoal until 1867. It was not until the railway line was built from Basel to Biel via Delémont that coke extracted from bituminous coal could be imported.

Prior to the exploitation of supposedly inexhaustible fossil energy sources, the scarcity of material resources was a prerequisite for economic design. The following four examples are intended to show how the consumption of materials was optimized in very different ways. Philibert de l'Orme, François Cointeraux, Camille Polonceau, and Joseph Paxton with Fox, Henderson & Co. all took a quite distinct approach to the challenges they faced. While all four found solutions that were closely aligned with their respective ideational, material, and technical contexts, these solutions were far from obvious.

François Renaud

↗ p. 106
Roof over the round court of the 'Halle au Blé'

1 ↗ p. 236
K.118 case study
Design and construction: Glossary

Innovation and invention

'Ce qui m'a ému de chercher cette invention n'a point été pour lucrative, … mais plutôt pour la nécessité des grands bois qui ne se trouvent plus en France.'[1]

In his book *Nouvelles inventions pour bien bastir et à petits fraiz* (Bk. I, Ch. III), Philibert de l'Orme (1514–1570) makes explicit reference to the acute scarcity of good timber in the 16th century—a shortage he ingeniously counters: instead of the large timbers used in traditional roof structures, he uses lightweight arched trusses stiffened by cross ribs. They consist of boards of about 1300 × 220 × 27 mm, sawn into a curved shape, that are joined, offset to one another, with wooden pegs in two or three layers depending on the load. The horizontal ribs are rigidly wedged to the planked arch, either passing through the arch or clamping around it in pairs.

De l'Orme's references to this in the work cited above are detailed and practical: the wedging is to be checked periodically, as timbers that would not normally be used might also be eligible as building material (Bk. I, Ch. I), even including pieces that would otherwise be burned. Aside from making use of scrap material, he sees an advantage in the addition[1] of small pieces, in that they are less likely to crack or shrink. He explicitly states that it is possible to reuse wood from demolished structures.

He supports his findings with rich experience. For instance, in Bk. I, Ch. XVI he describes how the roof over the hall of Limours Castle, with its span of 10 metres, was built with just a quarter of the amount of wood and at a third of the cost of a conventional roof structure. Moreover, the three-centred arch inscribed in the main structure permitted the insertion of an intermediate floor for the screed.

In the closing chapter (Bk. II, Ch. XIV), de l'Orme summarizes the advantages of his invention in ten points and stresses, among other things, that, thanks to the all-wood connections, the total cost of his roof structure is equal to that which would have to be spent in corresponding traditional structures solely for wrought-iron connecting parts.

In his own buildings, de l'Orme deployed spans of up to 17 metres, but in his book he presented two unbuilt projects that went far beyond this: the 'Salle ou basilique', with its span of 48 metres (Bk. I, Ch. XXIff.), and, for the building that replaced the Montmartre monastery which burned down in 1559, a dome that was over 50 metres in diameter. These were huge dimensions that became reality 200 years later: the roof over the round court of the 'Halle au Blé', the Parisian corn exchange, was built according to de l'Orme's principles with a diameter of 41 metres. Even in more modest rural and urban contexts, the construction principle came into widespread use over the centuries.

1   'What motivated me to search for this invention was by no means the desire for profit, … but rather the scarcity of large timbers for construction, which can no longer be found in France.'

Out of scarcity

 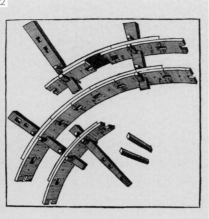 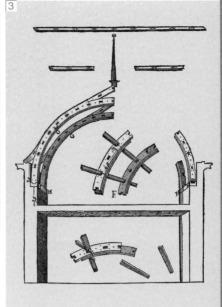

[Figs. 1–3]   In addition to spectacular halls, numerous simple buildings in rural France are also spanned by arched roofs based on de l'Orme's structural principle. The photo (left) shows an example from Occitania. The drawings are taken from the book *Nouvelles inventions pour bien bastir et à petits fraiz*.

Utopian earth

François Cointeraux was 50 years old and had garnered extensive experience as a master builder, surveyor, entrepreneur, and architect when he self-published a small essay with a big title in the spring of 1790: *École d'architecture rurale, ou leçons par lesquelles on apprendra soi-même à bâtir solidement les maisons de plusieurs étages avec la terre seule, ou autres matériaux les plus communs et du plus vil prix*.[2] The 50-plus pages of text are supplemented by ten elaborate illustrated plates and describe in great detail *construction en pisé*, or rammed earth construction. Beyond describing the tools, he gives a detailed explanation of the construction of the repositionable formwork, as well as matters of practical execution—namely, the importance of thorough tamping. The introduction refers to a subscription offer for another three booklets, which were to be issued later that same year and in the following year.

The four booklets appeared at a turbulent time. The years after 1780 in France were marked by a grave financial crisis and the unstable government of the lingering absolute monarchy. The increasing tax burden on the rural population, widespread poverty, extremely harsh winters, and ensuing crop failures prepared the ground for the French Revolution, which began on 14 July 1789. Another factor that needs to be taken into account is the publication of Diderot and d'Alembert's *Encyclopédie* between 1751 and 1772—probably not the first but a very extensive and successful attempt to collect the world's knowledge and to record human knowledge systematically in pictures and text.

2   'School of rural architecture, or lessons by which one can independently learn to build sound multistorey houses with earth alone, or with other common and inexpensive materials.'

↗ **p. 107**
Une petite Maison en Pisé

In this context shaped by scarcity and new beginnings, Cointeraux's writings aim to explore the expertise available in the greater Lyon area relating to traditional earthen construction, to identify the causes of its often-poor execution, and ultimately to describe with meticulous precision how the use of this traditional construction method could be expanded. The goal was to revitalize rural construction in an inexpensive, hygienic, and fire-resistant manner using locally available and reusable building materials. The insights were not just gained theoretically but were founded in local *savoir faire* as well as in the trials and experimental buildings of the *chantier-école*. The success of the writings, which were very soon translated into other languages and spread throughout Europe and overseas, is impressive. Although many structures were built using the improved technique of rammed earth construction, developments were not really in line with Cointeraux's expectations. Exponents of the traditional trades offered resistance. Could it be that his ideas fell victim to cheaper access to mechanical energy in the dawning fossil age?

From today's perspective, what made Cointeraux's writings innovative was not, first and foremost, the knowledge itself but the fact that he made it available to new audiences using a combination of text and images, an approach that was meant to replace the master craftsman's dissemination of proven traditional solutions.

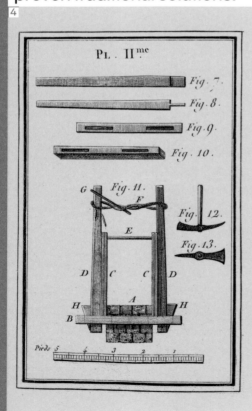
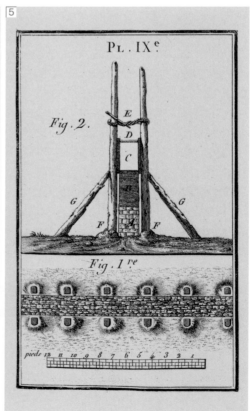

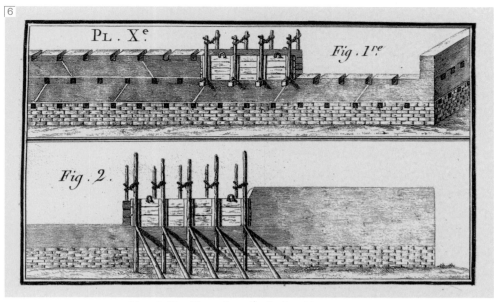

[Figs. 4–6]   Plates from *École d'architecture rurale* …: all the tools and procedures to build a house of rammed earth are depicted in detail.

Light system in tension

In 1836, after three years of training, Camille Polonceau (1813–1859) graduated *hors ligne* from the École centrale des arts et manufactures in Paris, where Gustave Eiffel, William Le Baron Jenney, and Armand Moisant would also train some 20 years later. Founded in 1829, the focus here, in contrast to the École polytechnique, was on the extremely close link between theory and practice. Auguste Perdonnet, who directed the railway course that Polonceau attended at the École centrale, immediately employed the graduate at the newly founded Compagnie du chemin de fer de Paris à Versailles (rive gauche), which was seeking less costly solutions owing to scarce funding. After Polonceau's premature death, Perdonnet's eulogy praised the many levels of innovative power exhibited by the young engineer, who not only improved the locomotive roundhouse as a building type but also achieved impressive increases in the efficiency of locomotive coke consumption. However, his best-known achievement is surely the Polonceau truss, which he began developing in 1837 to roof freight sheds between Paris and Versailles with spans of 8.4 metres in wood, cast iron, and wrought iron. Polonceau received the *mention honorable* for his perfected model of the truss exhibited at the 1839 *Exposition des produits de l'industrie française*.

↗ p. 108
Gare d'Orléans

What characterizes a Polonceau truss? Of course, Polonceau knew buildings such as the Marché de la Madeleine (1824) with a main span of 11.3 metres, which was discussed in Charles-Louis Mary's building course at the École centrale. The delicate but also extremely fragile structure—the roof of the market hall, designed as a king bolt truss, collapsed in 1842—made a distinction in material and form between the various load-bearing elements according to their stresses.

This also applies to the Polonceau truss, whose primary elements hark back to the traditional trussed beam. Two such elements, which Polonceau regarded as dimensionally stable planes, are joined by means of a tie rod to form a truss that needs a minimal amount of material. For the freight sheds of the Paris–Versailles railway line, the columns, rafters, and braces are made of wood; the elements in tension are initially made of 6 mm, and later 10 mm, wrought-iron wire. In his article 'Notice sur un nouveau système de charpente en bois et en fer', Polonceau meticulously describes how the dimensioning of the individual members was optimized by means of full-scale trials. He also notes that the trusses are reusable and can be easily transported in separate parts, and that the rafter can also be pieced together from two parts.

In addition to the structure just described, the illustrated plate accompanying his article shows detailed solutions for large spans in plates 6, 7, and 8. Here, cast-iron compression members that have been optimized in shape are now shown, as well as wrought-iron gusset plates that already exhibit a very controlled flow of forces. Soon, in addition to market and industrial halls, the train shed of the Gare de l'Est, with a span of almost 30 metres, would be built using the principle of the delicate Polonceau truss, followed by the train sheds of Lyon-Perrache, Gare du Nord, and Gare d'Austerlitz in Paris, as well as that of Budapest's Nyugati (western) railway station, designed by Gustave Eiffel, which has spans reaching over 50 metres.

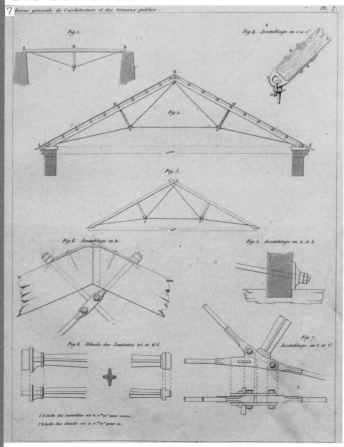

Illustrated plate for the article 'Notice sur un nouveau système de charpente en bois et en fer'.

Skeleton without meat

The bid submitted by Fox, Henderson & Co. in July 1850 to build the hall to house the *Great Exhibition of the Works of Industry of All Nations* according to the concept laid down by Joseph Paxton contains two options: one—to construct the building and dismantle it after the exhibition—for 79,800 pounds sterling, and another—with the on-site building to be assigned to the Royal Commission—for 150,000 pounds. The competition preceding the exhibition, which, primarily for reasons of cost, had failed to yield a viable project, had specified as a central requirement that the hall in Hyde Park should be capable of being dismantled after the exhibition. Joseph Paxton subsequently submitted a general concept to the building committee, which was grounded in his expertise in building greenhouses, and teamed up with Fox, Henderson & Co., who enjoyed a reputation as designers and contractors in railway and station construction.

The fact that the building could be erected within six months—from awarding the contract to completing the enclosure of the structure—is mainly thanks to two factors: on the one hand, Charles Fox and John Henderson began making construction drawings and working out the sequencing and scheduling three months before signing the contract; on the other, rules were formulated to optimize the individual components—in terms of space, geometry, dimensions, weight, and means of production—for efficient assembly and disassembly. The limitations of making glass with the hand-blown cylinder glass process resulted in the basic format for the glass panes of the roof, which in turn determined the basic grid size for the column spacing.

Paxton's concept, sketched in two dimensions, is thereby transformed by Fox, Henderson & Co. into a non-directional, spatially conceived framework.[3] Each basic unit of 24 × 24 feet (approximately 7.32 × 7.32 m) consists of four columns, column heads, and 3-foot-high beams. All the parts are made of cast iron according to the principle of modularity [2], each with the same external geometry. Differences in the loads imposed on the columns and beams are accommodated within the given geometric layout by adjustments to the wall or cross-sectional thickness of the members. In addition to standard girders of 24-foot length, girders built with a hybrid mix of wood, wrought iron, and cast iron are used for spans of 24, 48, and 72 feet. They are 3 or 6 feet high, and the same column head can be used at either height for all girder and column types. Both its ends, like those of the columns, are machined to obtain the greatest precision. The connections between columns and girders are designed to be rigid and also reversible: the girder is first set into a notch on the lower support and then fixed in place at the top with a wrought-iron wedge inserted into the groove between the upper support and the girder. The wedging

↗ p. 109
Crystal Palace

2 ↗ p. 236
K.118 case study
Design and construction: Glossary

3 The vaulted transverse hall was an exceptional case: it was stipulated by the building commission late in the process and led to a whole series of special structural solutions, which are of less interest here.

creates a certain amount of bending rigidity, which is supplemented by diagonal bracing at the stairs. After the exhibition, the building, which in the meantime had been dubbed the 'Crystal Palace', was dismantled and re-erected in Sydenham in south-east London.

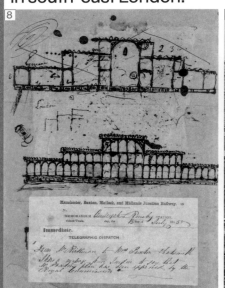 

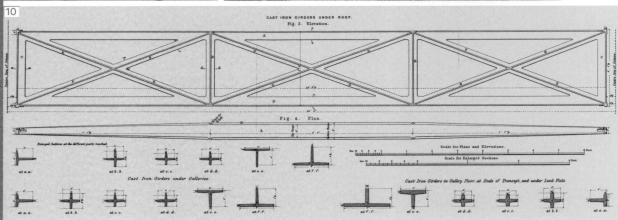

[Fig. 8] Paxton's earliest surviving sketches for the exhibition building.
[Fig. 9] Disassembly and reassembly change the original design. The Crystal Palace as rebuilt in Sydenham featured significant changes in configuration that did not correspond to Paxton's original concept. It was enlarged and made higher, and whereas only the transverse hall previously had a barrel vault, the vaulting now covered the entire building.
[Fig. 10] Structural details, Charles Downes, 1852.

Knowledge remains valid

Contrary to some disciplines in which new knowledge replaces old knowledge, the development of architecture and construction proceeds on the basis that earlier knowledge does not lose its validity but is supplemented by new knowledge: the history of construction technology is itself construction technology.

What can a curious look into the past bring us now? The four examples presented here all relate to scarcity, the lack of something: for Philibert de l'Orme, the lack of large timbers; for François Cointeraux, the lack of resources to renew the decaying rural built fabric; for Camille Polonceau, the lack of funding from an underfinanced railway company; and for Joseph Paxton and Fox, Henderson & Co., the lack of time, in competition with France, to open the *Great Exhibition of the Works of Industry of All Nations*—the first World's Fair—in the spring of 1851.

There is no way to dodge scarcity. Since it is not possible to fall back on assured knowledge, the questions that arise cannot, in principle, be decided. The ensuing freedom of choice demands a creative response. All four examples reflect an unbiased engagement with the matter at hand—an exploratory development—and they ultimately arrive at unexpected answers.

A big difference with the present day is that, for centuries, material costs were far more significant than they currently are for us. After a relatively inexpensive fossil fuel, bituminous coal, became abundantly available at the end of the 18th century, a development began that, over 150 years, turned the relationship between material and labour costs upside down. It is only recently that the value of material has regained importance and given new relevance to economical designs. The emphasis here is on diverse and urgent issues of resource conservation that are not tied to acute shortage but which counteract a prospective shortage using common sense.

Consequently, structures such as de l'Orme's arched truss, which found use not only in France but also in Germany, initially faded into obscurity over the course of the 19th century. But Friedrich 'Fritz' Zollinger, Merseburg's municipal architect, for example, adopted the basic principle and developed it as a self-supporting framework: a lamella roof structure called the 'Zollbau-Lamellendach', which he patented in 1923, at a time of severe housing shortage. Compared with traditional carpenter-built structures this roof structure halved the amount of timber used. In 2007, in an entirely different context, Samuel Mockbee returned to Zollinger's refinement when he and the Rural Studio of Auburn University used a high proportion of DIY work to build the second Akron Boys & Girls Club in an extremely impoverished region of the already poor US state of Alabama.

As mentioned, Cointeraux's commitment to rammed earth construction may also have reached its limits due in part to the cheap availability of fossil energy. However, this building technique's potential has been taken up repeatedly over the past two centuries. It gained renewed currency in France quite some time ago and has been embraced in Switzerland for a number of years now.

Maybe the Polonceau truss also offers approaches that could be of interest again today. In its resurgence over the past 30 years, the timber construction business has had a clear understanding that it is unwise to rely solely on structures made purely of wood—rather, wood should be used in composite structures, where it can perform best.

And finally, the lesson of the Crystal Palace touches on a central issue in circular construction—namely, how to join the components together in such a way that they can be conveniently taken apart again. This demand was catered to by the designs of Philibert de l'Orme and Camille Polonceau. François Cointeraux's *pisé* construction was also reversible, since the material of a building that falls into disrepair can always be reprocessed and reused.

At the outset of this conclusion, I stated that the development of architecture and construction proceeds on the basis that earlier knowledge does not lose its validity. We would be well advised to take these invaluable sources seriously and to study them in depth, again and again, while at the same time adopting a critical viewpoint.

[Fig. 11]　　　A duplex house with 'Zollbau' lamella roof, Merseburg, 1922.
[Fig. 12]　　　Akron Boys & Girls Club 2, Rural Studio of Auburn University, Alabama, 2007.
[Figs. 13, 14]　Riding hall in Flyinge, Sweden, AIX Arkitekter, 2005.

Literature:

Innovation and invention
- Blunt, Anthony, *Philibert de l'Orme*, London: Zwemmer, 1958.
- De l'Orme, Philibert, *Nouvelles inventions pour bien bastir et à petits fraiz*, Paris: Frédéric Morel, 1561.
- Erler, Klaus, *Kuppeln und Bogendächer aus Holz*, Stuttgart: Fraunhofer IRB Verlag, 2013.
- Graefe, Rainer, 'Die Bogendächer von Philibert de l'Orme', in id. (ed.), *Zur Geschichte des Konstruierens*, Stuttgart: Deutsche Verlags-Anstalt, 1989.
- Potié, Philippe, *Philibert de l'Orme—figures de la pensée constructive*, Marseille: Editions Parenthèses, 1996.

Utopian earth
- Baridon, Laurent, 'Le pisé de François Cointeraux—la terre pour utopie', in Robert Carvais (ed.), *Edifice & artifice—histoires constructives: Recueil de textes issus du Premier congrès francophone d'histoire de la construction* (Paris, 19–21 June 2008), Paris: Picard, 2010.
- Cointeraux, François, *École d'architecture rurale, ou Leçons par lesquelles on apprendra soi-même à bâtir solidement les maisons de plusieurs étages avec la terre seule, ou autres matériaux les plus communs et du plus vil prix*, vol. 1, Paris: self-published, 1790.
- Guillaud, Hubert, *Les carnets de l'architecture de la terre: Une grande figure du patrimoine régional Rhône-Alpes; François Cointeraux (1740–1830), pionnier de la construction moderne en pisé*, Grenoble: CRATerre-EAG, 1997.
- Seebass, Christian Ludwig, *Die Pisé-Baukunst, in ihrem ganzen Umfang, oder vollständige und fassliche Beschreibung des Verfahrens, aus blosser gestampfter Erde, ohne weitere Zuthat, Gebäude und Mauerwerk von aller Art wohlfeil, dauerhaft, feuerfest, und sicher gegen Einbruch aufzuführen*, Leipzig: Baumgärtnerische Buchhandlung, n.d.

Light system in tension
- Perdonnet, Auguste, *Camille Polonceau*, Paris: Simon Raçon, 1859.
- Polonceau, Camille, 'Notice sur un nouveau système de charpente en bois et en fer', *Revue générale de l'architecture et des travaux publics*, January 1840, 27–32 and plate 2.
- Polonceau, Camille, 'Neues Dachkonstrukzionssystem aus Holz und Eisen', *Allgemeine Bauzeitung*, vol 5, 1840, 273–280 (translation of the article in *Revue générale de l'architecture et des travaux publics*, January 1840).
- 'M. Polonceau (Camille) fils, à Paris', in *Exposition des produits de l'industrie française en 1839: Rapport du jury central—tome 2*, Paris: Bouchard-Huzard, 1839, 96.
- 'Polonceau (Barthélemy Camille) and Polonceau (ferme)', in Picon, Antoine (ed.), *L'art de l'ingénieur: constructeur, entrepreneur, inventeur*. Paris: Centre Georges Pompidou, 1997, 369–370.

Skeleton without meat
- Downes, Charles, *The Building Erected in Hyde Park for the Great Exhibition of the Works of Industry of All Nations, 1851: With Scientific Description by Charles Cowper*, London: John Weale, 1852.
- Peters, Tom F., 'The Crystal Palace', in *Building the Nineteenth Century*, Cambridge, MA: Massachusetts Institute of Technology, 1996, 226–254.
- Wachsmann, Konrad, *Wendepunkt im Bauen* (reprint edition), Dresden: VEB Verlag der Kunst, 1989 (1959), 9–21.

Project profiles

Roof over the round court of the 'Halle au Blé'

Paris, 1783 • Structural principle: Philibert de l'Orme (1514–1570) • Architecture: Jacques-Guillaume Legrand (1743–1808) and Jacques Molinos (1743–1831) • Timber construction: André-Jacob Roubo (1739–1791)

In the mid-16th century, Philibert de l'Orme developed a structural principle for joining small pieces of residual timber to form arched roofs with generous spans—a pioneering invention that has since been applied and further developed in countless variations and dimensions. More than 220 years later, the round courtyard of the 'Halle au blé' in Paris was roofed using the same principle to form a domed hall—creating an impressive structure with dimensions similar to the Pantheon in Rome. In 1802 the building was destroyed by fire.

[Fig. 15]   Construction details, Jean-Charles Krafft, Paris, 1805.
[Fig. 16]   Exterior view, Jean-Baptiste Maréchal, 1786.
[Fig. 17]   Bearing detail, Philibert de l'Orme.
[Fig. 18]   Interior view, Jean-Baptiste Maréchal, 1786.

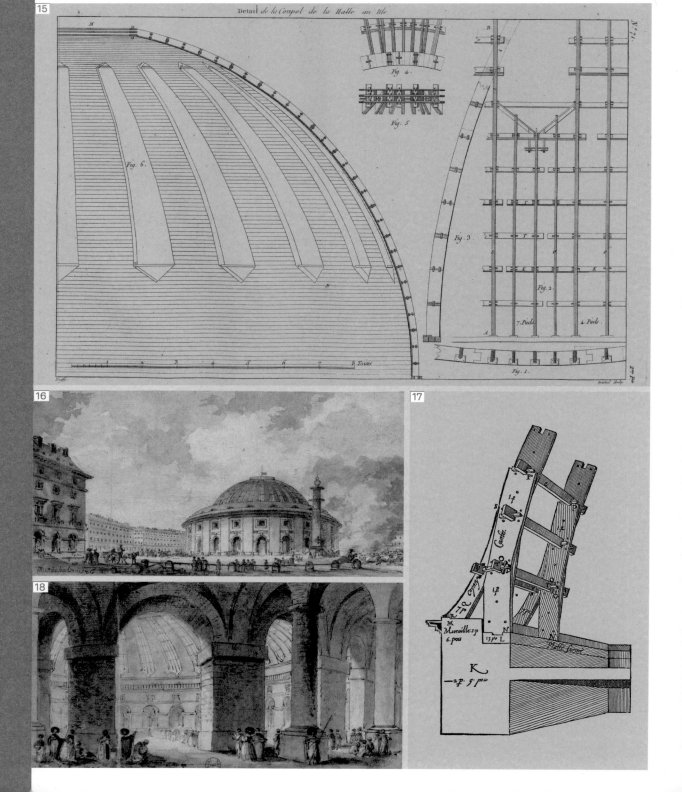

Une petite Maison en Pisé

Paris: self-published, 1790 • Structural principle: François Cointeraux (1740–1830) • Architecture: François Cointeraux

'La planche IV représente le plan d'une petite maison que nous allons bâtir avec lecteur, en Pisé'—this is how François Cointeraux introduces a prototypical house on page 20 of his standard work on rammed earth construction mentioned below, using it as an example to explain the advantages of rammed earth construction and to illustrate in minute detail the tools and individual steps in the work. His lavishly illustrated work is seen as a fundamental contribution to the scientific reappraisal and professionalization of this traditional, archaic means of construction.

from: François Cointeraux, *École d'architecture rurale, ou Leçons par lesquelles on apprendra soi-même à bâtir solidement les maisons de plusieurs étages avec la terre seule, ou autres matériaux les plus communs et du plus vil prix*, vol. 1

[Fig. 19] Plate VI: view of longitudinal façade.
[Fig. 20] Plate IV: floor plan.
[Fig. 21] Plate V: elevations of the end façades.
[Fig. 22] Plate VII: details of the exterior wall.

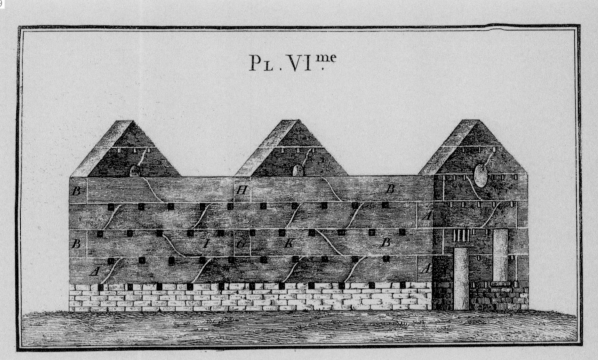

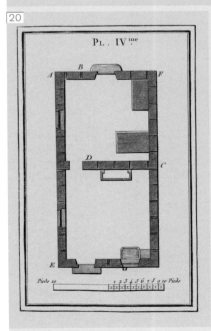

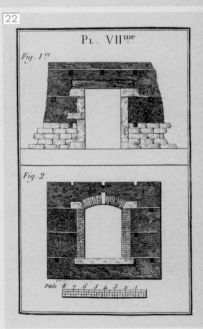

Project profiles

Gare d'Orléans

Paris, 1869 • Structural principle: Camille Polonceau (1813–1859) • Architecture: Pierre-Louis Renaud (1819–1897) • Structural engineer: Ferdinand Mathieu • Metal construction: Schneider & Cie, Le Creusot and Chalon-sur-Saône

After the former building was demolished, the new hall for Gare d'Orléans (now Gare d'Austerlitz) in Paris was built, between 1862 and 1867, as a light iron structure by Pierre-Louis Renaud, chief architect of the Paris à Orléans company. The roof is supported by delicate trussed beams derived from the principle conceived by Camille Polonceau. The additive structure, optimized in terms of material economy and reversibility, spans the 51.25 m wide and 280 m long train shed without columns—the second largest of its kind in France after Bordeaux.

[Fig. 23]   Interior view from Les Travaux publics de la France by Edouard Collignon, Paris, 1883.
[Fig. 24]   Exterior view during construction work to expand the station.
[Fig. 25]   Building section and detail drawings, Ferdinand de Dartein and J. Boulard, Paris, 1891.
[Fig. 26]   Detail of the roof structure.

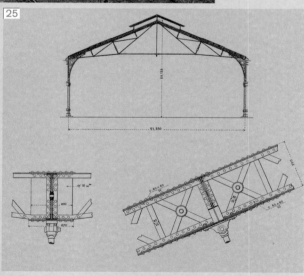

Crystal Palace

Hyde Park, London, 1850 / Sydenham, London, 1854 • Structural principle: Joseph Paxton (1803–1865), Charles Fox (1810–1874), John Henderson (1812–1858) • Architecture: Joseph Paxton • Structural engineers: Fox, Henderson & Co. • Contractor: Fox, Henderson & Co.

Joseph Paxton's building for the 1851 World's Fair in London anticipates much of what is discussed today in the context of reversible, reusable construction. Its modular design, the reversible connections, and the rational structure, which is optimized for flexibility of potential use, economy of material, and production factors, make the Crystal Palace an icon of design for disassembly [3]. The relocation from Hyde Park to Sydenham proved the practical feasibility of the pioneering concept. At its new location, however, the building later fell victim to a fire in 1936.

3 ↗ **p. 138**
A circular approach to architecture

[Fig. 27]   The 'Crystal Palace' from above, colour lithograph by Charles Burton, 1851.
[Fig. 28]   The Canadian Pavilion, coloured lithograph by Joseph Nash, London, 1854.
[Fig. 29]   Structural principle, after Tom Peter, 1996.
[Fig. 30]   Interior photograph of the main hall prior to dismantling for transport to Sydenham.

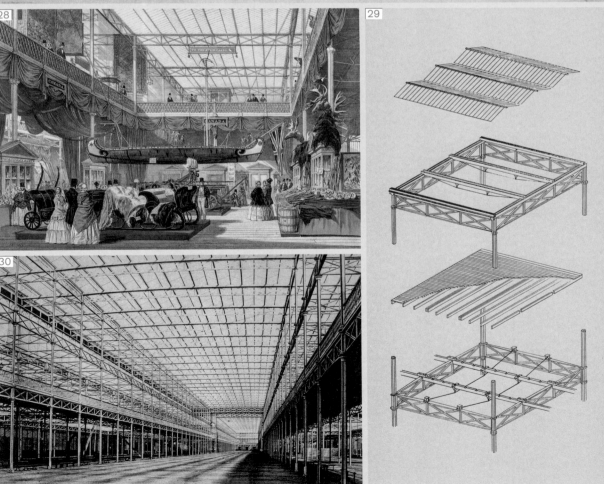

Patric Fischli-Boson

Circular load-bearing structures

Load-bearing structures account for a key portion of the resources and grey energy embodied within buildings, making it all the more important for them to be optimized. A Swiss pioneer and four contemporary examples drawn from university research projects in the local region illustrate how material-efficient, circular load-bearing structures can be designed—in steel, wood, stone, or concrete.

'Natura mensura est—Nature is the measure of all things.'[1] This is the statement with which Werner Sobek concludes a series of theses on the problems of today's building output and the potential of the reversible, resource-optimized lightweight structures of the future. After all, the construction industry is responsible for roughly 60 per cent of the worldwide consumption of resources. If resources are applied purposefully and the premise of the circular economy is adhered to, the possibilities for saving resources in the construction sector are enormous. The circular economy maximizes the useful life of elements by adding additional user loops, thus shifting the focus away from value creation and towards value preservation. Materials should no longer be consumed but instead put to temporary use. Connections should be designed to be detachable so as to allow components to be reused. Recycled materials should be incorporated into the construction process so as to enable recycling-friendly construction. Buildings should be designed as lightweight structures in order to save resources. Materials should be used where their potential can optimally unfold. Reducing resource and energy consumption in buildings can only be effective if construction is radically changed.

Current research in the building sector is engaged in investigating circular construction in general. At the ZHAW, research is being done on the potential intrinsic to the reuse of components and lightweight construction, especially in terms of the resource-efficient use of increasingly scarce raw materials aimed at reducing energy and greenhouse gases to achieve climate targets. The studies that follow are an initial outline of strategies for understanding how to deal with the reusability of building materials with the objective of moving the construction industry closer to a circular economy.

[1] Werner Sobek, laudatory remarks when presenting the 2019 Semper Prize, Sept. 2019, Saxon Academy of Arts, Dresden.

Patric Fischli-Boson

Toni el Suizo

The story of the Swiss bridge builder Toni Rüttimann is a singular one.[2] Having completed secondary school in 1987 he travelled to Ecuador to do social work, after the country had been hard hit by an earthquake. The adversities the people faced there encouraged him to help rebuild the destroyed infrastructure. Since then he has built 841 bridges around the world, connecting 2,265,000 people. His designs are a direct product of the materials that were available at no cost in the oil fields of the Ecuadorian jungle: used steel pipes, steel cables, and hardwood, as well as sand and stone contributed by the villagers. Even today, little has changed in the choice of materials, except the steel pipes and cables now come from sponsors in Argentina and Switzerland.

Rüttimann's bridges are suspended cable structures with different spans but always the same components: they consist of bridge pylons, main cables, suspender cables, a bridge deck, and anchorage blocks. Such a design uses materials very efficiently, since all the main elements except the bridge pylon are under tensile loading. The full capacity of the cross section can thus be activated without having to account for reductions linked to stability problems. However, the bridges have no redundancy. If one of the elements fails, the result is a total collapse, which is why the safety factors that Rüttimann uses for the engineering play a central role. They differ according to the bridge element and are dependent on the quality of the source material. The bridge components are stored in different countries and are inspected, assessed, and rated. This data is compiled in a spreadsheet and the safety factors are chosen as a function of the material assessment.

The works produced by Rüttimann exemplify the problems of reusing building components. All the data for a bridge project are gathered and processed in a central spreadsheet. It contains the basic geometric data, structural calculations, output data, the packing list with transport instructions, and the materials list, which is linked, in turn, to the inventory lists. By examining the supply of steel cables and steel pipes, the issue of inventory management can be better understood. Up until 2003, the steel ropes for the main cables came from oil drilling companies, and thereafter from cable car operators and manufacturers. Similarly, until 2003 the steel pipes for the bridge girders and the pylons came from oil pipelines. From then until 2020, they were obtained directly from a manufacturer. Since then, the quality of the materials has greatly improved. The prior function of the reused materials is well documented, which facilitates quality assessment. Auditing and evaluation rely on the detection of mechanical damage by means of visual inspection, and the quality of the utilized steel cables is well known on the basis of their previous use for aerial tramways.

↗ p. 123
Bridge No. 148

2   Toni Rüttimann (born 1967 in Pontresina) is a Swiss engineer who builds bridges in Southeast Asia and in Latin America, where he is known as 'Toni el Suizo'.

Rüttimann builds his bridges in such a way that they can later be dismantled and then rebuilt elsewhere. Only the juncture points of the pylon segments are welded. The rest of the nodes are made with bolted connections, which enables disassembly into segments of transportable size. It is thus theoretically possible to build a bridge of the same length or less without using additional components. That is the circular economy in action!

[Figs. 1, 2] Donated material: cable car cabling from Switzerland (left) and steel pipes from Italy, with Toni Rüttimann in the foreground (right).
[Fig. 3] Oil pipes awaiting reuse.

Load-bearing structures from electricity pylons

'Nothing is lost, nothing is created, everything is reused.'[3] That is the guiding principle behind the work of the research group led by Corentin Fivet and Jan Brütting at EPF Lausanne.[4] A resolute focus on circular construction necessitates a change in thinking on many different levels. With their case study for a railway station made of steel elements that were sourced during the dismantling of high-voltage electricity pylons, Brütting and Fivet's aim is to paint a picture of how a design practice for load-bearing structures might look in the context of the circular economy.

Rüttimann's work has already demonstrated that reuse involves optimizing the available materials. The material stock needs to be evaluated so that the best elements can be selected

3 Jan Brütting, Corentin Fivet, Structural Xploration Lab, École polytechnique fédérale de Lausanne (EPFL), 2020, thestructuralengineer.org.
4 Structural Xploration Lab, EPFL.

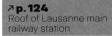
↗ **p. 124**
Roof of Lausanne main railway station

[1] ↗ p. 237
K.118 case study
Design and construction:
Glossary

from it for a specific use. With the help of an iterative allocation model, the research group led by Corentin Fivet has now delved into the details of optimal allocation at an academic level. The building parts repository contains a stock of elements whose characteristic values are known: modulus of elasticity; strength; density; specific gravity; cross-sectional shape; element length; and availability. This makes it possible to allocate elements as effectively as possible, which in turn ensures that 'downcycling' is avoided in the reuse and consequently that elements are not used below their potential.

For the case study of a railway station, 50 obsolete electricity pylons from the canton of Valais were analysed according to these requirements for allocation. They are constructed as trusses built of extruded steel angles (L-sections) bolted together at the nodes, which facilitates non-destructive dismantling. This enabled 19,000 load-bearing members to be harvested and divided into 332 groups according to the aforementioned parameters. The load-bearing members now form the material basis for the design of a roof consisting of three symmetrical central units (black) and two asymmetrical lateral units (grey). [fig. 20] As a result, the 75 × 200 m roof structure straddles four pairs of railway tracks. The design of these primary units was selected by taking into account the stock of available materials and optimizing the nodal geometry so that most elements did not need to be cut. This even made it possible for the existing bolt holes to be reused. On the other hand, though, the shape of the new structure was consequently limited by the existing options for a reconfiguration[1] of the existing elements.

From a mathematical standpoint, the reuse of components is an allocation problem that has been investigated using various different approaches (SAND, NAND).[5] The objective function takes into account the available structural members, the geometric constraints, the actions, the structural capacities of the elements—such as buckling behaviour and bearing-stress resistance—and the suitability for use of the nodal displacements. The objective function is linear, except for the compatibility constraints, which contain binary products. These are resolved by applying the so-called Big M method (simplex algorithm). The two-step procedure of defining allocations and topologies, combined with geometry optimization, leads to local optimality. On the one hand, given a fixed geometry, the allocation of members is iterated, while an attempt is made to minimize material consumption and waste. On the other hand, if the geometry is unconstrained, optimization of the layout can be achieved by varying the nodal position. This iterative optimization is concluded when no further mass is available and waste reduction has been achieved through successive iterations. In the case study, the central and lateral units were optimized individually to reduce the computational effort.

5   See Jan Brütting, Joseph Desruelle, Gennaro Senatore, and Corentin Fivet, *Design of Truss Structures through Reuse* (Lausanne: Structural Xploration Lab, Swiss Federal Institute of Technology (EPFL), Applied Computing and Mechanics Laboratory, 2018), elsevier.com/locate/structures.

This reduced the overall number of truss diagonals and even made it possible to save weight as well.

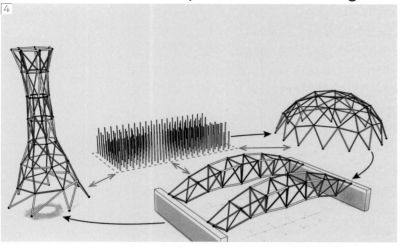

The available elements determine the formal possibilities.

Reciprocal frameworks—self-supporting structures

The self-supporting principle of reciprocal frameworks is first found in Chinese bridge structures of the 12th century, and Leonardo da Vinci also explored it in his studies of overhead structures in the early 16th century. Such frameworks have their archetypal origins in the interweaving of branches, evolving to become one of the first tectonic elements in architectural history. With his research work at ETH Zurich, Udo Thönnissen reveals how large spans can be bridged with a very specific principle using short load-bearing members.[6] The nodes do not need to be permanently attached, so the individual parts can subsequently be dismantled. The construction principle that has been handed down, with its mutually supporting linear elements, originated in various epochs and different regions. A commonality of the developments is that building materials and connectors were not available in the desired quantities and dimensions, which meant that spatial structures had to be developed with little material and often with short elements.

If the connections are established only by contact pressure, the reciprocal framework must be loaded under the force of gravity for it to be stable. The members are primarily subjected to bending moments and shear forces, which can vary greatly depending on the spacing of the connecting elements. Unlike other structures comprising stick-like members, reciprocal frameworks have no hierarchical levels; all the members are equal. Consequently, there is ordinarily no redundancy, and failure of one element or connection results in catastrophic failure. This can be avoided if the nodes are additionally secured by tension-resistant elements such as dowels or bolts. 'In reciprocal frameworks each individual slat functions as a single-span

6   Udo Thönnissen is an architect with offices in Zurich and Muralto. Ever since beginning research and teaching activities at ETH Zurich, he has been exploring reciprocal frameworks.

Patric Fischli-Boson

2 ↖p. 97
Out of scarcity
[fig. 2]

beam. If a random slat in the structural framework is stressed, then the load is transmitted to all the other slats. In the process, this slat also recursively loads itself.'[7] The recursive or self-impacting behaviour complicates the modelling and computation of these structures. Calculating the 'scattering' flow of forces was addressed by the mathematician John Wallis in the 17th century and described with progressive iteration in the studies of Kohlhammer and Kotnik in 2011/2013.[8] With these models, forces can be precisely calculated, and load-bearing elements such as nodes can be optimized.

 The insights that Thönnissen gained from his research at the ETH were applied to the project for a covered promenade at the Mkombozi Primary School in Tanzania, which he developed and implemented in collaboration with the architectural firm APC from Dar es Salaam. The pattern of the roof is based on triangles and hexagons. Although new wood was ultimately used here, because used material was not available in sufficient quality, the structure can be taken apart again and thus can theoretically be rebuilt in a new configuration. For assembly, falsework was erected in the shape of the vault, and the other timbers were installed from a mobile scaffold platform using a cantilever construction.

 Reciprocal frameworks are equally suitable for linear, planar, or spatial structures, as shown by the vaulted structures of Jean-Baptiste Rondelet and the roof structures of Philibert de l'Orme.[2] The initial cell defines the formal logic of the system through standard, edge, and aperture cells. Their basic configuration is essentially defined by the member length, member cross section, eccentricity, overlap length, and direction of rotation.

[7] Udo Thönnissen, *Hebelstabwerke: Tradition und Innovation / Reciprocal Frameworks: Tradition and Innovation* (Zurich: gta, 2015), 126.

[8] Thomas Kohlhammer, *Strukturoptimierung von stabförmigen Flächentragwerken mittels reziproker Analyse* (PhD diss., ETH Zurich, 2013).

5

6

Circular load-bearing structures

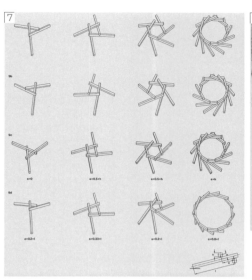
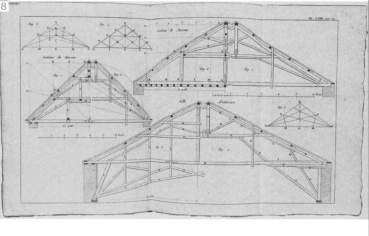

[Fig. 5]   Studies of floor/ceiling structures, Leonardo da Vinci, 1508–1510.
[Fig. 6]   Ceiling of the stateroom in Palazzo Piccolomini, Bernardo Rossellino, Pienza, 1462.
[Fig. 7]   Thönnissen: possible basic cells.
[Fig. 8]   Roof structure, Jean-Baptiste Rondelet, 1812–1814.

Shell structures reconceived

Shells are among architecture's most elegant structural elements. Spherical in shape, they rise up in a clockwise or anticlockwise direction above a defined floor area and form impressive spaces. Starting in ancient times, and then increasingly in the Renaissance, vaults were built, using stones and bricks, as pure compression arches. After the development of the Monier technique in 1868, these were also built of reinforced concrete, initially as thick-walled shells and later, through further development by Candela and Isler, also as thin-walled shells. Of groundbreaking importance for the construction of shell structures was their precise mathematical formulation on the basis of shell theory, as advanced by Eugène Cosserat (1909) and Paul Mansour Naghdi (1972).

The work of the Block Research Group at the ETH Zurich, led by Philippe Block,[9] builds on this knowledge and enriches the tradition of shell structures with innovative digital form-finding, calculation, and fabrication processes. This reinterpretation also makes shell construction interesting from the point of view of circular construction. The Armadillo Vault presented at the Venice Biennale in 2016, for example, was conceived as a structure purely loaded 'only in compression'. The junctures between the limestone blocks are mechanically connected solely using the tongue-and-groove method, without mortar or fasteners. They thus remain detachable and reusable. The shell's shape is chosen to ensure that the gravitational forces of the stone are transmitted in the plane of the shell as normal forces to the bearing points, where, depending on the angle of the apex block and the shell forces acting on the base, vertical and horizontal forces result. The latter are 'short-circuited' via steel tension bands to establish equilibrium. Imposed point

↗ p. 126
Armadillo Vault

9   Philippe Block is a professor at the ETH Zurich and co-director of the Block Research Group as well as director of the National Centre of Competence in Research (NCCR) Digital Fabrication.

loads as well as horizontal loads from earthquakes would likewise be transmitted through the shell structure as normal forces. Complex calculations with differing load cases ensure that the load vector always falls within the stone, as failure would otherwise occur.[10]

The form-finding process began with analogue means and the making of sketches and was then transferred to digital models. The shape was optimized with respect to the distribution of forces in the shell plane through the use of discrete element analysis software. Only recently has it become possible for the relationship between shape and force in cable and shell structures to be quantified during the design process. At the same time as the overall shape of the shell was being defined, the geometry and cut edges of the stone blocks were specified, and these were then cut to size with three-axis circular saws and given their final shape using a five-axis CNC circular saw. The entire structure relies on joining the blocks with great precision so that they fit together exactly. The apex stones at the crown were therefore fitted on-site, with the result that the contact pressure took effect as quickly as possible upon lowering the falsework, and the initial deformation was kept to a minimum. The individual blocks vary in dimension, weighing 45 kg at the crown and 135 kg at the bearing points.[11] In relation to the loading imposed on it, the stone's thickness increases near the bearing points. The structure's astonishing slenderness is the result of the process of optimizing the shell's shape and the relation of span to rise, as well as the strength of the material used and the node conditions at the element boundaries. If the ratio of component thickness to span width is taken as a measure of resource efficiency, the Armadillo Vault performs astonishingly well: it is proportionally half as thick as an eggshell, which is generally considered the perfect shell.

10 See Philippe Block, Tom Van Mele, Andrew Liew et al., *Structural Design, Fabrication and Construction of the Armadillo Vault*, thestructuralengineer.org, May 2018.

11 Matthias Rippmann and Philippe Block, 'Computational Tessellation of Freeform, Cut-Stone Vaults', *Nexus Network Journal, Architecture and Mathematics* (May 2018), doi: 10.1007/s00004-018-0383-y.

[Fig. 9] In 1926, the Zeiss Planetarium in Jena is completed as a thin-walled shell.
[Fig. 10] Félix Candela's double-curved concrete shells are just 4 cm thick.

Load-bearing structures built with CPC technology

The Fibre Reinforced Plastics group led by Josef Kurath at the School of Architecture, Design and Civil Engineering at the ZHAW has been working on components made of fibre-reinforced plastics (FRPs) for the construction sector since 1998.[12] Together with industry partners, it researches and develops practical applications such as CPC slabs, which are prestressed concrete units with carbon reinforcement.[13] The combination of carbon and concrete is promising in many respects. Carbon reinforcement has a tensile strength about ten times higher than B500B reinforcing steel with five times less mass. Furthermore, carbon reinforcement exhibits good chemical resistance, which is of central importance in combination with concrete to mitigate the impacts of use. The insufficient shear force behaviour and fire resistance is greatly improved when combined with concrete, thus proving to be a congenial complement to the composite material. The reasons for prestressing the carbon reinforcement mainly arise from the criterion of economic efficiency. Prestressing yields the same stiffness at a price that is five times lower.[14] In addition to this economic consideration, another advantage is that it is easy to work with CPC slabs. They can be freely customized with CNC milling machines, similar to working with wood. CPC technology results in very thin components, as has been shown in its application for the construction of the pedestrian bridge over the Eulach river.

The elements can be joined by means of CPC push-fit connections or with detachable internal bolted connections. The push-fit connection is friction locked with dovetail jointing and low-shrinkage, high-strength mortar. Studies on reversible connections are currently under way. CPC elements can thus be used alone or combined with steel or wood in a hybrid structure. Current developments demonstrate the potential for using CPC slabs in building construction as floor and wall systems. An integral CPC coffered slab with integrated utility lines reduces the slab's dead weight by 75 per cent compared with classic in situ concrete construction. This can be installed as a slab-column or slab-wall system. The reuse of CPC slabs is made easy by the inserted or bolted connections, which are similar to those used in steel construction. And additionally, if the recyclable material cannot be reused, it is possible to shred it like ordinary concrete demolition material, without it being necessary to separate the reinforcement, and it can then be utilized as clean concrete recyclate.

---

[12] Josef Kurath is a structural engineer and professor at the ZHAW School of Architecture, Design and Civil Engineering. Parallel to teaching, he heads the Fibre Reinforced Plastics research group there.

[13] CPC = carbon prestressed concrete.

[14] Josef Kurath, *CPC – eine neue Betonbauweise am Beispiel von Tunneldecken*, ASTRA Unternehmertagung, conference, Ittigen, 18 September 2020.

↗ p. 127
Eulach Bridge

Patric Fischli-Boson

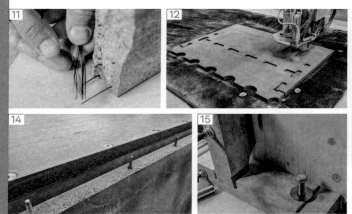

[Fig. 11] Reinforcement with carbon fibres.
[Fig. 12] Digital cutting.
[Fig. 13] Coffered slab with integrated conduits and piping.
[Figs. 14, 15] Screwed and push-fit connections.

Vision and reality

The approaches presented here span a broad field of inspiring ideas, but how do they address the specific realities of our building practice? And what clues do they give us about its future development?

Are structures à la Toni Rüttimann even conceivable in Switzerland? The Swiss and harmonized EU standards, which provide the normative foundations and reflect state-of-the-art technology, have a statutory character in Switzerland and must be applied and observed, also when reusing building materials and parts. Among other things, the standards regulate the execution conditions for load-bearing structures and building products, and require, for example, full traceability of the construction materials, including all test certificates. This is one of several problems in the reuse of building components. This circumstance complicates the seemingly simple and short decision-making paths in Rüttimann's case. Today's normative specifications are conceived for the use of primary materials produced under industrial conditions. The reusability of materials is not regulated by standards and thus requires that the body of standards be updated or expanded.

What Rüttimann develops empirically becomes the guiding idea of a complex computational model in the case of Jan Brütting and Corentin Fivet: how can one make optimal use of existing building component resources for new structures? The goal of reusing structural elements is to reduce environmental impacts. The fact that the developed method has potential in this respect is shown by the implemented life cycle assessment (LCA), which compares the difference between reused elements and new ones made of recycled steel. For the method presented, it was possible to show that the environmental impact can be reduced by 63 per cent, even though 50 per cent more material is needed compared with a new, weight-optimized solution.[15] To date, owing to the complexity of the computational

15 Mark D. Webster and Daniel T. Costello, 'Designing Structural Systems for Deconstruction: How to Extend a New Building's Useful Life and Prevent It from Going to Waste When the End Finally Comes', Greenbuild Conference, Atlanta, GA, November 2005.

model, this type of design has arguably remained the preserve of just a few specialists. Furthermore, it changes the dynamics between architects and engineers by leading to a design process that is sequential rather than concurrent and collaborative. In light of this, the need to develop a shared language and grammar seems evident.

Udo Thönnissen's research is based on age-old construction knowledge, which is given new relevance thanks to digital planning and fabrication processes. The shell of the Block Research Group's Armadillo Vault also exemplifies how traditional construction techniques combined with modern planning and production methods can unleash unimagined potential and how entrenched construction principles can be reconceived. In terms of circular construction, using vaults loaded 'only in compression' or reciprocal frameworks to span and cover spaces is a solution that permits disassembly and reassembly. The Armadillo Vault and reciprocal frameworks can fulfil a representative function, providing intellectual stimulus for reinterpreting building principles that have faded into obscurity by applying the digital means we now have at our disposal. Hollow clay block floors or ribbed slabs are ripe for reinterpretation in the light of digital and circular construction.

Josef Kurath's CPC system can be interpreted as a modern ribbed slab. This structural principle pursues the approach of offering a resource-optimized and digital alternative to conventional monolithic construction. The system is promising: its high degree of prefabrication, the low material consumption, rigorous separation of load-bearing structure and the routing of utility lines, the possible combinations with other materials, and its push-fit and bolted connections are all highly suitable for circular construction. Common to all lightweight structures, however, are preconceptions about economy, sound insulation requirements, and insufficient energy storage performance due to the lack of mass. The Hybrid Lightweight Construction research group, which is dedicated to these topics, was founded at the ZHAW in 2020. It focuses on issues relating to structural optimization (composite construction), detachable connections (reuse), fire protection, and sound insulation.

The increasing demand for raw materials and the associated global climatic changes are so drastic that the building sector must also deal with the consequences and mitigate the impacts. Switzerland would be well advised to initiate a resource-efficiency programme for the construction industry in order to emphasize the political dimension, because raw materials are a finite commodity. There are few who oppose resource conservation, and in general a positive attitude can be discerned in this regard. However, the incentives for change in the building sector are too modest and the social and political pressures too weak to prompt transition on a large scale. There are substantial untapped potentials for waste prevention through reuse. Optimized approaches such as 'cradle to cradle' and the concept of 'urban mining' are impulses that must be taken up, further developed, and put into practice. The construction industry has great potential to be a key contributor to decarbonization. Based on personal experience, however, a great deal of work needs to be done to persuade builders, both private and professional, to establish new methods of construction. Basic and applied research in the field of lightweight construction and in the reusability of building components can therefore make valuable contributions to reducing obstacles and increasing the acceptance of new construction methods. Konrad Wachsmann would be amazed that, even in 2021, the inflection point in construction has not yet been reached. It is time to progress a step further.

Project profiles

Bridge No. 148 Río Lempa, Honduras / El Salvador, 2000 • Civil engineering: Toni Rüttimann • Construction: Toni Rüttimann, local community

The 148th of Toni Rüttimann's suspension bridges, all made of decommissioned cable car cabling and other second-hand materials, crosses the Río Lempa on the border between Honduras and El Salvador. Numerous helpers participated in the construction process, which was literally a tightrope act: after the pylons were erected on the banks, the main cables were tensioned and then the horizontal beams for the bridge deck were hung, piece by piece, on secondary cables. After two weeks, the new bridge was finished. Since then, hundreds of other bridges have been built in a similar way in South and Central America and Southeast Asia.

[Fig. 16] The bridge is assembled piece by piece.
[Fig. 17] Material being transported to the construction site.
[Figs. 18, 19] The completed bridge.

Project profiles

3 ↗ **p. 180**
Values and processes
Reuse from a developer perspective

'We are currently running a pilot project, for instance, in which old, decommissioned overhead line masts are not disposed of but refurbished and then reused.'

Roof of Lausanne main railway station — Lausanne, 2019 (case study) • Structural principle: EPF Lausanne, Structural Xploration Lab

The Structural Xploration Lab at EPFL, led by Corentin Fivet, investigates methods of combinatorics for creating new structures with used building components. Jan Brütting and other researchers jointly studied possibilities for reconfiguring the extruded angles of electricity pylons, which are connected by plates and bolts, for a new roof over Lausanne's main railway station. The hypothetical case study was motivated by a real situation: the grid operator in Valais plans to replace six power lines from the 1950s with a high-voltage line. This means that about 50 masts per line with a total of up to 19,000 steel sections will be discarded. And Swiss Federal Railways is also thinking about the reuse potential of its overhead line masts.[3]

[Fig. 20]   The separate components of the pylons are reconfigured to construct the station roof.
[Fig. 21]   Pylon prior to reuse.
[Fig. 22]   Detail of connection.

Circular load-bearing structures

Promenade, Mkombozi Primary School

Chamazi, Temeke District, Dar es Salaam, Tanzania, 2018 • Client: Shirika ya Masista wa Mkombozi (Sisters of the Holy Redeemer) • Architecture: Udo Thönnissen, Zurich, in cooperation with APC Architectural Pioneering Consultants, Dar es Salaam • Civil engineering: Dr Neven Kostic, Zurich

The promenade, created by Udo Thönnissen in cooperation with APC, joins teaching and outdoor spaces of a church primary school in Dar es Salaam. While the columns and longitudinal girders are made of steel for protection against termites, the roof is supported by a reciprocal framework of slender solid wood elements—a response, both aesthetic and pragmatic, to the poor availability and transportability of large, industrially annealed components for engineered timber construction. The standardized linear elements, each with four slotted holes, are connected with flexible dowels and a wedge. in this way, they can be taken apart later and then reassembled in a different configuration.

[Fig. 23] Reciprocal framework of standardized members: the barrel vault has four types, and the 'apses' have seven.
[Fig. 24] Cross section.
[Fig. 25] Plan of roof structure.
[Fig. 26] Assembly of the reciprocal framework.

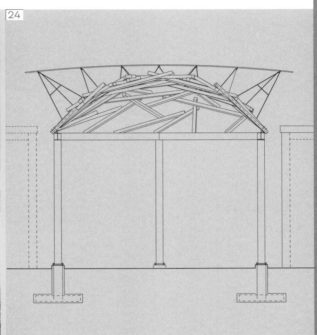

Project profiles

Armadillo Vault Arsenale, Architecture Biennale, Venice 2016 • Structural principle: ETH Zurich, Block Research Group • Civil engineering: Ochsendorf DeJong & Block (ODB Engineering) • Natural stone contractor: Escobedo Group, Mexico

With their limestone pavilion for the 15th International Architecture Exhibition in Venice, the research group led by Philippe Block at ETH Zurich stretches the possibilities of shell construction to the utmost: 355 unreinforced limestone slabs, some of which are only 5 centimetres thick, are assembled without mortar to form a shell spanning 16 metres, solely thanks to their sophisticated geometry. The spectacular installation shows how, with the help of today's precise digital planning and fabrication, it is possible to use even material of low tensile strength sparingly, and without additional fasteners, for masonry construction.

[Figs. 27, 28] The completed pavilion in the Arsenale in Venice.
[Fig. 29]   Assembly.
[Fig. 30]   Floor plan.
[Fig. 31]   Cross section.

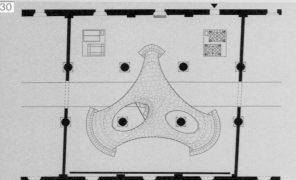

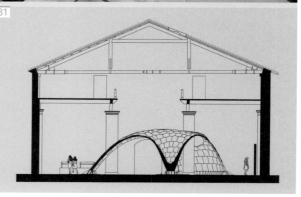

Circular load-bearing structures

Eulach Bridge

Winterthur, 2017 • Structural principle: ZHAW, Fibre Reinforced Plastics group, Winterthur • Civil engineers: Staubli, Kurath & Partner, Zurich • CPC contractor: Silidur, Andelfingen

On ZHAW's Campus T in Winterthur, the pedestrian bridge over the Eulach river was rehabilitated by replacing a segment with 40 mm thin CPC slabs reinforced with prestressed carbon fibres. Pairs of slabs were adhered full-surface for the frame, while one layer sufficed for the bridge's deck. The new bridge section was completely prefabricated and then installed in one day. It is a demonstration of how to build economically with concrete, requiring only one-fifth of the material (concrete and reinforcement) of a conventional reinforced concrete structure. The adhesive bonds also serve here as weather protection. Nevertheless, reversible screwed or push-fit connections are also possible.

[Fig. 32]   The rehabilitated bridge.
[Fig. 33]   Production and assembly of the CPC unit in the shop.
[Fig. 34]   Placement of the CPC unit.
[Fig. 35]   Construction details.

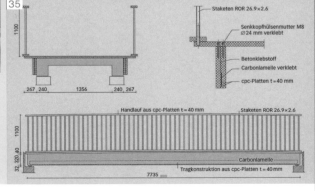

Guido Brandi

A circular approach to architecture

There are various approaches to circularity in architecture: these include using reclaimed products wherever possible, focusing on natural and local raw materials, tailoring construction to the life cycles of components, and ensuring component assemblies are reversible.

For now, circular construction is an idea that exists only as the inverse of linear construction, a process in which everything used in construction subsequently goes to waste. If we exclude operational energy use (which has, in recent years, been actively tackled and reduced and whose impact also depends on the primary energy source), then the ultimate goal of genuinely circular architecture would be a process in which no waste is ever generated and therefore all embodied energy is conserved. It goes without saying that achieving this goal will be a long and difficult process. But it should also be said that, as we move away from linearity towards circularity, there are numerous intermediate steps we can implement and design approaches we can realize.

Drawing on five different reference projects, this essay presents five possible strategies that can help us to achieve circularity in architecture. In some cases, these strategies are complementary; in others, they are mutually incompatible. Architecture, after all, is not simply a case of implementing lists of proposals. The approaches discussed here are all shaped by their relationship with modern architecture, which, in conjunction with the development of reinforced concrete in the late 19th century, continues to define the worlds of architecture and construction to this day. Circular architecture needs to understand the modernist movement—but also to move beyond it: in doing so, it should not, however, neglect the economic viability of its chosen resources. After all, modernist architecture was able to spread by virtue of its designs' ease of execution, the ubiquity of its materials, and the formal freedom afforded by building in concrete, as well as the material's outstanding fire and water resistance.

For it to be economically competitive enough to take hold, circular architecture needs to embrace the following principles:
- minimization of waste;
- use of fewer but more sustainable materials;
- use of components produced and processed in the building site's local area;
- separability of the various layers of a building;
- design amenable to disassembly.

Guido Brandi

Discard nothing—working with what is left over

If we are to avoid construction waste, the first step is to try to reuse demolition material wherever possible. Discarded building components contain the craft skills and design know-how that went into their making; they thus have an intrinsic value and a potential value that goes beyond just what they are worth as scrap.[1] In Europe, we are seeing a new public appreciation of the value of working directly with materials and of rediscovering as a society or community the feel for how individual components are assembled and disassembled.[2] One particularly notable example is the UK's Assemble Studio, a heterogeneous collective of architects, artists, and philosophers that gained international recognition—and won the 2015 Turner Prize—for its urban renewal project Granby Four Streets in Liverpool. Other examples include Rotor in Brussels[3] and the French group Bellastock, whose architecture festivals showcase pavilions made from waste material.

It's an approach Emanuele Almagioni, Giacomo Borella, and Francesca Riva of Milan's Studio Albori have been exploring since the 1990s. Demolition and disposal have always been anathema to the trio; instead, their projects always endeavour to reuse as much of the material and history of existing components and buildings as possible. Examples include their proposals for reviving Milan's abandoned San Cristoforo station, originally designed by Aldo Rossi and Gianni Braghieri, and their installation for the Chicago Architecture Biennial in 2015, which featured an old wooden staircase that the architects themselves transported piecemeal by bicycle then reassembled at the Chicago Cultural Center.

A recently rebuilt family home in the centre of Laveno, a town in the province of Varese, offers a particularly good example of the studio's approach. The initial plan was to preserve as much original structure as possible of the small two-storey house, which had been built with brick walls, a wooden roof, small windows, and views of Lake Maggiore, and to focus mainly on remodelling the interior, perhaps creating a larger opening towards the lake. Unfortunately, the structure turned out to be in such a poor state that the only option was to pull it down and start again, retaining the original volume in order to conform to the municipality's strict building regulations. Faced with the task of having to demolish the original building, Studio Albori's chief concern was how to reuse and integrate as many existing elements as possible in the new structure. Windows and doors were individually catalogued, and the traditional hexagonal cement tiles, stone thresholds and steps, as well as the wooden ceiling and roof beams were all dismantled and transported to the building contractor's storage facility, as were the roof tiles and metal railings, while the limestone and brickwork were used to fill in the excavated pit. Next the architects had

↗ p. 143
Casa a Laveno

1 ↗ p. 268
Eight theses

2
Value creation for new specialists

2 ↖ p. 13
Reuse!
[fig. 4]

3 ↗ p. 151
New generalists, new specialists
Rotor and the practice of reuse in Belgium

to decide what to use for the new supporting walls. They opted for a lightweight wooden structure filled with 36-cm-thick straw bales, which in themselves constitute a natural waste product; the wood was sourced from a local joinery and complements the existing roof and floorboards. When it came to the old hexagonal floor tiles, their initial idea was to reuse them as cladding for the blind façade looking towards the church, which would echo the red-and-white zigzag pattern that is typical for villages around the lake. This, however, was vetoed by the client, and the studio was left with no other choice but to use leftover terracotta tiles from the client's own stock.

It took ten years in total for the entire design and building process to be completed, due to a combination of long waiting times, sudden changes, and disagreements with heritage conservation officials, along with the great sensitivity shown towards the site. It's a way of practising architecture that, while not likely to becoming the global norm, does at least point the way towards a more sustainable and exhaustive approach to the built environment.

[Fig. 1] Granby Four Streets is an ongoing community-led project to rebuild Granby, a once lively multicultural area of Liverpool that had, after decades of failed regeneration efforts, almost been left to ruin. Working with the community land trust set up by residents in 2011, Assemble succeeded in renovating ten terraced houses on Cairns Street, establishing the Granby Workshop, which provides training for locals, and developing a public indoor garden for the use of residents.

[Fig. 2] To compensate for the lack of practical experience in courses, a group of Parisian architecture students established an annual full-scale building festival in 2006, during which several hundred participants designed, built, and inhabited a temporary settlement over the course of four days. Today, the Bellastock team organizes reuse projects on various scales. Pictured here: the temporary kitchen at the 2015 Playmobile Festival.

[Figs. 3, 4] Proposal for the reuse of an environmentally problematic hulk, in which new life is brought to the skeleton of the abandoned San Cristoforo station in Milan via a system of lightweight residential modules. A full-size model of the proposed design was presented at the Venice Biennale in 2008.

Guido Brandi

[Fig. 5] Casa a Laveno: the original house.
[Figs. 6, 7] The patterned render on a traditional dwelling by Lake Maggiore helped to convince heritage conservation officers that hexagonal tiles could be used to clad the façade.
[Fig. 8] For the building's foundations, efforts were made to minimize the use of concrete; instead, wire-mesh cages were filled with stones and fragments of the old brickwork.

↗ p. 144
Haus K

4 ↗ p. 236
K.118 case study
Design and construction:
Glossary

Materiality[4]—working with a single substance

In the late 19th century, as the Industrial Revolution drove rapid technological change, steel, cement, and celluloid began to enter the construction market, replacing traditional materials such as iron, wood, and stone. In his 1860 treatise *The Stones of Venice*,[1] Ruskin was already stressing the importance to the pursuit of an honest and pure architecture of taking heed of the material. One of the earliest such calls, it was an entreaty later followed by numerous architects, including William Morris with his Arts and Crafts movement, Adolf Loos with his 'material aesthetic',[2] and Joseph Albers with his Bauhaus courses on the meaning of materials.[3] Today, we are once again seeing calls for a true-to-material approach, but with a new, ecological slant: concentrating on locally available natural building materials has great potential as a way to reduce embodied energy. But what are the consequences for today's architects of limiting themselves to a few simple natural materials, given the vast range of choices available? And what are the consequences for sustainability and circularity in architecture?

1 Ruskin 1953: 391–392.
2 'Die Baumaterialien' (1898), in Loos 1962: 99–104.
3 Albers 1928: 3–7.

Wood is probably the most versatile of building materials. Not only does it save on embodied energy, it and its secondary products are also capable of meeting all the structural, acoustic, and fire-resistance requirements of a building. Even wood needs to be utilized with care, however; derivatives should be avoided and the natural character of the material shown to good effect. Engineered wood flooring, manufactured by combining multiple layers, uses eight times as much embodied energy as its solid-wood counterpart.[4] Glulam timber compares similarly badly.

    In Alpnach, architects Patrik Seiler and Søren Linhart have created a house that is also a manifesto. Made almost entirely of wood, this Swiss home was realized in close collaboration with the Küng family, who were both the clients and the manufacturers of the solid-wood system used in its construction. The entire structure—façade, internal walls, ceilings, and roof—consists of pieces of solid wood, namely of cross-layered spruce timbers joined using nothing but beechwood dowels, i.e. without recourse to glue, chemical additives, or metal connectors. The wood was all sourced from the surrounding region and processed locally in the Küngs' own workshop. Each single panel is 21 cm thick and fire resistant for 90 minutes (F90), while twinned panels can be used to create a solid façade that requires no additional insulation and is capable of supporting the ceiling boards, which are also made of dowel-laminated timber.

    It's a materially 'pure' building that consists inside and out of one single untreated natural product, a building whose raw materials, being neither impregnated, stained, nor otherwise processed, remain raw materials and can thus be directly reused. Such a structure might seem, at first glance, to involve inordinate amounts of material. In reality, it should be noted that all the timber from which the walls are made is of very low aesthetic quality and, had it gone into the manufacture of wood derivatives, would have been recycled anyway. In one sense, such a building simply skips an entire production stage, thus saving all the energy that would have been used in it.

    The only compromise is the concrete base that anchors the building to the steep slope. It forms the house's foundations, underlining that it's not about using one material for every function but about using the right material for every situation. Even here, though, we can learn from this pioneering project: the concrete's internal structural reinforcement is not steel but bamboo, meaning the concrete will be easier to break up and recycle later on. Going to such lengths to replace metal with renewable resources may seem exotic, but it underlines the seriousness with which this project explored architectural and structural means of combining more sustainable materials.

[4] Pfäffli 2020.

[Fig. 9] At the Küng AG workshop, robotic arms layer varying lengths of timbers crosswise on the assembly table, automatically leaving openings for doors and windows. At the points where the layered timbers intersect, a CNC mill is used to drill holes for the precisely inserted beechwood dowels. The fully automated machine shapes pieces, drills sockets, cuts mortices, and calibrates the various elements. These high-tech components are then assembled according to a traditional construction method that has been used for thousands of years.
[Fig. 10] Dry construction of solid wood walls.
[Fig. 11] Bamboo reinforcement for the concrete base.

↗ p. 145
Stone-built home in Montélimar

Continuing local traditions

People once built houses using existing materials and handed-down methods, but, above all, by looking to what had gone before, something the vernacular and spontaneous architecture presented in Bernard Rudofsky's *Architecture Without Architects* illustrates very well.

With the rise of industrial production, the discovery of more high-performance materials such as steel-reinforced concrete, and the globalization of transport thanks to standardized methods such as containerization, building components can be supplied to any place on Earth, even if they are alien to that area. As forces of commercial and geographical centralization, cities have brought a sense of interchangeability to construction: anything is possible, any material can be used, any construction method realized.

Perhaps the most striking example of this discourse between ubiquity and tradition can be seen in post-war southern France. In Marseille, a city devastated by air raids, two architects realized their respective visions of the architecture of the future: Le Corbusier built his Unité d'Habitation (1947–1952), thereby demonstrating the versatility of concrete, while Fernand Pouillon, who designed the La Tourette (1948–1953) and Immeuble au Vieux-Port (1951–1955) complexes, rejected this new mechanistic architecture, instead creating buildings from limestone from the surrounding region and working with local clients to develop rapid and commercially viable new techniques such as 'pierre banchée'.

Like Pouillon, Gilles Perraudin works with stone from the Fontvieille quarry and draws on handed-down knowledge. His designs demonstrate the underappreciated value of using natural materials to build houses that are easy to construct and deconstruct, economically viable, environmentally sound, and yet extremely long-lasting.

Perraudin's design for a house in Montélimar is a case in point: the walls were made of solid limestone and are 40 cm thick, while the ceilings and roof are of untreated solid larchwood—material choices that avoid industrial processing, eschewing preservatives and proofing agents, in order to reduce embodied energy.

The limestone blocks were assembled almost like a prefab system, being joined with lime mortar so that they can be taken apart again and reused. The simplicity of the execution, the avoidance of the usual wait for concrete to dry, and the usage of one single material allowed construction to proceed at pace. A secondary economic benefit is that using locally sourced solid stone not only keeps old building traditions alive, it helps keep quarries alive too, particularly when they are in sparsely populated areas far from major urban centres. These choices also aid the house's internal climate, creating a 'living shell': stone breathes and, thanks to its high specific gravity, also stores heat, enabling it to regulate humidity and temperature inside the house and counterbalance daily temperature fluctuations.

Perraudin's experiences, like Pouillon's on a larger scale, show us that traditional construction doesn't have to simply regurgitate lessons from the past; it can also actively reinterpret them and make them the starting point for innovation. That, however, requires building designers to have in-depth knowledge of materials, their local production, their construction, and the economics of the building site, to once again be organizers, economists, engineers, inventors, and artists, as Pouillon liked to say.[5] In short, it requires multifaceted architects.

5   Pouillon 1968: 78.

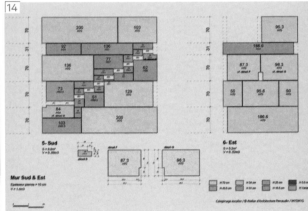

[Fig. 12]   Pierre banchée: limestone slabs from the Fontvieille quarry serve as formwork for the poured concrete while themselves forming the façade, a dual role that significantly speeds up the construction process. First used in the La Tourette housing complex.
[Figs. 13, 14]   As soon as the stone blocks arrive on site, work proceeds apace. Each stone is marked in a particular colour on the plans to save time during construction and avoid errors. Pictured here: the plan for the staircase wall, which is also supported by stone blocks.

↗ p.146
École Nationale Supérieure d'Architecture Nantes

5 ↗ p.236
K.118 case study
Design and construction: Glossary

Guido Brandi

System separation[5]—taking life cycles into account

'The main architect is time,' says Stewart Brand, founder of the *Whole Earth Catalog* (1968–1998), a highly successful US magazine that focused on ecology, DIY, and self-sufficiency.

It was Brand who defined the six layers that need to be taken into account in every new build or rebuild—site and foundations, structure, skin, services, space plan, and stuff (i.e. furniture)—stipulating that these should be easily separable without the replacement or alteration of one impacting on the lifespan of the whole.

This principle, however, is at odds with a commitment to using just one material wherever possible and standardizing building components as far as possible; here, each component is instead designed according to its function and its life cycle.

The early architects of the Industrial Revolution applied this latter concept extensively. They saw the need for large, modular, and flexible spaces in which the machinery of production could be installed, machinery that was likely to change rapidly over time and would thus necessitate constant remodelling. One of the first instances of architecture embracing this pragmatic way of thinking came around 1900 in Detroit following the birth of the motor car. The factories that Albert Kahn built for Henry Ford followed the principles of industrial production and recognized the need for highly adaptable, well-lit spaces. They represented a new architectural typology, providing a flexible infrastructure that could be reused again and again. While the Ford plant followed gravity, bringing raw materials in from above and, at ground level, churning out ready-for-testing Model-T Fords, the first FIAT factory turned the process on its head: at Giacomo Mattè-Trucco's 'Lingotto' building (1916–1926) in Turin, cars were produced at ground level then put through their paces on the rooftop test track. Based on a 6×6m grid of supports, this concrete structure with brick infill, which measures 510×72m and features four internal courtyards, has endured for a century and remains one of central Turin's key commercial hubs. Once the most important car-making plant in Italy, it is now home to an exhibition and business centre, a shopping mall, a museum, a hotel, and a university. It turns out the key to longevity was not the building's rooftop racetrack, but its versatile and flexible grid-based construction.

Parisian practice Lacaton & Vassal followed similar principles with their Nantes School of Architecture, the design of which allows students and staff to tailor spaces to different usages and needs. From the outside, it has a deliberately unfinished look, resembling an industrial building sandwiched between various dockland warehouses.

The supersized main structure consists of 80×80cm thick prefabricated concrete pillars and hollow concrete floors, a system more normally used for the construction of multistorey car parks. It's perhaps not surprising, then, that the building also boasts an entry ramp and a publicly accessible external ramp that winds its way from the ground floor up to the open-sided flat roof. The three concrete decks are two to three storeys high, allowing steel mezzanines to be inserted and the minimum floor area stipulated in the competition to be tripled. This secondary structure, which is in theory removable but in practice permanent, represents an additional and separate 'layer' in the building's construction. Each of the concrete decks can support up to 1 t/m², meaning the architecture students can even build 1:1 models if need be. The curtain façades are galvanized steel, glass, and polycarbonate, making them completely transparent and extremely light. And the aluminium and glass internal walls allow single-height spaces to be thermally isolated and intermediate climate zones to be created in the higher-ceilinged spaces. The latter were deliberately left unplanned so that they can be used and adopted as the students see fit, while the exposed technical services are designed to be easily disassembled or extended.

By their own account, the architects did not set out to create an architectural object—their response to the task before them was to put the people who work and live in the spaces centre stage. What you get here, therefore, are bare spaces, the result of a modular and mundane structure that, rather like Cedric Price's extravagantly envisioned Fun Palace,[6] has no fixed form other than that produced by its constantly changing configuration.

6   Cedric Price's Fun Palace is a recurring reference point for the work of Lacaton & Vassal. It is cited in numerous interviews and also influenced their renovation of Paris's Palais de Tokyo.

6 ↗ p.178
Values and processes
Reuse from a developer perspective

'How can we even begin to document the resources contained in such buildings? How can we collect and share the information we need to allow tomorrow's demolished structures to serve as material banks?'

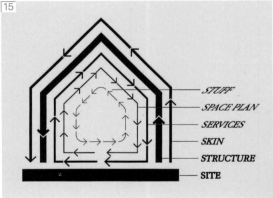

[Fig. 15]   Stewart Brand's six layers of a building, which Madaster uses to catalogue the existing elements of a building and create a materials passport.[6] In a sense, this harks back to Le Corbusier's principles of modernism.
[Fig. 16]   Exterior of Albert Kahn's 1909 Highland Park Ford Plant in Detroit.
[Fig. 17]   Artistic aerial shot of the Lingotto factory from 1928.

[Fig. 18] The primary structure's prefabricated concrete parts being assembled.
[Fig. 19] Façade of the Nantes School of Architecture.

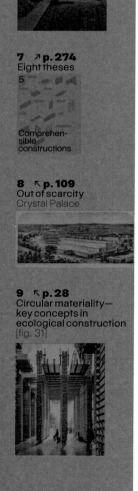

↗ p. 147
Haus R128

7 ↗ p. 274
Eight theses
5
Comprehensible constructions

8 ↖ p. 109
Out of scarcity
Crystal Palace

9 ↖ p. 28
Circular materiality—
key concepts in
ecological construction
[fig. 31]

Design for disassembly (DfD)— why construction details matter

In 1851, Gottfried Semper visited the Great Exhibition at London's Crystal Palace, where, amidst the 'Babylonian confusion',[7] he came across a reconstruction of a Caribbean hut, a simple timber-frame structure with walls of coloured cloth. It was this encounter that inspired Semper's theory of architecture as 'clothing'. From that point on, contemporary buildings were seen as products of a process of cultural evolution originating with that primitive, easily disassembled hut; the hut led to the temple, which led to the palace, which led to today's skyscraper. It is, though, surely time for us to view that evolution as concluded and start trying to reverse the process, to get back to a simpler architecture whose materials can be connected in reversible ways, and whose every element has a precise constructional and aesthetic function?[7]

Deliberate provocations aside, if we look back across modern architectural history, it's primarily been temporary pavilions and exhibition buildings that have addressed the issue of disassembly on a larger scale. Perhaps the most famous example is the iron-and-glass structure of the Crystal Palace,[8] but there are numerous others, too, such as the IBM Travelling Pavilion, created by Renzo Piano Building Workshop using glulam timber, polycarbonate, and aluminium, or Peter Zumthor's Swiss pavilion for EXPO 2000 in Hanover[9]—both lightweight structures capable of being disassembled and reassembled elsewhere. There are, though, also massy examples such as Anne Holtrop's Bahrain Pavilion for Expo 2015 in Milan, which was made entirely from concrete prefab sections and designed to be dismantled after the Expo and rebuilt in Bahrain.

Obviously, such structures don't have to negotiate the complexity of residential insulation standards. Arup's Circular Building,[8] on the other hand, aims to provide a more widely

7 Semper 1852: 3.

8 Stuart Smith:
The Circular Building:
https://www.arup.
com/perspectives/the-
circular-building

applicable blueprint, as does the Circle House project,[9] a development of simple residential units by Lendager Group, 3XN Architects, and Vandkunsten built as a practical demonstration of design for disassembly (DfD). These projects also illustrate how essential it is to make information such as product details, post-construction changes, and disassembly instructions available for each component; here, the use of BIM design and virtual digital twins to provide a parallel documentation of every component's life cycle will become standard practice.[10]

One way to achieve reversibility in architecture is by embracing the modularity[11] of standardized components and uniform connections. This is something already seen in system-based construction, a well-known Swiss example of which is the MIDI 100 system developed by Fritz Haller. By contrast, Antón García-Abril's research into structures and designs, which explores the possibilities of prefab elements for bridges and viaducts in unorthodox fashion, offers inspiration for those keen to avoid being constrained by repetitive systems. His Hemeroscopium House, for instance, is a structurally highly elegant prefab residence that is a far cry from the standardized architecture of catalogue homes.

A particularly tricky aspect of designing for disassembly is dealing with the various layers added on-site for insulation, sound absorption, or condensation control purposes, layers that are often irreversibly fixed in place using glue or bituminous materials. Likewise, technical services are frequently irreversibly embedded in walls or concrete slabs. Mechanical or plug-in connections within technical systems are an oft-cited solution to such problems but, really, there's one simple rule for true DfD: ensure all parts of a building can be disassembled simply by reversing the processes and steps used to assemble them.

A genuine trailblazer in the field of reversible architecture, the home that architect and engineer Werner Sobek designed for himself and his family more than 20 years ago makes an excellent starting point for an examination of this approach. Although planned with easy disassembly and relocation in mind, the house has so far stayed put and is therefore yet to prove its promised dismantlability in practice. Nonetheless, the principles underpinning its construction are a useful guide for any design with pretensions to circularity. First and foremost, Sobek's house is remarkably light (the superstructure, which sits on concrete foundations, weighs a total of 40 tonnes) and has net-zero energy consumption. Its simple cuboid form is built of standardized steel sections that can be transported by truck. The façade consists of triple-glazed standardized panels affixed to the structure via a system of steel cables and screw plates.

---

9 The Circle House: https://gxn.3xn.com/project/circle-house-demonstrator

10 ↗ p. 201
From part to whole and back again
Teaching reuse in architecture
'I think the digitization of planning processes will open up major possibilities here. It could allow detailed information for each component to be documented in BIM models, right from the new-build stage.'

11 ↗ p. 236
K.118 case study
Design and construction: Glossary

Internal partitions of hard-to-reuse materials such as plasterboard or brick were avoided; in fact, only the toilets were partitioned, using aluminium panels held together via a system of metal plates and magnets. A secondary solid wood structure supports the parquet flooring, which is also made of solid wood. There are suspended ceilings of removable aluminium panels that allow the copper pipes of the concealed heating and ventilation system to be accessed at any time, and the roof is completely covered by a photovoltaic array that collects solar energy while also keeping the rain out. Building work was completed in around one month and the prefab structure fitted in ten days. Technologically exemplary, Sobek's house remains as relevant today as it was 20 years ago. What's more, it proves that buildings designed with separability[12] in mind can still have a distinctive architectural aesthetic.

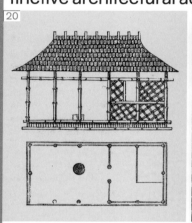

[Fig. 20] In Gottfried Semper's lectures in Zurich, the Caribbean hut he'd seen in one of the national pavilions at the 1851 Great Exhibition, held at London's Crystal Palace, served to symbolize the origins of built architecture.
[Fig. 21] Renzo Piano Building Workshop's IBM Travelling Pavilion (1982–1986): used to present IBM's technological innovations, this pavilion spent two years travelling between Europe's major capital cities. For ease of transportation, assembly, and disassembly, the enclosure was built using modular wood and polycarbonate elements with aluminium joints.
[Fig. 22] Anne Holtrop's Bahrain pavilion: the structure was made entirely of prefabricated panels of reinforced concrete, the joints of which were deliberately emphasized and are a determining factor in the aesthetic, with precision-fit bronze 'seams' sealing the roof joints against the elements.
[Fig. 23] Fritz Haller's MIDI 100 construction system.
[Fig. 24] Hemeroscopium House, Ensamble Studio, Antón García-Abril.

The many routes to circularity

For every architectural assignment, there is more than one appropriate solution—the five projects presented here thus merely outline a range of possible responses.

Studio Albori have adopted a radical and principled stance, namely that absolutely nothing should be thrown away. When thinking about a project, they always start from the position that all or as much of the existing materials as possible should be reused and repaired, thus creating architecture that allows the existing fabric of the building to live on in a new guise.

Both Gilles Perraudin and Seiler Linhart are practising a new form of regionalism, one in which the local area or region is the chief source not just of the raw materials but of the technical know-how too. Their use of a limited number of primary materials and their avoidance, wherever possible, of additional processing can also be read as a continuation of traditional local practices.

Lacaton & Vassal's architecture looks beyond a focus on material, stressing the need for flexibility in space plan and usage. They also design spaces that take into account the differing life cycles of various components, clearly separating structure and fit-out.

Lastly, Werner Sobek has developed an architectural approach in which concept and detail always go hand in hand. From design idea to detail execution, Sobek assiduously applies the principles of constructional logic and modularity, of assembly and disassembly, carrying them forward into the architectural aesthetic—from micro to macro and back again.[13]

In an increasingly interconnected world in which humanity's impact on nature, and nature's on humanity, is becoming more and more severe, it is imperative that we turn our back on today's steroidal architecture, on the constant quest for ever higher standards and ever greater convenience. Instead, we need to focus on going back to a critical examination of spatial requirements, to simpler materials, to less complex HVAC technology. It's no longer enough to build buildings that are net zero in terms of operational energy, we need to adopt a second net-zero goal—to ensure the construction and future deconstruction of our buildings is powered solely by renewable energy. Perhaps we should look afresh at Semper's Caribbean hut and see its constructional and functional simplicity not as the starting point for architectural evolution but as its ultimate goal!

[13] p. 197
From part to whole and back again
Teaching reuse in architecture

Literature:

Truth to materials—working with a single material
- Albers, Josef (1928), 'Werklicher Formunterricht', in *Bauhaus*, no. 2/3, ed. Hannes Meyer, Dessau.
- Cramer, Charles, and Kim Grant, 'Formalism II: Truth to Materials', smarthistory.org, 3 Apr. 2020 (accessed 28 Apr. 2021).
- Hillebrandt, Annette, Petra Riegler-Floors, Anja Rosen, and Johanna Seggewies (2018), *Atlas Recycling*, Munich: Detail, https://doi.org/10.11129/9783955534165.
- Loos, Adolf (1962), *Sämtliche Schriften*, vol. 1, ed. Franz Glück, Vienna/Munich: Herold.
- Pfäffli, Katrin (2020), *Graue Energie und Treibhausgasemissionen von wiederverwendeten Bauteilen: Methodik und Berechnung in Varianten am Fallbeispiel Gebäude K118 in Winterthur*, Zurich: ZHAW Institut für Konstruktives Entwerfen/Stadt Zürich.
- Rottau, Nadine (2012), *Materialgerechtigkeit: Ästhetik im 19. Jahrhundert*, Forschungsberichte Kunst + Technik, 2, Aachen: Shaker.
- Ruskin, John (1953), *The Stones of Venice*, vol. 2, London: Smith, Elder & Co.

Continuing local traditions
- Nequinha, Vicente (2016), 'Fernand Pouillon—The Modern Master Builder', in *Charta—On Relation in Architecture*, Zurich: Park Books.
- Noble, Allen G. (2007), *Traditional Buildings: A Global Survey of Structural Forms and Cultural Functions*, London / New York: I.B. Tauris.
- Perraudin, Gilles (2013), *Construire en pierre de taille aujourd'hui: Musée des vins et jardin ampélographique, Patrimonio, Haute-Corse*, Dijon: Presses du réel.
- Perraudin, Gilles (2018), 'Sobre et frugale', in 'Elogio della compressione', *archi*, no. 5.
- Picout, Laurie (2017), 'Utiliser la pierre est une position morale et éthique', *L'Architecture d'Aujourd'hui*, no. 417, Mar. 2017.
- Pouillon, Fernand (1968), *Mémoires d'un architecte*, Paris: Éditions du Seuil.
- Rudofsky, Bernard (1964), *Architecture Without Architects: A Short Introduction to Non-Pedigreed Architecture*. New York: Museum of Modern Art.
- Zerbi, Stefano (2011), *Construction en pierre massive en Suisse*, EPFL, thesis no. 4999.

Separability—taking life cycles into account
- Brand, Stewart (1994), *How Buildings Learn: What Happens After They're Built*, New York: Viking.
- Baldwin, Jay, and Stewart Brand (eds.) (1986), *The Essential Whole Earth Catalog: Access to Tools and Ideas*, with an introduction by Stewart Brand, Garden City, NY: Doubleday.
- Bergeron, Louis, and Maria Teresa Maiullari-Pontois (2000), 'The Factory Architecture of Albert Kahn', Architecture Week, 15 Nov. 2000, architectureweek.com/2000/1115/culture_2-1.html (accessed 1 Mar. 2021).
- Bürklin, Thorsten, and Jürgen Reichardt (2019), *Albert Kahn's Industrial Architecture: Form Follows Performance*, Berlin: Birkhäuser.
- Chan, Carson (2013), 'Lacaton & Vassal: Game Changer', interview, 4 Mar. 2013, 032c.com/o-architects-where-art-thou-game-changer-lacaton-vassal (accessed 26 May 2021).
- Lacaton, Anne, and Jean Vassal (2012), *Lacaton & Vassal: Recent Work*, 2G, no. 60. Barcelona: Gustavo Gili.
- Zimmerman, Claire (2019), 'If the price is right: The hard currency of architecture', *The Architectural Review*, 24 Sep. 2019, architectural-review.com/essays/if-the-price-is-right-the-hard-currency-of-architecture (1 Mar. 2021).

Design for disassembly (DfD)—why construction details matter
- Bell, Victoria Ballard, and Patrick Rand (2006), *Materials for Design*. New York: Princeton Architectural Press.
- Bell, Victoria Ballard, and Patrick Rand (2008), 'Detailing the Sobek House', *Architecture Week*, 19 Mar. 2008, architectureweek.com/2008/0319/building_1-1.html (27 May 2021).
- *db—Deutsche Bauzeitung* (2001), 'Experiment Wohnen', July 2001.
- Blaser, Werner, and Frank Heinlein (2001), *R128 by Werner Sobek*, Basel: Birkhäuser.
- Laugier, Marc-Antoine (1755), *Essai sur l'architecture*, Paris: Chez Duchesne.
- Rykwert, Joseph (1972), *On Adam's House in Paradise: The Idea of the Primitive Hut in Architectural History*, New York: Museum of Modern Art.
- Semper, Gottfried (1851), *Die vier Elemente der Baukunst: Ein Beitrag zur vergleichenden Baukunde*, Braunschweig: Vieweg.
- Semper, Gottfried (1852), *Wissenschaft, Industrie & Kunst: Vorschläge zur Anregung nationalen Kunstgefühles*, Braunschweig: Vieweg.
- Semper, Gottfried (1863), *Der Stil in den technischen und tektonischen Künsten oder Praktische Ästhetik: Ein Handbuch für Techniker, Künstler und Kunstfreunde*, vol. 2, Frankfurt/Munich: Bruckmann.
- Werner Sobek, wernersobek.com (accessed 20 May 2021).

Project profiles

Casa a Laveno
Laveno, Varese, 2021 • Client: private • Architects: Studio Albori, Milan

Tasked with creating a new build to replace an existing home close to Lake Maggiore, the architects aimed to ensure the environmental footprint would be as small as possible. To save on concrete, stone-filled steel cages were used as foundations. The external walls are built on a lightweight wooden structure and insulated with straw. Wherever possible, components such as doors, stairs, and windows were reused from the previous building or bought second-hand from local suppliers. In addition, the orientation of the site was harnessed with the aim of keeping net energy consumption to zero: large windows were inserted on the westerly aspect facing the lake, while the north elevation gained a closed façade.

[Fig. 25] The house's 'new' façade.
[Fig. 26] North elevation looking towards the church.
[Fig. 27] From bottom to top: plans of the ground and top floors.
[Fig. 28] Longitudinal section.

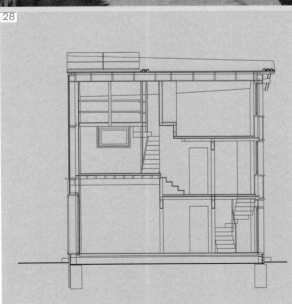
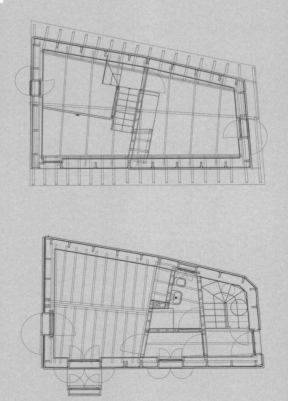

Project profiles

Haus K

Alpnach, 2018 • Client: private • Architects: Seiler Linhart, Lucerne / Sarnen • Load-bearing structure and building physics: Küng Holzbau, Alpnach • Timber construction: Küng Holzbau, Alpnach • Ornamentation: René Odermatt, Küssnacht am Rigi (decorative woodwork)

With this private residence in Alpnach, the architects and their clients, a timber construction firm, set out to demonstrate what can be achieved with natural, renewable building materials: using CNC machining, sections of regionally sourced solid spruce wood were manufactured, then assembled using nothing but wooden dowels—i.e. without glue or metal connectors—to create a three-storey home that needed no additional insulation. The fit-out used solid wood wherever possible too, while a rammed earth core made from spoil adds thermal storage mass. The one exception to the rule is the concrete base, though future reusability is ensured even here, thanks to bamboo rather than steel reinforcement.

[Figs. 29, 30] External view.
[Fig. 31]   Upstairs loggia.
[Fig. 32]   From bottom to top: plans of ground and first upper floor.
[Fig. 33]   Longitudinal section.

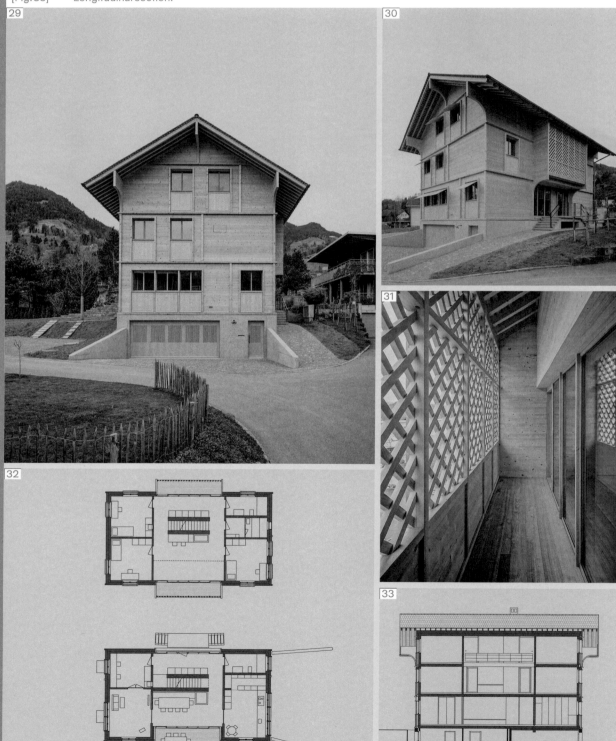

A circular approach to architecture

Stone-built home in Montélimar Montélimar, 2018 • Client: private • Architects: Gilles Perraudin architectes, Lyon • Build consultation and site supervision: WYSWYG Architecture, Nobouko Nansenet, Lyon • Construction: SAS Lionel Roux, Puygiron • Quarry: Carrières de Provence, Fontvieille

This square-plan house takes its cue from the site and surroundings. The floor plan is determined by the relative position of the sun and by the possibilities of the locally sourced material: the basic grid is formed by solid 40 cm thick blocks of limestone which, laid vertically, also constitute the façade, structure, insulation, and internal walls and thus—together with the wooden ceilings—define the internal spaces. The result is simple, almost primitive architecture realized using local knowledge, skills, and materials. The structure is weighty and durable yet, thanks to the unlimited lifespan of its stone blocks, can be repeatedly dismantled and reused.

[Fig. 34] External view.
[Fig. 35] Central hallway with staircase.
[Fig. 36] Bedroom with exposed stone.
[Fig. 37] Plan of upper floor.
[Fig. 38] Axonometry.

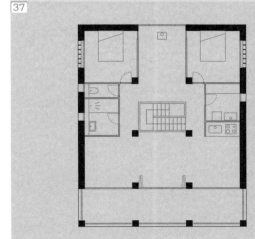

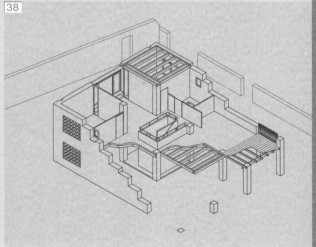

Project profiles

École Nationale Supérieure d'Architecture Nantes

Nantes, 2009 • Client: Ministère de la Culture – DRAC des Pays de Loire • Architects: Lacaton & Vassal, Paris • Civil engineering, concrete structure: Setec Bâtiment, Paris • Civil engineering, steel structure: Cesma, Merignac • General contractor: Savoie Freres

The Nantes School of Architecture is the foremost example of a building designed in separate layers and thus adaptable to future developments. To make full use of the maximum built volume, the architects created a supersized primary structure of prefabricated concrete sections, into which additional mezzanine levels could subsequently be inserted, thereby allowing for a flexible utilization of space. All partition walls and façade elements are lightweight and designed for disassembly. The result is architecture that does not have just one fixed interpretation but is more like a palimpsest whose current appearance is merely a snapshot in time.

[Fig. 39]   External view.
[Fig. 40]   Double-height space looking towards the studios.
[Fig. 41]   Section showing primary concrete structure plus secondary steel structure (the latter with dark shading).
[Fig. 42]   Ground-floor plans showing fixed spaces (dark shading) and flexible spaces (light shading); from left to right: street-level primary concrete structure, first mezzanine, second mezzanine.

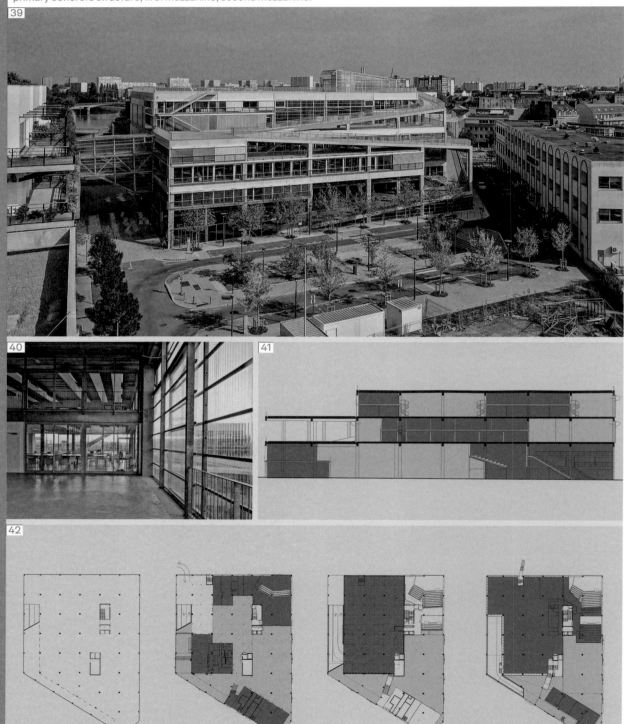

A circular approach to architecture

Haus R128

Stuttgart, 2000 • Client and architect: Werner Sobek, Stuttgart • Civil engineering: Werner Sobek Ingenieure, Stuttgart • Consultants, steel structure and façade: SE Stahltechnik, Stammham • Consultants, energy engineering: Transsolar Energietechnik, Stuttgart • Construction: Hardwork, Stuttgart

Completed back in 2000, Werner Sobek's own home in Stuttgart remains an exemplar of reversible architecture to this day. This low-mass, zero-energy house (its superstructure weighs a mere 40 tonnes) was erected in just one month and can be completely disassembled. Its individual elements all have standardized dimensions and use screw or magnetic joints for ease of disassembly, be it the screw-jointed steel structure made of standardized sections, the curtain façade, or the magnetically connected partition walls of the bathrooms.

[Fig. 43]   External view.
[Fig. 44]   The open interior, the spaces of which have no partition walls and are separated only by glass.
[Fig. 45]   Connecting joints in the primary structure.
[Fig. 46]   Structural axonometry.
[Figs. 47, 48]   Longitudinal section; from left to right: plans of first floor and top floor (with main entrance).

Discussion

New generalists, new specialists: Rotor and the practice of reuse in Belgium

Since 2005, the work of the Belgian collective Rotor has revolved around reusing building components. Here, it operates on a wide-ranging terrain: in addition to design and consulting work in the field of architecture and interior design, its portfolio also includes exhibitions and publications as well as research and teaching. In 2016, an offshoot, Rotor DC, was established as a separate reclamation dealer specializing in the salvage, reconditioning, and sale of reusable building components. Rotor thus typifies a whole host of architectural practitioners in Europe[1] who, in the service of a more circular architecture, creatively augment the scope of services provided by 'traditional' architecture firms. Sometimes their involvement also extends into areas that are typically the domain of companies and suppliers or even building contractors and specialist planners. After all, many issues and responsibilities that have been sorted out and delegated at an early stage in conventional construction processes remain unresolved in situations of reuse[2]—an experience also shared by the company baubüro in situ. Anyone who still wants to reuse must take a generalist approach as an architectural practice— or specialize as an expert in circular construction who fills this gap for others. To generate more understanding about how reuse is changing the concerns, organizational frameworks, and working methods of architectural professionals, and how it is even opening up new occupational profiles,[3] two 'summits' between Rotor and baubüro in situ took place as part of the ZHAW Circular Construction project. The first was held in Winterthur on 11 November 2019, coinciding with a guest lecture by Arne Vande Capelle in the ZHAW's 'Blue Monday' lecture series on component reuse, while the planned reciprocal visit to Brussels on 18 May 2020 had to take place online because of the pandemic. The exchange of experiences is summarized in the following conversation between Michaël Ghyoot **and** Arne Vande Capelle **of Rotor,** Pascal Hentschel **of baubüro in situ, and** Guido Brandi **from the ZHAW Institute of Constructive Design (IKE).**

In conversation:
ZHAW Institute of Constructive Design / baubüro in situ: Guido Brandi / Pascal Hentschel
Rotor: Arne Vande Capelle and Michaël Ghyoot

1 ↖ p. 13
Reuse!
[fig. 4]

2 ↗ p. 246
K.118 case study
Construction organization: Circular models

3 ↖ p. 36
K.118 reportage
Hunting and gathering
'Geraldine walks through the former bank building with the large window fronts. She measures the safety glass, notes its dimensions, takes pictures from a distance and up close: the corners, the mounting, and the seals. Geraldine is a building component hunter.'

New generalists, new specialists
ZHAW IKE / baubüro in situ   Rotor

Rotor DC

Guido Brandi:
Let's begin with a very specific question: why did Rotor—an architectural firm—start a dismantling business?

Michaël Ghyoot:
Very simply because Rotor DC enables us to reclaim more material than before. This way we can truly do something and actively gain experience in the reuse sector.
    Incidentally, we are not an architectural firm and never have been, even though more than half of us studied architecture. That said, we are engaged thematically in the broad field of architecture (with publications, courses, and lectures ...). But we are not registered with the Belgian Ordre des Architectes and are therefore not architects in the official sense. We work as interior designers and assist architects (as well as building contractors) in their project development.

GB: How did you get started? What was your chief motivation?

MG: We started Rotor in around 2005 and the focus was then on industrial waste. We visited many factories in and around Brussels and focused on what we could find in the waste containers rather than what was presented in the showrooms. At the very beginning, we had a somewhat utilitarian approach: that is, we wanted to find and reuse cheap material, but we realized quite soon that industrial waste ultimately reveals exactly how industrial production processes work, from both an economic and a social point of view. With one of our first projects, the exhibition *Deutschland im Herbst*, we sought to show how fine the line can be between products and waste.

Due to unwanted variations in colour, fully functional plastic boxes are designated as waste. With a series of art installations, Rotor highlighted the fine line between the useful and the useless in the exhibition *Deutschland im Herbst* (2008).

GB: So how did the connection to the built environment enter into it?

MG: In our research work on industrial waste, we increasingly focused on construction and reusing building materials. In 2007, we resolved to build our organization's headquarters out of industrial waste and reused scaffolding elements. It was a temporary building that only existed for one year, but it encouraged us to continue exploring how the construction industry can use alternative materials.

'We realized quite soon that industrial waste ultimately reveals exactly how industrial production processes work, from both an economic and a social point of view.'

GB: How is your business structured? For example, what legal form does your company have?

Since then, Rotor has continued to develop and work on different projects of that kind. An important milestone was the establishment of the Opalis website, a directory of dealers in Belgium who sell reclaimed and salvaged building materials. Its reach has meanwhile expanded to the Netherlands and France. In addition to this, we have increasingly become specialists in designing interiors with reused components.

MG: In 2014, Rotor DC started as a project run by the non-profit organization Rotor. After experimenting for a few years and completing a few dismantling projects, at the end of 2016 we established Rotor DC as an independent cooperative and formally organized company with suitable insurance and its own financial management and legal status.

[Figs. 2, 3] On the site of a former chocolate factory in the western part of the city, Rotor DC shares a large warehouse with other interim users until its planned demolition in 2022. Salvaged building components are stored here, and there are also offices and a public showroom. Heavy items such as stone slabs, floor tiles, and roof tiles are stacked in the yard out front, where they are first cleaned of mortar residues and reconditioned.

GB: How many employees does Rotor DC have?

MG: At the beginning of 2020, Rotor DC had about seven full-time equivalents, but there are actually more people, because not everyone is full-time. There's a team of three to four people who focus on dismantling (and who are sometimes aided by freelance workers). This team also operates in our workshop and is responsible for cleaning the materials as well as sorting and reconditioning them. One person is responsible for general logistics and another team of three to four people takes care of designing the showroom, cleaning and reconditioning the components, posting the products on our website, processing the orders, and handling customer service. In addition, there are new projects to be planned, inventory lists to be compiled, and many other tasks to be done. And lastly, two people are responsible for management: accounting, staffing, contracts, and so on.

Pascal Hentschel:
My impression is that the professional background of those who work at Rotor is very diverse. Is there also a specialist for inventory management and logistics?

MG: No, none of us has any training in logistics. The people here have very different educational backgrounds. For example, the person who is responsible for coordinating and executing the dismantling work in recent years had studied oceanography, which essentially has nothing to do with construction. He worked it all out on his own, is extremely competent, and brings a lot of healthy common sense to the table, which, in my opinion, are very important qualities to have when thinking in reverse about the construction process. After all, as a system, a building is not quite as complex as the underwater world or an ecosystem; maybe that's why it wasn't so complicated for him to retrain. (laughs)

'An important milestone was the establishment of the Opalis website, a directory of dealers in Belgium who sell reclaimed building materials.'

New generalists, new specialists
ZHAW IKE / baubüro in situ — Rotor

PH: A question about finances: you put a lot of work into what you do. Can you sell the material at a fair price and still make a profit?

MG: Most of the profits are actually generated by selling the materials, but sometimes we also charge the building owner for our dismantling work, with the rationale that everything we take with us will not have to be disposed of later by the owner at their expense. But, of course, cost is a topic of huge importance for us—it's ultimately the deciding factor—and we try to stock and sell elements that are profitable.

Since early 2020, we have also been officially working together with demolition companies. They bring us properly dismantled components and we resell them. The profit is then divided up. It's a win-win situation when they bring the material to us instead of transporting it to a landfill. It's also an interesting strategy when viewed in the long term, because it turns everyone in the construction industry into a potential salvager. After all, contractors are the ones who deal daily with potentially reusable building parts. With a concept like that, and provided there are good refurbishment options and sales channels, the amount of sensibly reconditioned and reusable material can be significantly increased.

PH: In our work, we have found that packaging and transport are two key aspects, and therefore we always try to use the same small company, Wick Upcycling GmbH, to transact this activity. Quite often materials break during transport, and what's even more common is for them to be incorrectly packed or loaded. How do you deal with that?

MG: That's a really important point. A big part of implementing the dismantling plan together with subcontractors is to make them aware of the requirements for packaging and transport. When we start working with a new provider, we generally meet on-site and make sure that materials are handled properly. Once everything becomes routine, such meetings are no longer necessary. But we're also constantly learning.

GB: What materials sell best?

Arne Vande Capelle: Mainly tiles, wood flooring, light fittings, good post-war materials ... Ultimately, they are always high-quality handcrafted products. Of course, you can buy new tiles, but they are quite expensive; in Belgium, for example, they cost about €100/m². We can sell them for about half the price; that's still five times more expensive than the super-cheap cement tiles from China or deep-discount sellers.

PH: Who are your customers?

MG: They are private individuals as well as construction companies. We try to appeal to both target groups, even though they have different needs with regard to opening hours, quality of materials, and reliability of delivery. Sometimes the architects are the ones who suggest their clients should visit our showroom, and sometimes it's the other way around. Construction companies generally come to us when the client wants reclaimed material. Hardly anyone comes spontaneously. In terms of the number of customers, there are more private building owners than contractors. But construction companies usually order larger quantities, whereas private individuals will often just buy 2m² of tiles or a sink.

'With a concept like that, ... the amount of sensibly reconditioned and reusable material can be significantly increased.'

Fundamentals of reuse

GB: At Rotor you work on many different projects that involve circular construction. What principles do you follow when you start a new project?

MG: Our biggest goal is always to preserve a building and ensure its continued use. We stay in contact with many neighbourhood councils and organizations that are actively involved in the preservation of buildings, since that should be the top priority. Often the goal should be to minimize the flows of materials to and from the construction site. Only after those opportunities have been exhausted should the share of salvaged and reused elements be maximized within these streams.

A good example of this approach is the 'MAD Project', where we convinced the architects from V+ to retain the existing building, since the demands of the building programme (a centre for fashion and design) were achievable with only relatively minor interventions. The different characters and sizes of the existing rooms offered a very special atmosphere and were reason enough not to raze the building.

With a radically conservative design, Rotor and V+ Architectes won the competition in 2012 for 'MAD', the new centre for fashion and design in Brussels. Instead of the expected new build, their compelling proposal preserved as much as possible of the fundamentally diverse existing buildings and interconnected them into an exciting spatial sequence.

GB: What's your position on demolishing buildings that are still in functional condition and are not even all that old?

MG: Our impression is that, when it comes to demolishing buildings, a lot of things frequently go wrong. Often there's a lack of imagination, or there's a special building programme that simply doesn't fit a certain situation. In such cases, form should not follow function, but rather vice versa: the functions should be aligned to the existing forms. Yet sometimes we get the impression that reuse is taken as a pretext to warrant demolition. These days, the decision to demolish a building is rarely a matter of public discussion. It's decided by the owners without public debate, even when the decision has an impact on the urban fabric as a whole.

GB: How can you convince a large business, such as a real estate company, to invest time and money in reuse?

MG: Reuse can be interesting for all sorts of reasons. It often yields materials that are no longer available and that bring more quality to a project. Of course,

'Our biggest goal is always to preserve a building and ensure its continued use.'

GB: Are CO_2 savings also an argument for you?

it's also vastly more environmentally friendly. For me, reuse is interesting because it requires rethinking the way something is done; this especially pertains to allocating funds in the construction budget, to the key project participants, to the message conveyed by the project, to the project's use of resources, to the project's economic impacts, and so on. Of course, such matters can hardly persuade clients whose processes are standardized and rigorously planned in minute detail and who do not want to rethink their way of working. But even then, reuse is possible.

MG: Reducing the environmental impact caused by construction is an important issue for us. Reuse is frequently more environmentally friendly than producing new materials and disposing of large amounts of waste. This needs to be recognized and we need to call attention to it—if only to justify the extra effort required to make the transition to a truly circular economy.

We are concerned, however, about the risk of reducing environmental and ecological issues to a purely bureaucratic approach, with countless new clerks occupied with calculating and managing an ever-growing number of variables and impacts. It would be terrible if every decision were taken only on the basis of data comparison, with no open discussion of the limitations of such approaches (what are the origins of the data, who compiles them, and for what purpose …) and with no room for unquantifiable arguments. The regulation of such processes should also be discussed. On a higher level, there are philosophers and historians of science (such as Alfred Crosby and Theodore Potter) who have been able to demonstrate that the mania to measure everything is essentially a symptom of modernity. In confronting the ecological challenges, we probably also need to fundamentally rethink our habits …

Rotor design assistance

GB: Nevertheless, I'm interested in quantifying it. Do you know how much material by weight, volume, and area you manage to salvage and then reuse in your projects? Do you have examples for which you know these figures?

AVC: Of course, that's very project-dependent. When we salvage material, we know how much it weighs and how much area it covers, but we don't always calculate how much that is in proportion to the whole building. We're more likely to do that with our design assistance projects. Percentages are also always good when it comes to communicating with clients.

A good example is the Multi project in Brussels, which began in September 2016. Our participation resulted from an invitation from Conix RDBM and Whitewood. We reached agreement on the ambitious goal that at least 2 per cent (by value and weight)[4] of the elements making up the project should be reused. These components could come from the building itself, the former Philips Tower, or from other buildings, supplied by specialized traders. For a build of that kind, 2 per cent is a significant amount and a great challenge.

'It would be terrible if every decision were taken only on the basis of data comparison … with no room for unquantifiable arguments.'

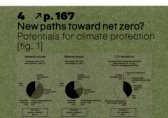

4 ↗ p. 167
New paths toward net zero?
Potentials for climate protection
[fig. 1]

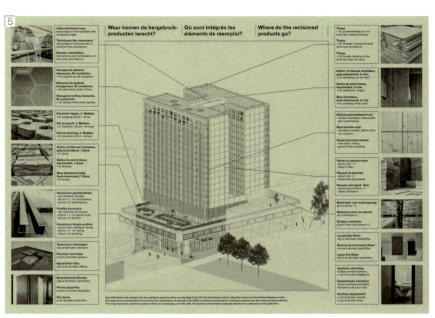

The Brouckère Tower represents a contentious chapter in the urban development of Brussels in the 1960s, marked by radical interventions in the mature fabric of the city. The Multi project was intended to give it a new lease of life: Rotor advised the architects and clients on using salvaged building components for the rehabilitation project. After its planned 2021 reopening, the tower will re-emerge as a landmark and stimulus for sustainability and the circular economy—and will be reconciled with the city.

GB: How do you start a project like that?

AVC: During the design and construction phases, we assist the architects in the integration of salvaged elements. The first step is to look for suitable materials. Given the size of the project, they must be available on the market in sufficiently large quantities. It is also necessary to choose those items that fit the project and its standards of quality and that offer added value. We especially look at buildings in the Brussels service sector that are undergoing renovation at the time.

GB: Can you give us some examples that explain how you achieve such a percentage on a project of this size and complexity?

AVC: Together with the architects, we identified 15 areas of action. One of them, for example, is the raised-panel flooring for the entire high-rise building. These 40,000 m² alone represent 2 per cent of the weight of the entire building!

At Mobius Réemploi, a dealer near Paris, impressive amounts of raised floor tiles are lined up in stacks, awaiting reuse.

GB: How is it possible to find salvaged panels of the same kind in such quantity?!

AVC: In Paris, there's actually a dealer whose business model is based on just such products. He's been around for three years. When we told him the quantity we were looking for, it didn't startle him. In principle, he could supply it without any problem. In the end, our client and the vendor agreed on a flooring type and half of the floor area in the building should be surfaced with it!

We see two to three such areas of action that are really big (in terms of quantity and cost), but then there are also other, much smaller areas, such as building a 300 m² public terrace out of reclaimed natural stone atop the base of the building. Another possibility is to install a salvaged kitchen on each floor.

To achieve the 2 per cent that I mentioned, it takes a mix of large- and small-scale measures. Although it is often the smaller measures that get people excited about the added value of reused materials, such as the reuse of stone paving from a well-known square in Brussels or Bruges. Maybe they witnessed the removal of the pavement on-site and didn't know that an agent was storing the slabs on their premises, and now they are excited about this kind of reuse. It's important to ignite this spark of enthusiasm.

GB: Do you also work towards recoding[5] architectural elements, giving them a new function or meaning?

AVC: How can individual building components be given a different function? Experiments on this are extremely difficult, yet it's also a very exciting area of work! For the Brouckère Tower project, for example, we're currently exploring the idea of working with glulam beams, sawing them to size, and using them to clad the interior walls. A whole series of steps is necessary for this change of function. To begin with, you need a workshop that can handle the material. We coordinate the initial experiments, ascertain the total cost, and coordinate everything with the architect or the developer to attain a feasible solution. In this case, our principal job is to coordinate the dialogue between the architects and the workshop that can repurpose the different components for their new function.

GB: Was Rotor DC also involved in the Brouckère Tower project?

AVC: Yes, most definitely. Rotor DC assessed the reuse potential of material present on site and orchestrated the dismantling, transport, and storage of the huge limestone blocks, which weighed nearly a ton, for the cladding of the entire base of the building.

A demolition company was also involved. It followed Rotor DC's recommendations for salvaging the materials, and consequently 70 per cent of this batch could be reused; we had estimated 50 per cent. The stone blocks will be used to clad the extension of the existing base (the existing part will be preserved) and also to pave the ground floor of the building.

Removal of a Belgian blue limestone block.

'How can individual building components be given a different function? Experiments on this are extremely difficult, yet it's also a very exciting area of work!'

PH: What form of contract do you have as consultants?

AVC: We generally have a contract for services and charge an hourly rate that is geared to the fees of specialist planners such as structural or technical engineers. For our consulting services, we are sometimes paid by the architects responsible for the project and sometimes directly by the client.

GB: When I look at your projects, it seems to me that you work mainly in the field of interior design and that with Rotor DC's assortment of materials you also concentrate mainly on fit-out materials. baubüro in situ, by contrast, actually manages to reuse structural and façade elements. Have I got that right? Why is this, and what's your attitude towards it?

MG: Yes, that's right. At Rotor DC, we indeed tend to focus on materials for interiors (although we certainly also have outdoor paving stones on offer). It's easier to start a business with such materials—this applies to the assessment of technical performance, the options for processing, the investments needed, and so on. We hope to be able to expand our palette of materials in the near future.

Our planning projects are generally restricted to the field of interior design. Again, it is clear that we are not registered architects. These projects do not always have the constraints that architects face, but they also provide a good environment in which to explore how reuse can change the role of designers. And in the process, our work routinely converges with the world of architecture.

GB: Do you have an example for that?

MG: A good example is the competition for the design of a temporary roof for the Christmas market on the central square in Antwerp. By chance, just as the competition had commenced, we got a call from a demolition contractor who was busy dismantling a large steel roof at Brussels-North station, which had been constructed as a space frame. He asked if we were interested in the components.

Our first concern was the issue of structural stability and safety. We asked a structural engineer firm to give their assessment, and they confirmed that the roof would certainly be stable for the duration of the Christmas market! Unfortunately, the project was not built, but it would actually not have been a problem to build such a roof.

 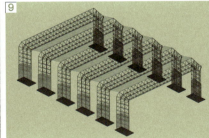

[Figs. 8, 9] Rotor's competition entry for the Christmas market in Antwerp: components of a scrapped space frame from Brussels-North station are reassembled in a different configuration to form the new roof. The Structural XPloration Lab at EPFL is one of a number of groups pursuing related topics.[6]

In connection with the support we provide to architects and building owners, we are also involved in 'real' architectural projects. For instance, we are involved in renovating the headquarters of Zinneke, a socio-artistic organization in Brussels. We're assisting the

'When I look at your projects, it seems to me that you work mainly in the field of interior design and that with Rotor DC's assortment of materials you also concentrate mainly on fit-out materials.'

'In connection with the support we provide to architects and building owners, we are also involved in 'real' architectural projects.'

6 ↖ p. 124
Circular load-bearing structures
Roof of Lausanne main railway station

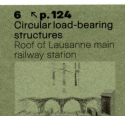

architects and the client in the reuse of building elements, which include second-hand windows for a rear façade. It's an interesting case study.

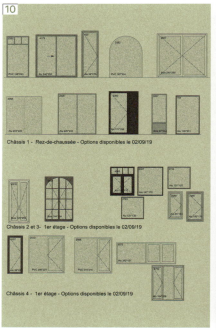

[Figs. 10, 11] Zinneke/Masui4ever project: a traditional house in the historical centre of Brussels is given a new façade of old windows. It is a long process that challenges everyone involved. A vague sketch of the façade must suffice for the building permit, while technical specifications tailored to the project serve as a guide in the search for suitable windows, the planning for which needs to remain highly adaptable—an experimental set-up reminiscent of the ELYS culture and business hub in Basel.[7]

In this case, we had to find the windows and assist the team in acquiring them. We also had to make sure the frames met the minimum requirements for energy efficiency, size, and availability. Our initial concern was that all these requirements would reduce the available options to zero. But in the end, there were then a number of possibilities on the market— enough to enable the architects to do some compositional studies!

Thus, as this example shows, reuse does not necessarily limit creativity. The opposite is actually the case. Among the available windows, one was arch-shaped. I'm pretty sure the architects would not have drawn such a shape for a new build. But since this window was on the list, it became interesting for them. They took a fancy to it and decided to integrate it into the façade … albeit upside down!

Opalis

GB: How did you find all those windows?

AVC: There are dealers who specialize in the dismantling, reconditioning, and storage of salvaged windows. Most of them also offer a guarantee on their products. They're real experts for this one type of building component. We recently even found a company in the Netherlands who only salvages skylights. They check whether they are still watertight and if the insulation is intact, and they assign a code to indicate the

7 ↖ p. 93
Where there's a will …
ELYS culture and business hub

'There are dealers who specialize in the removal, reconditioning, and storage of salvaged windows. … They're real experts for this one type of building component.'

GB: How exactly does Opalis work?

quality of each window. As far as I know, they discard one in five units because they don't meet the necessary quality standards. For Zinneke, the windows came from a dealer in a suburb of Antwerp, about 40 km from the site. That dealer, and many others who specialize in different building components, can be found on the Opalis website.

AVC: The website has detailed information about reusable building components and materials, about dealers and availability, and also has pictures of the companies' stock. Since 2012, more and more dealers from an increasing number of new regions have been added. Thanks to a European grant from the FCRBE project (within the Interreg NWE Programme), we are currently documenting the offerings in the Netherlands as well as in France, where we are working together with Bellastock and Les Aventuriers du Sixième Continent. With Salvo, we also have a project partner in the UK who has actually been maintaining a directory like this since 1992! On salvoweb.com you can find data for thousands of salvage dealers and antique shops. There are suppliers from all over the world, but the focus is on dealers in the UK.

One of the intentions behind such databases is to give reclamation and salvage dealers more visibility. The easier it is to contact dealers working in this sector, the more widespread we believe the use of such materials will become.

Opalis, an online directory that has hitherto been active in north-western Europe, brings architects and clients into contact with an impressive array of dealers of reusable building components. The aim is to help the market for reclaimed building components—which has thus far been fragmented and informal—to develop its full potential.

GB: I could imagine Opalis being useful in two ways: not only to promote the idea of reuse in general but also to foster the reuse of 'local' building elements and materials …

AVC: On the one hand, that's true, but the traders listed on Opalis (and their merchandise) are often more international than you might think and are also very diverse. One example is a demolition company that removes and stores a great many contemporary structural and decorative elements from the buildings. They can do that because, as a demolition company, they're on the premises anyway. A company like that works very locally and most of the materials are sold in small quantities to private people, although they do indeed also stock really large quantities.

New generalists, new specialists
ZHAW IKE / baubüro in situ

Rotor

[Figs. 13, 14] Two specialized dealers from the Netherlands: Vermeulen & Zonen and Regts Antieke Tegels.

But there are also other companies that mainly sell salvaged wood floors—from medium to high quality; their material comes from all over the world. These top companies even import reclaimed wooden elements from Southeast Asia. Or there's a company, for example, that sells traditional Dutch tiles. They are removed from buildings in the area, but then sold throughout the world to rich Americans, Russians, or Brazilians, because there's no market for them locally! Reuse is associated with certain ideals, but we have no wish to overly romanticize the topic and want to keep an eye on the commercial implications as much as possible.

GB: That doesn't sound all that optimistic!

AVC: We have seen too many people approach this issue with too much optimism; we simply want to be realistic. Our last exhibition in Brussels, titled *Life Under a Cherry Tree* (in November 2019), was about this very topic. We presented a collection of materials that, despite having some potential, are not currently reusable—such as everything with asbestos, or anything that does not meet the usual standards, or things that it's much cheaper to buy new. Our aim with the exhibition was to get people to give thought to the subject. After all, there are also systemic limitations to reuse. That must not be forgotten. It simply isn't enough for architects to be enthusiastic and project managers motivated; structural changes also need to take place.

The exhibition *Life Under a Cherry Tree* (2019) gathers building components and materials that stubbornly resist reuse—be it because they are difficult to salvage or because they are simply incompatible with today's needs.

In Brussels, we believe it's possible to go a step further when it comes to reuse and give a realistic assessment of the issue of sustainability (with all its problems). What we at Rotor absolutely do not want is a neoliberal appropriation of this issue, with people in Morocco cleaning wooden floorboards which are then sold on Amazon! Reuse should not be understood as 'the solution', but as a gentle form of progress and of thoughts about a possible new future.

PH: Considered from that perspective, it could actually become a big problem if, in 20 years' time, there is a requirement in Europe to use 20 per cent reclaimed material in every new building!

MG: That's exactly what we mean! There is a grim example from the United States that was reported in *The New York Times*. It concerns a company that imports salvaged tropical wood components from Southeast Asia. The journalist reported that the demand for such components was so high in the United States that it impacted the real estate market in the country of origin. There, as it turns out, old and valuable houses were actually being demolished to meet the demand. So even with reuse, which is in itself sensible, perverse situations like this can arise. As with everything else, here, too, a lack of clear rules can have destructive effects.

Reusers as generalists

GB: Your work is very diverse, and you have established, as we can confirm, a new player in the construction industry. Do you believe that you are thereby helping to define a new understanding of the role that architects play in Belgium and in Europe? How do you see yourselves?

MG: Yes, our spectrum of activities is very broad and also very multilayered and diverse. But there are also some limits. Because we do a great many things and deal with all sorts of different materials, we often lack the opportunity to delve deeper into the matter in question.

Nowadays, our feeling is that we are often intermediaries. We try to connect different people and different worlds with one another. That's a thoroughly satisfying job but also a very fragile position, because such an intermediary role is basically always only temporary. As soon as the connections have been made and the knowledge has been transferred, the intermediary is no longer needed. Personally, I take a relatively relaxed view. If we become superfluous because everyone is able to implement reuse strategies in their projects, that could be seen as a successful outcome of our efforts! But again, Rotor is so heterogeneous that we're all bound to give slightly different answers to this question.

GB: Where do you see yourselves in ten years? Was it the right decision to found Rotor DC? Is there more to come along those lines?

MG: There are currently two companies with two different objectives. Rotor's goal as a non-profit organization is to promote reuse generally, and this can be achieved by means of a wide variety of measures. Examples include courses for prospective architects on how to integrate reuse into the design process, or lecturing, or compiling and sharing information, or assisting architects, or carrying out

'What we at Rotor absolutely do not want is a neoliberal appropriation of this issue, with people in Morocco cleaning wooden floorboards which are then sold on Amazon!'

research projects ... This diversity opens up numerous opportunities for the future.

By contrast, Rotor DC is a business that actually dismantles building materials and reconditions them for reuse. Hopefully this service will still be needed in the future and we'll be able to continue doing it. The chances are good that our business model will continue to evolve.[8] Right now, a lot is still in flux, as can be seen from the current shift: away, that is, from a decidedly vertical way of working, where we do the dismantling work ourselves, to a more horizontal one, where we work with lots more traditional companies that can properly dismantle the materials. Speaking very generally, I think there's a need for what we're developing. How does one process material that's suitable for reuse and where does the necessary technical know-how come from, as well as the knowledge of the legal matters involved? That might be the greatest added value that Rotor DC has to offer. We hope that will continue.

New paths toward net zero? Potentials for climate protection

[1] Katrin Pfäffli, *Graue Energie und Treibhausgasemissionen von wiederverwendeten Bauteilen: Methodik und Berechnung in Varianten am Fallbeispiel Gebäude K118 in Winterthur*, ed. (ZHAW Institut Konstruktives Entwerfen / Stadt Zürich, Zurich, 2020).

Reusing components in order to reduce one's environmental footprint naturally makes a lot of sense. In her June 2020 study entitled *Graue Energie und Treibhausgasemissionen von wiederverwendeten Bauteilen*,[1] Katrin Pfäffli used the example of K.118 to examine and quantify this in detail for the first time. The findings from this investigation allow us to draw some initial conclusions about the potentials of reuse as a means to decarbonize our construction industry.[1] They also offer methodological tips on how it can establish itself in existing instruments for assessing energy efficiency in the future. The journey toward this goal was accompanied by a series of workshops involving Philipp Noger and Michael Pöll of the City of Zurich's Office for Sustainable Construction Kerstin Müller and Marc Angst of baubüro in situ, and Eva Stricker of the ZHAW Institute of Constructive Design (IKE). The following conversation took place on 11 May 2020 as part of these workshops.

In conversation:
ZHAW Institute of Constructive Design / baubüro in situ: Eva Stricker / Marc Angst, Kerstin Müller
ZHAW / preisig:pfäffli: Katrin Pfäffli
Office for Sustainable Construction, Zurich: Michael Pöll

1 ↗ p. 256
K.118 case study
Greenhouse gas emissions

New paths toward net zero?
ZHAW IKE / baubüro in situ   ZHAW / preisig:pfäffli   Office for Sustainable Construction, Zurich

Eva Stricker:
Katrin, you have calculated the energy balance of the K.118 project in comparison with a hypothetical building using new components. This revealed that said construction could be built with approximately 40 per cent of the embodied energy and greenhouse gas emissions of an identical, conventionally built house. What do these figures tell us?[2]

Katrin Pfäffli:
The energy savings achieved here are hugely significant. They are particularly high in terms of the greenhouse gas emissions. I cannot think of any other strategies that would be similarly effective—obviously with the sole exception of the continued use of the on-site structures. By way of comparison, a CO_2-optimized wooden construction reduces greenhouse gas emissions by a maximum of 15 per cent as opposed to a solid construction. Reuse is in a different league altogether, even if the data of your pilot construction cannot be directly transferred to other projects.

Kerstin Müller:
Was this surprising to you?

Michael Pöll:
Your construction appears to have broken some serious new ground—if I had had to submit an estimate, I don't know what I would have arrived at. And it is all the more valuable in that you have succeeded in turning your experiment into reality. The figures that are now available instil a sense of hope for the future. We have been optimizing buildings to help reduce greenhouse gas emissions for many years. Our highs, when there have been any, have come in the form of improvements within the single-digit percentage range. By comparison, the figures of your project are sensational—particularly in light of the fact that several new construction materials were used that had not yet been optimized in terms of their greenhouse gas emissions.

Marc Angst:
Wherever we were unable to work with either the existing material or used components, we tried to avoid burdening the CO_2 balance as much as we possibly could, even when using new parts. We use concrete as infrequently as possible, and only where it is absolutely essential for the structure or for the purposes of sound insulation and fire protection. We utilize natural *materiali poveri* wherever possible, such as straw for thermal insulation or clay as plasterwork. The savings made in the overall balance can be attributed to the entire catalogue of measures used, whereby the reused parts achieve the greatest effect.

2   ↗ p.262
K.118 case study
Greenhouse gas
emissions:
Overall balance

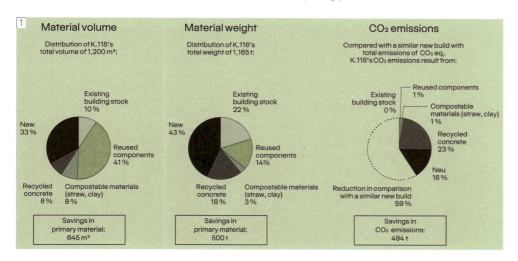

New hope for 'urban mining'

KM: We are just concerned about the fact that while we've made significant progress in reducing industrial energy and CO₂ consumption in building operations over the past decades, the efforts in the area of construction have been stagnating.

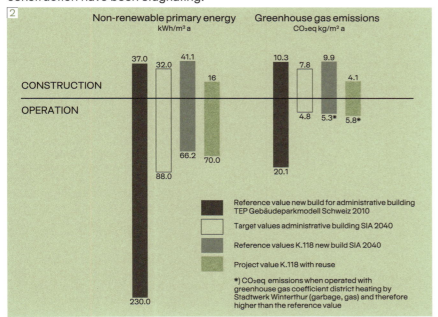

KP: Yes, with regard to the CO₂-neutral operation of buildings, there are certainly a number of viable solutions now. However, in terms of construction we are currently lagging quite a long way behind and simply have no idea how the building materials industry will implement the required savings at a technical level. Even CO₂-optimized cement only saves around 15 per cent to 20 per cent compared with fresh cement, which is a start, of course, but obviously still a long way from where we're trying to get to.

New paths toward net zero?
ZHAW IKE / baubüro in situ ZHAW / preisig:pfäffli Office for Sustainable Construction, Zurich

MP: And time is short ... For example, if we scale down Switzerland's greenhouse gas budget to the level of the City of Zurich, as the commissioning client, we will have exhausted our entire CO₂ quota by 2023—and that's just with the buildings that are currently planned. Until such time as we succeed in developing key processes to make the construction materials industry more CO₂-neutral—I'm thinking here, for example, of the production of rebar or cement—we need to find substitutes for critical materials and components, and for this we need strategies that are effective, pragmatic, and, most importantly, capable of being immediately implemented.

ES: This means that reuse could serve as a type of bridging technology, so to speak, until we succeed in developing CO₂-neutral production processes. What kind of role does 'classic' recycling play? Haven't the selective separation of construction waste and the utilization of new construction materials already been implemented to a significant extent in Switzerland?

KP: That's correct; a large proportion of construction waste is currently recycled over here. However, the recycling of construction material usually only saves a small amount of energy and greenhouse gas emissions at best. For example, the embodied energy and emissions from recycled concrete are on a par with those generated by conventional concrete. Of particular ecological interest here are the reduction of gravel usage and the conservation of landfill capacities.

MP: The list compiled by the Coordination Conference of Building and Property Bodies of Public Sector Developers (KBOB) illustrates the current state of construction material recycling. 'New' steel has practically ceased to exist in Switzerland. All the structural steel is made of material that is almost 100 per cent recycled and is also listed as such by the KBOB. In spite of this, however, the embodied energy and greenhouse gas emission values are still relatively high. The same is true for concrete, as you have already mentioned, Katrin. We will not make much progress in reducing CO₂ consumption just by recycling construction materials. In this regard, the hopes placed by the construction industry on the wonderful concept of 'urban mining' have so far not been fulfilled. The reuse of components now has real potential to breathe new life into this idea.

Accounting for reuse

ES: Katrin, you calculated these promising figures in detail during the evaluation of the K.118 project. Can you briefly explain how you went about this?

'Construction material recycling usually only saves a small amount of energy and greenhouse gas emissions at best.'

'For example, if we scale down Switzerland's greenhouse gas budget to the level of the City of Zurich ... we will have exhausted our entire CO₂ quota by 2023.'

KP: Basically, I referred to the new SIA 2032 data sheet that was published in August 2020 and now also takes existing buildings into consideration. In order to obtain a realistic picture, my first step was to determine the energy consumption and emissions generated by dismantling, transporting, and preparing (where necessary) the reused components and then reinstalling them. However, the original manufacture of the components was not factored into this—as stipulated by SIA 2032, e.g. for existing buildings undergoing conversions. To make a comparison with a hypothetical construction consisting of new parts, my second step was to discount all the elements that are also generally neglected when the accounting is done for a new construction in accordance with SIA 2032: the transportation from temporary storage facilities to the construction site and the outlay involved in installing the components there.

ES: Lining this up with the SIA 2032 life cycle model, you equated the dismantling, or 'harvesting', of the components with the supply of raw materials (R1 = A1), the refurbishment of these components with manufacturing (R3 = A3), and their reintegration with installation, and then, component for component, you factored in (or discounted) the energy consumption of these activities, including the required transportation, analogous to a conventional new build.[3]

KP: Correct. As a result, certain portions of the energy required for construction, which can account for up to 10 per cent of the overall balance, are not taken into consideration—this is a methodological simplification and imprecision that we must learn to live with in all accounting models. The consistent methodology will allow us to make a comparison between a construction using new parts and one built with reused parts.

Materials and construction methods in a new light

ES: Which components have benefited most significantly from reuse?

MA: The aluminium sheeting we use for the façades in the K.118 project is one such example: it is an extremely high-quality and long-lasting product which we would otherwise never have been able to afford—either economically or ecologically speaking. The same is also true for windows and doors; these are often high-tech products of superior design and craftsmanship that are almost impossible to recycle owing to their material composition.

MP: I generally get the best results when I substitute new components with high embodied energy values for used ones.

3 ↖ p. 10
Introduction

New paths toward net zero?
ZHAW IKE / baubüro in situ   ZHAW / preisig:pfäffli   Office for Sustainable Construction, Zurich

KP: I also find the experience with steelwork quite exciting, as it has the reputation, from a historical point of view, of being the 'naughty child' of embodied energy optimization. Steel is one of the costliest materials in terms of CO_2 emissions and embodied energy. But it has become apparent that it also provides huge benefits: the largely standardized components are low-wear and have good separability properties. As a result, steel components are tailor-made for reuse.

ES: What I also find interesting about the example of steelwork is that it can be reused for the supporting structure, too, which is responsible for a significant proportion of the embodied energy within a building. In practice, this is still quite rare. However, the example of the K.118 project shows that the reuse of components no longer has to be limited purely to cladding or interior design, it can also play an important role in developing the structure of a house from scratch—something that makes the topic of reuse an even more exciting subject in teaching architectural and constructive design.[4,5]

MA: However, it will still take a lot of constructive development work in this area, especially in the context of the reinforcements required for sound insulation and fire protection: in spite of all our sustainability efforts, concrete was still largely used for this purpose in our project. For example, our ceilings now consist of used steel trapezoidal sheets bonded with concrete, which limits their reversibility. In that area, we still have a long way to go before we reach the optimal solution. At the same time, we are experimenting with concrete encasement solutions where the steel beams and supports are already filled with concrete at the factory and are then bolted together on the construction site.[6] I think that is extremely exciting, because it means we are building composite parts that can still be joined in a way that allows them to be removed later. The next step could be to replace the concrete that is used for fire protection with clay. However, we don't yet have the documentation and tests to substantiate this.

Construction vs operation

ES: Are there also components—unlike with the steel structure—where reuse is not worth it from an environmental perspective, especially when taking into account the operating energy? For example, does it really make sense to build the thermal envelope with reused parts? Aren't new

---

4 ↖ p.95
Out of scarcity

5 ↖ p.111
Circular load-bearing structures

6 ↖ p.46
K.118 reportage
Constructing and coordinating [fig. 1]

'Steel is one of the costliest materials in terms of CO_2 emissions and embodied energy. But it has become apparent that it also provides huge benefits.'

7 ↗ p.195
Uncharted legal territory
Reuse under Swiss law

'An important basic principle comes into play with preserving in situ—the right of continuance … But as soon as [buildings] are demolished, the right of continuance no longer applies, nor is it passed on to components removed from the building.'

building components so superior in terms of their structural properties that the savings in terms of energy and greenhouse gas emissions ultimately offset any embodied energy and greenhouse gas emissions resulting from the building process?

KM: We were not allowed to consume more operating energy than a conventional new build. Even though we are building with reused components, legally speaking it is considered a new build, which has to comply with the applicable energy laws and requirements.[7] In the case of the K.118 project, this was the SIA Energy Efficiency Path[2], which actually went a long way beyond the minimum legal requirements. If we want to use older windows with poor insulating properties, then we have to offset that somehow—by compensating in the system verification process or by turning the openings into box-type windows.

ES: In the case of your project at the Lysbüchel site in Basel,[8] you even relied on used materials for the thermal insulation …

KM: That's true. We worked with pre-fabricated façade elements whose wood frames were filled with leftover insulation material. These were sections of new mineral-wool façade panels combined with clean dismantled materials.[9] To ensure that there would be no cavities, we then sealed them with granulate. That means we always used relatively new, high-quality materials. However, for the thermal insulation certificate, we still had to calculate it as a 'non-monitored' building material according to the SIA standard. That means the certificate is based on a worst-case scenario even though the real λ value of the insulation is probably much better. As a result, an additional 20 per cent of insulation material had to be used, above what was theoretically needed to achieve the required U-value. This means, in reality, that our reused façade insulation should perform much better than shown in the calculations for the energy audit.

MP: I tend to take a fairly relaxed view of this debate. Our operation is about 20 years ahead in terms of what we are thinking about, and we are just now beginning to catch up when it comes to the materials. When we're building, we need to strive for a net balance in which operation and construction are given equal consideration. This is a realization that must—and will—prevail.

---

2 The SIA Energy Efficiency Path (SIA 2040 information leaflet) is published by the Swiss architects and engineers' association as a guideline for the implementation of the 2000-Watt Society in buildings of the categories housing, offices, and schools. Aside from operational energy, it also factors in grey energy and site-specific mobility and uses both non-renewable primary energy and greenhouse gas emissions as assessment criteria.

8 ↖ p. 93
Where there's a will
ELYS culture and business hub

9 ↖ p. 87
Where there's a will
[fig. 23]

'When we're building, we need to strive for a net balance in which operation and construction are given equal consideration.'

Evaluation and approval

ES: If you look at the building permit process, it is usually necessary to have an SIA 380/1[3] energy certificate, which only takes the operating energy into account. That begs the question of how, as a building contractor or architect, I can argue the benefits of reusing materials?

KP: Yes, that is correct, most cantons only require a heating energy calculation for standard buildings. However, in the case of special building permits, you can see that things are changing. Here, a statement on the energy consumption during the construction phase is increasingly being requested for the development of a site (*Arealüberbauung*) and for the design plan (*Gestaltungsplan*). That may be based on the SIA Energy Efficiency Path, as in the case of K.118, or be in line with Minergie ECO[4]. I am sure that as soon as enough of a track record has been compiled and people notice that this does not make construction significantly more complicated and expensive, then this practice will also be adopted for standard buildings.

ES: But even if an embodied energy certificate is required, there is still no uniform methodology for how the reuse of components could be recorded. Katrin, you were explaining earlier that you retraced the energy and CO_2 consumption for each component of the K.118 project, including all the transportation and processing steps. That effort paid off for the evaluation of this pilot project. However, what kind of solution could we arrive at here that would be easy to manage in the regular approval process?

KP: I think it is obvious that it would have to be simplified. If only because it is impossible to know at the time the building permit is submitted—or even when an initial evaluation is done during the competition phase—where the components will come from.

MP: I have also been thinking about how we can illustrate that in the KBOB list. When, on the one hand, I see how little is spent in adapting and transporting the reused materials and, on the other, how much difference there is to a comparable new material, I tend to put a very low uniform value for reused components in the KBOB list. From an energy perspective, 'reused' is simply a new material category like wood or steel or aluminium—just with extremely low levels of energy and CO_2 consumption. For the evaluation, we need a strategy that is as pragmatic and simple as possible in order to help promote this truly promising approach.

KP: That is why I think it is very important that this data is used in the KBOB list and that anybody calculating life cycle assessments has access to them. That is

---

3 cf. Norm SIA 380/1 Heizwärmebedarf, 2016
4 Minergie-ECO is an established Swiss certification standard by the Minergie and ecobau associations. Minergie-ECO adds health and construction ecology concerns to the existing Minergie building standards. This includes topics such as 'sustainable building cioncepts', 'materialization and processes', as well as 'embodied energy', among others.

'From an energy perspective, 'reused' is simply a new material category like wood or steel ... just with extremely low levels of energy and CO_2 consumption.'

the basis for establishing a uniform assessment practice. As a second step, the methodology for the calculation must then also be codified in SIA 2032 itself. Unfortunately, these insights come after the recently concluded revision. In this regard, we have to make a lot of improvements, and, in addition to calculating the life cycle assessment, we also have to integrate reuse as a binding methodological foundation on which all labels and standards can be based—from the 2,000-Watt Site[5] to Minergie-ECO.

KP: That's right, but it shows that this issue is gaining traction. In the past, we have often seen Minergie taking up an issue and then gradually tightening the requirements—after a while, this then finds its way into the normal legislative process.

MP: In an older version, Minergie took the initiative and demanded a limit value for embodied energy. However, that was not very ambitious and I don't think I've ever seen a building that would have fallen short of this lax requirement.

ES: When I reuse a material, I do not just save the energy used for its production. There is also no waste disposal or, at least, it is delayed until the next cycle of use. Should that not be taken into account when assessing reused parts?

KP: I believe that the costs for the disposal of the components should remain where they originated, i.e. when they are used for the first time. That provides the most consistent incentive. Because, in spite of being reused, a component will not stay in the cycle forever. The only thing we can say with certainty when the component is first installed is that it has to be disposed of at some point—whether that's after one or multiple cycles of use.

MA: What opportunities do you see for providing incentives so that fewer buildings are demolished after 20 or 30 years?

ES: Yes, we have talked a lot about the approval of new buildings, but what about the approval for tearing them down? In some way, is reuse not a type of damage limitation for a problem that only arises if buildings that are intact are demolished much too soon? And, in order to be consistent, shouldn't there also be some sort of demolition energy certificate?[10]

KP: In theory, there is already a lever in the form of the embodied energy certificate. Only in rare cases will the demolition and a new building that replaces an old one be more efficient than preserving or converting an existing one. However, it is not the energy consumption or the CO_2 emissions that decide whether a building should be demolished or not. When competitions for new buildings are announced, it is often stated that, unfortunately, the previous building has to be torn down because it no longer meets energy standards. The real

---

5 The 2000-Watt-Site (*2000-Watt-Areal*) describes a sustainability certificate for urban planning endeavours that was developed by the Federal Office of Energy as part of the Energie-Schweiz programme.

10 ↗ p. 183
Values and processes
Reuse from a developer perspective

'What if I was unable to get permission to demolish unless I reused 100 per cent—or whatever the maximum achievable amount might be—of the building? This kind of thing is also possible for beef cattle, for instance: the cow is only slaughtered once 100 per cent of it is sold.'

New paths toward net zero?
ZHAW IKE / baubüro in situ   ZHAW / preisig:pfäffli   Office for Sustainable Construction, Zurich

reason, however, is nearly always financial. That means it is about utilization and returns and not a life cycle assessment. The new social relevance of the call for net zero and the consistency of people's compliance with its demands will certainly have an impact here.

CO₂: Costs vs value

ES: And that brings us back to the problem that the value of material is simply no longer relevant in our affluent society. Kerstin, you did some experiments with issuing CO₂ certificates for the components you reused at the Lagerplatz site. Wouldn't that be a way to counter this?

KM: Yes, we talked to two agencies specializing in CO₂ certificates. In principle, people are interested. However, we would have to prove that there was no way to save even more CO₂ with another type of construction, and that is impossible. This and other uncertainties have caused this initiative to sputter a bit. In order to blaze a trail that others can follow, this would take a lot of pioneering work, and, unfortunately, we just don't have the capacities for that right now.

ES: Wouldn't the results of our evaluation help in that regard?

MP: If, in addition to the value for reused materials, the value for new ones in terms of greenhouse gas equivalents were to be shown in the KBOB list, then that should also help convince the certification agencies.

KP: All this stands and falls with the sad reality that CO₂ certificates are not worth enough to make a significant difference financially. We should really aim to ensure that new materials reflect the full costs and that all external costs are internalized—not just in the greenhouse gas balance but also in Swiss francs. For example, the disposal would have to be paid in full during production. That would result in more realistic material costs. When you work with reused components, you realize that you need to reformulate design and planning processes, and by the same token, you need to reconsider the economic processes involved in construction.

MA: I am wondering what price for CO₂ would be appropriate. A ton currently costs CHF 25–30 on the EU market, and that is certainly too low.

MP: In the case of the Kunsthaus Zürich, we did a competition where the CO₂ was internalized in the material supply, and that was pointless. Relative to the contract value, this CO₂ price had no impact.

'We should really aim to ensure that materials which are as good as new reflect the full costs and that all external costs are internalized.'

MA: But even when we use CHF 108 per ton, which is the fixed price for compensation in Switzerland, our building at the Lagerplatz site only amounts to a total of CHF 53,000. That constitutes only a bit more than 1 per cent of the total construction budget.

KP: Yes, if we consider the impact of climate change and factor that into the CO_2 price, then we would probably have to operate with an entirely different set of numbers.

MP: In terms of new construction, we usually assume between CHF 200 and 300 for each ton of CO_2 that was saved, and we consider that 'economical' and socially acceptable.

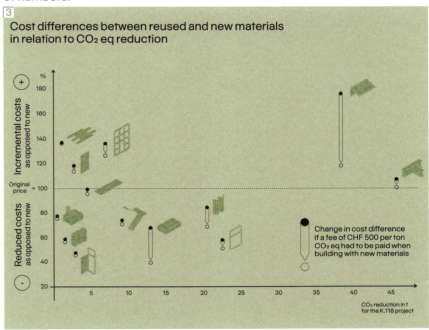

3 Cost differences between reused and new materials in relation to CO_2 eq reduction

Rethinking standards, creating space

MA: There also need to be some demand-side shifts. Given the climate crisis, we have to contemplate what is worth more: a stylish floor plan or the energy and the CO_2 invested in a house with a slightly outdated arrangement of rooms? In my opinion, the same applies to our perception of perfection. Are signs of wear on functional building components a flaw or a patina? In far too many cases, fully functional existing materials are discarded as waste because of a few superficial imperfections. I think this is an area where we have to fundamentally rethink our requirements.[11]

KP: I agree, that is a discussion we need to have. It makes sense to value existing buildings and to continue to use them for as long as possible—and not just because of the embodied energy. We often see that older buildings, which make do with a

'We have to contemplate what is worth more: a stylish floor plan or the energy and the CO_2 invested in a house with a slightly outdated arrangement of rooms?'

[11] ↗ **p.266**
Eight theses

Challenging the demands

ES: When it comes to reusing individual components, I think the question of surface perfection seems to be more of a design-related or financial issue. In most cases, it is possible to give used components a 'facelift', so that signs of use disappear. In the case of the K.118 project, you largely avoided doing that because the narrative of the history of these parts is an element of the design and because it allowed you to stay within the budget. Would it really have strained the life cycle assessment and the CO_2 footprint if you had done things differently in that regard?

KM: I think it is very important to emphasize that there is definitely room for different architectural styles when reusing materials. They can be visible or invisible. Everybody can deal with that as they see fit.

ES: And that is precisely what makes this topic so exciting in teaching architectural design. There are many strategies for sustainable building. Most of them are burdened with many regulations and restrictions. In the case of reuse, however, there is a new kind of architectural scope.[12]

ES: Are you considering building with components in the City of Zurich?

minimum of technology, are far better in terms of maintenance and adaptability than more recent 'machines' packed to the gills with technology.

KP: Obviously the costs of treating the components are a factor. However, it is a long way before this would negate the benefit of the savings in the construction. Even if you had spent three times as much effort on the preparation of components for K.118, you would still be in an excellent position, environmentally speaking.

KP: When future laws feature a threshold for embodied energy and greenhouse gases, then reuse will turn into a lever with which certain architectural visions can still be implemented.

MP: I think it is very important to use exemplary buildings to demonstrate this to the public.

MP: Yes, we are planning to announce an architecture competition on that basis for a specific construction project. Right now, we are still trying to overcome some legal hurdles with regard to the submissions, but we are definitely still on track. When it comes to CO_2 reduction, we won't get much further going down the beaten path. We need innovative solutions—the sooner the better. Time is running out and we simply have to make progress!

Values and processes: Reuse from a developer perspective

The reuse of building components upends established processes in planning and construction. Embracing it anyway requires courage and initiative from all concerned. Developers, in particular, will need to adopt reuse if industry practices are to change in such a way that it doesn't remain the exception. This is something Guido Brandi, Michael Eidenbenz, and Andreas Sonderegger of ZHAW's Institute for Constructive Design (IKE) wanted to explore in their discussion of 18 June 2020. First, Oliver Seidel and Marc Angst, project managers at baubüro in situ, presented their K.118 project in Winterthur and their conversion project in Basel's Lysbüchel site. These case studies then formed the basis of a discussion with figures from the construction and real estate sectors about their experiences with and expectations for reuse. The following people took part: Tina Puffert from the Stiftung Abendrot pension fund, which commissioned the K.118 project and supported the academic evaluation thereof that underpins this book; Barbara Rentsch, head of municipal portfolio management for the city of Basel and thus the public sector client for the Lysbüchel conversion project; Barbara Zeleny, lead senior project manager at SBB Immobilien, the real estate arm of Swiss rail operator SBB, who has been exploring the potential for reuse and supported ZHAW's 2019 autumn semester master's studio 'On-Site Component Reuse';[1] Cyrille Veron from general contractors and property developers Losinger Marazzi AG, who, as head of acquisition, renovation, and conversion for German-speaking Switzerland and in his work at Madaster Switzerland, is committed to promoting circularity in the construction and real estate sector; Nathanea Elte, board member at the housing cooperative Mehr als Wohnen and president of the non-profit housing cooperative Allgemeine Baugenossenschaft Zürich (ABZ), which has more than 5,000 apartments in the Zurich metropolitan area; and finally Christian Kohler from the Alternative Bank Schweiz (ABS), a specialist in real estate finance.

In conversation:
ZHAW Institute of Constructive Design: Guido Brandi, Michael Eidenbenz, Andreas Sonderegger
From the construction and real estate sectors: Nathanea Elte, Christian Kohler, Tina Puffert, Barbara Rentsch, Cyrille Veron, Barbara Zeleny

1 ↗ p.323
ZHAW IKE: Teaching
[fig. 2]

Values and visions

Michael Eidenbenz:
First I'd like to ask you to consult your collective crystal ball: how would you assess the future potential for building component reuse? How significant a role might it play?

Barbara Zeleny:
I'm really fascinated by the idea that, with its 3,600 properties, SBB could create 2,400 new buildings from its own resources if we were just able to reuse 70 per cent of our existing buildings' materials and components. We could regenerate from within, as it were!

ME: Is that a realistic scenario?

BZ: In my eyes, it's certainly conceivable that we could head in that direction—despite the numerous practical challenges it would of course bring. We supported ZHAW's investigation of our Neugasse site in Zurich for the very reason that we wanted to study, using a real-world example, how such existing buildings are put together, just what components they contain, how we can quantify them, and how we can set in motion the process of dismantling obsolete buildings and incorporating the components into new designs. Prefabricated industrial and functional buildings are already designed to be disassembled and reassembled elsewhere, but an important part of our current construction and development activity is the conversion of obsolete infrastructure sites for new usages. Naturally, the question of how we can adapt structures—either partially or in their entirety—to new functions is of great interest to us here. Understanding just what resources they contain and how we can use them is a first step in that journey.

ME: Cyrille Veron, you represent a large general contractor. If component reuse took hold in a big way, would that mean major changes for your firm? Do you think it's conceivable that reuse could become established to the extent that Barbara Zeleny just outlined?

Cyrille Veron:
To me, it seems not just conceivable but also desirable. Alongside my work at Losinger Marazzi AG, I also serve on the board of Madaster Switzerland, an organization that aims to address the very questions that Barbara Zeleny just identified as our first challenge. How can we even begin to document the resources contained in such buildings? How can we collect and share the information we need to allow tomorrow's demolished structures to serve as material banks? These questions require a whole new way of thinking, particularly among firms like ours. In my view, clients are generally open to the idea of reuse. The construction industry needs to step up and develop the requisite practical solutions. Often, we as developers or general contractors are not even able to give reliable information about whether a reuse scheme is even feasible. This is partly to do with the building norm constraints within which we have to operate, but often uncertainties around liability are also an obstacle.[2]

ME: There is already a willingness to trial reuse in pilot projects: in conjunction with baubüro in situ, Stiftung Abendrot and Basel's municipal property department are currently realizing two projects in which reclaimed components play a key role: the K.118 project in Winterthur and the ELYS[3] culture and business

2 ↗ p.244
K.118 case study
Building organization:
A legal vademecum

3 ↖ p.93
Where there's a will ...
ELYS culture and
business hub

'I'm really fascinated by the idea that, with its 3,600 properties, SBB could create 2,400 new buildings from its own resources .... We could regenerate from within, as it were!'

hub in Basel's Lysbüchel site. I'd be interested to know whether the durability of previously used components was factored into any risk analysis. Does this impact on assessments of future operating costs? Do you plan for different refurbishment cycles because you assume components will have shorter lifespans?

Tina Puffert:
We expect the building components we reuse to have a lifespan no shorter than that of equivalent new products. As a pension fund, Stiftung Abendrot doesn't just consider the return on its investments, we are also always looking for added value in terms of social and environmental sustainability. The reuse of building components encapsulates this principle on a variety of levels. It's by no means a new idea either. Throughout history, serviceable parts have been reused, it's only in recent times that this has got rather lost. We've already incorporated the principle of reuse in numerous projects. A pilot project such as K.118 serves as a test bed that can help us assess which components can be reused most viably— both environmentally and economically. That involves a certain degree of risk, but it also allows us to learn a great deal for future projects.

CV: When assessing the value and longevity of reclaimed components, their physical properties naturally play a key role. Often older components have a quality of material and craftsmanship that just wouldn't be affordable today. That was our motivation for reusing components in the renovation of AXA's Winterthur offices we carried out with MOKA Architekten;[4] it would have been simply criminal to dispose of the existing solid-wood fixtures and replace them with new and less durable wood-veneered board.

Barbara Rentsch:
Obviously, with projects such as the one we are currently realizing in the Lysbüchel site, you have to assess in advance the potential risks that reuse might pose. To my mind, though, the danger is not so much that reclaimed components will be of inferior quality or longevity. Statutory regulations and norms have to be met either way, so the scope for divergence in quality is relatively low. We also share the belief that pilot projects are largely about what insights we can gain. There is always some cost involved in trying out new things. We work out our return on investment across the entire property portfolio, and that affords us a degree of freedom in individual pilot projects.

BZ: Often the reason we demolish a building and replace it with a new one is not necessarily because it has come to the end of its service life. Mostly, it's driven by write-down periods: once a building is written off, it no longer has any value in the accounts. Only when we understand that written-off materials still have value can we start to think differently about them. We need to stop calculating lifespans across entire buildings; each component has its own individual lifespan and, via basic refurbishment processes, many elements of a building can be given a new life that won't necessarily be any shorter than their first one. We are only just beginning to take this on board, but the results of our first efforts are very promising: we are currently running a pilot project, for instance,

4 ↖ p.90
Where there's a will …
Renovation and refurbishment,
Römerstrasse office building

'Once a building is written off, it no longer has any value in the accounts. Only when we understand that written-off materials still have value can we start to think differently about them.'

in which old, decommissioned overhead line masts are not disposed of but refurbished and then reused. This results in a 23 per cent reduction in costs per mast—given Switzerland's 30,000 overhead line masts, that's a significant potential saving.

ME: That's an important message. The way we account for or determine the asset value of real estate definitely plays a key role here. Obviously, it makes a big difference whether the value of a property is determined via predicted revenue and expenditure (DCF method) or via write-downs of the asset's value. Doubtless the practices of, say, housing cooperatives and institutional investors differ greatly here. But the added or decreased value of reclaimed components is not just determined on the basis of accounting procedures. Potential users would surely also have their own view—and this would influence potential revenues for a property. A question, in particular, for the housing professionals among us: how would you assess the acceptance of component reuse among your tenants? Do you expect it to impact rentability and thus the risk of vacancy?

Nathanea Elte:
I'd say it depends very much on how you communicate it and, of course, on the target group. If you have an overall concept that is environmentally forward-thinking, in everything from operational energy to transport to permeable surfacing and biodiversity in landscape design, then reused building components would be a very good fit. I can easily imagine this attracting tenants who also appreciate the aesthetics of that way of building. Smaller-scale lighthouse projects could thus work really well and also act as multipliers, helping to spread the underlying ideas. At ABZ, however, we also occasionally build larger housing estates—200 to 300 units— for people who are genuinely reliant on the availability of affordable housing and don't have any particular idealistic agenda. I'm not sure that they would be as accepting of visible signs of use in a new apartment.

TP: Given the relatively low levels of vacancy in Switzerland, I think it's definitely possible for developers to set their own standards for sustainability. Location, layout, and rent are the primary criteria for tenants' decisions. They generally don't have that wide a choice and are often not able to be particularly choosy when it comes to fit-out and materials. If we as developers recognize that reusing building components has a significant potential benefit for the environment,[5,6] then I think we have an opportunity, a duty even, to also put that into practice—even if the results may not initially conform to the aesthetic expectations of users. After all, such expectations are to a large extent informed by what they are accustomed to and are thus also shaped by what we build.

ME: Is it necessary for such reuse to be visible?

TP: I'm convinced that visible traces of reuse needn't necessarily have negative connotations. Reused components might have a story a tell that could be marketed in a positive way. I'm confident that this way of building is very appropriate for our times.

NE: My experiences have been a little different. In our Mehr als Wohnen project, we've got 13 very different buildings. Two are timber-built, which, from an

[5] p. 256 K.118 case study Greenhouse gas emissions

[6] p. 165 New paths toward net zero? Potentials for climate protection

'If we as developers recognize that reusing building components has a significant potential benefit for the environment, then I think we have an opportunity, a duty even, to also put that into practice.'

environmental point of view, should have positive connotations. In one of them, the timber structure is visible inside; in the other one, it isn't. In the one where you can see the wood, we've witnessed a significantly higher churn of tenants and more requests to move to a different building, though the lack of private outdoor spaces and some initial problems with the acoustics are doubtless also factors. On the other hand, it also has its fans, but people do very specifically mention these particular issues.

BR: Reclaimed items sourced from salvage or heritage experts have long featured in the renovation of listed buildings, be it a historic staircase, an especially finely crafted kitchen, or really high-quality parquet or stone flooring. With their particular patina and history, there's huge potential for such things to be used in the rental sector. With larger-scale residential developments, the real obstacle, to my mind, is not so much tenants' acceptance as economic viability: after all, we have a political obligation to build affordable homes, and this becomes very difficult if every building component is a bespoke solution and you can't guarantee efficient workflows that will be completed on schedule.

Funding reuse

ME: I'd be interested to hear the Alternative Bank's perspective on this: Christian Kohler, as a financial services provider, how do you assess the risks around vacancy and structure when approving mortgage lending? Has the Alternative Bank already thought about whether and how the risks of building with reused components differ from conventional construction?

Christian Kohler: Essentially, we view building component reuse as a good thing that is worth supporting. Alternative Bank Schweiz is already funding various developments on different scales in which reused building materials play a role. If the reused material is cheaper than new and this reduces construction costs, then obviously it becomes economically interesting. Such cost benefits should then also translate into lower rent. We don't therefore see a risk of greater vacancy rates, this is much more likely to be caused by location. Essentially, we make decisions to provide funding on a case-by-case basis. From our point of view, it doesn't make any difference from an aesthetic quality perspective if reclaimed material is used. But, as I said earlier, it should be cheaper than new material. Our preference is to fund component reuse in new-build projects. If necessary, we can adjust the value via the standard, especially in the fit-out. We always make sure a building's age-related depreciation is set against an appropriate amortization of the property.

ME: Do you as a lender also offer specific incentives for the reuse of building components?

CK: No, we haven't got to that stage yet. At the moment, we don't have a product that provides targeted incentives for reuse, but we're certainly open to the idea. We regularly review and refine our lending instruments, and we're very keen to see what we can do in this area in future, too.

CV: Mr. Kohler, you said that if we develop projects using reclaimed material, it should be cheaper than it would be with new material. Have I got that right?

CK: You can't really judge it across the board like that. It's just that we've noticed that if a customer can choose between a new building component and a reused one, then, in the end, price is usually the deciding factor.

CV: What if your loan assessment criteria included not just financial aspects but CO_2 footprint as well? If a better CO_2 footprint got you more favourable lending terms, that would be a powerful incentive for sustainable construction.

TP: When providing funding, it's not just where the money comes from that matters, but also when it comes: if you're talking about structurally important building components or façade elements, there is a strong probability that the original design will be significantly influenced by what components are available. That means components and design have to be harmonized even before the planning application stage, and investment in those components made.[7] Anyone relying on third-party investment will struggle to secure funds for that these days.

Economics and organization

ME: That's an interesting debate, and one that leads us on to our next subject: construction costs. Here, the question of what kind of costs are considered is particularly relevant. If carbon consumption is factored in, that obviously changes how the economic viability of reuse is viewed. An advance disposal levy, such as we've already seen for electrical appliances, could of course offer a huge incentive here. Conversely, it would significantly increase construction costs for new builds. Cyrille Veron, how would you view a disposal levy that translated a component's embodied carbon into a monetary cost?

CV: That would certainly be one way of providing incentives. There has definitely not yet been enough focus on the issue of CO_2. Without a subsidy or advance levy, we will struggle to ensure this issue is given the proper weight.

BR: It's also true, though, that the K.118 project is an ideal case in which perfectly suited steel girders etc. happened to be available at just the right time. For me, it's a great example of what can be done and I admire the dedication behind it, though I also wonder whether such an exceptional case can really be a blueprint for a universally applicable, low-carbon way of building. The biggest CO_2 savings are still achieved not by deconstructing but by repurposing a building.

ME: You're right, of course; we should obviously aim to preserve buildings for as long as possible. But if they have to be demolished, then reusing the components is surely the most sustainable solution.

TP: In ten years' time, it will hopefully be a matter of course that we have to take responsibility for the resources contained in our buildings, that we have to pay for carbon according to consumption. Earlier,

[7] ↗ p.254
K.118 case study
Costs: Construction
costs and financing

'Components and design have to be harmonized even before the planning application stage, and investment ... made. Anyone relying on third-party investment will struggle to secure funds for that these days.'

Barbara Zeleny mentioned how the value of materials should be determined not by write-down periods but by their actual lifespans. I would add another aspect here: the carbon needed to manufacture the material should be given a price that I have to pay if I dispose of the component before the end of its lifespan. If reclaimed components had a value, then a market for them would develop.

BZ: A similar thought occurred to me: what if I was unable to get permission to demolish unless I reused 100 per cent—or whatever the maximum achievable amount might be—of the building?[8] This kind of thing is also possible for beef cattle, for instance: the cow is only slaughtered once 100 per cent of it is sold.

NE: Obviously my ears immediately prick up at such a proposal. In the city of Zurich, housing cooperatives are currently the main drivers of densification, the ones chiefly responsible for providing more housing for ever increasing numbers of people. And to be honest, we do struggle with the protracted and complicated nature of the processes we have to go through in order to redevelop an estate. For us, it's a balancing act: we also need to ensure we can deliver the affordable housing we urgently require. A levy of the kind Barbara Zeleny describes would genuinely be a massive obstacle for us. I worry that we would then simply not be able to meet our obligation to build affordable housing.

Logistics and liability

ME: If we could look again at the process from the other angle, i.e. not in terms of demolition but in terms of seeking and finding components, I can see two related strategies: we can either hunt around for used components on demolition sites or resort to new products that, for whatever reason, are left over— be they returns or surplus goods. The windows at the ELYS[9] culture and business hub on the Lysbüchel site are an example of the latter strategy—did you make a conscious choice to opt for new windows, Ms. Rentsch?

BR: Actually, the aim with this project was to draw resources for the building from the material available on-site wherever possible. Large parts of the existing concrete structure were retained, while dismantled sections of the site served as a reservoir for additional building components. However, windows weren't available in sufficient quality and quantity, so baubüro in situ hit upon the idea of asking window manufacturers in the surrounding area if they had any surplus stock. This proved surprisingly successful: within a short space of time, 200 good-as-new windows had been found. And to be honest, I'm glad we've now got new windows whose physical performance data is known. I don't know how we'd have fared in terms of energy efficiency rating otherwise.

ME: Can the canton just buy material? Normally in the public sector, you have to put these things out to tender.

BR: That's true, but it's also possible for us to buy materials on our own account and put their processing out to tender. Of course, you then have to bear the

---

8 ↗ p. 192
Uncharted legal territory
Reuse under Swiss law
'In accordance with the precautionary principle, ... the increased recycling of components from the waste cycle [could be promoted]—for example, through an obligation to prove that a component may only be disposed of if reuse is impossible, or only possible at unreasonable cost.'

9 ↖ p. 93
Where there's a will ...
ELYS culture and business hub

Values and processes
ZHAW IKE

From the construction and real estate sectors

risk for any flaws in the material yourself. This is something we resolved via a reserve fund, a budget item in the tender that's earmarked for any repairs.[10]

ME: That brings us to the question of who should take on the role of reuse specialist in tomorrow's construction processes. Is it a role best assigned to architects, as it has been with baubüro in situ? Should it instead be performed by dedicated specialists? Or should developers perhaps do it themselves, given that they know their existing buildings better than anyone and are thus able to consider where those buildings' components could be reused, even before they're dismantled?[11]

BR: In my view, it needs to be part of the sustainability strategy of any larger property owner. But planners with relevant expertise also have an important role to play here. In practice, such tasks will probably ultimately be shared out between clients and planners.

ME: Would it not also be a viable business model for general contractors to, say, store any surplus material produced and retain it for use in future projects?

CV: We have at least already begun reusing our temporary site structures, transferring them from one site to the next. That's a first step, but there's a long way to go before this way of working really takes hold. We could, for instance, start by no longer choosing products specific to each project; that way, we'd have more generic leftover components that could later be reused. To facilitate reuse projects, however, you don't just need components, you also need skilled planners. Most planners simply find lots of reasons as to why something cannot be done. There are only a few who are prepared to embrace this issue and to seriously try it out.

ME: It would surely help if there were good networks among those who do have that willingness. That would enable a market for specialist reuse-oriented planning services to develop.

TP: It's at least as important to have networks of suppliers and companies so that a client or planner can get hold of suitable building components.[12] I'm not usually a great fan of state intervention but, in this case, I do think there needs to be measures to kickstart their development. In addition, we need CO_2 pricing to prevent serviceable material from simply being thrown away. That's the only way to ensure a market for building components can develop.

BZ: I'm intrigued by the thought of what would happen if, in future, a given resource was simply no longer available new. Let's say that no more trees can be felled in Switzerland over the next 30 years. Suddenly, no one would even dream of throwing away used timber. At a stroke, all the material that, for convenience, currently just gets chucked in the ground would instead come onto the market.

Existing buildings—preservation and documentation

Guido Brandi:
A large-scale marketplace for reclaimed components will only function, though, if we can find a consistent way of capturing and making available the data required for planning. That's why using a standardized component catalogue was a key theme of our courses. As a first step, we thus worked with SBB's property arm,

---

10 ↗ p. 238
K.118 case study
Construction organization

11 ↗ p. 246
K.118 case study
Construction organization:
Circular models

'Of course, you then have to bear the risk for any flaws in the material yourself. This is something we resolved via a reserve fund, a budget item in the tender that's ring-fenced for any repairs.'

12 ↖ p. 161
New generalists, new specialists
Rotor and the practice of reuse in Belgium [fig. 12]

on whose Neugasse site we based our semester project, to try and document the components contained in the existing buildings …

BZ: One time, the students went hunting around for components and then measured their 'spoils' as best they could. At the same time, we did a walk-through of all the sheds with BIM Facility and measured the components via point clouds to see just how quickly we could get an idea of the resources contained in our 3,600 properties, only a handful of which had already been documented in BIM models. Such 3D models can be created relatively quickly using laser scans, but then the real detective work begins: what material is this made of? How do I find out what I can use this component for? What is its performance, its remaining lifespan? And what specifications do I need to record to be able to subsequently take my component catalogue to an architect or contractor, who can then use it to plan or construct a new building?

[Figs. 1, 2] How can components that are still in place be documented to facilitate future reuse? A laser scan of the train sheds at the Neugasse site resulted in a 3D point cloud model that could subsequently be translated into a precise line drawing using CAD software.

GB: At ZHAW, we were, of course, primarily focused on the didactic aspect. How can finds be used to develop new architectural solutions?[13] And what questions should you ask about the components you find? You've found a steel truss frame—but do its dimensions and the quality of its material match the requirements of your design?

BZ: That's exactly where testing engineers come in; they can take my 3D model and go to the existing building to assess the capability of the material. After all, some of our buildings are, of course, over 100 years old—that means you don't have precise details about

13   p. 197
From part to whole and back again
Teaching reuse in architecture

'Such 3D models can be created relatively quickly using laser scans, but then the real detective work begins: What material is this made of? How do I find out what I can use this component for?'

GB: But if we wait for 30 to 50 years until we can exploit today's BIM-planned buildings for reuse, it'll be too late. That's why documenting and cataloguing the existing fabric is so important.

the materials. That's not a problem with new buildings: in today's BIM world, you can get such information straight from the models.

Housing—a particular challenge

NE: We've just heard lots of intriguing examples, but these have all been either industrial buildings or non-standard building types, where it's sometimes possible for the building to follow the requirements of the material. But how would you persuade developers like us to engage with such processes? Our core business is housing; in a nutshell: a 4½-room apartment, for instance, has to be no more than 98 m² and the more identical apartments we can produce, the more affordable these will be—that goes for running costs, too. I do wonder how we can manage to engage with such processes and still meet our obligation to build as much good and affordable housing as possible as quickly as possible.

BZ: One thing that occurs to me here: we both have to tackle the issue of replacement new builds. In your case, they are for legacy housing estates; in ours, for station or service buildings with 100 years of history. These have their own distinctive architecture and are mostly of solid construction. Replacing them would inevitably mean being unable to reuse probably 90 per cent of the materials. Perhaps we need to ask ourselves more often if it's possible to retain and augment the existing buildings instead.

NE: In the housing sector, the problem is exacerbated by the real difficulties we face around space and costs …

BZ: Perhaps space isn't the main paradigm for what we need to achieve right now. It's always a question of prioritization, of which objectives we give what weight.

NE: Which brings us back to the question of balancing competing interests. Here, I really think that only via economical space utilization and occupancy policies can we succeed in offering great new homes to as many people as possible.

BR: Densification is, of course, a key issue. And there are genuinely estates that take up a great deal of space but are almost impossible to densify. Often heritage conservation is another important factor.

NE: At the moment, we've got a project in which we're able to almost quadruple the utilization rate via a replacement new build. To be honest, I just can't imagine how this could be achieved without replacement and don't know of any good, realistic examples. I would genuinely be very interested in concepts for incorporating reuse into optimized, standardized

'But if we wait for 30 to 50 years until we can exploit today's BIM-planned buildings for reuse, it'll be too late.'

Andreas Sonderegger:
At ZHAW, we explored this very issue in our 'Shaping Housing Estate Biographies' project: as part of a master's studio, we and our students analysed three residential estates in Winterthur and Zurich, seeking to find strategies for their ongoing densification that wouldn't require total replacement.[14] The results were really inspiring. They showed that it is in fact possible to achieve a significant level of densification without starting again from scratch.

AS: Agreed! Even within associations of architects and engineers, there have been debates about whether our pursuit of norms has taken us down a blind alley in recent years. The SIA lighting norm is a case in point.

AS: Often the building materials industry is very well represented on standards committees. To stretch

14 ↗ p. 207
From part to whole and back again
Teaching reuse in architecture

'... in the 2019 spring semester, we used three housing estates in the canton of Zurich to explore how we might meet pressures to redevelop such buildings, without simply replacing them with new builds.'

housing. It would be great if the university's research in this area could progress to the extent that it takes away the uncertainty for developers. That's why I think it's important that major developers such as the city of Basel or SBB are getting involved; we too can learn from their early experiments.

NE: For our inventoried Kanzlei estate, we spent years studying every conceivable variant of preservation and partial preservation, only to ultimately end up demolishing it—which was incidentally also the recommendation of external experts and heritage conservation officials. There was just no other way to achieve a meaningful redevelopment.

BR: Reuse and regeneration are appealing and convincing ideas, but in reality, there are also snags. At our Rheinacker site, we're currently adding two new storeys to an existing three-storey building. Getting permission was a long process, and it's not an easy situation for those who have to carry on living there during the work.

CV: When it comes to circularity in the housing sector, I think we need to look first and foremost to the future. We need concepts that allow residential buildings to be easily dismantled and reused. Here, working with optimized standardization can actually be a boon.

BR: I agree that building systems offer a lot of potential in this context. It's surely no coincidence that the Netherlands, where system-based construction is much more widely used, is way ahead of us in terms of building for circularity.

TP: To be honest, though, I wonder whether we don't need to question the standards that put so many obstacles in our way. We ask an awful lot of our buildings these days. That means regulations on noise control, fire safety, accessibility, etc., the standards of comfort and convenience we now apply, and much more besides. I think it's time we started to concentrate on what matters most. The costs—in particular, the environmental costs—of such luxury are now just much too high.

NE: I'd throw in noise control here too …

TP: It's also worth asking how these norms were drawn up, by whom, and in pursuit of what ends.

'We ask an awful lot of our buildings these days. … The costs—in particular, the environmental costs—of such luxury are now just much too high.'

Values and processes
ZHAW IKE

From the construction and real estate sectors

a point, you could even say that the obstacles we have to overcome in order to build with reclaimed components were thought up by those who want to sell us newly manufactured products instead. It's environmental and economic madness, what we allow our construction industry to get away with, and this urgently needs reassessing and rectifying. It's up to us to force politicians to change tack!

Uncharted legal territory: Reuse under Swiss law

Within the Circular Construction project, an interdisciplinary working group has devoted itself to the legal aspects of reuse. Taking the K.118 case study as their starting point, Andreas Abegg and Meinrad Huser from the ZHAW School of Management and Law, attorney Annatina Menn, an expert on matters of private law, and Marc Angst and Eva Stricker compiled the basic principles, identified legal particularities, and formulated questions for the future legal handling of reuse in construction. The results of this collaboration are documented in the publication *Die Wiederverwendung von Bauteilen: Ein Überblick aus rechtlicher Perspektive (The Reuse of Building Components: An Overview from a Legal Perspective)*[1] and will be examined in greater depth in the context of an Innosuisse (Swiss Innovation Agency) project. One aspect of the Circular Construction project was to summarize the most important findings on contractual and liability issues[1] and examine fundamental questions from the perspective of public law. The following discussion retraces conversations which took place in several workshops between spring 2019 and summer 2020. Even though these statements refer to a Swiss case study, in particular, and therefore can only reflect the specific legal situation in Switzerland, the greater issues addressed here can also be seen as being of relevancy in an international context.

[1] Andreas Abegg and Oliver Streiff (eds.), *Die Wiederverwendung von Bauteilen: Ein Überblick aus rechtlicher Perspektive* (Zurich: Dike, 2021).

In conversation:
ZHAW Institute of Constructive Design (IKE): Eva Stricker
ZHAW School of Management and Law: Andreas Abegg, Meinrad Huser
baubüro in situ: Marc Angst

1 ↗ p. 244
K.118 case study
Construction organization:
A legal vademecum

Uncharted legal territory
ZHAW IKE — ZHAW School of Management and Law — baubüro in situ

Eva Stricker:
Marc, your work with reused building components is primarily aimed at making the construction process as sustainable as possible …

Marc Angst:
Yes, because reused building components have potential benefits in three respects: they don't consume new raw materials, they don't have to be disposed of for now, and there's no CO_2 used in making them. In this way, we can make a significant contribution not only to conserving resources and avoiding waste but also to protecting the climate.[2]

ES: At the same time, however, you have encountered repeated obstacles in practice. In many ways, circular construction appears to be uncharted territory, particularly from a legal point of view. You need a real pioneering spirit and a willingness to take risks to venture there. Andreas and Meinrad, can you briefly outline the extent to which the reuse of components as a strategy for sustainability can be based on legal foundations in Switzerland? Which areas of law are affected by this?

Meinrad Huser:
Although the Swiss Federal Constitution declares sustainable development to be a national objective, this does not result in the comprehensive protection of natural resources. Rather, the constitution provides a general direction: on the basis of the constitutional principle of sustainability, the Confederation and the cantons must strive for a permanently balanced relationship between nature and its capacity for renewal, on the one hand, and its use by humans on the other (Art. 73 BV). This constitutional obligation applies to government actions in general and must therefore be observed by legislators, the courts, and public authorities. In the context of the planning and approval of construction projects, all government authorities must therefore strive for sustainable solutions. It seems obvious that the reuse of existing and functioning components promotes sustainability in several ways.

Andreas Abegg:
However, there is a degree of tension between the protection of the climate and resources on one side of the divide and economic freedom on the other. This is because, in principle, every natural person and legal entity can decide for themselves what they do economically and in what way. They can decide to use new building components. On the other hand, anyone who wants to bring to market existing components or use them in buildings can also invoke this fundamental right.

MH: But at the same time these freedoms are limited by legal barriers, which often

---

2 ↖ p.165
New paths toward net zero?
Potentials for climate protection

'In the context of the planning and approval of construction projects, all government authorities must therefore strive for sustainable solutions.'

serve to secure the freedoms and rights of other people. The standard that is required is defined by technical specifications or the guidelines of the building authority, which, in practice, are often in conflict with reuse.

MH: The Environmental Protection Act is fundamental, particularly the regulations governing the avoidance and disposal of waste, and the corresponding ordinances of the Bundesrat. Product safety law also plays an important role, especially the regulation of construction products.

MA: How are these constitutional principles specifically reflected in terms of legislation? Or, rather, who writes the regulations that are relevant to me as a user?

Reuse and waste legislation

ES: So when we are talking about reuse, we are talking, on the one hand, about waste and on the other about building products. What exactly is a reused building component from a legal point of view?

AA: Legally speaking, a distinction should be made between two situations. If the owner wants to reuse parts of a building, these parts remain in the economic cycle and are treated as goods in the usual way. The owner or occupier decides the fate of the component, irrespective of whether it is a new item they had made or comes from a demolished building. The component remains a component and thus falls within the scope of construction product law. But if the building owner—for whatever reason—no longer wants to use them, these components initially become waste. This is because, under the Environmental Protection Act, all movable objects that the owner is disposing of or whose disposal is required in the public interest are regarded as waste. The provisions of waste legislation then apply to the further handling of the component concerned.

ES: What are the practical consequences of this?

MH: Environmental law is based on the precautionary principle. Consequently, the object of environmental legislation is to avoid waste from the outset where possible. If this is not possible, the recovery chain should be followed. The Act recognizes four types of recovery: direct reuse, material recovery, energetic utilization, and recycling. The more environmentally valuable option must be selected from the various recovery processes. So direct reuse takes precedence over recycling. So far, the only examples of direct reuse mentioned in the Act are clothes, glass bottles, and returnable products. However, the reuse of existing building components can be seamlessly added to this list.

'But if the building owner—for whatever reason—no longer wants to use the components, they initially become waste.'

AA: Based on the legal situation, we can indeed conclude that the reuse of existing components is the most important form of recovery. The waste ordinance already includes detailed special regulations for handling materials that derive from excavation and demolition. These stipulations could, for example, be a model for regulating the reuse of building components in the future. In accordance with the precautionary principle, government measures could be used to promote the increased recycling of components from the waste cycle—for example, through an obligation to prove that a component may only be disposed of if reuse is impossible, or only possible at unreasonable cost.

MA: So the reuse of intact components is actually a legal requirement already. Do you see any potential for expanding that?

Reuse and the law on construction products

ES: This would at least address the problem that reuse is attempting to counter where it arises, namely the premature disposal of intact components. What is the legal situation, then, if I bring a component that has been declared waste back into the economic cycle via reuse and make it a construction product again?

AA: The law on construction products regulates the basic requirements for the design and execution of built structures. Most importantly, it also serves to protect consumers. Construction products may only be put on the market if they are safe—i.e. they do not endanger health and safety under normal or reasonably foreseeable conditions of use. This applies not only to products when they are first brought to market but more generally when they are put up for sale or incorporated into a structure. Anyone offering components for sale or use must comply with these safety regulations, regardless of whether these elements are new or used.

MH: If a construction product is covered by a harmonized technical standard, it may be put on to the market if the manufacturer has drawn up a performance declaration for the product. With this declaration, the manufacturer takes responsibility for the conformity of the construction product based on this performance.

MA: But often it's not quite so easy to trace who originally manufactured a component …

MH: … but it's worth looking, because if the manufacturer can no longer be determined, the distributor automatically takes their place and bears responsibility for the after-market obligations for the product. They are responsible for the safety, identifiability, and documentation of the component.

'Anyone offering components for sale or use must comply with these safety regulations.'

AA: Yes, that's right. So it's worth properly researching the origin of components, and, where possible, getting a copy of the manufacturer's performance declaration. Otherwise, as a reuser, you yourself become liable. But the aftermarket obligations specified by the law on construction products should not just be seen as obstacles. Rather, they reduce the complexity of checking the components by making it possible to refer to the original manufacturer's performance declaration when reusing construction products.

MA: Does that mean that as a designer or retailer, I am liable for components whose manufacturer I don't know?

MH: But the law also supports reuse in other respects: it expressly stipulates the sustainable use of natural resources. The structure must be designed, constructed, and demolished in such a way that natural resources can be used in a sustainable way. In particular, it should be ensured that the structure, building materials, and components are reusable and recyclable.

ES: That's interesting. So future reusability and the non-destructive dismantling of components are already set out in the legislation!

AA: However, the law does not then follow up on these objectives with any obligations to reuse components that are binding in individual cases. So here, there is definitely potential for further development.

Reuse in the approval process

MA: To be honest, I am almost surprised that reuse has evidently already made it into the legislation at so many different levels. With our K.118 project, we often have the feeling that, legally speaking, we are operating in somewhat uncharted territory. This applies to contractual relationships and liability issues,[3] while at the same time, particularly in the institutional approval process, we were repeatedly faced with new questions that had to be clarified in each individual case. Without the basic open-mindedness of the City of Winterthur, we might well have failed in the approval process.

ES: Meinrad and Andreas, could you briefly explain what the legal conditions we were talking about earlier mean, specifically, for the formal approval of a building made from used parts?

AA: In the context of building permits, a balancing of interests not only makes sense but is a legal requirement. The sustainability principle and economic freedom must be balanced with protective objectives such as the preservation of health, nature,

[3] ↗ p.244
K.118 case study
Construction organization:
A legal vademecum

'So it's worth properly researching the origin of components.... Otherwise as a reuser, you yourself become liable.'

and historic building substance, provided the legislator has not explicitly excluded this. The precautionary principle from environmental law should also be considered in the process of granting a building permit.

MH: In practice, however, the reuse of existing components has so far been given little weight in these considerations. As an expression of the constitutional sustainability principle, it should be afforded more importance in the balancing of interests, a requirement that also corresponds with the objectives of waste and construction products legislation.

ES: But in practice, standards like those for safety and fire protection are often made a blanket requirement for acquiring a building permit. This makes it almost impossible to give individual consideration to the question of whether, thanks to its sustainability, a used component can also be used with minimal deviations from the standard. What legal significance do such technical standards actually have?

AA: Public planning and building law is strongly linked to technology and is based on the relevant empirical values. In individual cases, the building code and the building authorities regularly refer to guidelines and recommendations ('standards'). However, technical standards such as these are not legal propositions but expressions of experience; they are of particular importance in liability law.

MH: The building approval authority may deviate from such standards if safety can be provided in another way. No waiver is required for this, the acknowledgement of important reasons is sufficient. The reuse of existing components can certainly be regarded as one such reason.

MA: When we were looking for components for our K.118 project, it often happened that components deviated very slightly from the specified requirements stipulated under the approval process. How could more latitude be created to accommodate contingencies like this?

AA: The degree of latitude that is actually allowed by the balancing of interests and the principle of proportionality is often obscured by directives or standards. So, for example, technical standards are regularly updated—with consequences for the reusability of components: older components can legally remain installed without problems, despite changes in the standards. But once they have been removed, they must usually be adapted to current standards. Here, it would be necessary to work towards a practice whereby components could be reused if they were compliant with the regulations at the time when they were first installed. The authorities routinely have the necessary

'The building approval authority may deviate from such standards if safety can be provided in another way. No waiver is required for this.'

ES: For the conversion of existing buildings, there is already a whole series of regulations that makes it possible to preserve building fabric, even if it no longer fully meets current requirements. The City of Zurich, for example, defines a tolerance range for the mass of existing guardrails. This creates certainty in the planning process and relieves the planning authorities of the task of having to assess each individual case. What do you think about the future possibility of defining such tolerance ranges for reused components as well?

discretion to do this, and they should actually make full use of it.

AA: The community must always consider carefully whether it wants to introduce a norm for everyday situations on a mandatory basis or whether it wants to take account of individual cases. If they do, then these regulations must be formulated in such a way that deviations are possible in individual cases. For example, the planning authority should give priority to those variants that can satisfy the sustainability principle.

MA: In fact, in the case of alterations, regulations have already been established that are based on sustainability considerations. For example, existing buildings can be retrofitted with external insulation, even if this causes separation distances to fall below those specified in the building regulations.

ES: Wouldn't it be possible to put reused components on an equal legal footing with those preserved in situ?

AA: An important basic principle comes into play with preserving in situ—the right of continuance—and many special regulations for alterations are based on this. It applies to all buildings and structures, as long as they remain in a particular place in the way they were previously approved. But as soon as they are demolished, the right of continuance no longer applies, nor is it passed on to components removed from the building.

MH: We are familiar with the subject from our dealings with fire protection regulations: existing buildings and systems only need to be adapted to the regulations if substantial structural or operational modifications, extensions, or changes of use are made—and then only within the bounds of proportionality. By contrast, once a component has been dismantled, it may only then be reinstalled elsewhere if it complies with current regulations.

ES: It is precisely this approach, which links the component to the first place of installation, that makes it so difficult to keep components in circulation.

AA: Here a rule would have to be found that extends the right of continuance to functioning individual parts, which are also available on the market as individual parts. That would be in line with the constitutional

'An important basic principle comes into play with preserving in situ—the right of continuance—and many special regulations for alterations are based on this.'

principle of sustainability. This is a very new topic, though, and one that has barely been considered in legal circles. However, in the legislation and practical administrative work of the authorities, there is an openness to helping sustainability achieve a breakthrough.

MA: We are very curious to see how this develops!

From part to whole and back again: Teaching reuse in architecture

The interaction with existing buildings is an integral part of the master's course in architecture at ZHAW's Institute of Constructive Design (IKE), which has been exploring the potential of reclaimed components in architecture and construction since 2018. For the 'Readymade—Building with Found Objects'[1] master's studio in the 2018 spring semester, 22 students each developed their own responses to the actual brief for the K.118 project. The class was led by Marc Loeliger and Andreas Sonderegger, who then revisited the subject with the 2019 spring semester master's studio 'Shaping Housing Estate Biographies'[1,2], which looked at the preservation of buildings and the reuse of building components within a wider urban planning context. For three long-in-the-tooth housing estates in Zurich and Winterthur, students devised regeneration strategies that would retain and reuse the existing fabric. In the 2019 autumn semester master's studio 'On-Site Component Reuse',[3] Alain Roserens and Marc Loeliger then asked students to explore the possibilities of using components found on the site in the design of a new primary school, to be built on one of the last remaining pieces of brownfield land alongside the main Zurich railway line. These classes were complemented by the taught module 'Constructive Research', in which Alexis Ringli, Eva Stricker, and Guido Brandi examined key issues around the reuse and reusability of building components via 1:1 scale models. In the following conversation, which took place on 15 July 2020, the key protagonists take stock.

[1] See Marc Loeliger, Andreas Sonderegger, Tanja Reimer, and Philippe Koch, *Siedlungsbiografien entwerfen: Transformation statt Totalersatz*, ed. ZHAW Institute of Constructive Design (Zurich: Werk Verlag, 2020).

In conversation:
ZHAW IKE, research: Guido Brandi, Eva Stricker
ZHAW IKE, teaching: Marc Loeliger, Alexis Ringli, Andreas Sonderegger

From part to whole and back again
ZHAW IKE research   ZHAW IKE teaching

When deconstruction comes before construction

Eva Stricker:
Let's start by going back to the beginning of our first master's studio in reuse: in spring 2018, the 'Ready-made' semester kicked off with a deconstruction workshop at Zurich's Orion buildings, an office complex from 1989/90 that was then scheduled for demolition.[4, 5] Supervised by Marc Angst and Pascal Hentschel from baubüro in situ, the students examined and personally disassembled building components at the site, both for the actual K.118 project and for their own designs.

[Figs. 1, 2]   Deconstruction workshop, Orion complex: ZHAW students attempt to remove one of the aluminium windows. Inspecting the day's haul.

Marc Loeliger:
Marc Angst and I went to have a look around the Orion complex, accompanied by its caretaker, to see what might possibly lend itself to reuse. That's when it really hit me for the first time just how fundamentally wrong the current approach to construction is. A perfectly maintained property with just a few decades under its belt was being torn down just like that, to make way for a new build that is only marginally bigger. For me personally, that was a really pivotal moment, one that opened my eyes to how current and urgent this issue is. And I think the students felt exactly the same.

After less than 30 years in use, Zurich's Orion office complex makes way for a new build.

ES: Your finds included the triple-glazed aluminium windows that featured in the baubüro in situ project—and in almost all the students' projects. There were also huge granite facing slabs available in vast quantities—ageless materials!

---

4 ↗ **p. 215**
K.118 case study
Component map

5 ↖ **p. 35**
K.118 reportage
Hunting and gathering

'During the tour of the building, Pascal is trying to identify which parts might be used for K.118. ... As a result, the steel fire escape, the façade slabs, various types of windows, and other items … will eventually find their way to Winterthur.'

↗ **p. 227**
K.118 case study
Component catalogue:
Orion window

↗ **p. 225**
K.118 case study
Component catalogue:
Orion cladding slab

ZHAW IKE research

ZHAW IKE teaching

ES: At any rate, using deconstruction as a way into the design assignments proved a worthwhile exercise. You repeated it in the next semester, taking students to the renovation of the Adliswil swimming pool complex …

ML: Yes, it's hard to believe such stuff is normally just recycled or thrown out. Ultimately, it was the same here because baubüro in situ were only able to use a small fraction of the available components in their Lagerplatz project.

Alexis Ringli:
That time, it wasn't so much about gathering components for students' actual designs; as per the semester's theme of on-site component reuse, we wanted students to utilize components reclaimed from existing buildings on Zurich's Neugasse site. Instead, our intention here was for students to get a feel for what deconstruction for reuse actually entails. While they attempted to painstakingly remove grouting by hand so as to salvage the bricks of a limestone wall for reuse, the neighbouring wall was demolished mechanically in just a fraction of the time.

Guido Brandi:
It was really striking to see how much more effort is required for disassembly than for demolition. They are two completely different jobs; one involves manual craft, the other is just destruction.

[Figs. 4, 5] Deconstruction workshop, Adliswil swimming pool: left, students painstakingly salvaging components for reuse; right, mechanical demolition.

ES: It's not just about the process of finding and salvaging components though. It's also about understanding—in reverse, as it were—how you need to assemble things to make sure structures are reversible.

ML: That's true. Experiencing at first hand that there are components you can't reuse because some absurd adhesive prevents you from disassembling them is much more instructive than any textbook's perfectly planned design details.

Systematizing reuse

AR: Another aim of the exercise was to systematically log and document found components. Here, we were able to build on the work already done by baubüro in situ, who had devised forms for their own haul of salvaged components. These we gave to the students, tasking them with finding out what information we

'While they attempted to painstakingly remove grouting by hand so as to salvage the bricks of a limestone wall for reuse, the neighbouring wall was demolished mechanically in just a fraction of the time.'

really needed in order to have a meaningful component catalogue that would help us to design and plan projects. That information was then to be entered into a digital database and combined with measured drawings and 3D models of each component.

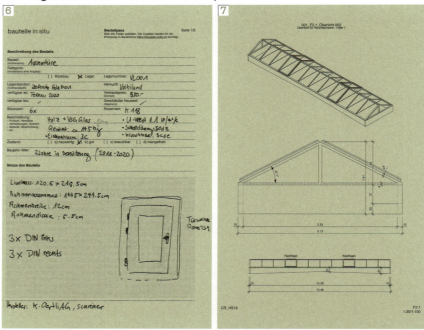

[Figs. 6, 7]   From initial record to detailed catalogue: after two days of taking measurements at the Neugasse site, students document more than 160 components via dimensional drawings and 3D models; these are then linked to a digital database.

GB: We used the IFC (Industry Foundation Classes) standard for the databases. With this open international standard, which conforms with Switzerland's element-based cost classification system for construction (E-BKP), every component can be linked to a data set outlining dimensions, characteristics, and specifications. The problem, of course, is that you don't have all of this information when working with components from existing buildings. Also, certain parameters that are specific to reclaimed components may not be known, such as length and place of usage in earlier life cycles. These additional descriptions need to be added in separate tables.

ES: You explored this issue in more depth in your work with the Swiss rail operator SBB to document existing buildings on its Neugasse site. How did you go about that?

GB: As one of the largest professional developers in Switzerland, SBB is looking for ways of documenting and cataloguing the fabric of its existing buildings. After all, infrastructure buildings offer particular potential for reuse thanks to their repetitive structures. One of the key challenges is how to document components that are still in situ in a building. For the existing buildings on the Neugasse site, SBB worked with BIM Facility. The latter's 3D colour laser scans of indoor areas and drone imaging of the outside allow a highly accurate point cloud to be created, which then has to be translated into a 3D model of the building.[6]

ZHAW IKE research   ZHAW IKE teaching

AR: Certain intermediate steps are still required to get from these measurements to a viable component catalogue. In addition to detailed measurements, you need to also record technical data relating to such things as the properties of the material or the component's physical characteristics. A uniform structure is also required for such a catalogue. The database created by Madaster Switzerland is a step in the right direction. It allows users to input information on what kind of components are available where and in what quantity. However, this data is nowhere near detailed enough to allow architects to then actually work with the components.

GB: I think the digitization of planning processes will open up major possibilities here. It could allow detailed information for each component to be documented in BIM models, right from the new-build stage. Once the building is due to be renovated or demolished, all that information would then already be on hand.

ML: Accurate 3D modelling will be an extremely valuable tool in component reuse. It's crucial to know the exact dimensions and material properties of parts from the outset. After all, it's hard to adapt components to a building. It's more a case of buildings having to adapt to components. That's something we hadn't yet formalized by the time of our 'Readymade' semester, but the students started using such 3D models off their own bat and exchanging them among themselves. They created a sort of virtual 'construction kit' that everyone was able to draw on.

ES: This three-dimensional construction kit is one aspect; another deals with the fact that, when planning a design, you'll have precisely predefined elements in some places and, in others, there will be gaps that you have to source components for, which requires a certain flexibility on your part. In its execution plans, baubüro in situ uses a colour code to reflect that fact.[7] For the student designs, you drew on established practice in renovation projects to develop your own colour code: black for existing fabric, yellow for demolition, red for new elements, and green for reused.[8]

Andreas Sonderegger:
At first there was some resistance among students, who felt this marred the aesthetics of their plans. Really, though, it proved to be the only way to ensure the projects could be discussed in depth and progressed. When reusing components, your plan needs to convey more information than is possible with a conventional idealized black-and-white design drawing.

Variation through limitation

ES: It's not just specific planning methods and tools that are required, though. The design approach has to change too.

AS: Yes, it's a bit like when we played with building blocks or Lego as kids. There is a predefined set of parts and we have to try to find the ideal combination of them for the task at hand. That is fundamentally different from the conventional notion of a design project which in a continual process gets developed from the bigger idea to the smallest detail.

ML: That rather makes it sound as though it's primarily just a case of putting together a construction kit.

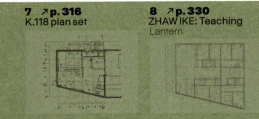

7 ↗ p.316
K.118 plan set

8 ↗ p.330
ZHAW IKE: Teaching Lantern

'Accurate 3D modelling will be an extremely valuable tool in component reuse. It's crucial to know the exact dimensions and material properties of parts from the outset.'

But I think it's extremely important that we as architects are also responsible for developing the structure and the architectural expression of a design. After all, the skill lies not just in assembling predefined building blocks and fulfilling spatial requirements—we are only just beginning to explore what component reuse entails for architects—and what opportunities it offers.

AS: I don't know what you did with your childhood building blocks … but surely that is exactly what it's all about—developing an overarching idea using a limited repertoire of parts.

ES: The 'Readymade' semester offered pretty convincing proof that a limited choice of resources can indeed inspire various ideas. The students not only tackled the same real-world design assignment as baubüro in situ, they also had recourse to the same catalogue of components, though they were allowed to add finds of their own as well as new elements. Despite the constraints of the brief, they came up with 22 totally different designs. How did the students initially react to these constraints? And how did they end up taking such divergent paths? Does working with limited materials perhaps spur designers to make full use of the possibilities available?

ML: Alongside the reuse of building components, another specific feature of our semester assignment was the need to add a storey to a historic building incapable of bearing the additional load itself. That's why, after the deconstruction workshop, we started the design work with an exercise exploring load-bearing structure. This allowed the students to test out different structural approaches from the outset, and these remained evident in the completed projects.

AS: Over the course of the semester, the gap between structural concept and available building components steadily decreased. In Alexandra Vier's project, for instance, the effective depth of the castellated beams salvaged from the Emil Frey car dealership was not sufficient to span the pillarless interior envisaged in the design. Instead, twin stacked girders were used to top off the external load-bearing structure, crowning the building's roof in striking fashion.

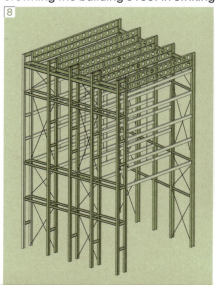

[Figs. 8, 9]   'Readymade' master's studio, Alexandra Vier.

ML: Parallel to developing the load-bearing structure, many students also had strong visual references in mind from the start, and these helped them ensure the heterogeneous mix of found components added up to a coherent whole. Selina Putzi, for instance, took her cue from Hilla and Bernd Becher's photographs of water towers, while Sean Schättin's design draws on Jules Saulnier's iconic façade for the Menier chocolate factory.[9]

1:1—The immediacy of objects

ES: This method of tackling multiple design processes and different levels of scale at the same time is typical of the 'synchronous design' methodology we teach at the institute: instead of progressing step by step from large scale to small, the design evolves via constant dialogue with structural, atmospheric, and urban planning aspects …

ML: That's why I find the interaction with reclaimed components so didactically valuable: it positively compels students to adopt a synchronous design process. Before they're even able to articulate an initial abstract design idea, they find themselves directly confronted with very specific physical components.

ES: To foster this process, we devoted an entire exercise in the autumn 2019 'Constructive Research' class to using the immediate formal, physical, and atmospheric qualities of reclaimed components as inspiration for designs. Each group received a short literary text to set the mood as inspiration for constructing a lighting object out of found elements and materials.

AR: For a lot of them, it felt like a strange way to start, but perhaps that very bewilderment helped spark something. Manual interaction with an existing piece, something many of our students are familiar with from their professional training, combined with abstract atmospheric imagery invited students to extract new qualities from a familiar thing.

ES: We thus ended up with solutions that we would probably never have hit upon had we not used found objects. Take the weighty desk lamp for which a compressed air canister was cut open and repurposed as a shade, its metal inner coating suddenly revealing itself to be an excellent diffusor. Or the two students who used a minimalist tension cable system to turn discarded fluorescent tubes into columnar shades, inside which the backlit remnants of the tubes' spent gas shimmer like alabaster—thereby turning traces of demise into a sophisticated texture.

AR: The found objects acted as catalysts—in just a few weeks, we ended up with surprisingly mature designs. In the case of the prototype fluorescent tube lamp, our colleagues at the ZHAW Centre for Product and Process Development are even interested in developing it professionally.

9 ↗ p.324
ZHAW IKE: Teaching
Trellis

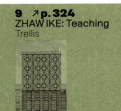

'Before they're even able to articulate an initial abstract design idea, they find themselves directly confronted with very specific physical components.'

From part to whole and back again
ZHAW IKE research ZHAW IKE teaching

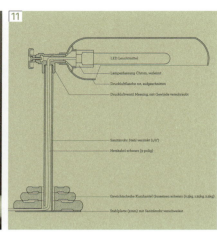

[Figs. 10, 11] 'Constructive Research', Thomas Papritz and Michael Steiger.

[Figs. 12, 13] The lamp designed by students Luca Hänni and Bardhyl Krasniqi was refined in conjunction with the ZHAW Centre for Product and Process Development and readied for a limited production run: six lamps made using a total of 200 spent fluorescent tubes are set to illuminate the entrance level of the K.118 building.[10]

ES: We also find similar examples in the master's studio designs. Here, too, found components triggered processes that would otherwise not have occurred. One such example is Nina Röthlin's project, which she aptly titled 'Lampion' (Lantern).

ML: Nina took a very intuitive and open-minded approach to experimenting with different combinations of materials, some quite adventurous, meticulously refining the composition[11] of components in collage-like visualizations. She drew on various strategies that could prove very useful in future projects featuring

10 ↗ **p. 307**
Creating K.118
[fig. 23]

11 ↗ **p. 236**
K.118 case study
Design and construction:
Glossary

ES: What I also find interesting about her design is the way it deals with the material's apparent deficits. For fire safety regulations, the load-bearing structure of reclaimed steel wouldn't be as suitable as it is for housing; it would need strengthening. Nina thus used the granite slabs from the Orion office complex for retrofitting[13], inserting them between the flanges of the sections. It's open to question whether or not that will actually get approved, but it's still fascinating to see how necessity can give rise to such highly aesthetic and refined details.

ES: These visual references serve not just to unify a somewhat audacious mix of diverse components. The shared industrial heritage also helps to unite very different atmospheric worlds: reclaimed OSB panelling was repurposed as wainscoting, industrial glazing reborn as a room partition, and double doors from lifts used to connect configurable spaces. In conjunction with its intended usage as student accommodation, these double meanings lend the design a certain almost ironic quality.

reclaimed components. For instance, she enveloped her building in a rhythmically structured second skin of reclaimed wire-reinforced glass panels, which acts as a visual filter that compensates for the heterogeneity of what lies behind. In other projects too, this kind of visual Rhythmization[12] has proven its worth as a means of unifying visually diverse components.

AS: Another recurring theme that features in various different forms is the pictoriality[14] of many of the projects. Selina Putzi's design, for instance, combines multiple visual references to create a really unconventional collage.[15]

ML: Yes, the exterior may nod to the Bechers' water tower images but, in the octagonal-plan interior, you suddenly find references to bourgeois 19th-century homes.

AS: Other projects stick with the industrial aesthetic. Ursina Bislin, for instance, based the spatial structure and ambience of her apartments around a load-bearing structure of reclaimed castellated beams, which the interiors show off to great effect. Together with the resulting high ceilings, they allow for a successful transfer[16] from industrial atmosphere to loft-like living spaces.

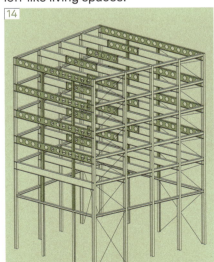

[Figs. 14, 15] 'Readymade' master's studio, Ursina Bislin.

12 ↗ p. 237
K.118 case study
Design and construction: Glossary

13 ↗ p. 237
K.118 case study
Design and construction: Glossary

14 ↗ p. 236
K.118 case study
Design and construction: Glossary

15 ↗ p. 326
ZHAW IKE: Teaching
Residential silo

16 ↗ p. 237
K.118 case study
Design and construction: Glossary

From part to whole and back again
ZHAW IKE research   ZHAW IKE teaching

ES: Such a transfer can also work on a typological level. The industrial components at the students' disposal inspired some of them to develop load-bearing structures that you wouldn't initially expect in the context of student accommodation.

AS: Take Steffano Crameri, for instance, whose project uses the wealth of available steel sections to create new trussed beams that wrap around the entire existing building, a load-bearing structure that allows for a pillarless rec room between the two floors of student rooms. This feat of reconfiguration[17] seems more redolent of complex structural engineering than of conventional residential development.[18] The motivation, by the way, was the wish to protect the old building. The fabric of the latter can be left intact and a wraparound structure was an entirely logical response—albeit a rather sumptuous one …

ES: On the other hand, that's balanced out to a certain extent by the reuse of components. If the components are already there and would otherwise have to be disposed of, conventional measures of what is economically and ecologically appropriate are put into a new perspective. The apparent opulence[19] of this solution suddenly becomes acceptable simply because the material is already available—Nina Röthlin's use of granite can be read in the same way.

ML: Reusing components does often result in especially generous solutions. When looking for suitable building components for a given task, it's often just not possible to optimize everything all the time. The minimum requirements define the lower limit, but there's no upper limit when it comes to dimensions and quality. So a certain degree of oversizing[20] is inherent in such reuse.

AS: Another example of the creative use of industrial building components in a new context is the school premises Leonie Frommenwiler devised for the Neugasse site. Her proposal combines elements of the site's previous buildings such as Y-shaped pillars and the lattice girders of the roof lights yet departs dramatically from the industrial shed structure for which they were originally intended. It's also a design that has little in common with conventional school architecture. Instead, it features rows of two-storey classroom units clustered together like terraced houses. The regular rhythm of their roofs, on the other hand, ensures the units also work together as a single large form. The result is a surprising typological transformation[21] of an industrial shed structure into an innovative new type of school.[22]

AR: She also wasn't afraid to adapt certain components to the new context. The width of the roof lights, for instance, was reduced to tailor them to the requirements of the new usage context.

ES: This is another important aspect that sets reuse apart from a mere 'construction set' approach. As architects, we have to decide what we want to adopt wholesale, what needs adapting to the requirements of the new task, and what might need adding. The individual part and the whole are always mutually dependent.

---

17 ↗ p. 237
K.118 case study
Design and construction: Glossary

18 ↗ p. 328
ZHAW IKE: Teaching
Industrial living

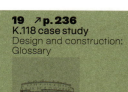

19 ↗ p. 236
K.118 case study
Design and construction: Glossary

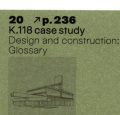

20 ↗ p. 236
K.118 case study
Design and construction: Glossary

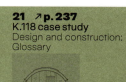

21 ↗ p. 237
K.118 case study
Design and construction: Glossary

22 ↗ p. 336
ZHAW IKE: Teaching
Buildings within a building

Working with what's there

AS: In his design for a school building on the Neugasse site, Sean Hoskyn addressed these issues with genuinely radical sensitivity.[23] The proposal, which could even be classed as preservation of an existing building conversion, involves preserving the fabric of a railway depot that, in and of itself, was not particularly worth saving, and inserting into it all the educational and ancillary functions of a primary school. Working with the existing roof lights, he devised a spatially intriguing school building that also boasts an extremely efficient access design. The latter is based on the principle of buffering,[24] which has also proven its worth in other projects: here, a secondary façade is inserted for the classrooms, allowing the thermally deficient building envelope to be retained. Corridors are located in this buffer zone.

ML: Sean's proposal reminds us that the most sustainable form of circular construction is the in situ preservation of the existing fabric. When facing an architectural assignment involving existing buildings, we first need to ask ourselves: what can we preserve? How much do we need to intervene to make the project workable? How much can we intervene without compromising the existing building?[25]

ES: That's why we need to define our task—or rather our students' task—a little differently, we need to ask: what kind of school building can be realized on this site using the existing fabric?[26] That opens up an entirely different range of scenarios than if we expected them to perfectly fulfil the brief via demolition and total replacement. Similar thinking underpinned your master's studio 'Shaping Housing Estate Biographies', albeit on a larger scale.

ML: Yes, in the 2019 spring semester, we used three housing estates in the canton of Zurich to explore how we might meet pressures to redevelop such buildings, without simply replacing them with new builds. These pressures related to densification and new usage requirements as well as to the buildings' physical deficits, something often cited as reasons for replacement. In conjunction with the developers, we worked with students to explore ways of regenerating the existing buildings in order to facilitate the requisite transformation of the estate.

AS: In Jean Hartmann's design, for instance, a first phase of densification would see new modular wooden structures set between the existing buildings of GWG's Flüeli-/Bürglistrasse estate in Winterthur. When the older buildings come to the end of their useful life, these can then be replaced by new builds and the modular first-phase structures mounted on top—a process-based model that, from the outset, anticipates the reuse of entire building sections.

ML: Ideally, anything that we add should not just increase density but also improve the existing estate. Linda Eisenbart's proposal initially retains the old buildings, merely introducing small annexes that add a small number of apartments plus new accesses and communal areas—an intervention that also enhances

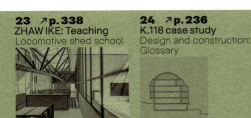

23 ↗ p.338
ZHAW IKE: Teaching
Locomotive shed school

24 ↗ p.236
K.118 case study
Design and construction:
Glossary

25 ↖ p.10
Introduction

26 ↗ p.266
Eight theses
Challenging the demands

From part to whole and back again
ZHAW IKE research

ZHAW IKE teaching

the existing estate, providing greater convenience, generosity, and a new lift. In a second phase of densification, replacement new builds would then make symbiotic use of these new accesses.

[Figs. 16, 17] 'Shaping Housing Estate Biographies' master's studio, Jean Hartmann.

ES: Working in this way requires the designer to appreciate that the objective is not a perfect, finished project. Instead, it's about understanding what is there and improving it in a meaningful way, using your interventions to create the best possible foundation for future phases of development. As architects, we are always part of a larger process that others have already contributed to and others still will take forward.

AS: In the master's thesis projects I coach, you can see how this kind of thinking really does upend students' previous way of working. Interaction with existing buildings—their regeneration, modification, and augmentation—needs to be included in architectural teaching as a matter of course.

Design for reuse

ES: Also worth mentioning in this context is Thomas Papritz's proposal for the Neugasse site, which takes a very nuanced approach to the existing buildings.[27] Here, the stone-built central tract and the listed wooden shed are retained and used to accommodate parts of the school, while the eastern shed is

'As architects, we are always part of a larger process that others have already contributed to and others still will take forward.'

27 ↗ p. 332
ZHAW IKE: Teaching
Reciprocal frame structure

deconstructed and the reclaimed parts used to create a compact new build that's precisely tailored to the concept of the school.

ES: For the fit-out of his school, Thomas Papritz devised a series of standardized sections and infill panels that can be combined in different arrangements, while Raphael Bitzi's proposal envisages the entire load-bearing structure as a set of standardized, separable elements. The modularity[32] of these designs addresses many of the questions raised by a circular approach to construction. Might that involve building systems playing an increasingly important role once more?

AS: For the ceilings of the new building, he combined existing steel sections to create a reciprocal frame structure. This process of addition[28], the joining together of relatively small remnants, allowed him to create more generous spans, while the windmill-like arrangement seems ideally suited to the spatial requirements of the school cluster. A reversible subsystem of non-load-bearing internal partitions and built-in furniture follows the geometry of the beams but can also be altered or removed at any time should requirements change. By ensuring system separation[29] of the load-bearing structure, technical services, and fit-out throughout the design, he has come up with an adaptable building that manages to be specific and flexible at the same time.

ML: This is key to allowing the building to be remodelled or retrofitted in future, and eventually broken down into its individual parts. Separability[30]—designing systems such as connections or assemblies so that they can be deconstructed—is the cornerstone of circular construction. Making it clearly visible can help us cultivate a specific design language for circular architecture that's accessible and easy to understand. If we can see how the elements of a building are connected, then that not only facilitates reparability, it also helps to counter the alienating effect that some of today's highly complex façade systems can have—even on architects. Our students' designs give us some early pointers as to what that might look like in practice: cladding panels are not glued but held in place via visible screws or brackets. They are not set flush but shingled or fitted with cover strips—this allows for the tolerance[31] required to accommodate varying formats or imperfect edges.

AR: For Raphael's school building, he devised a crosswall system whose sections are made from the concrete and trapezoidal sheet metal composite ceilings salvaged from the site. These are combined with ceilings made of lightweight wooden panels.[33] It's an interesting approach that combines components of differing ages and with differing 'life expectancies' in such a way that they can be swapped out at a later date if required. It also became apparent, however, how difficult it is to devise reversible connections while still meeting relevant fire safety and noise control regulations. With Thomas's internal wall system, the latter proved a particularly hard nut to crack.

AS: The systems-based approach has a lot of promise. However, we also know—at the latest since our research with ICOMOS Suisse into post-war modernist Swiss building systems—that attempts to develop

---

28 ↗ p. 236
K.118 case study
Design and construction:
Glossary

29 ↗ p. 237
K.118 case study
Design and construction:
Glossary

30 ↗ p. 237
K.118 case study
Design and construction:
Glossary

31 ↗ p. 237
K.118 case study
Design and construction:
Glossary

32 ↗ p. 236
K.118 case study
Design and construction:
Glossary

33 ↗ p. 334
ZHAW IKE: Teaching
La machine

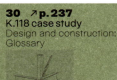
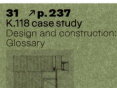

From part to whole and back again
ZHAW IKE research

ZHAW IKE teaching

construction solutions that are universally and enduringly applicable rarely succeed. Given today's constantly changing building norms, now more than ever.

ES: The issue of reusability not only impacts how we plan and design, it also affects what we build with. It's not for nothing that the great majority of our students chose steel-based designs—steel components are long-lasting, standardized, and often feature reversible connections. This predestines them for reuse. Traditional timber construction featuring linear components also offers potential in this regard. By contrast, solid construction, especially using concrete, compares increasingly unfavourably from a sustainability point of view—not just because of the large amounts of resources and energy required for the material's production but also because it's generally almost impossible to disassemble and reuse such components without damaging them, even in prefabricated buildings.

AR: There is some progress in concrete construction though. At the Institute of Constructive Design (IKE), for instance, Josef Kurath and his team have developed high-performance concrete components that are reinforced with carbon fibre. As with timber construction, pieces can be precisely CNC-milled from sheets just a few centimetres thick; these can then be assembled and later disassembled if required. So far they have been used primarily in the construction of balconies and bridges[34] but, in our 'Constructive Research' semester of spring 2020, we also looked at potential applications within buildings.

Teaching reuse

ES: Looking back over your experiences of the past three years: how do you think this kind of circular construction will, or at least should, change the way we teach architecture?

AS: We've already established that incorporating reuse into their projects practically obliges our students to design across different levels of scale from the outset. If we hadn't already made synchronous design an integral part of our teaching methodology, we would definitely have to start doing so now.

ES: To my mind, working with 1:1 scale models and specific building components is particularly key here. It inspires chains of thought and experiments that you can hardly imagine arriving at via theory alone. On the other hand, you can't hide behind the abstraction of a rough scale, where unconventional ideas for using found components can quickly seem very hypothetical—and questions of whether those ideas would actually work in practice remain unanswered.

AR: Our students are greatly helped here by their background in building design. Almost all of them have completed vocational training before coming to us; most are trained architectural draughtsmen or women. Obviously that helps a lot when you're faced with very specific construction-related issues from the start of the design process.

ML: On the other hand, this 1:1 work requires you to already know what components you can use. When looking for reclaimed building components, however, you're often on your own, because there's

34 ↖ p.127
Circular load-bearing structures
Eulach Bridge

ZHAW IKE research   ZHAW IKE teaching

just not yet a big or professional enough market here in Switzerland. In our 'Readymade' semester, we were very fortunate that we could draw on the huge amount of groundwork done by baubüro in situ and 'borrow' the practice's component catalogue, virtually at least. But this lack will make itself felt in future design projects—and in the competitions now being launched in this area.[35]

ES: That's one of the reasons why, in the subsequent master's studio, you limited students to using the components available on the Neugasse site—despite all the challenges this brings in terms of cataloguing and documenting components that are still inside buildings.

GB: Our conversation with Belgian firm Rotor shows that north-west Europe is way ahead of us in this regard. Over there, a network of companies and suppliers offering used building components is already up and running and working pretty well.[36] I think, though, that we're allowed to be a little bit ahead of reality in our teaching and that we should remain hopeful that Switzerland and the rest of Europe will soon start to catch up. Even the issue of logging and documenting components can present an opportunity for our teaching: here, students can practise making effective use of digital planning tools in their design work, something that, thanks to BIM, has already become the norm in reality.

AR: For me, though, the integration of used components is just one of the many issues a circular approach to construction poses for building design courses. Another equally fascinating issue is that the need to make tomorrow's buildings repairable and disassemblable will change how we build them and with what.

AS: That's an area where it's definitely worth experimenting in all kinds of directions. After all, our view of what construction methods are feasible and sustainable is closely linked to the life cycle model used in evaluations. Brick buildings, for instance, fare relatively badly because the assumed life cycle is determined by depreciation of worth and not by the actual lifespan of the materials. If we were to genuinely start preserving and reusing components and materials in line with their actual lifespans, it would upend a fair few apparent certainties.[37]

ML: That's looking forward to how things might be in the future. But, to my mind, it's also worth looking back at how things have been done up until now. We have to make sure we find a different, more sensitive approach to existing buildings. That's true for practitioners and educators alike. We can't carry on simply preserving and protecting buildings of historic importance and declaring everything else up for grabs—we need to find ways of preserving the existing fabric while allowing for regeneration. The reuse of building components is one such way.[38]

---

35 ↗ p. 285
Reuse in construction
A look ahead
[fig. 2]

36 ↖ p. 161
New generalists, new specialists
Rotor and the practice of reuse in Belgium

'The website has detailed information about reusable building components and materials, about dealers and availability, and also has pictures of the items on offer. Since 2012, more and more dealers from an increasing number of new regions have been added.'

37 ↗ p. 272
Eight theses
4

Diversity of building methods

38 ↗ p. 270
Eight theses
3

Inherited identity

K.118 case study

3 ↖ p. 36
K.118 reportage
Hunting and gathering
[fig. 3]

4 ↖ p. 42
K.118 reportage
Testing and planning

'They found a high-bay warehouse with hundreds of steel sections in the Zellweger textile machine factory.' ...
'Yes, that sounds good. When do we have to get them out by?'
'The demolition excavators will be here in three days.'

K.118 case study
Component map

⌂ Place of origin

October 2016

1 Letzigraben housing development
Zurich
Letzigraben letter boxes

May 2017

2 Werk 1 Sulzer Areal site
Winterthur
Werk 1 window
Werk 1 mesh balustrade infill
Werk 1 electrical distribution board

3 Siemens Albisrieden site
Zurich
Siemens photovoltaic system

October 2017

4 Coop distribution centre, Lysbüchel[3]
Basel
Lysbüchel load-bearing steel structure

January 2018

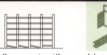

5 Zellweger textile machine factory[4], Uster
Zellweger interior door
Zellweger steel section
Zellweger acoustic panel
Zellweger radiant ceiling panel

April 2018

6 Orion office buildings[5]
Zurich
Orion window
Orion external staircase
Orion cladding slab

August 2018

7 Ziegler print shop
Winterthur
Ziegler window
Ziegler façade metal cladding
Ziegler insulation board

September 2018

8 Burghalde school
Baden
Burghalde finned radiator

October 2018

9 Building 190 Sulzer site
Winterthur
Lagerplatz roof tiles

October 2018

10 Glattpark surgery
Zurich
Glattpark IEi30 interior door

November 2018

11 Cafe Sorglos
Zurich
Cafe Sorglos ventilation plant

December 2018

12 Coop distribution centre
Pratteln
Pratteln parquet flooring

January 2019

13 SBB station temporary solution
Aarau
SBB sandwich panel

14 Neomontana factory workshop, Zurich
Neomontana steel trapezoidal sheeting
Neomontana steel beam
Neomontana front door

15 Vogelsangstrasse housing development
Winterthur
Vogelsang floorboards
Vogelsang radiator

Februar 2019

16 Eulerstrasse residential building
Basel
Eulerstrasse kitchen

September 2019

17 Badenerstrasse office building, Zurich
Badenerstrasse flat roof balustrade

February 2020

18 Buckheimerstrasse office building, Zurich
Buckheimerstrasse WC cubicle partition

April 2020

19 Hunziker temporary buildings
Willisau
Eventbau marquee floor panel

May 2020

20 Temporary solution Volkiland shopping centre
Volketswil
Volkiland exterior door

August 2020

21 BauTeilLaden
Winterthur
BauTeilLaden washbasin

September 2020

22 Eglistrasse housing development, Zurich
Eglistrasse windows

✩ Destination

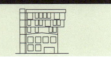

★ K.118
Winterthur

5 ↖ p. 198
From part to whole and back again
Teaching reuse in architecture
[fig. 3]

Component catalogue: A selection of components involved in the study

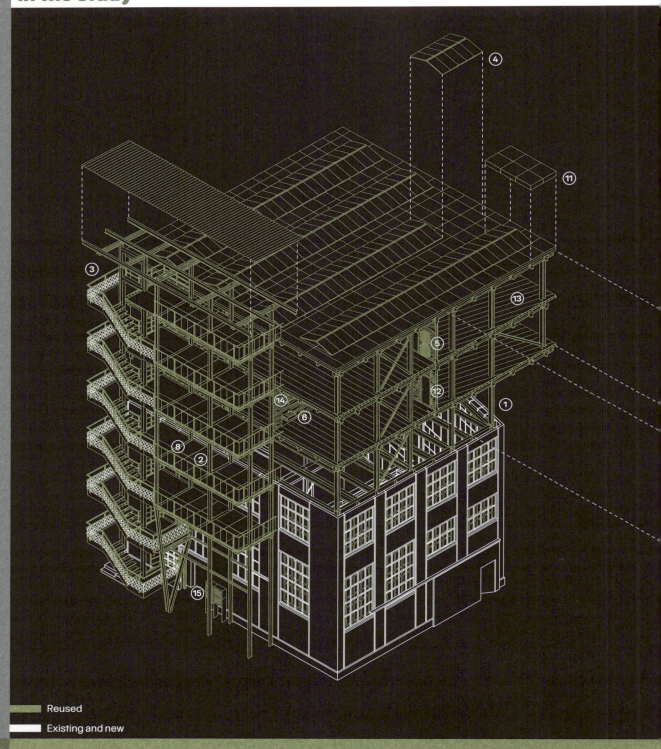

Reused
Existing and new

K.118 case study
Component catalogue

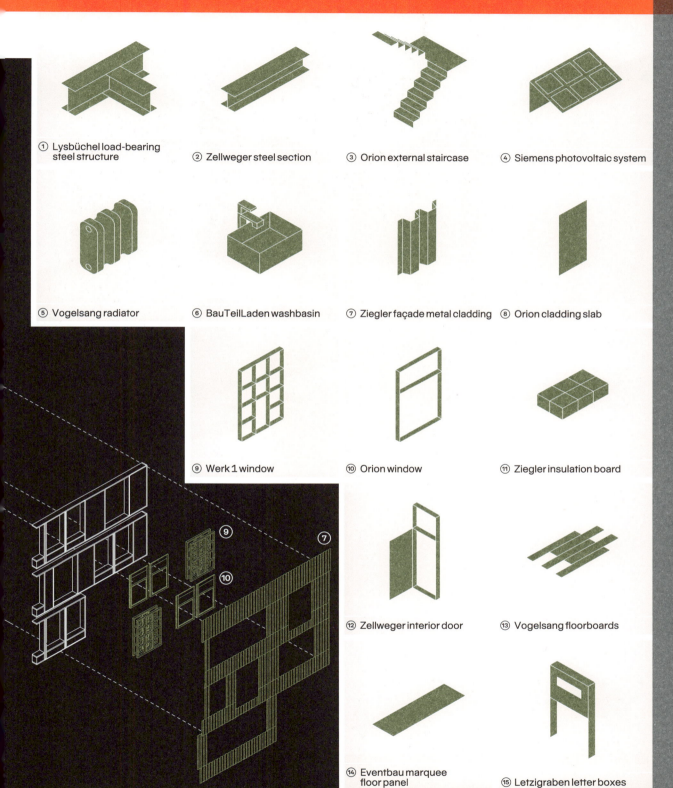

① Lysbüchel load-bearing steel structure
② Zellweger steel section
③ Orion external staircase
④ Siemens photovoltaic system
⑤ Vogelsang radiator
⑥ BauTeilLaden washbasin
⑦ Ziegler façade metal cladding
⑧ Orion cladding slab
⑨ Werk 1 window
⑩ Orion window
⑪ Ziegler insulation board
⑫ Zellweger interior door
⑬ Vogelsang floorboards
⑭ Eventbau marquee floor panel
⑮ Letzigraben letter boxes

↖ **p. 36**
K.118 reportage
Hunting and gathering
[fig. 4]

Lysbüchel load-bearing steel structure

Two-storey steel structure comprising bolted HEA and IPE sections

e-BKP*	C 3	Type	HEA 200
Qty.	63 t		IPE 400 and 450
Manufactured	2004		IPE 270 and 330
Weight	63 t	Properties	–
Dimensions	200 × 190 × 5.0 × 10.0 × 6400 mm	Preparation	Doubling the number of secondary beams, shortening 50 per cent of the secondary beams (one bay), concrete encasement (partial) as fire protection
	450 × 190 × 9.4 × 14.6 × 8400 mm		
	270 × 135 × 6.6 × 10.2 × 8300 mm		
Material	S235 steel		
Finish	painted		

*Swiss standard element-based construction cost plan

[4] 13 km, HGV → [VI] 58 km, HGV → [E] 48 km, HGV → ★

Coop distribution centre Lysbüchel, Basel, October 2017 | Coop distribution centre warehouse, Pratteln | Steel construction company, Stetten | K.118

↖ **p. 38**
K.118 reportage
Hunting and gathering
[fig. 6]

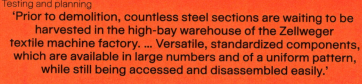

↖ **p. 42**
K.118 reportage
Testing and planning

'Prior to demolition, countless steel sections are waiting to be harvested in the high-bay warehouse of the Zellweger textile machine factory. ... Versatile, standardized components, which are available in large numbers and of a uniform pattern, while still being accessed and disassembled easily.'

K.118 case study
Component catalogue

Zellweger steel section

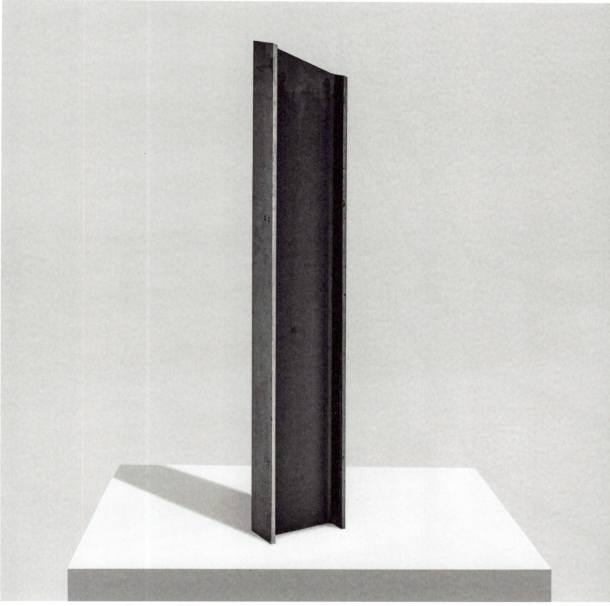

Single-span IPE beam

e-BKP	C 3	Material	S235 steel
Qty.	382 lin. m	Finish	zinc dust paint
Manufactured	unknown	Type	IPE 120
Weight	–	Properties	–
Dimensions	120 × 64 × 4.4 × 6.3 × 3600 mm	Preparation	Processing for welded floor frames

▶ 5 ▶ 25 km, HGV
Zellweger textile machine factory, Uster,
January 2018

▶ IV ▶ 55 km, HGV
Tössallmend storage, Winterthur

▶ E ▶ 55 km, HGV
Steel construction company, Stetten

K.118

↖ **p. 45**
K.118 reportage
Hunting and gathering
[fig. 7]

Orion external staircase

Seven-storey steel dog-leg staircase with half landings

e-BKP	C 4.2	Material	steel, steel grating treads
Qty.	1 pc.	Finish	galvanized
Manufactured	1990	Type	dog-leg stair with half landings
Weight	–	Properties	stair width 1.2 m
Dimensions	7 storeys	Preparation	additional handrail, mesh infill panels
	2600 × 4860 × 21900 mm		for child safety

6 ▸ 75 km, HGV   VI ▸ 95 km, HGV
Orion office buildings, Zurich, April 2018   Coop distribution centre warehouse, Pratteln   K.118

↖ **p. 49**
K.118 reportage
Constructing and coordinating

'In addition, a 20-year-old photovoltaic system from the Siemens site in Zurich-Albisrieden will be installed and operated on the roof.'

K.118 case study
Component catalogue

Siemens photovoltaic system

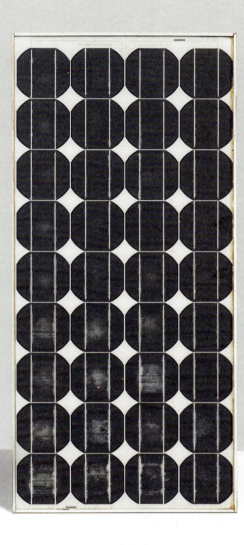

Consisting of 264 panels, output 20 kWp

e-BKP	D 1	Type	Siemens Solar M75S
Qty.	264 panel system	Properties	output 20 kWp (complete system)
Manufactured	1997		installation east-west, 15° slope
Weight	7.8 kg	Preparation	cleaning, replacement of plug
Dimensions	1 panel: 330 × 1219 × 50 mm		connectors, new substructure for
Material	glass, aluminium, solar cell		east-west installation on green roof
Finish	–		

▣ 3 km, HGV   ▭ 25 km, HGV
Siemens Albisrieden site, Zurich, May 2017   Aargauerstrasse storage, Zurich   K.118

Vogelsang radiator

600-mm-high column radiator, painted steel

e-BKP	D 5	Material	steel
Qty.	34 pcs.	Finish	painted, white
Manufactured	unbekannt	Type	Zehnder Charleston, 4–6 columns, 16–19 elements
Weight	–	Properties	–
Dimensions	15 pcs. each of 6 columns × 19 elements 870 × 210 × 600 mm	Preparation	cleaning, pressure testing, replacement connections

15 1 km, HGV   **II** 1 km, HGV   ★
Vogelsangstrasse housing development, Winterthur, January 2019   Old bus depot storage, Winterthur   K.118

K.118 case study
Component catalogue

BauTeilLaden washbasin

White fine ceramic basin, chrome finish standard H/C fitting

e-BKP	D 8	Finish	white
Qty.	10 pcs.	Type	unknown
Manufactured	varies	Properties	standard H/C fitting
Weight	–	Preparation	descaling, cleaning
Dimensions	400 × 600 mm		
Material	white fine ceramic basin, chrome finish fittings		

21 5 km, HGV
BauTeilLaden, Winterthur   K.118

↖ **p. 39**
K.118 reportage
Hunting and gathering
[fig. 1]

Ziegler façade metal cladding

0.7-mm-thick aluminium trapezoidal sheeting, stove-enamelled

e-BKP	E 2.3	Finish	paint, colour: red-orange approximating to RAL 2001
Qty.	609 m²		
Manufactured	2006 and older	Type	SP40/121 smooth
Weight	–		SP45/150 textured
Dimensions	900 × 800 – 4200 × 0.7 mm	Properties	–
Material	aluminium	Preparation	none

▶ 100 km, HGV ▶ 95 km, HGV
Ziegler print shop, Winterthur, August 2018   Coop distribution centre warehouse, Pratteln   K.118

↖ **p. 44**
K.118 reportage
Testing and planning
[fig. 5]

K.118 case study
Component catalogue

Orion cladding slab

Granite natural stone slabs, smoothed and polished

e-BKP	E 2.3	Material	Baveno Bianco granite from Italy
Qty.	75 m²	Finish	polished on one side, back rough-hewn
Manufactured	1990	Type	–
Weight	78 kg/m²	Properties	–
Dimensions	various × 1320 × 30 mm	Preparation	none

 6 | 75 km, HGV
Orion office buildings, Zurich,
April 2018

VI | 95 km, HGV
Coop distribution centre warehouse,
Pratteln

K.118

↖ **p. 45**
K.118 reportage
Testing and planning
[fig. 6]

Werk 1 window

12-pane industrial window with aluminium frames and double glazing

e-BKP	E 3.1	Finish	anodized aluminium
Qty.	18 pcs.	Type	12-pane industrial window
Manufactured	unknown	Properties	1 opening light
Weight	–		frames not thermally separated
Dimensions	1770 × 2960 × 50 mm	Preparation	cleaning, adjustment of fittings,
Material	Aluminium frame and double glazing		replacement bottom-closing seal

 2 | 1 km, HGV
Werk 1, Sulzer Areal site, Winterthur,
May 2017

 IV | 5 km, HGV
Tössallmend storage, Winterthur

 F | 5 km, HGV
Timber construction company,
Winterthur

K.118

K.118 case study
Component catalogue

Orion window

Casement window with top light, aluminium frame, and triple glazing

e-BKP	E 3.1	Finish	anodized aluminium
Qty.	44 pcs.	Type	top light and opening sash thermally broken frame
Manufactured	1990		
Weight	90 kg	Properties	U-value of frame: 1.5 W/(m²·K)
Dimensions	1368 × 2165 × 75 mm		U-value of glass: 1.4 W/(m²·K)
Material	anodized aluminium triple-glazed	Preparation	replacement of seals, cleaning

6 | 75 km, HGV **VI** | 95 km, HGV **F** | 5 km, HGV
Orion office buildings, Zurich, April 2018 | Coop distribution centre warehouse, Pratteln | Timber construction company, Winterthur | K.118

↖ **p. 198**
From part to whole and back again
Teaching reuse in architecture
[fig. 1]

Ziegler insulation board

120-mm-thick expanded polystyrene insulation board, double layer

e-BKP	F 1	Type	Sika Sarnatherm® Norma
Qty.	265 m²	Properties	thermal conductivity (λ value): 0.034 W/mK
Manufactured	2006		Density: 27 kg/m³
Weight	–		specific heat capacity: 0.39 Wh/kgK
Dimensions	1000 × 1000 × 120 mm	Preparation	none
Material	EPS		
Finish	–		

▶ 7 100 km, HGV ▶ VI 95 km, HGV
Ziegler print shop, Winterthur, August 2018   Coop distribution centre warehouse, Pratteln   K.118

↖ **p. 38**
K.118 reportage
Hunting and gathering
[fig. 7]

'The moment when the architects wanted to pick up doors at the Uster textile machine factory was also a learning experience.'

K.118 case study
Component catalogue

Zellweger interior door

Single-leaf door with top light, steel frame with melamine-faced, solid timber leaf

e-BKP	G 1.4	Finish	melamine-faced grey-white
Qty.	16 pcs.	Type	12 DIN left
Manufactured	unknown		6 DIN right
Weight	–	Properties	previously fire doors in a lightweight partition
Dimensions	900 × 2600 × 126 mm		
Material	steel frame solid timber leaf	Preparation	door leaves repainted

▬ 5 25 km, HGV   Ⅳ 5 km, HGV
Zellweger textile machine factory, Uster,   Tössallmend storage, Winterthur   K.118
January 2018

↖ **p. 51**
K.118 reportage
Adapting, repairing, reinstalling
[fig. 2]

Vogelsang floorboards

Spruce floorboards, 22 mm thick

e-BKP	G 2	Material	spruce
Qty.	983 m²	Finish	oiled, stained, sealed, unfinished
Manufactured	unknown	Type	floorboards approx. width 80-120 mm
Weight	–	Properties	solid timber
Dimensions	thickness: 21-24 mm	Preparation	cleaned, de-nailed
	length: varies 2950-3950-4900 mm		

15 ▸ 1 km, HGV
Vogelsangstrasse housing development, Winterthur, January 2019

II ▸ 4 km, HGV
Old bus depot storage, Winterthur

F ▸ 5 km, HGV
Timber construction company, Winterthur

★ K.118

↖ **p. 49**
K.118 reportage
Constructing and coordinating

'The 3-ply boards came from a company that does event construction. They were used as floor panels for different major events, such as gymnastics and wrestling meets or trade fairs and then discarded at some point.'

Eventbau marquee floor panel

3-ply spruce plywood boards, 27 mm thick, phenolic resin coating

e-BKP	G 3	Finish	brown phenolic resin
Qty.	760 m²	Type	27 mm 3-ply plywood
Manufactured	unknown	Properties	–
Weight	–	Preparation	cut to size, planed over the whole surface
Dimensions	1000 × 4000 × 27 mm		
Material	spruce		

19 | 75 km, HGV   K.118
Hunziker temporary buildings, Willisau,
April 2020

Letzigraben letter boxes

12 compartments with aluminium letter and parcel boxes

e-BKP	G 5	Finish	anodized aluminium
Qty.	1 pc.	Type	Schweizer Metallbau, module M30
Manufactured	unknown	Properties	12 compartments with letter and parcel boxes
Weight	–		
Dimensions	1 module = 310 × 330 × 410 mm	Preparation	cleaning, spare parts, replacement locks
Material	aluminium		

 3 km, HGV
Letzigraben housing development, Zurich, October 2016

 5 km, HGV
Aargauerstrasse storage, Zurich

 20 km, HGV
Apprentice workshop, Zurich

K.118

Design and construction

The reuse of building components changes the way we design and construct—both in terms of process and results. Every success in the search for components triggers a chain reaction, which to some extent reverses the traditional design process or provokes surprising about-turns. Certain materials, forms, finishes, and connection details are suddenly specified one-to-one with the found component and demand design and constructive responses. But the future reusability of building components also requires a new perspective in the design process that goes beyond the current project. The particular design and constructive conditions and possibilities of the architecture of reuse were investigated on two parallel tracks in the context of the ZHAW Circular Construction project.

The following graphic retraces the process ↗ p. 234 using the K.118 project as an example. It illustrates the main design steps in relation to the found components recorded in the component map ↖ p. 214 as a quasi-evolutionary development.

Of course, the architectural possibilities of reuse transcend the individual pilot project—their (re)discovery is still in its infancy. Based on the analysis of further references and the design studios, lecturers and researchers at the ZHAW Institute of Constructive Design have, in a series of workshops, set out to identify those features and possibilities which characterise the architecture of reuse and future reusability.[1] An (incomplete) selection of these can be found in the glossary ↗ p. 236.

1 ↖ p. 197
From part to whole and back again
Teaching reuse in architecture

1 ↖ **p. 44**
K.118 reportage
Designing and joining

'In the case of the small, glazed, industrial windows from Sulzer Werk 1, which is located across from Hall 118, different questions arose.'

2 ↖ **p. 36**
K.118 reportage
Hunting and gathering
[fig. 4]

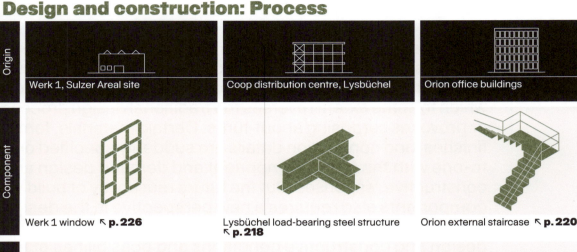

Design and construction: Process

Origin

| Werk 1, Sulzer Areal site | Coop distribution centre, Lysbüchel | Orion office buildings |

Component

Werk 1 window ↖ **p. 226**

Lysbüchel load-bearing steel structure ↖ **p. 218**

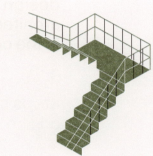
Orion external staircase ↖ **p. 220**

K.118 reuse

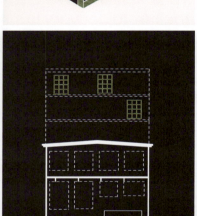

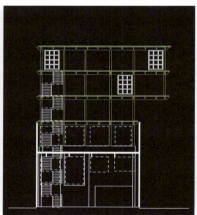

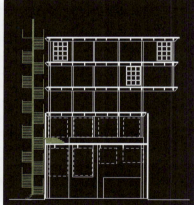

Effect

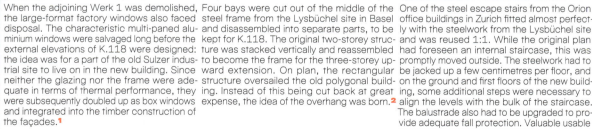

When the adjoining Werk 1 was demolished, the large-format factory windows also faced disposal. The characteristic multi-paned aluminium windows were salvaged long before the external elevations of K.118 were designed: the idea was for a part of the old Sulzer industrial site to live on in the new building. Since neither the glazing nor the frame were adequate in terms of thermal performance, they were subsequently doubled up as box windows and integrated into the timber construction of the façades.[1]

Four bays were cut out of the middle of the steel frame from the Lysbüchel site in Basel and disassembled into separate parts, to be kept for K.118. The original two-storey structure was stacked vertically and reassembled to become the frame for the three-storey upward extension. On plan, the rectangular structure oversailed the old polygonal building. Instead of this being cut back at great expense, the idea of the overhang was born.[2]

One of the steel escape stairs from the Orion office buildings in Zurich fitted almost perfectly with the steelwork from the Lysbüchel site and was reused 1:1. While the original plan had foreseen an internal staircase, this was promptly moved outside. The steelwork had to be jacked up a few centimetres per floor, and on the ground and first floors of the new building, some additional steps were necessary to align the levels with the bulk of the staircase. The balustrade also had to be upgraded to provide adequate fall protection. Valuable usable space was gained on the inside.

3 ↖ **p. 42**
K.118 reportage
Testing and planning

'Pascal's just made a nice discovery. IPE 120 steel beams. What do you think we can use them for? We were thinking the balconies. ... We've already got the large granite slabs for the floor.'

4 ↖ **p. 41**
K.118 reportage
Designing and joining [fig. 4]

K.118 case study
Design and construction

Orion office buildings

Zellweger textile machine factory

Hunziker temporary buildings

Ziegler print shop

Orion office buildings

Orion cladding slab ↖ **p. 225**

Zellweger steel section ↖ **p. 219**

Zellweger interior door ↖ **p. 229**

Eventbau marquee floor panel ↖ **p. 231**

Ziegler façade metal cladding ↖ **p. 224**

Orion window ↖ **p. 227**

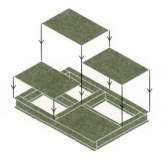

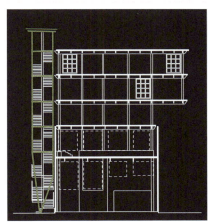
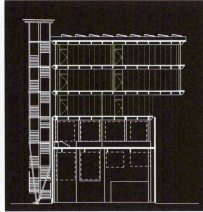
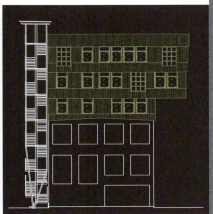

The new configuration of the IPE beams from the high-bay warehouse of the Zellweger textile machine factory allowed the landings of the new external staircase to be widened into a large balcony. The 30-mm-thick, grey granite slabs which previously clad the façades of the Orion office buildings in Zurich are laid on the steel structure as floor slabs—with the non-slip rough-hewn side face up and a sheet metal reinforcement on the underside. The width of the balcony was adjusted to the dimensions of the stone slabs. **3**

The decision to subdivide the floors with demountable lightweight partitions was made in the preliminary project stage. The substructure in new timber is boarded with large-format 3-ply panels which were previously used in stage construction–hence the generous thickness of the material. The melamine facing was planed on one side in an elaborate process and the surface of the wood was oiled. The timber doors with top lights and steel frames from the Ziegler print shop are integrated into the construction with repainted door leaves.

The windows from the Orion office buildings are used in the new build along with the reclaimed blind system and, where possible, the coupling profiles–the latter determining the spacing of the units. Intended for the upper floors, the top frame disappears above the ceiling on the inside. On the outside, it is masked by the trapezoidal cladding of the floor above. The scale-like overlapping storeys of the façade create tolerances for windows with predefined dimensions and deviations in the profiling and colour of the external cladding sheets from the Ziegler print shop. **4**

1 ↖ **p. 97**
Out of scarcity
[fig. 2]

2 ↖ **p. 92**
Where there's a will ...
DomaHabitare cohousing project

3 ↖ **p. 75**
Reusers
Hexenhaus

4 ↖ **p. 144**
A circular approach to architecture
Haus K

5 ↖ **p. 109**
Out of scarcity
Crystal Palace

6 ↖ **p. 140**
A circular approach to architecture
[fig. 24]

7 ↖ **p. 77**
Reusers
Villa PO-2

Design and construction: Glossary

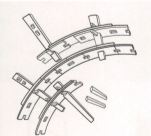

Addition[1]
Load-bearing structures with great potential can be created through the addition of small elements and left-over pieces: the small-scale jointed, arched timber roof constructions of Philibert de l'Orme span impressive distances.

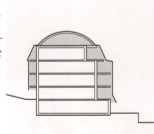

Buffering[2]
Double-layered façades allow the integration of thermally inadequate components and establish new architectural themes: Christian Jelk encloses the generous balconies and terraces of the cooperative residential building in Sainte-Croix with a collage of used, single-glazed windows.

Composition[3]
Collage, assemblage, *objet trouvé*– fine art techniques are applied to old components in new combinations to generate unusual aesthetic appeal: in 'Hexenhaus', Alison Smithson designs the expressive garden window from old doors and new parts.

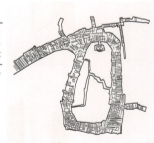

Continuity
The use of locally available components creates an inseparable connection between new things and the place and its history: Dimitris Pikionis reassembles ancient fragments for the visitor centre and outdoor areas of the Acropolis.
↖ **p. 22** [figs. 13, 14]

Legibility
Detachable connections can create a new constructive impression which makes the connection of parts comprehensible: the external tension springs on Peter Zumthor's pavilion for Expo 2000 announce the detachability of the parts.
↖ **p. 28** [fig. 31]

Materiality[4]
This relates to constructions which are developed from the intrinsic qualities of a material or component. With their Haus K project, Seiler Linhart Architects have developed a building with innovative solid timber construction. A house made only of timber, without metal or glue and without chemical additives.

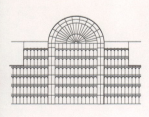

Modularity[5]
Systems designed to be demountable and remountable from the start determine the conception of structures from the ground up to the last detail: Joseph Paxton made use of his experience in building greenhouses in his modular design of the Crystal Palace.

Opulence
The oversizing of found components for their new use introduces rich spatial qualities and leads to an expressive appearance. Once forming the prestigious perimeter of the largest theatre in ancient Rome, the arcades of the Theatre of Marcellus have served as the plinth for a private palazzo since the 16th century.
↖ **p. 21** [fig. 8]

Oversizing[6]
Minimum requirements restrict the choice of found components downwards—but not upwards. In his Villa Hemeroscopium, Antón García Abril orchestrates giant precast bridge construction elements as an exciting installation of 'found objects'.

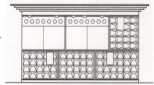

Pictoriality[7]
Strong forms and memorable image references prove to be a robust frame for the inclusion of heterogenous found elements: in his PO-2 villa, Alexander Brodsky combines discarded concrete elements to form a palazzo.

10 ↖ **p. 46**
K.118 reportage
Constructing and coordinating [fig. 1]

14 ↖ **p. 41**
K.118 reportage
Designing and joining [fig. 4]

236 237
K.118 case study
Design and construction

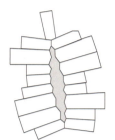

Recoding[8]
Old materials and components can take on an unexpected significance in their new use: In his conversion of the Kleines Café in Vienna, Hermann Czech covers the floor with tombstones cut into slabs.

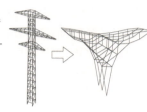

Reconfiguration[9]
This refers to the reassembly of elements with specific characteristics in a different configuration. In Jan Brütting and Corentin Fivet's project for the main station in Lausanne, electricity pylons are broken down into their individual parts and reassembled to form new load-bearing structures.

8 ↖ **p. 67**
Reusers
[fig. 19]

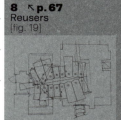

Retrofitting[10]
Inadequate components can be upgraded for new requirements by measured retrofittings. That may involve, for example, the structural design, building physics or fire protection: the steel beams and columns of K.118 are equipped with concrete encasement to comply with current fire protection requirements.

Rhythmization[11]
Defining strata and segmentation integrate structures made from diverse one-off elements into a whole in terms of design. In the Lysbüchel project by baubüro in situ, a rhythmic order of trapezoidal sheeting overlays the free play of various formats of reclaimed windows.

9 ↖ **p. 124**
Circular load-bearing structures
Roof of Lausanne main railway station

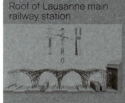

Separability[12]
Design connections between used and new components need to be accessible and demountable: Werner Sobek has built himself a house in which every element is demountable, including the structure, cladding, and building services.

System separation[13]
Consistent system separation makes it possible to adapt to future usage scenarios. In their project for the École d'architecture in Nantes, Lacaton and Vassal differentiate between the massive, basic structure shaping the urban space and the inserted internal room division and façade in lightweight construction.

11 ↖ **p. 93**
Where there's a will...
ELYS culture and business hub

12 ↖ **p. 147**
A circular approach to architecture
Haus R128

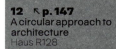

Tolerance[14]
Tolerances in the conception of joint configuration and fastening technology introduce scope for the incorporation of used parts which deviate from the nominal dimension. The floor-by-floor overlapping of the external cladding of K.118 allows the integration of various cladding panels and window formats.

Transfer[15]
Used building components give expression to the atmospheric world of their origin at their new location: industrial aluminium panels from Jean Prouvé's own production in combination with other parts give his home in Nancy a new kind of homeliness.

13 ↖ **p. 146**
A circular approach to architecture
École Nationale Supérieure d'Architecture Nantes

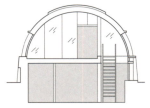

Transformation
Parts of 'alien' building typologies introduce structural and spatial potential for new builds with a different use. In Pierre Chareau's work for Robert Motherwell, decommissioned barrack huts are supplemented with elements from greenhouse construction to complete the studio.
↖ **p. 24** [fig. 19]

15 ↖ **p. 73**
Reusers
Maison Prouvé

Construction organization

The practical application of reuse is probably as old as building itself. Nevertheless—or perhaps precisely because of this—in many ways it challenges the general conditions of our modern construction, focused as it is on standardized and technologized planning and production. As a basic framework for a systematic investigation of these phenomena in the context of this study, and—based on the K.118 case study—specific services and processes of reuse were defined and considered from different points of view. Which stakeholders are involved? What services do they undertake and how do they relate to each other? What consequences can result from liability issues, for example? And which organizational models are conceivable to make the building process more circular? The key findings from this review are illustrated in the following four graphics:

Ten specific services can be derived from the K.118 case study that only become necessary as a consequence of reuse (e.g. dismantling and preparation) or need to be reallocated (e.g. transport and storage) on the basis of it: they are the search, assessment, documentation, acquisition, dismantling, transport, storage, preparation, reinstallation, and maintenance of the components. Each component search triggers a cascade of actions and decisions which can be assigned to these services. The following representation of the services and processes ↗ p. 240 shows possible variants, with the Orion window ↖ p. 227 serving as an example for illustrative purposes.

It is also the subject of our next focus of consideration: in the component organigram ↗ p. 242 the above services are assigned to all stakeholders who are involved, from the search process to reinstallation and maintenance; compared with the conventional construction process, there is a considerable variety of participants, which, in the K.118 project, is still growing with each new component that is found.

It is obvious that this complex web brings with it a variety of different contractual relationships and issues of responsibility. Starting from the specific case study and ordered according to the services formulated at the outset, the lawyer Annatina Menn, in collaboration with the ZHAW School of Management

[1] Andreas Abegg, Oliver Streiff (ed.), *The Reuse of Building Components: An Overview from a Legal Perspective* (Zurich: Dike, 2021)

and Law, has addressed these issues[1] and, together with general recommendations for action, summarized them in tabular form in A legal vademecum ↗ **p. 244**. Although the contracts discussed here can all be concluded orally and can develop validity accordingly, it is strongly recommended that all contracts be concluded in writing. The actual crux in the utilization of used components lies in the issues of liability and warranty. In the current market situation, the sellers of used components and the contractors who reinstall them will be careful to exclude, or at least limit, their warranty. Thus, in practice, in addition to the time-consuming procurement process, the risk is borne by the client and designers, as illustrated by the example of the aluminium windows. In this case, the problem was solved by the client making a provision for any repairs that may ensue. In addition, a maintenance contract was agreed with the company that had prepared the windows and fitted them into the façade elements.[2]

[2] The issues of warranty and maintenance are particularly important for components subject to wear (see Costs ↗ **p. 248**). In every other case, previous usage can instead be viewed as a practical test successfully passed.

The complexity of the illustrated processes and configurations is closely related to the mode of organization practised in the K.118 project. In this case, almost all the reuse services were undertaken or coordinated by the architectural practice, which took on an overall management role—including services that, in a conventional process, are usually assigned to contractors or suppliers. This is not something that can be taken for granted: the Circular models ↗ **p. 246** graphic shows in schematic form how the various actors involved in construction can contribute to the component cycle and refers to relevant examples mentioned elsewhere in this book.

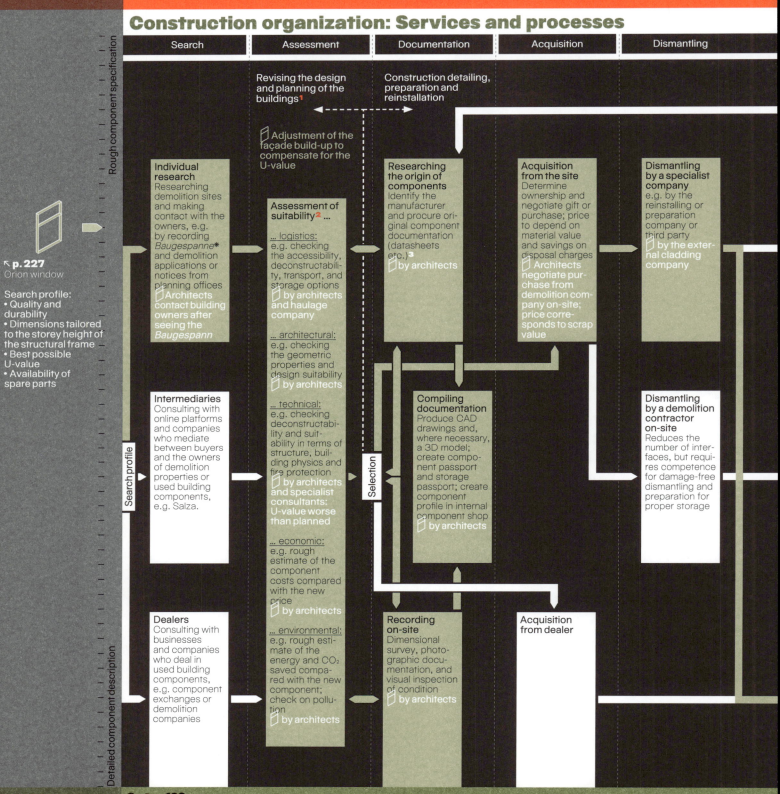

K.118 case study
Construction organization

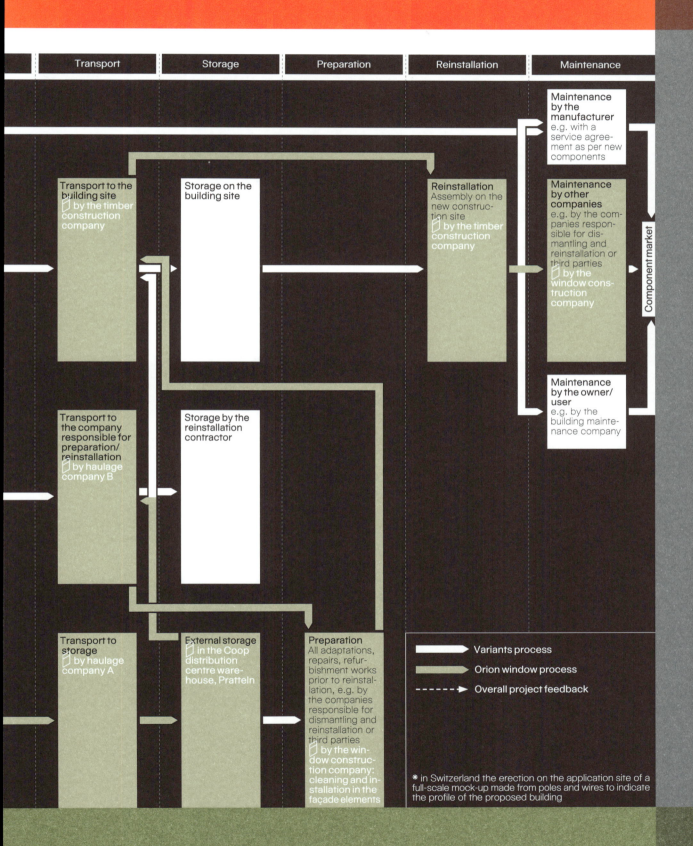

Construction organization: Component organigram
Conventional windows

Remit	**Client**	Contract for work and services
Contract for specific work	**Architect** Overall management responsibility	
	Authority to issue instructions / Coordination	
Specialist consultant Building physics		**Company** Window installation

Employer
Contractor

242 243
K.118 case study
Construction organization

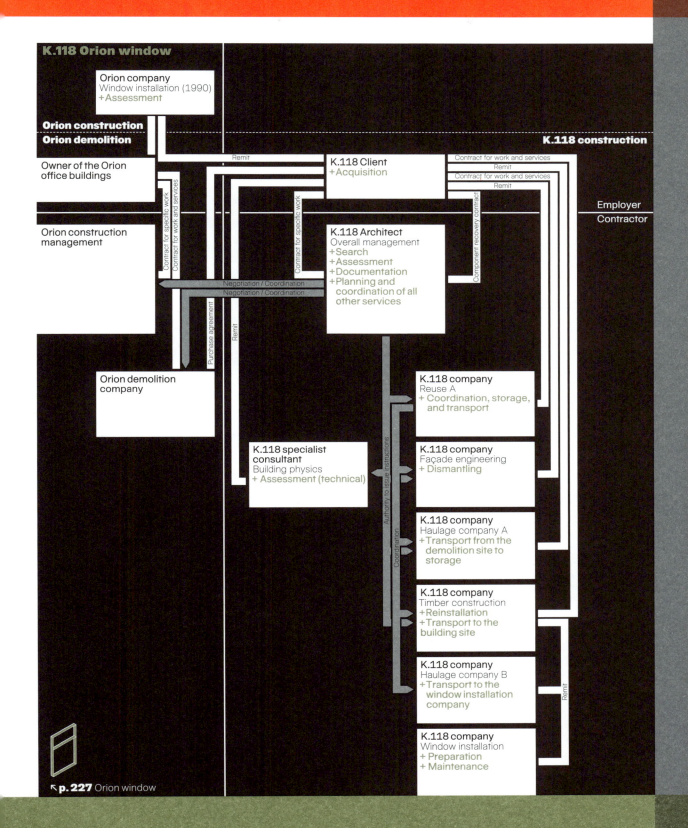

↖ p. 227 Orion window

1 ↖ p. 35
K.118 reportage
Hunting and gathering

'When he rides down Förrlibuckstrasse on the other side of the tracks, Pascal notices the batter boards that indicate a new building project at the site of the two Orion office buildings. At home, he does some research to find out what is going on.'

Construction organization: a legal vademecum

Example: Orion window ↖ p. 227

	Search, assessment, documentation + coordination of the other services	Acquisition
	The client of the K.118 project assigns the search, assessment, and documentation of components to the architect—this also applies to the windows. At the same time, the client assigns to the architect the coordination of all other services that will become necessary in the course of the reuse. These services are not part of the basic services of the usual planning contract but must be agreed separately as special services. In the case of K.118, an additional contract was concluded (a component procurement contract). The architect eventually finds suitable aluminium windows in the Orion office buildings in Zurich.[1]	The client, represented by the architect, concludes a purchase agreement with the owner—in this case, the demolition company—and pays the agreed purchase price, which corresponds to the value of the material. The seller disclaims any warranty in a written agreement. However, it is agreed, to the benefit of the buyer, that the risk of accidental loss shall only pass to the buyer upon handover (and not at the conclusion of the contract). It is further agreed that dismantling and transport costs shall be borne by the buyer.

Contract: agency contract or contract for work and services or mixed contract	Contract for the complete dismantling of the Orion office buildings		Acquisition of component: purchase agreement or gift or 'partial gift' [where the consideration is below the market value]
	Orion office buildings		Orion office buildings

Contract

Parties and contract qualification

Depending on the scope of performance, the contract between the client and the architect is qualified either as a contract for work and services (Art. 363 ff. OR*), as a contract of agency (e.g. construction management contract, Art. 394 ff. OR), or as a mixed contract (overall contract for planning and construction management).
• Depending on the contract qualification, the contractor undertakes to either produce drawings (contract for work and services) or to provide a service, e.g. for the coordination of the component procurement (contract of agency). Its warranty obligations and, in particular, its liability will differ accordingly.

If the payment of a purchase price is agreed upon, the client and owner of the component conclude a purchase agreement (Art. 184 ff. OR). If the components are handed over without payment, the transaction qualifies as a gift (Art. 239 ff. OR), at best, or a 'partial gift'.
• The owner of the components must be identified before conclusion of the contract. In the case of demolition/dismantled material, this could be owner of the property, the owner of one of the building's floors or a company already contracted with the demolition of the property. In case of doubt, it is advisable to obtain the consent of both the landowner and the demolition contractor.

Content

The contract is concluded upon agreement on the objectively essential terms.
• The specific scope of the designer's basic services should be clearly defined, as should their specific duties in connection with the selection, testing, purchase, and reuse of building components (in particular, for example, duties of examination and testing), if necessary with the involvement of (material) experts, power of representation in the purchase of building components, negotiation and representation of the client in the conclusion of all contracts with third parties, and coordination and organization of storage, transport, and preparation. Documentation in accordance with construction products law also plays an important role.[2]
• The client's obligations in the procurement of the components must also be defined. If, for example, the fiduciary acquisition of building components is part of the architect's scope of services, the client will be required to pay in advance. ↗ p. 254

The contract is formed upon agreement on the objectively essential terms of the contract. In the case of a purchase contract, these are the items to be purchased and the price. Unless otherwise agreed in the contract, in a purchase agreement the costs of handover or dismantling are borne by the seller, the costs of transport to a place other than the place of performance are borne by the buyer (Art. 188 f. OR).
• The contract should contain an exact description of the quantity, condition, and quality of the components and precisely regulate the time and place of handover.
• Any regulations deviating from the law regarding the bearing of costs for dismantling and transport are to be made individually.

Liability and warranty

The statutory regulations for liability and warranty according to the law of agency or contracts of work and services are discretionary in nature. The parties may contractually deviate from this and tighten or limit the liability/warranty or, to the extent permitted by law, exclude it altogether.
• Specific liability and warranty provisions, as well as notice and limitation periods deviating from the law, must be agreed upon individually.
• Liability for intentional or grossly negligent acts cannot be waived.

The seller is causally liable by law, i.e. also without fault, for defects of title and material defects in the purchased item. The buyer's rights in respect of defects are rescission and reduction of the purchase price and, in the event of fault, damages. On the other hand, the donor is only liable for defects if this has been specifically agreed, and otherwise only for damage caused intentionally or by gross negligence (Art. 248 OR).
• A very low price may indicate tacit exclusion of warranty. The fact that an item is used does not automatically justify that assumption.
• If the seller wishes to exclude their warranty, this must be expressly agreed.

Notes

In practice, the model contracts based on the services and fee schedules (LHO) of the Swiss Society of Engineers and Architects (SIA) are widely used. However, these contracts, as well as the SIA LHO 102, do not contain specific rules for the architect's tasks in relation to components that are to be reused. Accordingly, a supplementary agreement is needed.

In the case of a purchase, the benefit and risk of an object pass to the buyer by law as soon as the purchase agreement is concluded (Art. 185 OR). Thus, as a rule, the buyer bears the risk of accidental loss of the component, even if it is still installed in the predecessor structure. If this risk is to be transferred to the buyer only upon handover of the item, this must be agreed individually.

* Obligationenrecht = Code of obligations

2 ↖ p. 193
Uncharted legal territory
Reuse under Swiss law

'So it's worth properly researching the origin of components, and where possible, getting a copy of the manufacturer's performance declaration. Otherwise as a reuser, you yourself become liable.'

3 ↖ p. 41
K.118 reportage
Designing and joining
[fig. 6]

K.118 case study
Construction organization

Dismantling	Transport, storage	Preparation, reinstallation, maintenance
For the dismantling of the windows, the client concluded a contract with the window and cladding installation company, in which the damage-free dismantling of the windows and their placement on the ground floor for removal is agreed. Acting on behalf of the client, the architect orders pallets from a joinery firm that are specifically prepared for the proper storage and packing of the windows.	Finally, the aluminium windows have to be put into storage until they are actually reused. The client rents a warehouse for this purpose. A haulage company is commissioned to transport the windows to the warehouse, where an operative is tasked with storing the windows properly and drawing up an inventory for the architect's component management.	The invitation to tender for the contractor's services allows for the client to provide the windows. A contract for work and services is concluded with a timber construction firm for the construction of the façade. A subcontractor cleans and overhauls the windows and fits them into the façade elements.[3] Because there is no warranty from the manufacturer/supplier, the subcontractor is not prepared to offer the usual warranty.

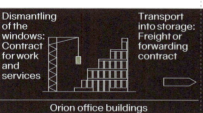

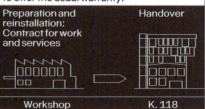

Client and (demolition) contractor conclude a contract of work and services (Art. 363 ff. OR).	Client and carrier or freight forwarder conclude a contract of carriage or forwarding contract (Art. 440 ff. OR; Art. 439 OR), the client and landlord of the warehouse conclude a lease agreement (Art. 253 ff. OR), and the client and bailee conclude a contract of bailment (Art. 472 ff. OR).	Client and contractor conclude a contract of work and services (Art. 363 ff. OR).
The contract is formed upon agreement on the objectively essential terms of the contract: the production of the work and the payment of remuneration. • The scope of services and the characteristics of the work should be precisely defined. As the components are to be reused, the dismantling contractor should undertake to dismantle them without causing damage. • Removal and professional storage by the contractor as well as the preparation of the components (type of containers, packaging, palletizing) should be precisely defined. • It is advisable to agree on the exact place and time of the handover.	The various contracts are formed upon agreement on the objectively essential terms of each contract: • In the case of a lease, the landlord only has to provide rooms and the owner of the components is responsible for their careful storage. • In the case of a contract of bailment, however, the bailee (warehouse operative) is responsible for the careful storage of the components on their premises. • Under certain circumstances, it is advisable to make compulsory insurance a part of the contract, or to insure the components oneself as the new owner.	The contract is formed upon agreement on the objectively essential terms of the contract. • The supply of materials by the client is not typical in construction. The associated due diligence and the contractor's duty to warn are regulated by law. Deviations from individual contractual provisions are possible, including more extensive inspection and testing obligations. • The scope of service including all necessary reconditioning measures or subsequent maintenance should be precisely defined.
The legal provision for the liability for defects in the work is discretionary in nature. Whether a defect exists shall be assessed according to the specifically agreed scope of services or the agreed characteristics. • Any exemption or limitation of warranty, as well as an individual regulation of any notice of defects and limitation periods must be explicitly agreed in the contract.	By law, each contract has its own liability rules, but these are usually discretionary in nature. • Individually agreed limitations or exemptions from liability are possible to the extent permitted by law.	By law, the contractor is liable for defects in the work and they are obliged to issue a warning if there are defects in the component provided by the client. • A warranty exemption or limitation as well as any notice and limitation periods deviating from the law must be agreed individually.
In the Swiss construction industry, the SIA-Norm 118 (General Conditions for Construction Work) is very often included in contracts for work and services. Insofar as this standard does not contain any suitable rules for the dismantling of components intended for reuse, such rules must be agreed on an individual contract basis.	Landlords, warehouse operators and forwarders/hauliers operate a bulk business and are in practice therefore likely to offer their services on the basis of general terms and conditions (GTC). These must be examined in detail. Any rules deviating from these must be agreed individually.	In the Swiss construction industry, the SIA-Norm 118 (General Conditions for Construction Work) is very often included in contracts for specific work and services. Insofar as this standard does not contain any suitable rules for reuse, such rules must be agreed on an individual contract basis.

3 ↖ p. 50
K.118 reportage
Constructing and coordinating

'This complete service of Wick Upcycling GmbH allows circular construction to take place where there is no corresponding industry.'

Construction organization: Circular models

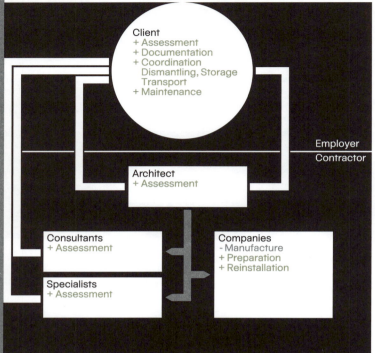

Circular client

A building owner activates his own component resources for future new buildings. Components in existing and new buildings are systematically recorded and documented for this purpose and are available as a component catalogue for new construction projects. Especially in the case of a large existing building and/or recurring requirements for new buildings, the company's own resources can be utilized in the best possible way. Irrespective of the individual construction project, structures for documentation, storage, and logistics are established within the company or in cooperation with external partners.

The project organization of individual construction projects can then be carried out in a largely conventional manner; specialization of the other project participants is not absolutely necessary. On the designer's side, the usual scope of services is expanded to add the inclusion and review of the existing component catalogue in alignment with the specific requirements of the project. On the contractor's side, the scope of services changes, since only preparation and installation—but not the delivery of the component itself—are required, because, to some extent, the client assumes the function of a supplier.[1]

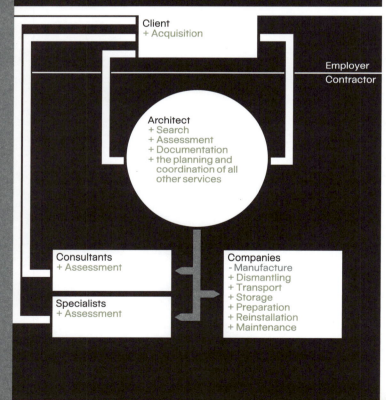

Circular planners

A large, non-specialized architectural firm, as in the K.118 case study, undertakes the coordination, as general planner, of all additional services required by reuse (**Services and processes ↖ p. 240**, **Component organigram ↖ p. 242**). This requires a broad-based team specialized in the reuse of components, especially since many of the additional services normally fall more within the sphere of influence of contractors and suppliers. In addition to architects and architectural technicians, skilled tradespeople and experts in logistics are therefore also part of the overall manager's team for the hunting down and documentation of components. The project-specific search for parts with close interaction between component, design, and planning is possible because the designing, planning, and hunting for these parts are all done by one party. This widens the architectural scope, while also increasing the complexity of coordination because potential items first have to be tracked down on various demolition sites and then salvaged in a coordinated manner and integrated into the new building. The remaining project partners similarly undertake partial services of reuse, but because of the coordination by the general management, specialization is not absolutely necessary. Alternatively, an architectural office that lacks the experience or capacity for the additional services of reuse can bring in a specialist, either in an advisory or operational capacity.[2,3]

---

1 ↖ p. 178
Values and processes
Reuse from a developer perspective

'I'm really fascinated by the idea that, with its 3,600 properties, SBB could create 2,400 new buildings from its own resources if we were just able to reuse 70 per cent of our existing buildings' materials and components. We could regenerate from within, as it were!'

2 ↖ p. 157
New generalists, new specialists
Rotor and the practice of reuse in Belgium

'During the design and construction phases, we assist the architects in the integration of salvaged elements.'

4 ↖ p. 53
K.118 reportage
Adapting, repairing, reinstalling

'The photovoltaic system ... remains in the possession of Alteno Solar AG, which will continue to operate it for the rest of its service life .... This means that the roof will be rented out by the operator of the system.'

6 ↖ p. 37
K.118 reportage
Hunting and gathering

'Way back in 1936, the grandfather of the current co-managing director Martin Hiltbrunner founded Hiltbrunner AG to get a foot in the door of the scrap material trade. Since then, the company has repeatedly had to adapt to changing market conditions.'

K.118 case study
Construction organization

Circular business

A company not only offers the manufacture and installation of new components but also has its own stocks of used components and/or maintains contacts with appropriate suppliers, demolition companies, and logistics partners. Beyond that, its business model changes little, because even in the conventional model, raw materials are not usually exclusively purchased on a project-specific basis and storage and transport facilities are often available. Provided that components are purchased very cheaply and preparation and logistics can be solved in-house, in this model economically attractive profit margins are also presumably possible for large companies which anyway have access to the corresponding infrastructure. No particular specialization is necessary for the remaining project participants. The designers only have to check the suitability of the components on offer for the specific construction project.

Alternatively, self-produced components can be provided to various customers within the framework of a contracting model.**4** They remain the property of the company and are simply used in a building for a certain period of time against payment in order to be subsequently overhauled and, if possible, installed in a new location. On the one hand, this requires a suitable infrastructure for storage and repair and, on the other, it sets incentives for the manufacture of durable, robust, and repairable products.

Circular suppliers

Specialist suppliers offer used, documented goods, whether as dealers for second-hand goods of various trades (see component exchange), a specialized building materials merchant that sells used components as well as new goods,**5** or as a demolition company that salvages usable components on its own demolition sites and sells them instead of disposing of them.**6** What is important, in any case, is the mediation between the source of the component and possible buyers, e.g. as practised in Switzerland by the Salza platform. In order to establish a functioning market, a sophisticated system of recording and documentation is necessary, as well as a network or trade directory that connects potential suppliers, clients, and architects. Even for building owners whose own stocks are recorded, the network can serve the sales of components surplus to their needs.**7**

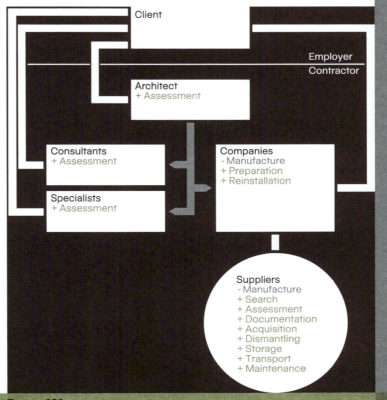

5 ↖ p. 162
New generalists, new specialists
Rotor and the practice of reuse in Belgium

'Two specialized dealers from the Netherlands: Vermeulen & Zonen and Regts Antieke Tegels.'

7 ↖ p. 161
New generalists, new specialists
Rotor and the practice of reuse in Belgium

'Opalis, an online network that has hitherto been active in north-western Europe, brings architects and clients into contact with an impressive array of dealers of reusable building components.'

Costs

Is it still possible in Switzerland today to build with reused components for the same price as with new ones? In order to get to the bottom of this question, the effective costs at component level were established, based on the construction accounting for K.118, and compared with equivalent new components. Not only is the final price relevant, but also the time when payment is due: while in conventional construction, materials can be ordered according to the construction programme of the new building, the availability of used components obeys the logic of demolition sites and the stocks of dealers who have been scarce up to now. Michael Eidenbenz, from the ZHAW Building Sector Platform, stood by in an advisory capacity during the subsequent investigations. Sources and methodology are referenced with each graphic.

    In the first step, the composition per component ↗ **p. 250** is investigated using ten components with different manufacturing processes and material properties as examples: what is the effective composition of their costs when all the services and processes ↖ **p. 240** relevant to reuse are taken into account? The planning costs directly related to the search and documentation of the components are also recorded here. The actual purchase price—at most, usually the scrap value—is generally negligible. On the other hand, labour costs for dismantling, preparation, and reinstallation are significantly higher in Switzerland, a high-wage country. For components subject to mechanical wear (e.g. the Orion window , Zellweger interior doors , Letzigraben letter boxes) special maintenance work and provisions for warranty replacement must also be taken into account. In the case of K.118 they are part of the contracts for work and services.

    The next step is the comparison per component ↗ **p. 252** with values for equivalent new components. Although they are mostly reinstalled with only minimal preparation, in some cases it was not possible to undercut the price of new components. For example, despite its untreated surface patina, the Lysbüchel load-bearing steel structure , which requires heavy lifting gear for dismantling, transport, and reinstallation, turned out slightly more expensive than a new one.[1] From a purely economic point of view, the Vogelsang floorboards were also not 'profitable'. The dismantling, preparation, and reinstallation of the small timber elements require a great deal of expensive manual work. However, had they been made from valuable high-grade timber instead of cheap spruce, the ratio would quickly have looked more favourable. Also relevant is the amount of work stored in the component in terms of embodied craft. Thus, reuse is financially worthwhile, especially for components with complex manufacturing processes, such as doors or windows, provided they are easy to salvage. Considerations such as these need to be taken into account when estimating the costs of reusing components.

Considered overall, reuse also affects the construction costs and financing ↗ p. 254 of the project: whereas in the conventional design and construction process, only design and approval costs are incurred up to the start of construction, for K.118, component costs of about 11 per cent of the construction costs had already accumulated during this time. The real design effort is also higher as a percentage of the total effort in the early project phases than provided for in the service model of SIA Order 102.[2] The effect is only relativized in the implementation phase, when the planning costs exceed that of a pure new build by about 15 per cent, similar to a conversion. In the case of K.118, that amounts to about 2 per cent of the construction costs. The client must therefore invest a considerable amount long before the construction permit is issued—over 60 per cent more than usual by the start of construction. In the end, the question posed at the beginning can nevertheless be answered with 'almost': at the component level, the reused components in the K.118 case study are on average cheaper than new ones. However, in the aggregate, additional expenses arise in the planning, and in the case of construction costs, 2–3 per cent savings due to rational construction methods are offset by the subsequent costs of reuse. That has to do not only with individual connection details but also with material residues that are difficult to calculate, and the lack of established processes and markets.

---

1 In view of strongly fluctuating steel prices, the result could have been more favourable at a different point in time.

2 SIA Order 102 regulating the services and fees of architects is published by the Swiss architects and engineers' association. It outlines the rights and obligations of all parties involved in the closing of a new contract for architectural services, lists an architect's duties, and contains a description of relevant services as well as a guideline to determine appropriate remuneration.

1 ↖ **p. 36**
K.118 reportage
Hunting and gathering
'Once the beams have been removed, something may go wrong in spite of the logistical planning: differently sized beams may get bundled together, which means that the packages are nearly impossible to handle. And that, in turn, means that the transportation costs go way up.'

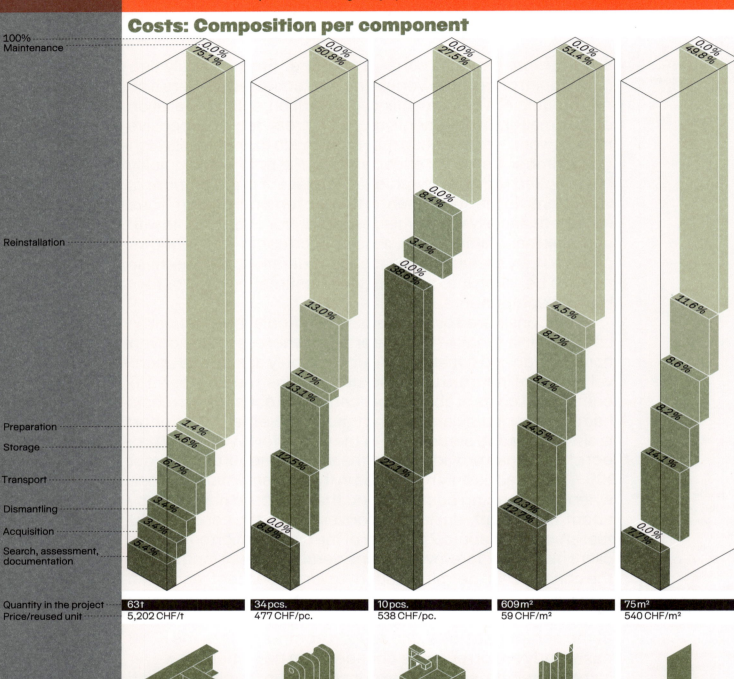

Costs: Composition per component

K.118 case study
Costs

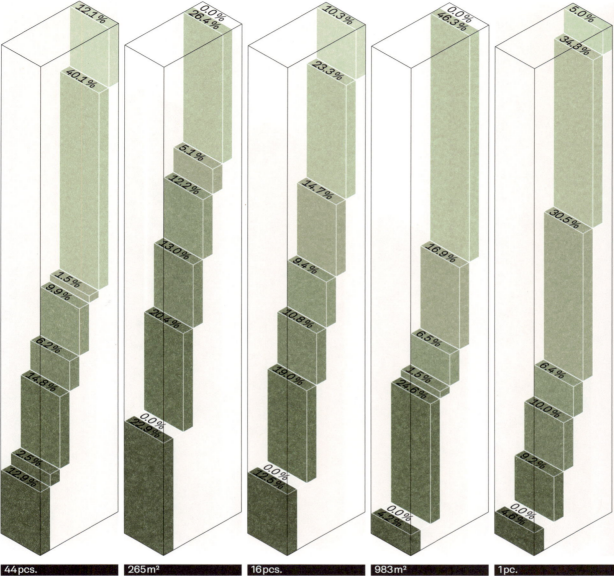

44 pcs.	265 m²	16 pcs.	983 m²	1 pc.
1,132 CHF/pc.	23 CHF/m²	1,051 CHF/pc.	124 CHF/m²	1,643 CHF/pc.

Orion window
Casement window with top light, aluminium frame, and triple glazing

Ziegler insulation board
120-mm-thick expanded polystyrene insulation board, double layer

Zellweger interior door
Single-leaf door with top light, steel frame with melamine-faced, solid timber leaf

Vogelsang floorboards
Spruce floorboards, 22 mm thick

Letzigraben letter boxes
12 compartments with aluminium letter and parcel boxes

Sources and methodology

All values are based on the K.118 project cost accounting and are stated exclusive of VAT. The values include all cost-relevant services of reuse: Search/assessment/documentation and coordination of all other services (architect's fee in accordance with component recovery contract ↖ **p. 244**), acquisition (purchase price), dismantling, transport, storage, preparation (cleaning, upgrading, and adaptations), and reinstallation. Costs for maintenance are taken into account, provided specially agreed warranties and maintenance work are included in the scope of services of the contracts with contractors. Not taken into account are any follow-up costs, which result from deviations of the component compared with new goods, e.g. in connection with other components.

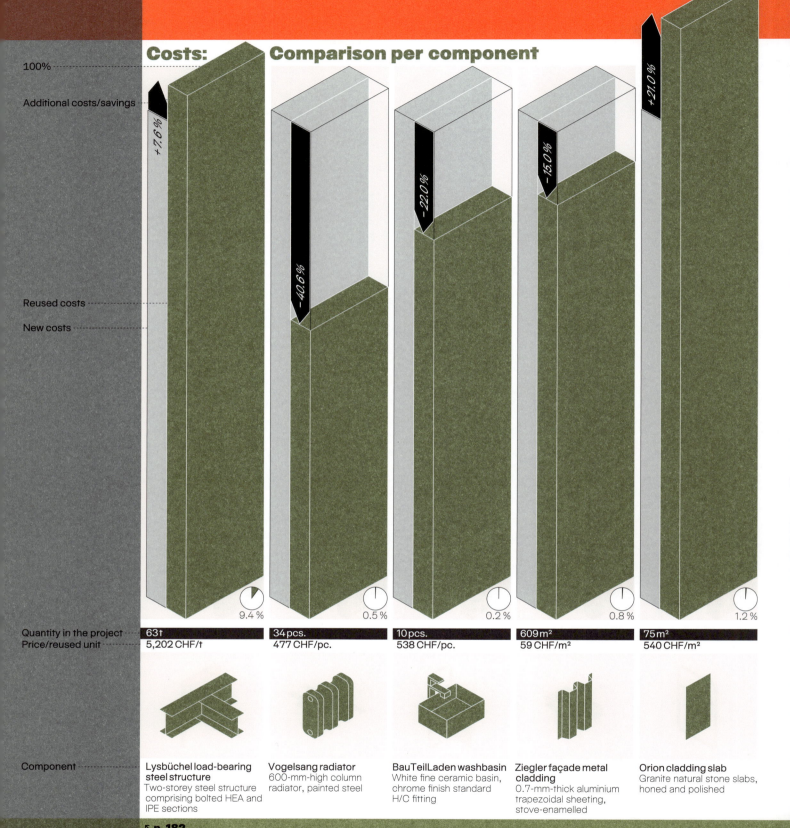

Costs: Comparison per component

100% — Additional costs/savings
Reused costs
New costs

+7.6% | −40.6% | −22.0% | −15.0% | +21.0%
9.4% | 0.5% | 0.2% | 0.8% | 1.2%

Quantity in the project: 63 t | 34 pcs. | 10 pcs. | 609 m² | 75 m²
Price/reused unit: 5,202 CHF/t | 477 CHF/pc. | 538 CHF/pc. | 59 CHF/m² | 540 CHF/m²

Component

Lysbüchel load-bearing steel structure
Two-storey steel structure comprising bolted HEA and IPE sections

Vogelsang radiator
600-mm-high column radiator, painted steel

BauTeilLaden washbasin
White fine ceramic basin, chrome finish standard H/C fitting

Ziegler façade metal cladding
0.7-mm-thick aluminium trapezoidal sheeting, stove-enamelled

Orion cladding slab
Granite natural stone slabs, honed and polished

↖ p. 182
Values and processes
Reuse from a developer perspective

'It's just that we've noticed that if a customer can choose between a new building component and a reused one, then, in the end, price is usually the deciding factor.'

252 253
K.118 case study
Costs

−41.4 %	−39.0 %	−54.8 %	+37.2 %	−61.3 %
1.4 %	0.4 %	0.5 %	3.5 %	0.0 %
44 pcs.	265 m²	16 pcs.	983 m²	1 pc.
1,132 CHF/pc.	23 CHF/m²	1,051 CHF/pc.	124 CHF/m²	1,643 CHF/pc.

Orion window
Casement window with top light, aluminium frame, and triple glazing

Ziegler insulation board
120-mm-thick expanded polystyrene insulation board, double layer

Zellweger interior door
Single-leaf door with top light, steel frame with melamine-faced, solid timber leaf

Vogelsang floorboards
Spruce floorboards, 22 mm thick

Letzigraben letter boxes
12 compartments with aluminium letter and parcel boxes

Sources and methodology

The 'Reused costs' values are based on the K.118 project cost accounting and are stated exclusive of VAT. Their build-up is explained on the preceding double page ↖ **p. 250 / 251**. In each case, the average of three values is recorded as the comparative value for an equivalent new component ('New costs'): the price of a component as similar as possible from the database of the Swiss Research Centre for Rationalization in Building and Civil Engineering CRB (status 10.2010/ 10.2019/04.2020, indexed in accordance with the Swiss Construction Cost Index 10.2019); the price of an equivalent new component in accordance with the quote provided by the contracted company (provisional item in all tenders), and the price of an equivalent new component in accordance with the comparative offer of a general contractor prepared for the evaluation.

In the case of components that have been installed divergently from their normal use, the comparative price was determined on the basis of a comparable standard design. Thus, the comparative price for the Orion cladding slabs used as balcony flooring refers to a cast stone element suitable for this purpose.

Relevance:
Share of the component in the construction costs according to eBKP-H*

* The component-based building construction-cost plan eBKP-H was developed by the CRB as an instrument for cost calculation, defined by Swiss norm SN 506 511 eBKP-H.

1 ↖ **p. 39**
K.118 reportage
Designing and joining
'Finding the material and the decision to use the metal sheeting come at an important time, making it possible to have the design of the façade ready for the planning application submission.'

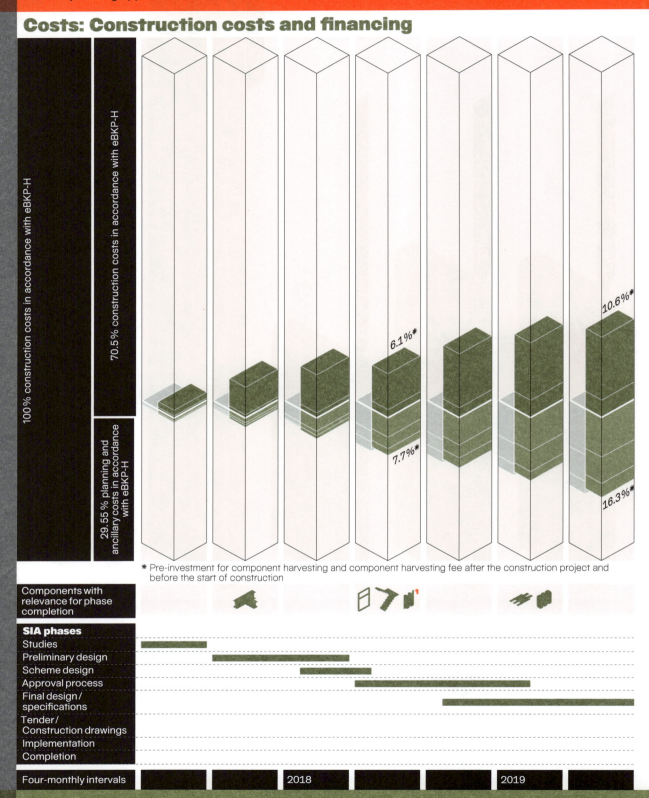

254 255
K.118 case study
Costs

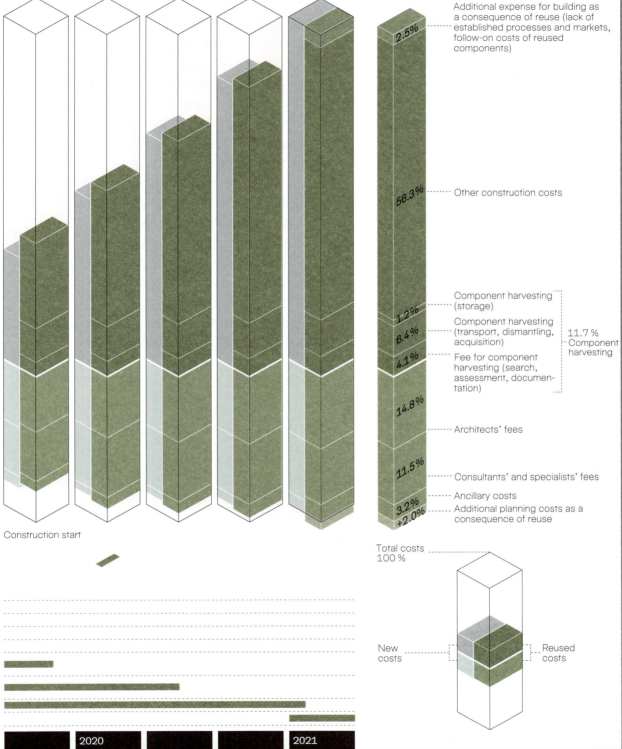

Sources and methodology

The values of 'Reused costs' are based on the construction cost accounting of the K.118 project, in accordance with the Swiss component-based building construction-cost plan eBKP-H. The chart shows the cumulative real construction costs of the K.118 project at four-monthly intervals compared with a hypothetical project using the same but new components. The planning and ancillary costs (eBKP-H V1, W) are shown below the x-axis; the construction costs (eBKP-H C, D, E, F, G) are shown above the x-axis.

The total cost of the K.118 project corresponds to the construction final account. Accordingly, the actual construction costs, including the follow-on costs for reuse, correspond quite closely to the comparative values. These are based on the pre-tender cost estimate calculated for the implementation of the K.118 project using new components. The cost trend from the start of construction is interpolated in the area above the x-axis. The area below the x-axis shows the partial services percentages in accordance with the service model of SIA Order 102.

Greenhouse gas emissions

As part of ZHAW's Circular Construction research project, the energy expert Katrin Pfäffli has investigated the energy consumption and greenhouse gas emissions associated with the creation of the K.118 project. Her June 2020 study 'Graue Energie und Treibhausgasemissionen von wiederverwendeten Bauteilen'[1] (Grey energy and greenhouse gas emissions of reused components) serves as the basis for the following investigation, which was supported methodologically by a workshop with the participation of Michael Pöll and Philipp Noger of the City of Zurich's Office for Sustainable Construction.[1] The following questions are thus of particular importance: what is the composition of greenhouse gas emissions for individual components? How big are the possible savings compared with new components? To what extent can the emission of greenhouse gases from construction be reduced through reuse if this is implemented as consistently as in the present case study? The sources and methodology of the investigation are explained with each graphic.

In the first step, the greenhouse gas emissions are analysed analogously to the economic study with regard to their composition per component ↗ p. 258. In order to provide as realistic a picture as possible, all services and processes ↖ p. 240 of reuse relevant to emissions were taken into account, including dismantling, transport, and preparation. This also includes transport from the interim storage facility to the construction site and reinstallation, processes which are usually neglected in the life cycle assessment according to SIA 2032.[2] A clear picture emerges: although all components originate within a maximum radius of 100 km, transport is key to the remaining greenhouse gas emissions. Dismantling and reinstallation are then only significant if heavy equipment is used, as in the case of the Lysbüchel load-bearing steel structure. On the other hand, preparation proves to have negligible effects for all the components under consideration.

The potential of reuse becomes obvious with the comparison per component ↗ p. 260 with the same but new parts. Even the transport within the stated radius is comparatively

1 Katrin Pfäffli, *Graue Energie und Treibhausgasemissionen von wiederverwendeten Bauteilen: Methodik und Berechnung in Varianten am Fallbeispiel Gebäude K118 in Winterthur*, ed. (ZHAW Institut Konstruktives Entwerfen / Stadt Zürich, Zurich, 2020).

2 The SIA 2032 information leaflet 'Graue Energie von Gebäuden' (Grey energy of buildings) is published by the Swiss architects and engineers' association. It regulates the balancing of ecological effects for the construction of buildings

1 ↖ p. 165
New paths toward net zero?
Potentials for climate protection

insignificant. Emissions are usually reduced more than 98 per cent, particularly if the manufacture requires thermal processes (e.g. the melting of metal or glass). The balance is somewhat less clear only with components whose handling during reuse requires the costly use of machinery, such as the Lysbüchel load-bearing steel structure, or those made from natural materials, whose manufacture hardly emits any greenhouse gases, e.g. the Vogelsang solid timber floorboards. Here, too, however, the savings are extremely high at about 90 per cent—reused components act as wild cards for the life cycle assessment.

Even if the values from a single case study cannot be generalized, the overall balance ↗ p. 262 of the K.118 case study does indicate the possible potential savings from reuse. Compared with a hypothetical building constructed from the same but new components, a total of 494 t CO_2eq are saved—i.e. about 59 per cent. The reused components are only responsible for about 6 t of the remaining 349 t of greenhouse gas emissions. If one considers the contributions of the various component groups to the savings, then, as expected, the load-bearing structure, windows and façade turn out to have lucrative potential savings. Overall, however, it is noticeable that the reductions of greenhouse gas emissions are not attributable to a few elements, but that it is the aggregate effect of many different elements that makes the difference.

The enormous potential of reused components for the reduction of greenhouse gases also casts the economic evaluation in a different light: If, when making the comparison per component ↗ p. 260, a realistic monetary value were attached to the CO_2eq savings shown, this would also significantly shift the cost per component in favour of reuse.[2]

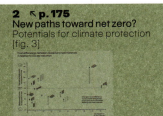

2 ↖ p. 175
New paths toward net zero?
Potentials for climate protection
[fig. 3]

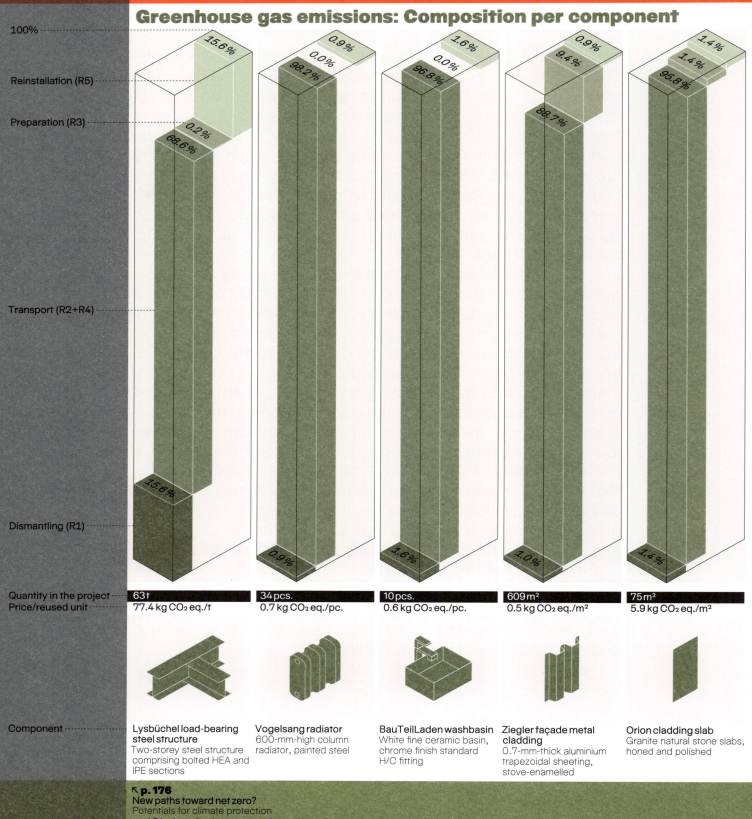

> **↖ p. 176**
> New paths toward net zero?
> Potentials for climate protection
>
> 'Obviously the costs of treating the components are a factor. However, it is a long way before this would negate the benefit of the savings in the construction. Even if you had spent three times as much effort in the preparation of K.118, you would still be in an excellent position, environmentally speaking.'

K.118 case study
Greenhouse gas emissions

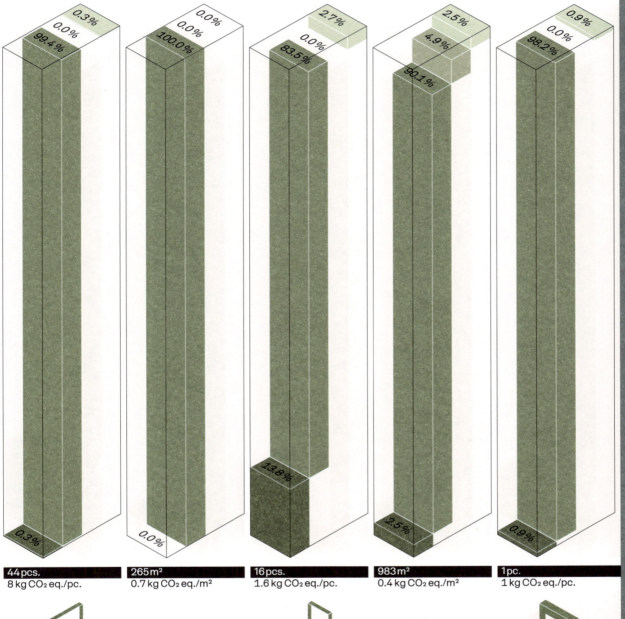

Orion window
Casement window with top light, aluminium frame, and triple glazing

Ziegler insulation board
120-mm-thick expanded polystyrene insulation board, double layer

Zellweger interior door
Single-leaf door with top light, steel frame with melamine-faced, solid timber leaf

Vogelsang floorboards
Spruce floorboards, 22 mm thick

Letzigraben letter boxes
12 compartments with aluminium letter and parcel boxes

Sources and methodology
All values are based on the June 2020 study: *Graue Energie und Treibhausgasemissionen von wiederverwendeten Bauteilen: Methodik und Berechnung in Varianten am Fallbeispiel Gebäude K118 in Winterthur*, carried out by Katrin Pfäffli (preisig:pfäffli) as part of the ZHAW Circular Construction research project, based on the SIA 2032 information leaflet *Graue Energie von Gebäuden* (Grey energy of buildings).

The values include all reuse services relevant to greenhouse gas emissions: Dismantling (R1), Transport (R2 + R4), Preparation (R3) and Reinstallation (R5). The graphic on ↖ **p. 10** shows the assignment of the services to the life cycle model SN EN 15804+A1 / SIA 490.052+A1.

Greenhouse gas emissions: Comparison per component

100%

Saving

New emissions:
Manufacture (A1, A2, A3, A4, A5)
Disposal (C1, C2, C3)

Reused emissions:
Reinstallation (R5)
Preparation (R3)
Transport (R2+R4)
Dismantling (R1)

−91.0 %	−98.0 %	−98.7 %	−98.6 %	−85.0 %
8.4 %	0.4 %	0.2 %	6.3 %	0.8 %

Quantity in the project
Price/reused unit

63 t	34 pcs.	10 pcs.	609 m²	75 m²
77.4 kg CO₂ eq./t	0.7 kg CO₂ eq./pc.	0.6 kg CO₂ eq./pc.	0.5 kg CO₂ eq./m²	5.9 kg CO₂ eq./m²

Component

Lysbüchel load-bearing steel structure
Two-storey steel structure comprising bolted HEA and IPE sections

Vogelsang radiator
600-mm-high column radiator, painted steel

BauTeilLaden washbasin
White fine ceramic basin, chrome finish standard H/C fitting

Ziegler façade metal cladding
0.7-mm-thick aluminium trapezoidal sheeting, stove-enamelled

Orion cladding slab
Granite natural stone slabs, honed and polished

↖ **p. 169**
New paths toward net zero?
Potentials for climate protection

'I generally get the best results when I substitute new components with high embodied energy values for used ones.'

K.118 case study
Greenhouse gas emissions

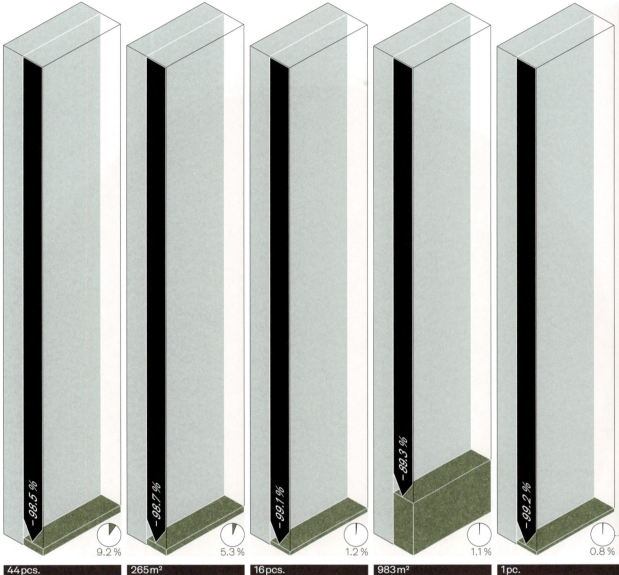

−98.5 %	−98.7 %	−99.1 %	−89.3 %	−99.2 %
9.2 %	5.3 %	1.2 %	1.1 %	0.8 %
44 pcs.	265 m²	16 pcs.	983 m²	1 pc.
8 kg CO₂ eq./pc.	0.7 kg CO₂ eq./m²	1.6 kg CO₂ eq./pc.	0.4 kg CO₂ eq./m²	1 kg CO₂ eq./pc.

Orion window
Casement window with top light, aluminium frame, and triple glazing

Ziegler insulation board
120-mm-thick expanded polystyrene insulation board, double layer

Zellweger interior door
Single-leaf door with top light, steel frame with melamine-faced, solid timber leaf

Vogelsang floorboards
Spruce floorboards, 22 mm thick

Letzigraben letter boxes
12 compartments with aluminium letter and parcel boxes

Sources and methodology

All values are based on the June 2020 study *Graue Energie und Treibhausgasemissionen von wiederverwendeten Bauteilen: Methodik und Berechnung in Varianten am Fallbeispiel Gebäude K.118 in Winterthur*, carried out by Katrin Pfäffli as part of the ZHAW Circular Construction research project, based on the SIA 2032 information leaflet *Graue Energie von Gebäuden* (Grey energy of buildings).

In order to compare the actual expenditure for the components of K.118 ↖ **p. 258/259** with values for new components, the services associated with reuse were compared with the life cycle model as per SN EN 15804+A1 / SIA 490.052+A1 ↖ **p. 10**. The comparative values for new components are based on the 2016 data set of the Swiss Coordination Conference of the Building and Property Bodies of the Public Building Owners (KBOB), plus the expenditure for phases A4 and A5, which is not considered in the KBOB data or set out in the SIA 2032 leaflet. Since there are no statistical values for these phases, the values determined for K.118 were used (A4=R4, A5=R5). They represent, on average, 50 per cent of the reused value of K.118 and 4 per cent of the new comparative value.

Share of the component in the total saving of CO₂ equivalents in the K.118 project, taking into account the service life as per the SIA 2032 leaflet: *Graue Energie von Gebäuden*.

Greenhouse gas emissions: Overall balance
Composition of the saved CO₂eq emissions

↖ **p. 166**
New paths toward net zero?
Potentials for climate protection

'The energy savings achieved here are hugely significant. They are particularly high in terms of the greenhouse gas emissions. I cannot think of any other strategies that would be similarly effective.'

K.118 case study
Greenhouse gas emissions

59% saved CO₂eq emissions

15.1% Existing building

21.4% Building construction
8.4% Lysbüchel load-bearing steel structure
4.5% Neomontana steel trapezoidal sheeting
4.5% Orion external staircase
3.2% Zellweger steel sections
0.8% Orion cladding slabs

18.5% Building services
13.5% Siemens photovoltaic system
0.4% Vogelsang radiators
2.7% Various heating installations
0.2% Washbasin component exchange
0.6% Various water installations
1.1% Ventilation ducts

30.7% Façade
9.2% Orion windows
5.0% Werk 1 windows
5.8% Other windows and external doors
6.3% Ziegler façade metal cladding
2.6% Façade construction
1.8% Façade insulation (straw)

7.3% Flat roof
5.3% Ziegler insulation board
2.0% 3-ply plywood ceiling boards

7.0% Building fit-out
1.1% Vogelsang floorboards
0.4% Other floor finishes
1.8% Eventbau marquee floor panels
1.2% Zellweger interior doors
2.5% Various internal partitions and doors

100% SAVING

59% 494 t CO₂eq Saving

100% 843 t CO₂eq TOTAL

1% 6 t CO₂eq Reused components

40% 343 t CO₂eq New components

K.118 | New comparison building

Sources and methodology

The method of calculation is based on the June 2020 study *Graue Energie und Treibhausgasemissionen von wiederverwendeten Bauteilen: Methodik und Berechnung in Varianten am Fallbeispiel Gebäude K118 in Winterthur*, carried out by Katrin Pfäffli (preisig: pfäffli) as part of the ZHAW Circular Construction research project, based on the SIA 2032 information leaflet *Graue Energie von Gebäuden* (Grey energy of buildings).

Left-hand graphic: shows the proportions of different component groups (according to element-based construction cost plan eBKP-H.) in the savings of CO₂eq achieved in the K.118 project, taking into account their service life according to the information leaflet SIA 2032 (Annex C).

Right-hand graphic: the K.118 project is compared with a hypothetical, conventionally constructed new build. Reclaimed and reused building components are replaced, like for like, with new elements, the straw insulation of the façade is replaced by mineral wool insulation with the same insulation value. The carbon footprint has been calculated in accordance with the information leaflet SIA 2032, i.e. without the expenditure for the construction phase in accordance with SN EN 15804+A1 / SIA 490.052+A1 (variant 2b of the study by K. Pfäffli), which is normally excluded there.

Eight theses

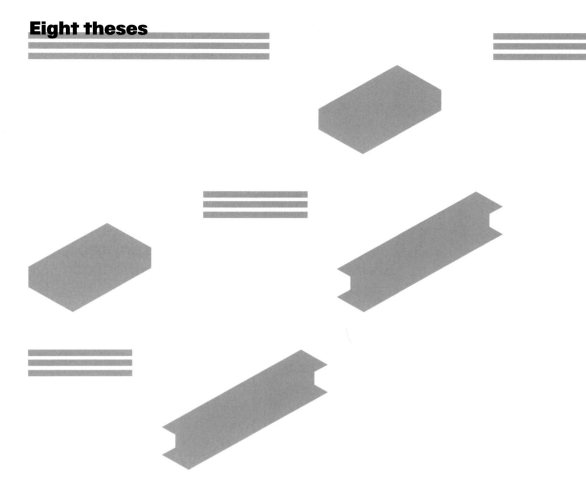

1

Reuse makes it possible to align the building process with the pursuit of sufficiency. Continuously escalating demands unnecessarily curtail the service life of our buildings and lead to enormous wear and tear. Throwaway building culture fails to recognize not only the finiteness of our resources but also the seriousness of the climate crisis.

Challenging the demands

Barbara Buser

Cultivating an architectural approach in line with thesis eight means that, for every building project, thought must be given to whether an intervention makes sense and what the consequences will be from a holistic point of view in terms of energy and material. It is crucial to know whether a built solution is sensible and unavoidable or whether a perceived physical problem can be resolved through organizational means or by scrutinizing the need. Given the urgency of the climate crisis, the question of what criteria should govern interventions has clear priority and has already been laid down in principle in waste and construction product law: preserve and reuse first, before then turning to replacement and recycling. Preservation, in particular, demands that we question certainties. Which means reducing and doing without. Technical and regulatory requirements, along with renewal rates spurred by fashions, habits of use, expectations of perfection, and cheap money, ignore the actual material and qualitative service life of our built fabric and fuel an immense waste of resources and energy. We have it in our hands to resist the seductive logic of 'ever better, faster, and more' and the unrestricted availability of resources, raw materials, and technology. The profusion of cheap options is the only thing that casts the act of embracing sufficiency in a negative light. And yet the familiar durability and adaptability of well-built houses is actually testimony to the fact that their service life can easily reach the 60 years we currently assume several times over, and that preserving and continuing to use what already exists, as well as reducing demand to the essentials, has, first of all, a liberating effect and can be viewed positively. Thus, the most important lever for creating change is in our minds. This is illustrated by the insights gained by Ellen MacArthur on her circumnavigation of the globe, when she radically confronted the concept of finiteness and sufficiency. This led her to devote herself to promoting the circular economy, whose overriding principle is to prolong the service life of things through maintenance. Yet even the reuse of building components can at best simply reduce waste. The resulting insight not only allows sufficiency to be understood as a fourth principle of architecture, but actually necessitates this.

2

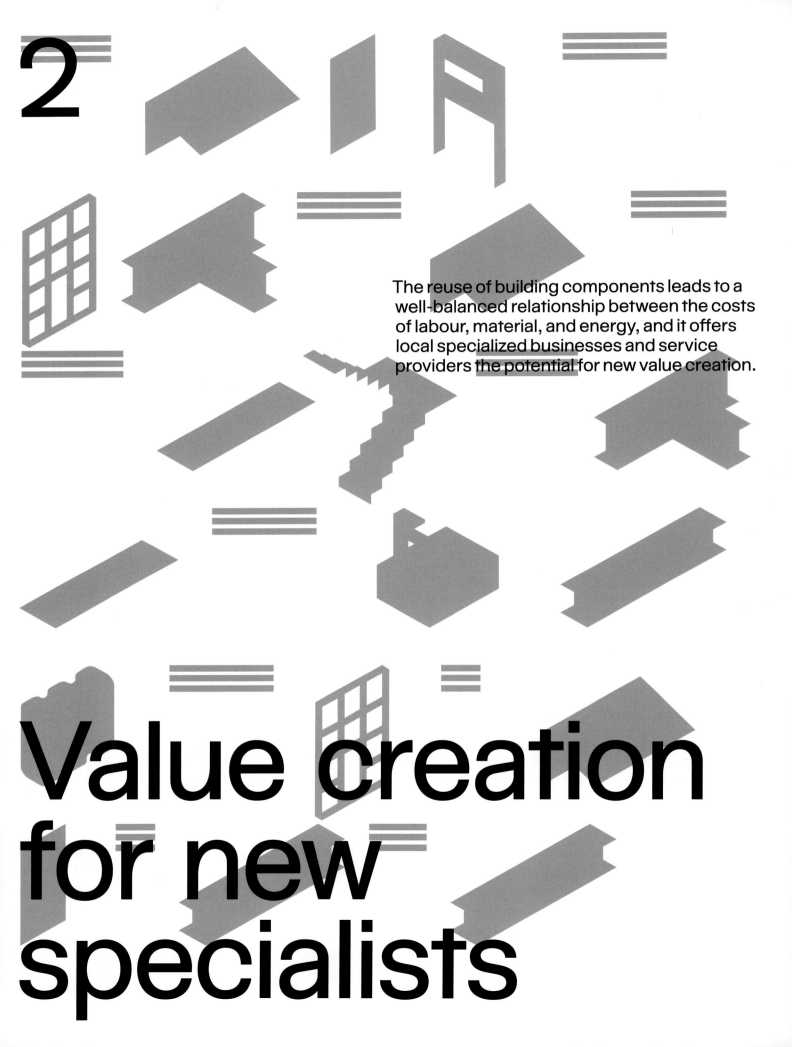

The reuse of building components leads to a well-balanced relationship between the costs of labour, material, and energy, and it offers local specialized businesses and service providers the potential for new value creation.

Value creation for new specialists

Andreas Oefner

If we compare current levels of building component reuse in Switzerland with those in Europe, it is striking that in Belgium, for example, both the number of companies and the range of materials involved are much greater. The promotion of supplier directories is, on its own, indicative of the market's importance there, even though it must still be considered a niche sector. The reason for its marginalization here in Switzerland, apart from a distrust of used goods that stems from prosperity and orderliness, is that Swiss wage levels are noticeably higher—meaning that material and energy costs, as well as disposal costs, are low in relation to wages. At present, it remains profitable to throw away building parts that are still serviceable and, instead of reusing them, produce new components for construction projects—which is wasteful and has a negative impact on the climate. This throwaway building culture not only fails to recognize that the costs of new production, with all its internalized environmental and climate damage, are actually many times higher than when building components are reused, it also ignores the fact that raw materials and landfill space are a finite commodity that will become more expensive as scarcity increases. Even today, choosing reuse over new products does not necessarily involve additional costs, despite high wages. If elements produced in a labour-intensive and technically advanced manner can be efficiently refurbished and put back into use, costs can be reduced even further. Not least thanks to the high quality and durability of the products used in this country, reuse is seldom a problem from a technical point of view, and early disposal is fundamentally antithetical to the proud local tradition of craftsmanship, design, and quality, which it negates. Incentive taxes and emission limits on greenhouse gases and environmental factors will probably help make reuse more competitive in the future. Today, the economic potential is already becoming apparent: components no longer have to be produced using large amounts of energy and resources, and long transport routes can be avoided. Further, (dis)assembly skills and component expertise are in demand along with a knowledge of materials and construction supporting the assessment, refurbishment, and distribution of high-quality material. Costs are shifting from international industrial sectors to new, local value chains where regional skilled trade firms accumulate the know-how to reclaim components from urban sources, logistics experts ensure expedient transport routes, and an emerging group of specialists support the process through to reinstallation and warranty coverage. This has resulted in the persistent utilization of high-quality reused and reusable components, local value creation, and an environmental and material footprint that is vastly superior to that of the throwaway building culture.

3

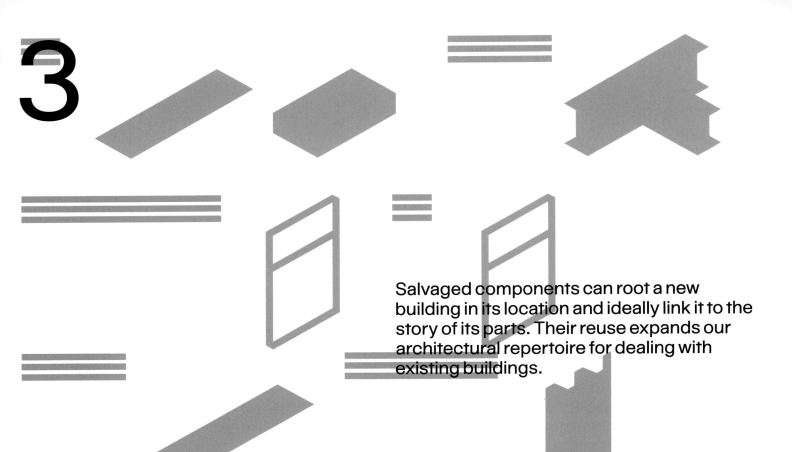

Salvaged components can root a new building in its location and ideally link it to the story of its parts. Their reuse expands our architectural repertoire for dealing with existing buildings.

Inherited identity

Eva Stricker

Building components not only store embodied energy, they also harbour memories—of craft skills and expertise, of social values and customs, of the history and purpose of the places for which they were once made.

The atmospheric richness of buildings, neighbourhoods, and cities that have developed over time is fed by the sediments of their architectural history. Medieval dwellings encode the labyrinthine alleyways of the old town onto the ancient Palace of Diocletian in Split. The Great Mosque of Córdoba grew from fragments of ancient temples before the Christian basilica interjected itself into its centre. Even today, what we build usually has a background history, making it a part and expression of social and economic transformations: granular garden cities are densified, and industrial wastelands and infrastructural sites within city centres are converted into residential and business districts. The spatial and narrative power that can be unleashed by preserving and appropriating the existing is something we experience every day inside the hall that was originally built as a boiler manufacturing site for the Sulzer company and now houses our school of architecture. ↖ **p. 52** [fig. 5]

When dealing with the existing fabric, the reuse of building components offers the potential to add nuances that enrich the preservation spectrum. Between heritage-conscious conservation, adaptive reuse, and total replacement, history can still live on in distinct parts, even when structures of mixed quality or drastic typological changes require new construction. Continuity and renewal are not mutually exclusive, as demonstrated by ZHAW students' designs for a school building on the Neugasse site in Zurich. The existing infrastructure buildings inspire solutions that range from sensitively fitting the programme within the existing spaces to inventing new school building types that use the constraints of the components found on site to develop not just atmospherically rich spaces but also a distinctive identity anchored in the place. ↗ **p. 332**

Of course, when new structures are being built, there are also other architectural ways to draw on the history of the site and to paraphrase what previously existed. The reuse of tangible parts, however, thrives on the immediacy of a verbatim quotation. Their physical and haptic qualities make the past perceptible to the senses. The genius loci gains an ally: the 'genius partis'.

4 Diversity of building methods

If one considers not only the production and assembly of building parts but also their previous history and possible future, the question of the sustainability and salience of building methods is posed anew for every place and every project.

Guido Brandi

If calculation of the embodied energy of a component takes into account not only the effort required for production and disposal but above all its potential for (multiple) reuse, then versatility and adaptability become key criteria. Indeed, a steel beam can be longer lasting and more sustainable than a glulam beam bonded together with polyurethane adhesive from pieces of wood of dubious origin. The K.118 building is a perfect example of this. A construction method that seems exotic at first glance—a steel frame with composite concrete slabs and a straw-insulated, unitized timber façade with aluminium sheet cladding—suddenly makes sense in light of the origin and reuse of its components. If the same aluminium sheet for the façade were new, then its use would not be ecologically sensible. The fact that it is salvaged from a nearby property slated for demolition means that its lifespan is extended and the need to manufacture new cladding is eliminated. Aluminium's devastating environmental footprint as a building material is not due to its intrinsic properties but to our inability to use it to its full potential: in perpetuity.

This paradigm shift means that natural mines are now being joined by new, artificial 'mines': our cities and settlements. Each building becomes a potential reservoir of building components and local construction processes that can be rediscovered and reused. A city can become 'vernacular' again. And in this case, 'vernacular' means using and rediscovering locally available materials and systems of construction.

The challenge for every architect is to interpret this new architecture while keeping one fundamental concept in mind: a component's sustainability is dependent on its cycles of reuse.

The extension of each building component's service life and its continuous reuse can become the motor behind a new architectural language that has yet to be discovered, in which the expression of a building is determined first and foremost not by the choice of construction method or structural system but rather by the type of building components found on site. The construction method goes from being a basic principle to a result.

5

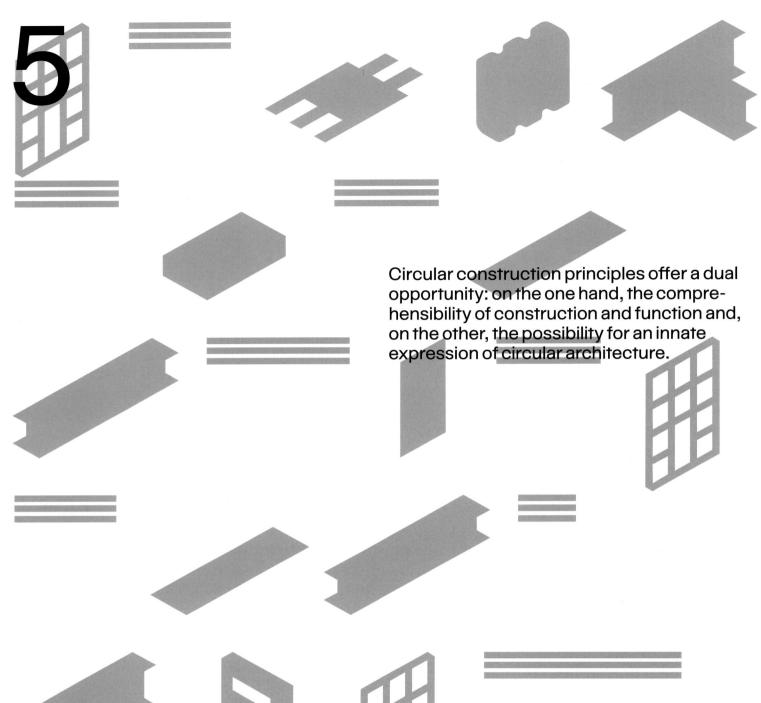

Circular construction principles offer a dual opportunity: on the one hand, the comprehensibility of construction and function and, on the other, the possibility for an innate expression of circular architecture.

Comprehensible constructions

Marc Loeliger

In his four-volume study *Die Tektonik der Hellenen*, published from 1844 to 1852 (translated by Harry Francis Mallgrave as *Greek Tectonics*), Karl Bötticher speaks of the core-form (the structure) and the art-form ('the artistic dressing applied to the core-form, symbolizing in effect its ... structural function'). Might the call for circular construction allow internal structure and manifest architecture to converge again?

In today's building sector, means of construction are becoming more complex due to increasing structural requirements and regulatory density. Whereas the composition of a wall was understandable in the past even to laypeople, today's common multilayered façade constructions are barely comprehensible even to experts. Making connections as invisible as possible by using concealed anchors or adhesives and applying foam to fix items in place renders it impossible to understand the tectonics of the parts, and ever more complex building installations can barely be grasped any more. The goal of reusing building components presupposes that elements are joined in a comprehensible way and can be disassembled. The aspirations of circular construction thus lead directly to intrinsic designs that counteract our increasing alienation from the built environment: structural elements that rest on top of one another, composite materials that can be disassembled, and self-explanatory connection details make the composition and tectonics of the components easier to understand. Repairable and upgradeable, visibly routed utility lines and comprehensibly configured technical installations allow one to understand how our 'machines for living' work.

However, the principle of separating systems should not be seen merely as the technically correct assembly of puzzle-like components. Peter Zumthor's pavilion for Expo 2000 ↖ **p. 28** [fig. 31] boasts an intrinsic expression through its narratively showcased logic of assembly. The airy way in which the timber elements are stacked and their fastening with steel cables and oversized springs are understood primarily as a design principle. Thus, what is at issue is not a dogmatic insistence on 'truthfulness' of construction but rather a new, narrative form of architectural rendition in Bötticher's terms, and consequently an intrinsic architectural language of circular architecture.

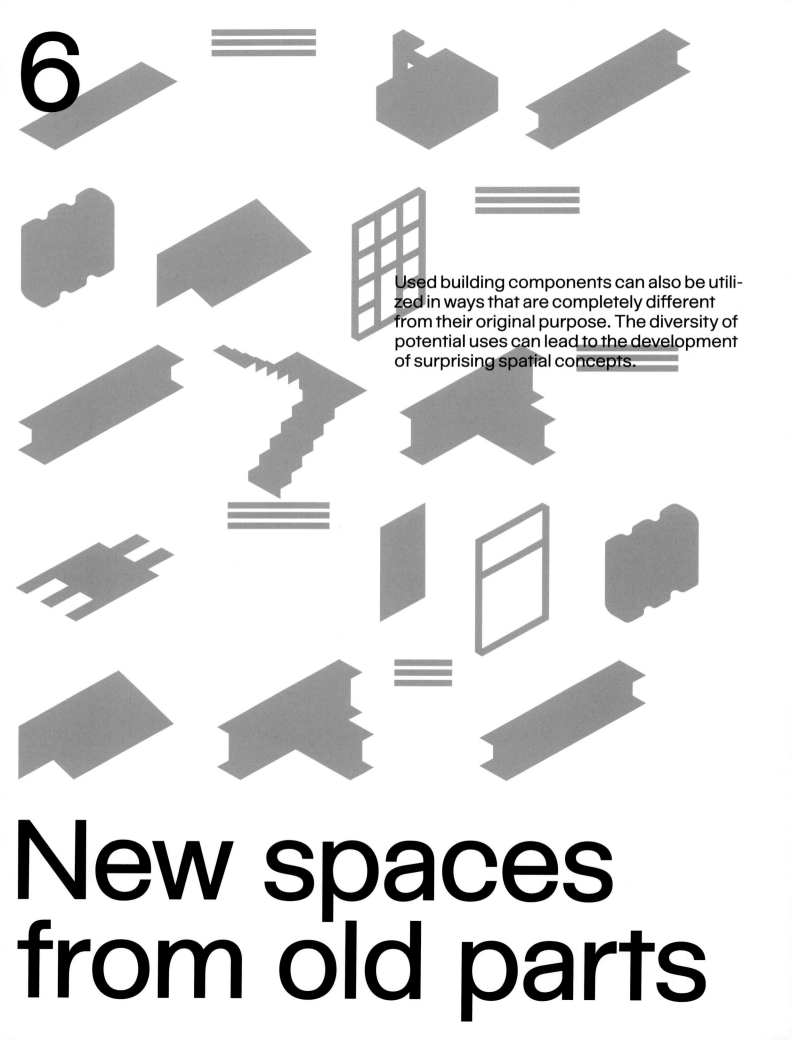

6
New spaces from old parts

Used building components can also be utilized in ways that are completely different from their original purpose. The diversity of potential uses can lead to the development of surprising spatial concepts.

Andreas Sonderegger

The bones of mammoths as load-bearing structures: this happened during the last Ice Age, when Neolithic hunters used these strange building parts as load-bearing structures for their huts in the treeless plains of Eastern Europe. These structures are echoed by the unexpected potentials that ZHAW students found for building components salvaged from the demolition of industrial and commercial shed buildings. Steel components once intended for heavy loads and large spans were now available in substantial quantities for straightforward design tasks. This convenient opportunity not only spurred invention but also facilitated unexpectedly lavish solutions. In light of the prosaic goal of cutting back on embodied energy, in some cases the solutions seem downright luxurious. The treasures gained from dismantling seduce us into material and spatial opulence—but given the alternatives made of new materials, this 'sin' can still be accepted with a clear conscience.

The spatial potentials of the unfamiliar building materials become evident in, for example, residential construction. Steel beams conceived to span industrial halls automatically yield generous room heights when used for the floors of residential buildings. The height of the girders, in and of itself, has an exciting spatial impact, whether as articulation of the ceiling or as a split residential level. The haptic qualities of the salvaged industrial materials and the direct perceptibility of the load-bearing structure, of interior fit-out, and technical installations enrich the housing ambiance and make the apartments transparent and spacious—loft living in an environmentally exemplary new building!

Opulence can also be rooted in the deficiencies of building physics. Salvaged windows, with all their shortcomings, can be combined into box-type double windows that meet today's legal requirements. Analogously, the same windows are used for unheated buffer layers to create an intermediate climate that can be used as a vestibule. But there is also the opportunity, at virtually no cost and beyond the scope of the programme, to gain architecturally and spatially engaging additional spaces—verandas, bay windows, winter gardens, and so forth—which can ideally become lively places of encounter and exchange.

Deindustrialization and the concomitant disruption of the building stock offer a finite, potentially rapidly diminishing source of raw materials for building component reuse in this country. However, the experimental spirit these building materials unleash today can surely be transferred to entirely different areas of circular construction.

7

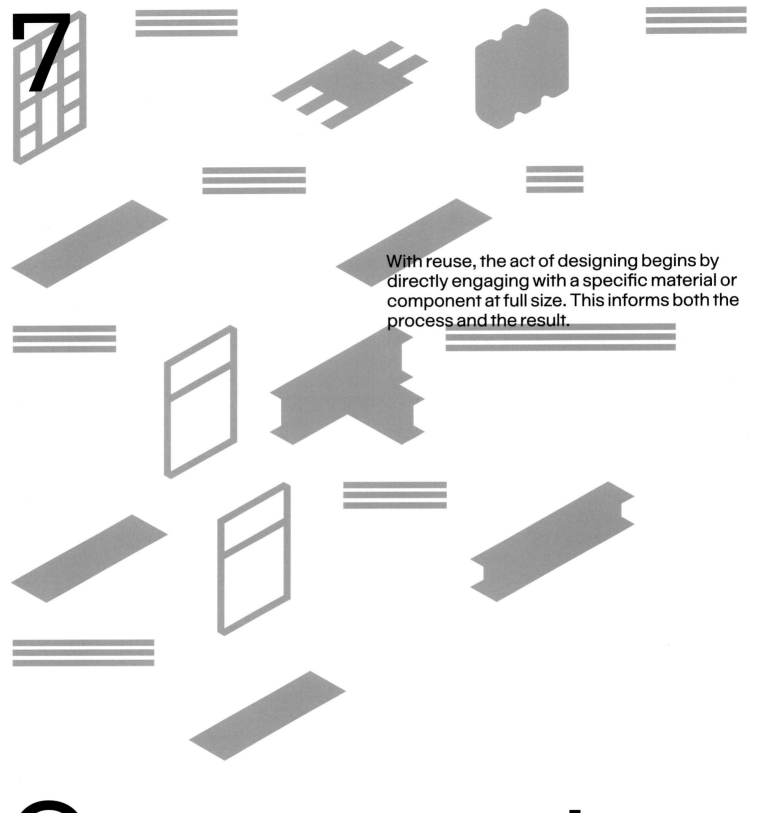

With reuse, the act of designing begins by directly engaging with a specific material or component at full size. This informs both the process and the result.

Component-
driven design

Alexis Ringli

For centuries, economics meant that the reuse of building components was a matter of course. Downgraded in industrial construction processes to a negligible presence, this practice has, for ecological reasons, taken on new and existential importance today. Circular construction methods enable the retention of stored energy and thereby sustainably reduce CO_2 emissions in the construction process. Conserving energy has become the top priority and must be taken into account over the long term. For us architects, this poses a challenge when dealing with reclaimed building parts—namely, to cultivate working methods and design processes that lead us to an intrinsic architectural expression.

The direct approach to reuse, once developed at the level of manual craft by master builders and carpenters, can serve us as an example. What traditional handicraft is to the carpenter, adept manipulation of construction is to the architect. The path to development of an intrinsic language for circular architecture requires that architects engage with the building components intended for reuse. It takes careful examination and interpretation of what is given, the 'found' component, to reveal hidden and random qualities of salvaged parts and to establish latitude to implement conceived space and atmospheric ideas as built structure and architectural image. By skilfully adapting, supplementing, and assembling building components—old and new—surprising, expressive architecture can be created. Environmental and economic needs are best met when necessary adjustments are kept to a minimum. This supposed restriction can be countered perfectly well—as initial designs show—with a painstaking search for potential in what already exists and with intelligent strategies. The 'functionally identical' use of a component should be distinguished from its 'interpreted' use. Whereas the former generally ensures easy continued use, the latter, with its greater design freedom, can never completely rule out the risk of constructive error. Circular construction poses a new challenge for architects, as it entails guaranteeing architectural quality while maintaining a favourable ecological balance. The design approach to engaging with the component is both the starting point and an opportunity for success.

8

When all that will be used is what is already there, finding becomes a key task and the result becomes a narrative of materials that are appropriate and locally available only at that exact moment.

Sampling and serendipity

Marc Angst

In the words of Claude Lévi-Strauss, this is 'the contingent result of all the occasions there have been'. The 'universe of instruments is closed and the rules of [the] game are always to make do with "whatever is at hand".' Form follows availability. By no means should we regard this as a hopeless constraint, but rather as an inspiring creative task and a hopeful alternative to the way we design and build. Spoilt by all that is always available everywhere around us and that which is newly devised for every imaginable purpose, we are caught up all too often in the dogmas of a modernity that continually presents us with the separation of new and old, of necessary and useless. We would do well to rely more courageously on the power of narratives that reveal to us a real reason for hope and a path towards other designs for life, as Ursula K. Le Guin (1929–2018) pointed out. An expression of this kind of confidence has been cultivated for some years now by the sci-fi genre 'solarpunk', to which Le Guin's work is assigned. It contradicts the fiction of eternal growth and unfettered technologies by exploring a kind of design space that accords a self-evident role to careful reuse. Narratives can help us in two ways: through the narrative of its origin and original function, the salvaged component loses its imperfection and gains a new identity, while the patina ('as found') reflects the impact of time on the material and literally manifests its durability. In lieu of a creative imperative, the narrative of the design process conveys the curatorial dialogue between what is already there, what is to be added, and what is actually available. Component by component, this iterative sampling follows a recurrent pattern of finding, evaluating the parts themselves and their suitability for the intended use, weighing alternatives, and ultimately deciding to incorporate specific elements or consciously forgo them. In this way, the art of combining comes to mean more than just the literal sum of disparate parts—and creativity helps overcome the resistance of those parts, which at first may not appear to fit the sum. Through robustness and the breakdown of dependencies, assembly must also ensure that the project that has been conceived does not collapse because of unsuitable building parts added at a later stage in the process. More than ever, reusing means being able to also imagine something else.

Andreas Sonderegger

Reuse in construction—a look ahead

As we often remind ourselves, our participation in this research and book project has fundamentally changed the way we think (we, all working architects with our own practice, teaching and researching at the ZHAW, who have contributed to this publication). Once more, we find ourselves rudely awakened from our modernist dream, underpinned as it was by the assumption that an endless reservoir of raw materials and cheap energy existed to create architecture. The oil crisis of the 1970s may have shaken the construction industry, but evidently not hard enough. In recent decades, reducing energy consumption used in the heating and operation of buildings has been a key focus for architectural practitioners and a driver of construction industry development, but now attention is finally turning to grey energy.

The abundance of cheap, predominantly fossil-based fuels has, for many decades, led us to severely neglect the importance of grey energy, the energy involved in the making of all industrial products and, in particularly large quantities, in the production of buildings. Now, though, we are beginning to realize the extent to which industrialization has devalued the manufacture of building components and materials, not only in financial terms but also in terms of their physical qualities and the associated resource and energy requirements. As that realization grows, we are increasingly coming back round to the pre-industrial master builder's view of construction, in which the work behind every single component, behind specific forms and finishes, was recognized and celebrated. These individual, mostly handcrafted components were appreciated as artefacts that encapsulated human endeavour

The ruins of Dresden's Church of the Holy Cross, as painted by Bernardo Bellotto in 1765. After its destruction in the Seven Years' War, the ruined medieval church was dismantled; the foundation walls of its replacement are visible in the foreground. The building has been destroyed five times over the course of its history, most recently during the Second World War.

and skill. In a sense, reusing building components or exploring such reuse, in conjunction with the thoughtful consideration and selection of appropriate parts, allows us to regain that way of seeing. We find ourselves in a very different and finite world, in which loss and destruction also have to be factored in, even with processes characterized by careful change. So what lessons for the future can we learn from our years spent examining this subject? Below I shall attempt to outline three key conclusions.

**Building with reused components:
Drivers and barriers**

Just a few years ago, the reuse of building components would have foundered on real-world practicalities but, suddenly, this new and still-unfamiliar practice seems a genuine possibility. It fits well with the digital age. It's only thanks to digital technology that we are now able to rapidly document building parts and details of existing buildings, to catalogue their components and efficiently administer and use the vast volumes of data that arise. That capability means we will need actors with the appropriate skills: tomorrow's planners will thus be digital natives who are well versed in handling such data, using it creatively, and turning it into 3D models.

The creative possibilities of building with reused components are incredibly varied, despite the prejudices some might have. Realizing those possibilities would perhaps result in a different kind of architecture, but it certainly wouldn't make architecture a poorer discipline. On the contrary, the constraints inherent in this new way of working seem to inspire inventiveness, as the divergent design proposals developed by our own students show. Even a narrowly defined design task drawing on the same pool of building components can, it seems, produce a surprisingly broad range of conceptual and constructional approaches.

Encouragement can also be found in the legal situation of building with reused components, which, in Switzerland at least, is remarkably clear on matters of liability law, product warranties, and so on. There are, on the other hand, a surprisingly large number of other practical obstacles that have to be overcome in the actual building process. What would be prudent in terms of material use—and urgently necessary in terms of energy footprint—encounters an ill-equipped construction practice which is not prepared to deal with such an approach. Throughout construction and planning, processes need to be completely rethought and reorganized. When building with reused components, you also quickly encounter difficult financial questions: who will shoulder the additional early-stage planning, logistics, and warehousing costs? And who should bear the associated risks?

The domestic market for reclaimed building components is small and, despite some progress, developing at a slow pace. But in countries where numerous suppliers in reclaimed parts do exist (Belgium, for example), it is notable that the components offered and their reuse contexts have mainly related to the building envelope and fit-out. For much of the fabric of existing buildings, on the other hand, the potential for reusing components remains limited. The solid primary structures that make up their bulk are particularly difficult to deconstruct without destroying them, hence these are instead broken down into their raw materials and recycled. Timber and steel structures are better suited to reuse, as are internal fixtures and fittings, but only if their constructive connections can be dismantled without damage, which is often not the case.

When you consider the obstacles to building with reused components, it's hard not to feel even greater respect for the practice's pioneers. Often those pioneers are planners, builders, and clients in one. If, however, the non-philanthropically minded are to also embrace reuse, then regulatory incentives will inevitably be required. More urgent still is the need for a new mindset among all construction industry actors. It's perhaps no surprise to find a property market behemoth such as the SBB, Switzerland's national rail operator, inventorying its entire infrastructure and building stock in order to optimize utilization; after all, for many of its facilities, reuse makes economic sense too. But it's among architecture practitioners that a mental shift is most urgently required.

In 2021, a competition for Stiftung Habitat's Lysbüchel Süd project in Basel saw Loeliger Strub's proposal chosen as the winning entry. Their design for a mixed residential and commercial block will reuse building components and materials (such as wooden ceiling beams, roof tiles as façade, and window shutters) that were salvaged during the redevelopment of a housing association estate (Libellenhof in Lucerne, planned by the same practice).

Architects need to learn to adopt what you might call an 'autophagous' approach, autophagy being the process in which the body recycles parts of its own cells. After all, who could be better placed to notice when viable components for reuse become available than those devising replacement buildings? And why, when a site is being redeveloped, is it not routine for material from torn-down buildings to be reused in their replacements? If such questions were given serious consideration, architectural practice would soon feature modes of operation that are dramatically different from those we see today.

The value of existing buildings

Transporting building components for reuse from the demolition site to a storage facility and then on to the construction site is often complicated and expensive; it also requires a lot of energy. Our master's class on on-site reuse attempted to get around this logistical problem, asking students to find ways to use components from a dismantled building (a railway depot) directly in its replacement (a new primary school). Not unexpectedly, the results illustrated once again that the most efficient way of reusing building components is to avoid demolition in the first place and instead convert and repurpose existing structures. A large proportion of a building's embodied energy is stored in its primary structure. That alone should motivate us to take a more considered approach to existing buildings.

As urban areas have been densified in recent years, it has become almost a matter of course to replace existing buildings with new builds, a process in which valuable building structures, affordable living space, and much embodied energy has often been unthinkingly destroyed. But what if we saw new buildings as an intelligent exception and not simply the rule? Obsolete building stock would then no longer be regarded as an obstacle to overcome, but instead form the basis for redevelopment. Alongside ecological and economical considerations, there are also social and cultural reasons why it makes sense to value the existing structures. Rather than developing new 'low-cost' housing, it would be better to use the housing already available to us for longer, while ensuring neighbouring new buildings are constructed to a high standard of quality and with a high longevity based on environmentally sound design. Moving forward, greater emphasis will be placed on the preservation of existing buildings, something that can no longer be simply dismissed as the hobby horse of heritage conservation bodies and enthusiasts but will, in future, also find favour for entirely rational environmental and financial reasons.

New criteria for structural design

To what extent will tomorrow's buildings feature reused components? The aforementioned issues surrounding the way our existing buildings are constructed mean it's hard to say for sure. Let us then at least draw inspiration from these issues for today's new constructions and factor in one more criterion when designing sustainable buildings, namely the future reusability of their components. For that to be guaranteed, structural design needs to incorporate reversible connections, modular design and easily disassembled components from the start.

Given that so much grey energy is contained within load-bearing structures, the latter need to be slimmed down as far as possible. With many methods of construction, however, disassembly is either hard or simply impossible to implement. In such cases, it is all the more important that structures are flexible or adaptable enough to facilitate future repurposing and that their various systems are easily separable. The system of slabs and columns Le Corbusier developed for his Maison Dom-Ino skeleton frame more than a century ago seems, in this context, remarkably ahead of its time.

If we are going to make tomorrow's buildings more reversible and flexible, will they also then be significantly lighter and make more efficient use of materials? This at least should be the aim, even if conflicts between contradictory objectives are not so easily overcome. Take noise insulation requirements within apartment blocks, for instance, or the much-discussed heat storage capacity of buildings: these are both factors that entail increased mass.

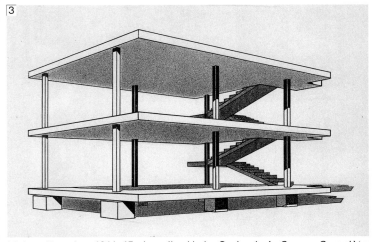

3 Maison Dom-Ino, 1914–15, described in Le Corbusier's *Oeuvre Complète*: "L'ossature 'Dom-ino' étant portante, ces murs ou ces cloisons pouvaient être en n'importe quels matériaux et tout particulièrement en matériaux de mauvais choix, tels que pierres calcinées par les incendies, ou des agglomérés faits avec les déchets des ruines de la guerre, etc. etc."

Here, too, norms driven by excessively high expectations of comfort and safety should be reassessed to ensure they are also environmentally compatible and reasonable. Professional associations and politicians thus need to take action to redefine standards and laws; in view of the competing interests at play, it is imperative that a more frugal approach to our finite resources is finally given due regard.

Creating K.118

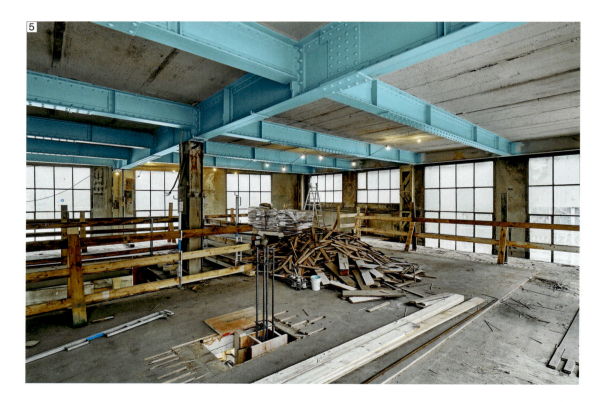

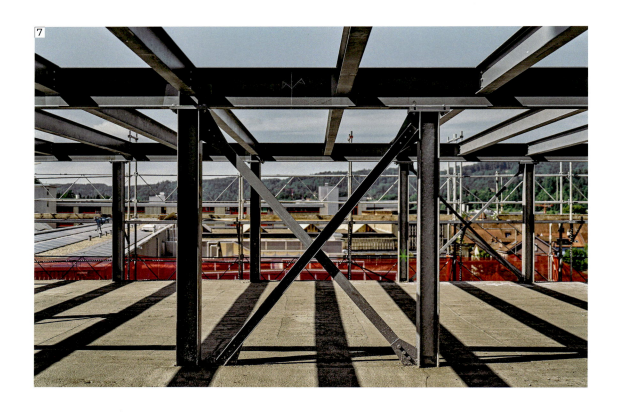

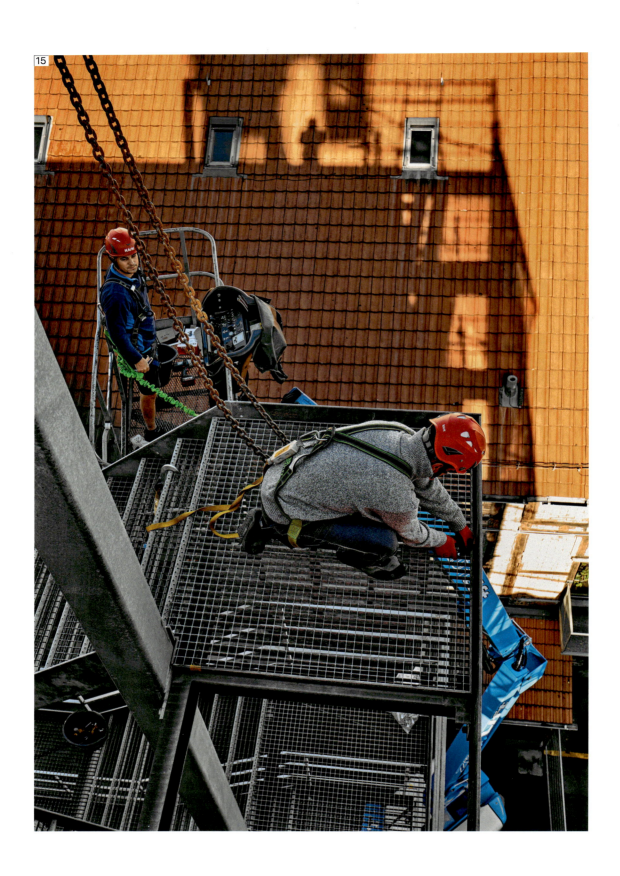

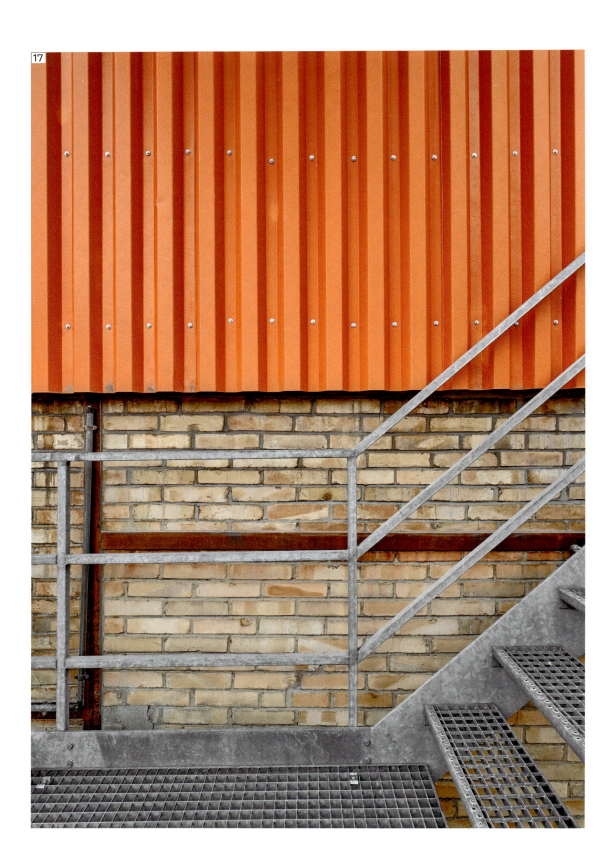

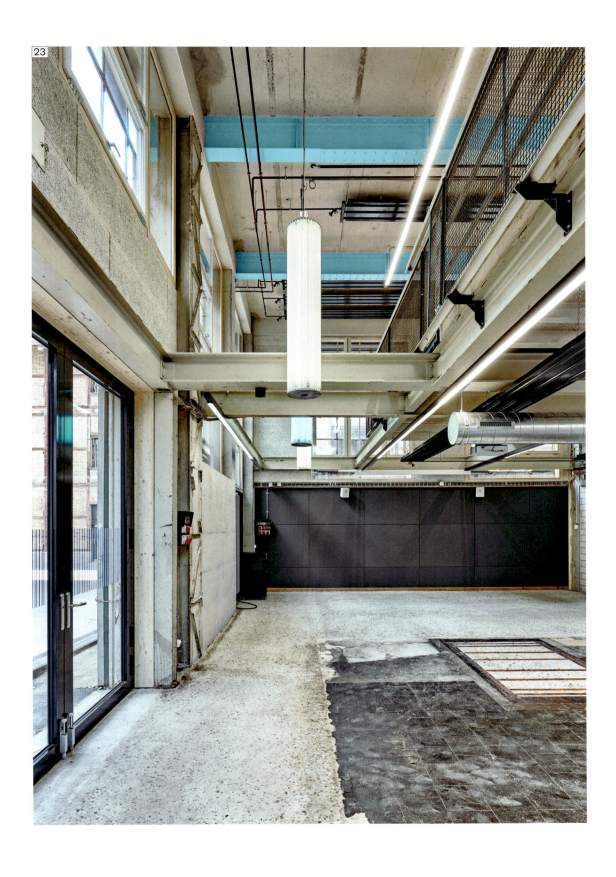

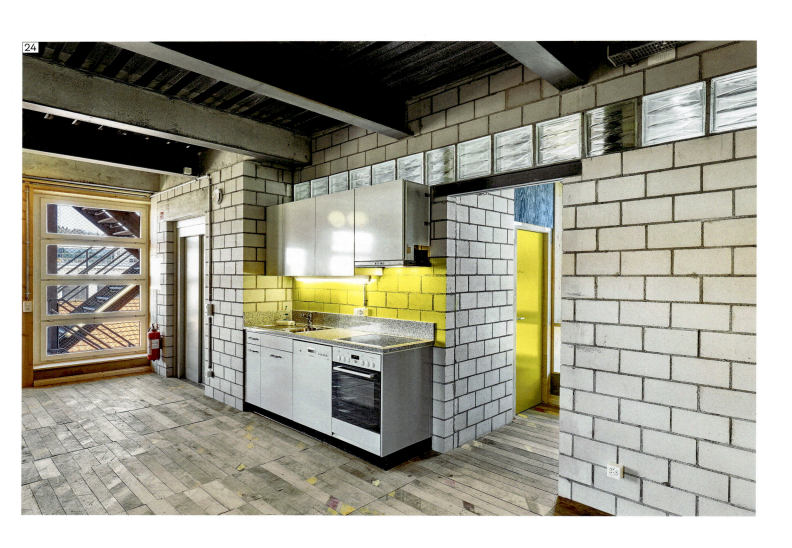

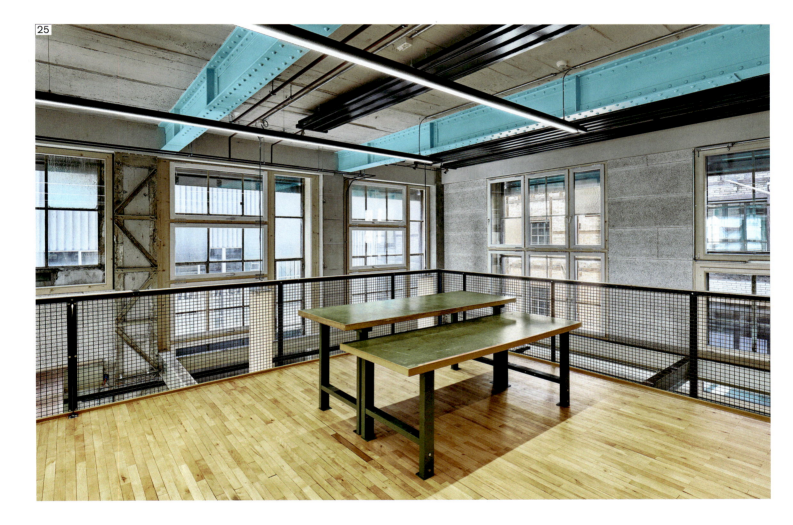

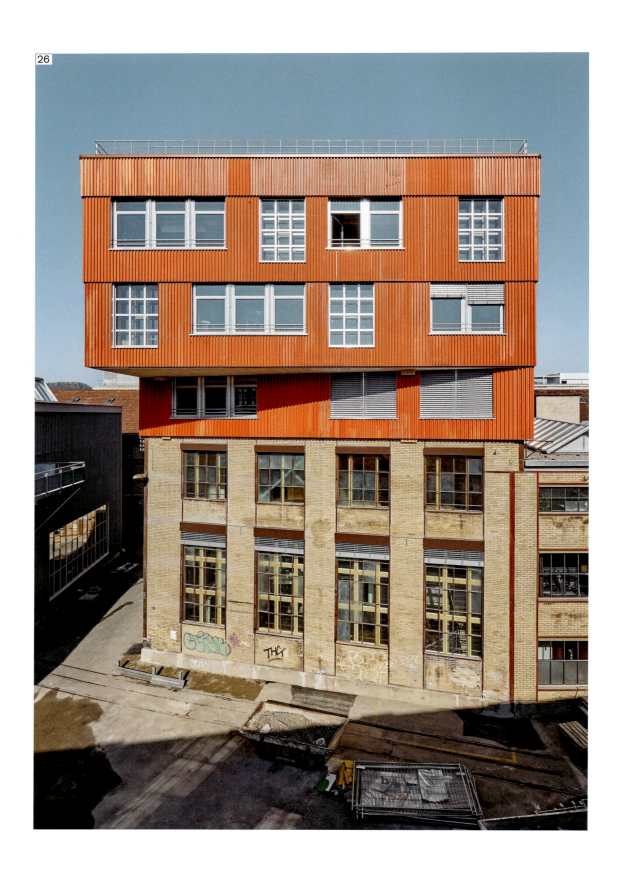

Creating K.118

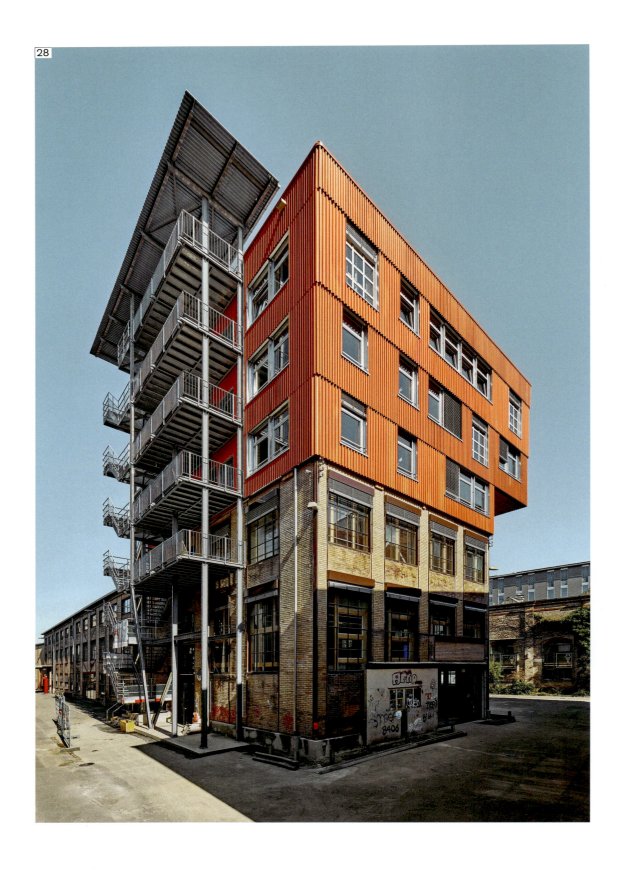
28

K.118 plan set

Designing for reuse means planning for possible scenarios. The two sketches show how the design of K.118 was changed and finalized as a result of the found components. The architects' initial sketch (below, left) visualizes the volume of the building based on the general conditions and constraints of the project. The façade of the existing building, consisting of panels of 120-mm-deep bricks set in iron frames, is to be retained. Three to four new floors can be built on top of this, the materiality of which is purposefully left open at this stage. The external stairs are already anticipated in this first sketch. It is only when the salvaged staircase is discovered that it becomes a reality and even adopts one of the urban design principles of the Lagerplatz. The various components needed for this vertical extension are highlighted or indicated with the first finds from the neighbouring Werk 1 project.

Using lists, the component hunters set out to find suitable building components. They found a suitable steel structure, windows, doors, and a staircase tower, granite slabs, sheets of metal cladding, etc. Every find opened up new possibilities, although some were rejected. What remain are the three storeys of the vertical extension and the external staircase. It was originally one floor higher than needed and has become an observation tower. Horizontal bands of trapezoidal metal sheeting mark the floors on the façade, into which various windows are 'hung'. Fortunately, the red colour fits in perfectly with the colour palette of the old Sulzer Areal industrial estate. If it hadn't been found, it would have to have been designed!

The steel frame oversails the trapezoidal plan of the existing hall. It has not been modified but now forms an overhang. The available meets the discoverable. This is illustrated by the difference in colours in the following drawings: 'Form follows availability.'

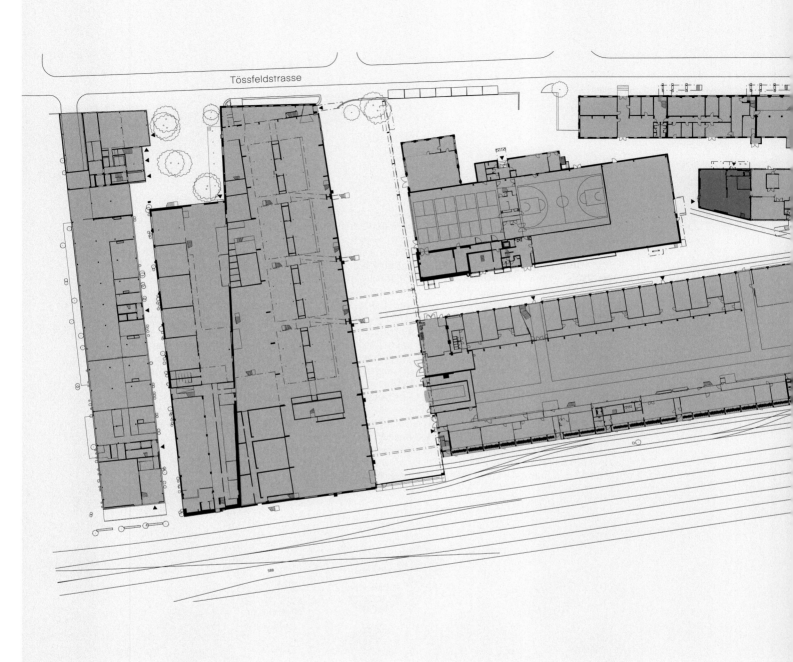

Site plan, Lagerplatz

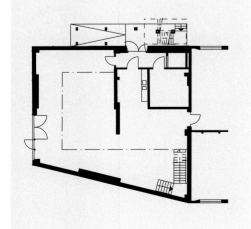

Floor plans: Ground floor

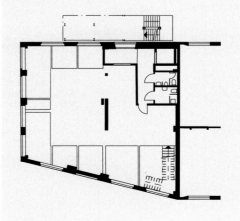

Gallery level

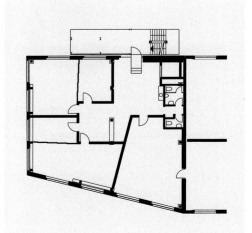

1st floor

K.118 plan set

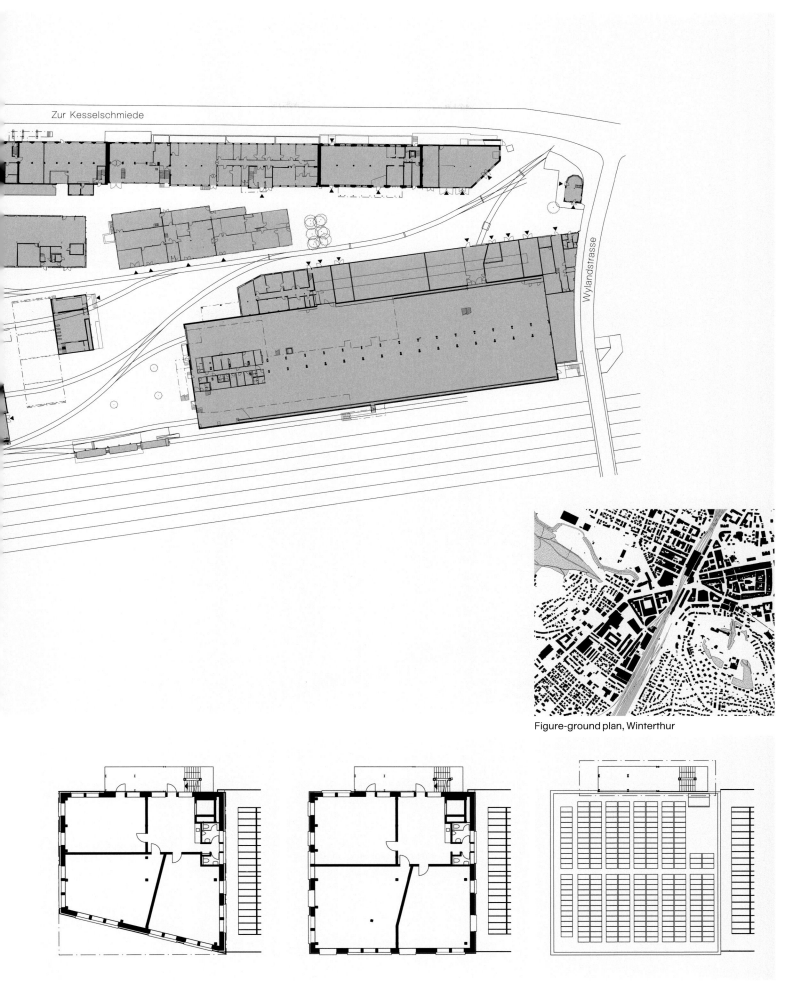

Figure-ground plan, Winterthur

2nd floor   3rd/4th floor   Roof

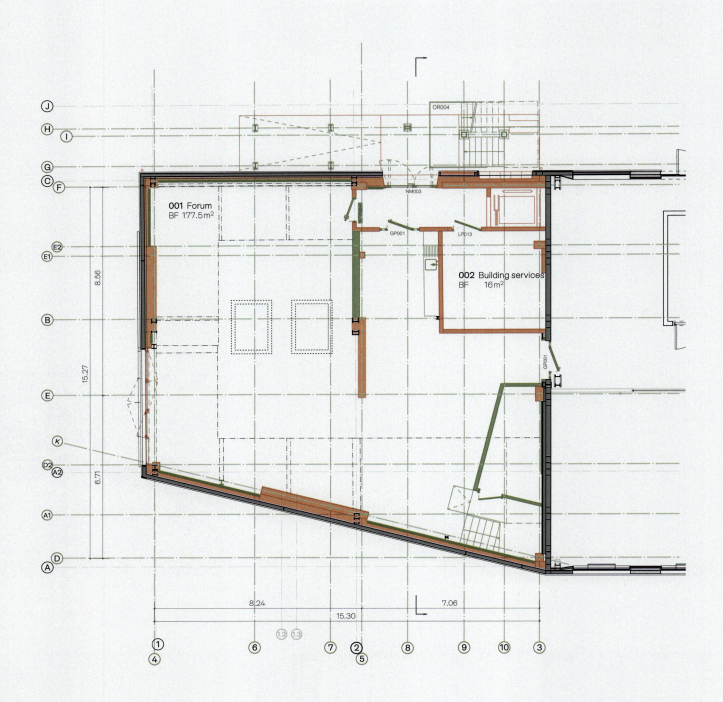

Ground-floor plan

K.118 plan set

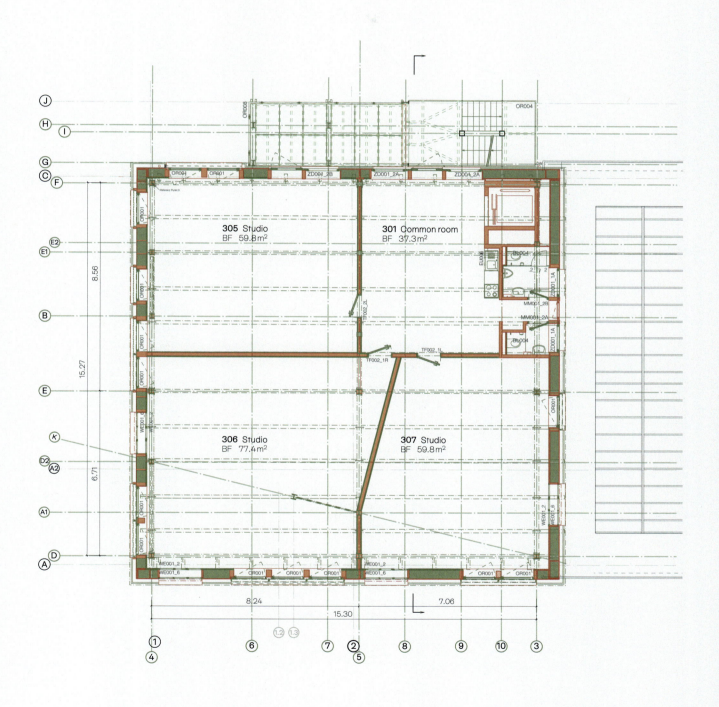

3rd-/4th-floor plan

South-west elevation

K.118 plan set

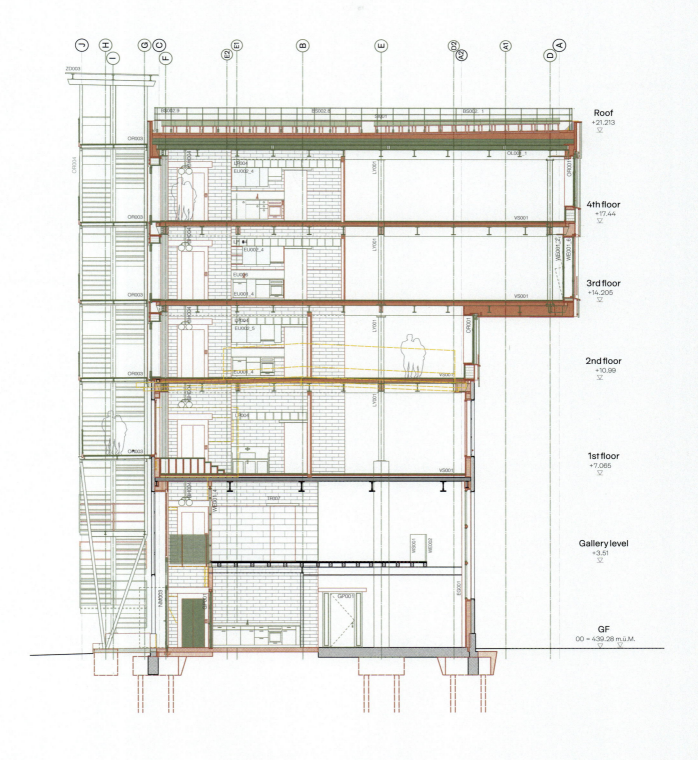

Cross section

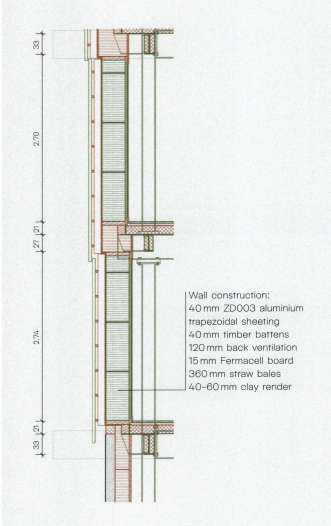
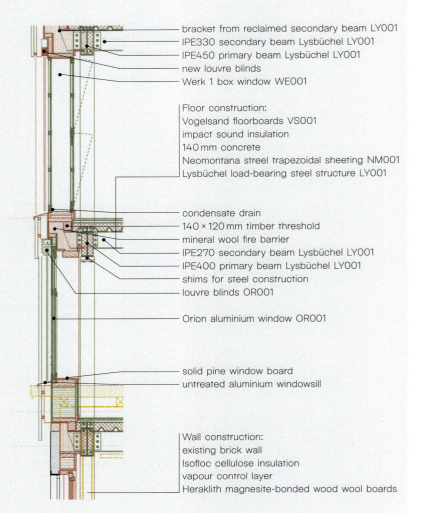

Vertical sections through the façade

K.118 plan set

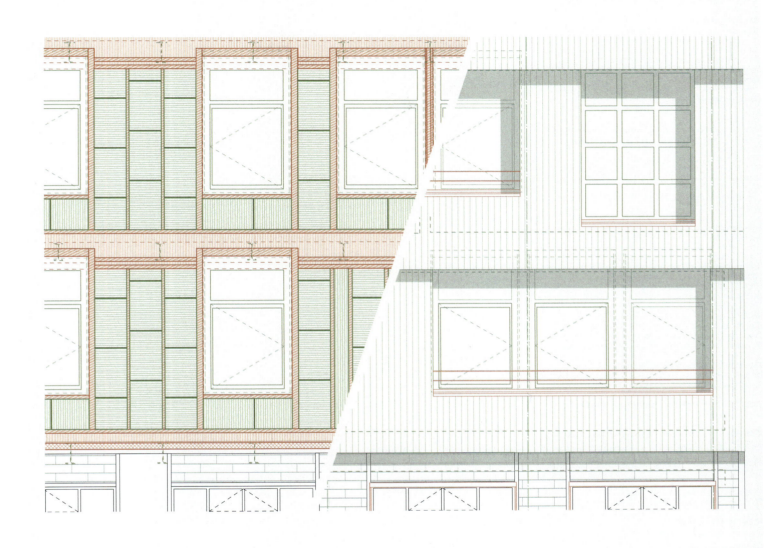

Façade elevation unclad/clad　　　　　　　　　　　　　　2.5 m

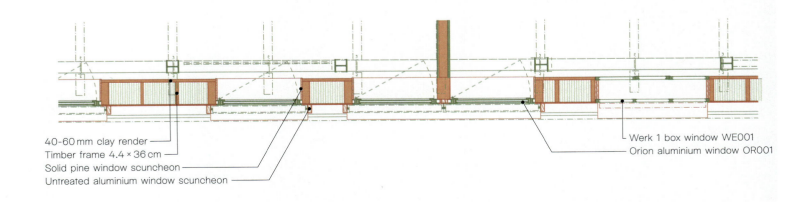

40–60 mm clay render
Timber frame 4.4 × 36 cm
Solid pine window scuncheon
Untreated aluminium window scuncheon

Werk 1 box window WE001
Orion aluminium window OR001

Horizontal section through façade　　　　　　　　　　　　2.5 m

K.118 plan set

K.118—Head-end building Hall 118
Address: Lagerplatz 24, 8400 Winterthur

Building owner
Stiftung Abendrot, Güterstrasse 133, 4053 Basel

Architecture
baubüro in situ ag, Hohlstrasse 400, 8048 Zurich,
Pascal Hentschel and Marc Angst with
Benjamin Poignon, Michèle Brand, Kerstin Müller,
and Barbara Buser as well as Fabian Kuonen,
Nina Hsu, Geraldine Clausen, Michèle Toboll,
Jan Bauer, Laia Meier

Consultants
Structural engineer: Oberli Ingenieurbüro AG, Winterthur
Timber engineering: Josef Kolb AG, Winterthur
Building engineering physics: 3D Bauphysik Huth GmbH, Glashütten
Acoustics: Raumanzug GmbH, Zurich
Fire protection: ProteQ GmbH, Schaffhausen
Building services: Russo Haustechnik-Planung GmbH, Winterthur
Electrical design: EGO Elektriker Genossenschaft, Winterthur

Implementation
Main contractor: BWT AG, Winterthur
Steelwork, structural frame: Wetter AG, Stetten
Timber construction, façades, and interior design: Zehnder Holzbau, Winterthur
Cladding, metalwork: Ninger AG, Rikon
Flat roofs: Zasag AG, Eglisau
Metal windows and doors: Geilinger AG, Winterhur
Heating: Staub Heizungen AG, Steckborn
Plumbing: Markus Steimer, Winterthur
Electrical system: Elpag AG, Winterthur
Decorations and clay renders: Malerei Wülser & Partner GmbH and Ralph Künzler, Winterthur

Design and implementation
baubüro in situ ag, with Pasquale Baumanagement, Zurich, and Valérie Waibel Architect, Winterthur

Total construction cost (incl. VAT)
CHF 5.28 m

Building volume according to SIA 416
5,809 m^3

Floor area according to SIA 416
1,534 m^2 gross / 1,168 m^2 main usable

Energy standard
SIA 2040 energy efficiency path

Heat generation
District heating

Project timeline
Design and component hunt: Summer 2017 onwards
Building application: Autumn 2018
Construction start: Summer 2019
Occupation: Spring 2021

ZHAW IKE: Teaching

Lagerplatz Master's studio 'Readymade—building with found objects', spring semester 2018 • Lecturers: Marc Loeliger and Andreas Sonderegger • Researcher: Eva Stricker

The collaboration between ZHAW and baubüro in situ began with this architectural design semester. Without knowing anything about the real project, the entire class were given the same brief as baubüro in situ: to add floors to the head-end building K.118 on the Lagerplatz site in Winthertur, in the immediate vicinity of the school of architecture. The ZHAW design assignment was also based on the same catalogue of salvaged components for K.118 as baubüro in situ had used. Everyone was surprised by the variety of work produced, which was hardly to be expected, given the common starting point. A nice beginning to the research project.

Neugasse site Master's studio on 'Component recycling on-site' and constructive research, autumn semester 2019 • Lecturers: Alain Roserens, Marc Loeliger, and Alexis Ringli • Researchers: Eva Stricker and Guido Brandi

After the first design semester, the task was modified: how does the reuse of building components work on-site when buildings are approved for demolition? The project partner SBB (the Swiss rail operator) was also interested in this issue. The construction task—a primary school building in Zurich on the site of the former Neugasse SBB depot—is aligned with the planned reality. As part of the research course, the students looked at how to create component catalogues. The environmental and design potential of component reuse on-site is obvious.

Lagerplatz: Projects

Trellis
Sean Schättin

The inspiration for this project was Jules Saulnier's Menier chocolate factory in Noisiel, built in 1872, a pioneering work of steel-frame construction. A network of steel beams encompasses the vertical extension. As in the historic model, the exposed, almost decorative, steel diamond shape serves as both a constructional and design element. The two-tone granite slabs once clad the Orion office buildings in Zurich—two buildings from the 1980s which were only granted a brief lifespan.

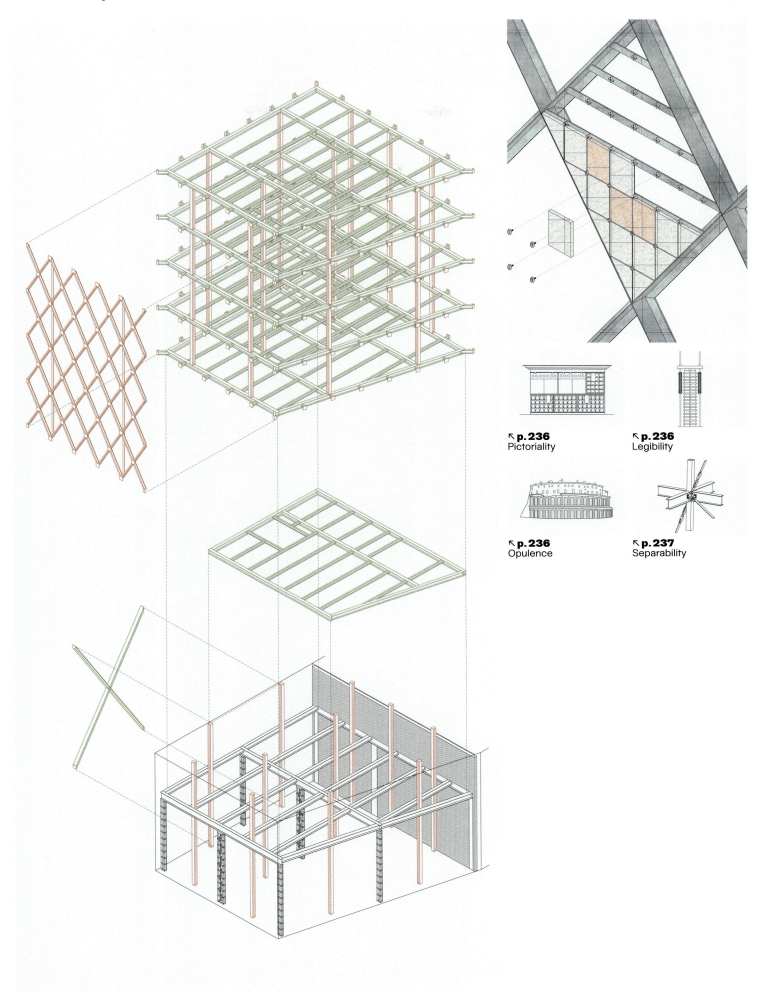

↖ **p. 236**
Pictoriality

↖ **p. 236**
Legibility

↖ **p. 236**
Opulence

↖ **p. 237**
Separability

Lagerplatz: Projects

Residential silo
Selina Putzi

A strong geometric form proves to be a robust framework for the use of foreign, in this case mostly reused, building components. From the outside, the existing top-heavy, octagonal building has an industrial look, reminiscent of the photographic portraits of gas tanks from the Ruhr area by Bernd and Hilla Becher. The inner life of the project is revealed as a surprising contrast to this. Consistently following the idea of reusing building components, spatially varied interiors are developed that have an almost bourgeois, homely character.

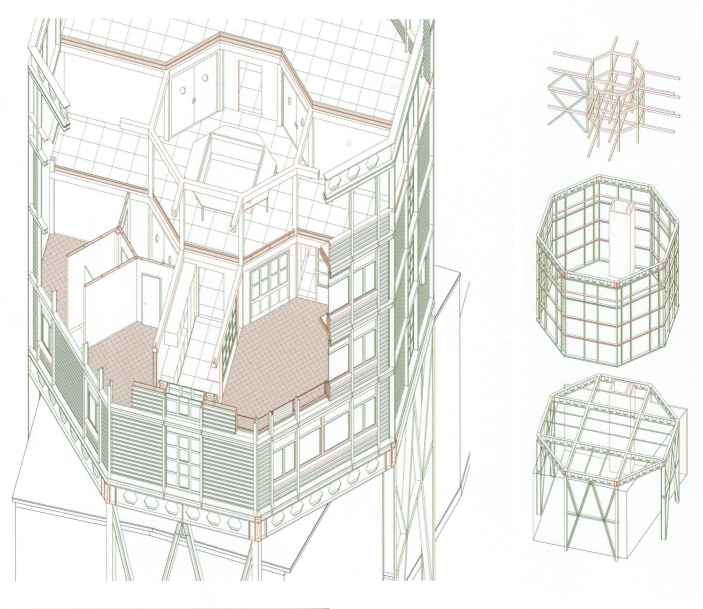

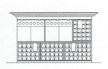

↖ **p. 236**
Pictoriality

↖ **p. 236**
Composition

↖ **p. 237**
Recoding

↖ **p. 237**
Transfer

Industrial living
Steffano Crameri

Thanks to the reuse of parts from industrial buildings, the non-neighbourhood residential use is seamlessly integrated into the industrial Sulzer Areal site. The existing hall is spanned on two floors by exposed steel trusses. This results in a variety of potential spatial possibilities, in both the floors with trusses and the intermediate, column-free residential floor. The building components are combined in a kind of bricolage to emphasize the specific atmospheres of the spaces. The individual constructional elements remain clearly legible and appear almost like staged objects.

ZHAW IKE: Teaching

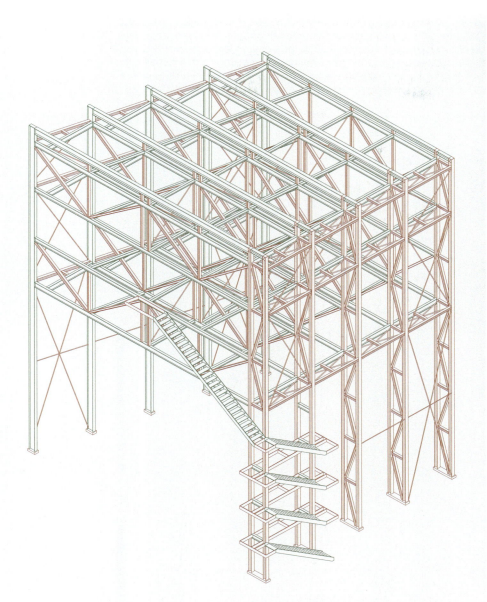

↖ **p. 237**
Reconfiguration

↖ **p. 237**
Transformation

↖ **p. 236**
Oversizing

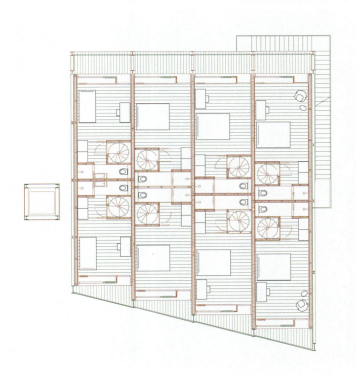

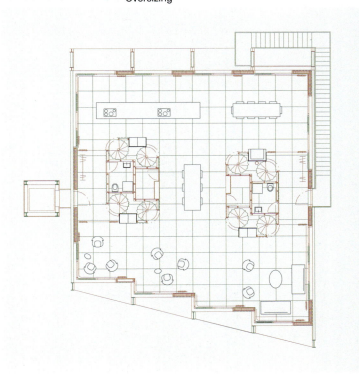

Lantern
Nina Röthlin

A minimal load-bearing structure provides a framework for an atmospheric collage of reused parts which, in their new function and sometimes daring compositions, are surprisingly appealing. The structural frame of existing steel trusses divides the building into two-storey units. The south elevation is characterized by projecting balconies, which hang from the massive roof beams with slim steel sections. Internally, the necessary fire-resistant cladding of the steel beams is refined into a decorative element—using salvaged red granite slabs as linings.

↖ **p. 236**
Composition

↖ **p. 237**
Recoding

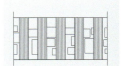

↖ **p. 237**
Rhythmization

↖ **p. 237**
Retrofitting

Neugasse site: Projects

Reciprocal frame structure
Thomas Papritz

This project responds to the partially listed existing building in a situational, pragmatic, and sensitive manner. The depot, built in the 1960s, now functions as a quarry. The spatial structural invention, originating from a deficiency, is a memorable feature of the project. The found steel beams, which were actually too short, were assembled into a reciprocal frame structure, which not only spans the new build but also configures the entire spatial arrangement of the classroom cluster. The trapezoidal sheet metal-concrete composite floor deck is cut into elements which are reused in the new build, along with the concrete slabs of the external cladding.

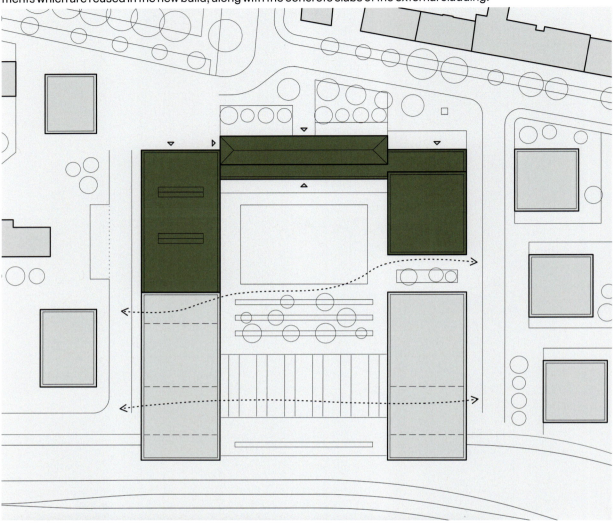

ZHAW IKE: Teaching

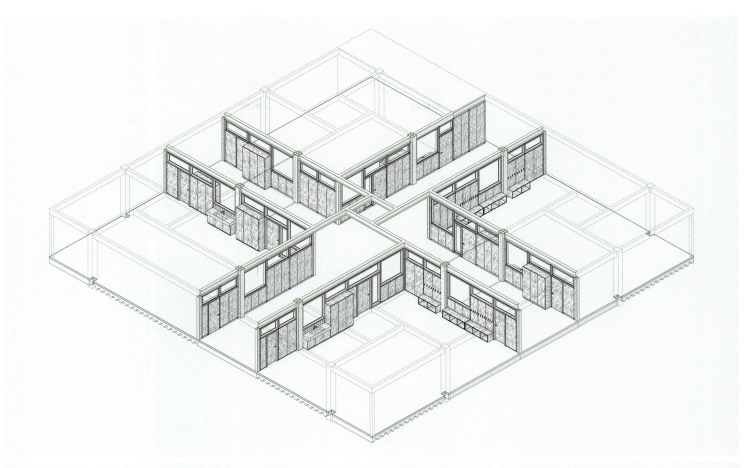

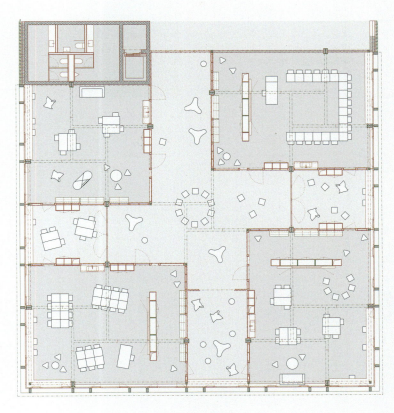

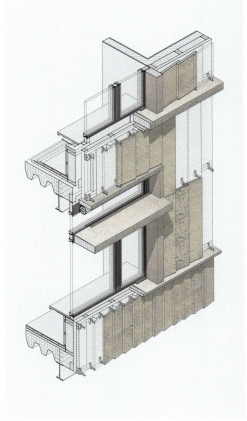

↖ **p. 236**
Addition

↖ **p. 237**
System separation

↖ **p. 236**
Modularity

↖ **p. 237**
Tolerance

↖ **p. 237**
Separability

Neugasse site: Projects

La machine
Raphael Bitzi

All that remains of the east wing of the locomotive shed are the brick walls of the end buildings. Spanned between them is the new three-storey school, topped by a huge roof terrace—an apparently new building that in reality attempts to exploit the full potential of the elements found on-site. The characteristic saw-tooth façade is formed from the tilted skylights. Consequently, the unheated corridors behind the façade have the appearance of verandas. We encounter the broken-off steel-concrete composite floor in the cross walls of the classrooms.

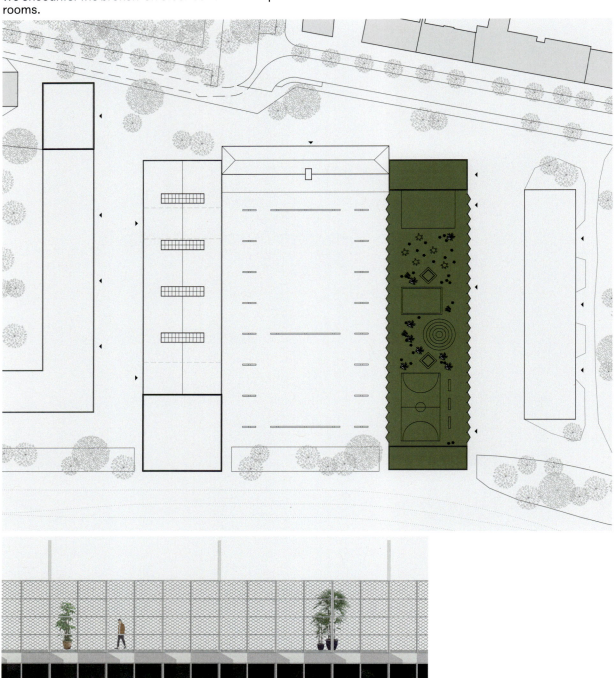

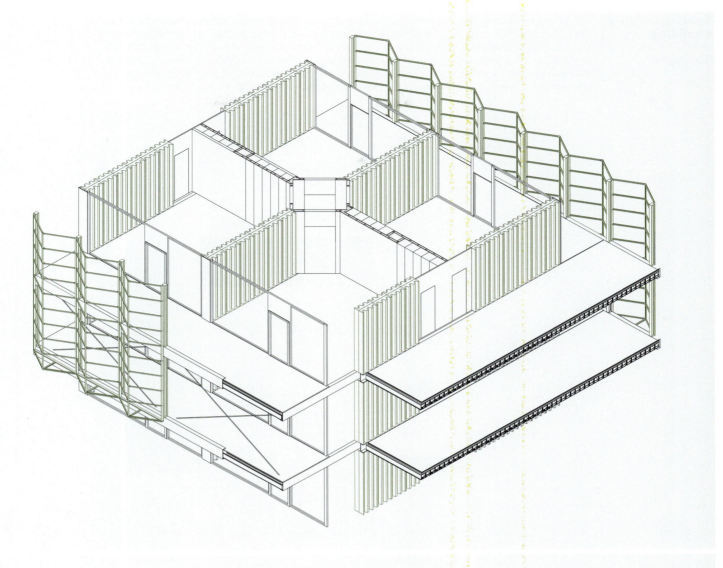

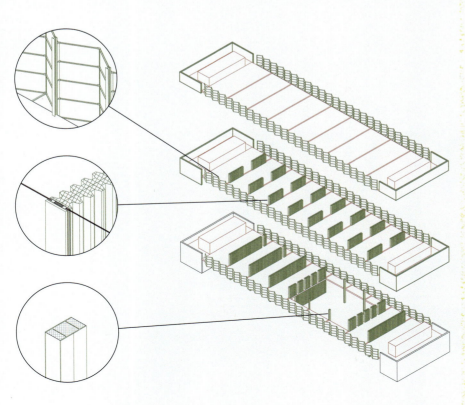

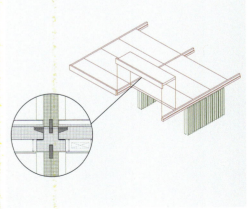

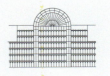
↖ **p. 236**
Modularity

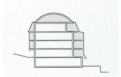
↖ **p. 236**
Buffering

↖ **p. 237**
Recoding

Neugasse site: Projects

Buildings within a building
Leonie Frommenwiler

The project aims to create child-friendly units and scales, coupled with a cheerful expression that almost lets you forget the industrial origins of the components. The combination of U-shaped roof trusses and the Y-shaped columns from the demolished train sheds provide inspiration for a new building type for a primary school. The units are lined up like Dutch townhouses, each with a classroom cluster: the communal rooms are on the lower floor, while on the upper floor, flooded with overhead daylight, are the more intimate classrooms.

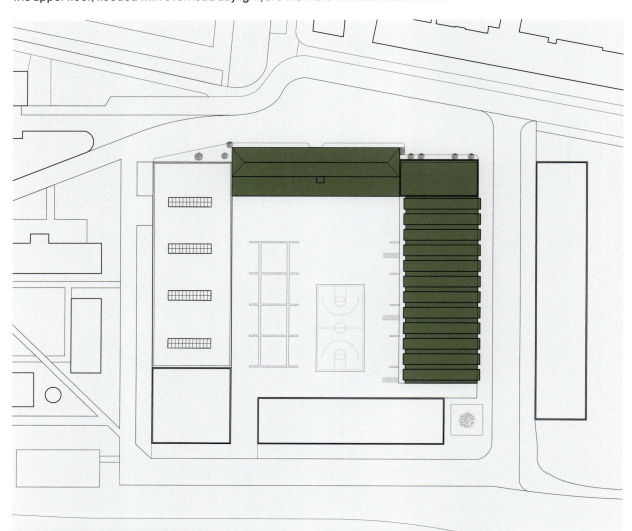

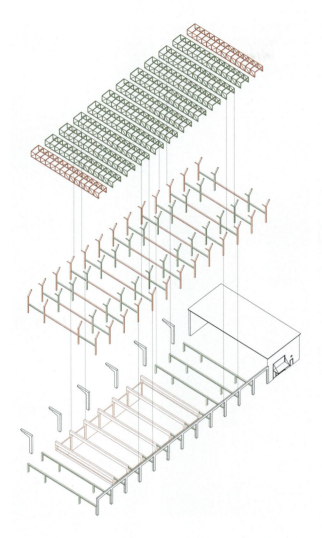
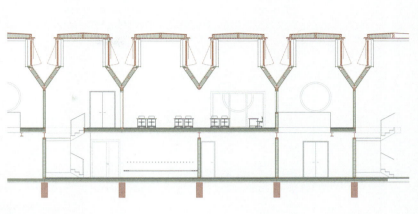
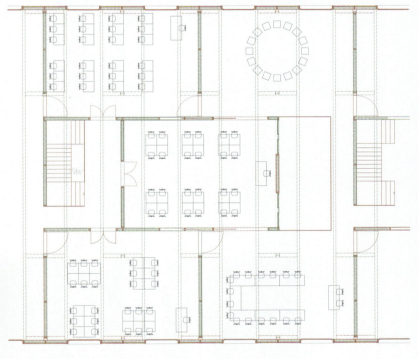

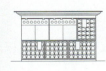
↖ **p. 236**
Pictoriality

↖ **p. 237**
Transfer

↖ **p. 237**
Transformation

Locomotive shed school
Sean Hoskyn

A new school building type is created from the radical reinterpretation of the existing building. In the locomotive shed, which underwent minimal alterations, the classroom clusters were positioned under the roof girders with skylights to optimize the distribution of daylight. Access to the units is via corridors along the façades, which function climatically as buffer spaces. They are able to compensate for any thermal shortcomings in the existing exterior envelope and the interior glazing, thus allowing for reused components to be utilized.

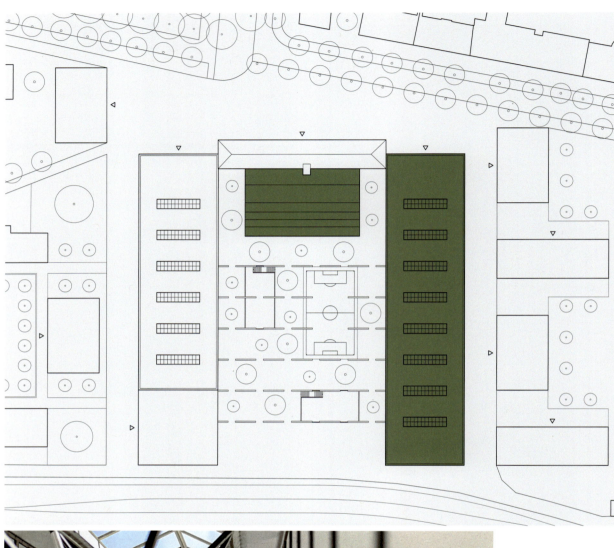

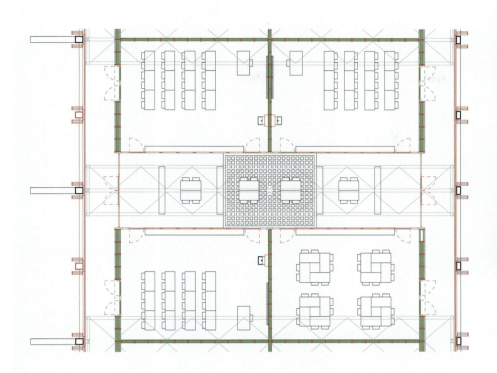

↖ **p. 236**
Continuity

↖ **p. 236**
Buffering

↖ **p. 237**
Transfer

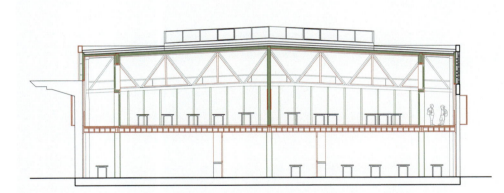

Circular construction—terminology

In the current discourse, the terminology of circular construction is heavily influenced by its origins in waste management. In various linguistic regions and contexts, certain terms have become established to designate the strategies of circular construction. However, these are not used uniformly. The following is a summary of some of them, without claiming to be exhaustive.
- In the Dutch parliament in 1979, Ad Lansink formulated a hierarchy of waste handling measures ('Lansink's ladder') aimed at reducing waste, which attracted a great deal of international attention. Reduce, Reuse, Recycle, Incinerate with energy recovery, Incinerate, send to Landfill.
- Since then, the waste hierarchy has been continuously refined and adapted in line with new technical possibilities. For example, in 2000, the Technical University of Delft differentiated the hierarchy for the construction industry, known as the 'Delft ladder': Prevention, Object renovation, Element reuse, Material reuse, Useful application, Immobilisation with useful application, Immobilisation, Incineration with energy recovery, Incineration, Landfill—see C. F. Hendriks, *Nationaal congres Bouw- en Sloopafval, kwaliteit in de keten* (Rotterdam: Nederlands studiecentrum, 2000); B. J. H. te Dorsthorst, T. Kowalczyk, C. F. Hendriks, and J. Kristinsson, 'From Grave to Cradle: Reincarnation of Building Materials', in *Proceedings of International Conference on Sustainable Building 2000* (Maastricht, 2000).
- In the English-language technical literature, the term reuse or re-use subsequently established itself in construction for the reutilization of components, irrespective of their function on the new site, as distinct from recycling, which merely describes the recovery of materials—see Bill Addis, *Building with Reclaimed Components and Materials: A Design Handbook for Reuse and Recycling* (New York: Routledge, 2006); Duncan Baker-Brown, *The Re-use Atlas: A Designer's Guide towards a Circular Economy* (London: RIBA Publishing, 2017).
- In the French-language technical literature, the term recyclage is used analogously to the English recycling for the recycling of building materials with loss of form. On the other hand, réutilisation (reuse with retention of form and the same function) and réemploi (reuse with retention of form for another function) are differentiated. The term récupération is used as an umbrella term for the reuse of obsolete building fabric—see Jean-Marc Huygen, *La poubelle et l'architecte: Vers le réemploi des matériaux* (Arles: Actes Sud, 2008); Julien Choppin and Nicola Delon (eds.), *Matière grise: Matériaux/réemploi/architecture* (Paris: Edition du Pavillon de l'Arsenal, 2014); Michaël Ghyoot, Lionel Devlieger, Lionel Billiet, and André Warnier, *Déconstruction et réemploi: Comment faire circuler les éléments de construction* (Lausanne: EPFL Press, 2018).
- However, in two more recent German-language publications, the term recycling is used in its original sense as meaning the recycling of building materials and components back into the materials cycle. If this involves a loss of form, the term Verwertung is used, with a differentiation made between Wiederverwertung (same production process) and Weiterverwertung (another production process with inferior results). Similarly, the term Wiederverwendung is defined as reuse for the same purpose, while Weiterverwendung denotes reuse for another, inferior purpose. At the same time, the terms upcycling and downcycling are used to describe the quality gradient between the materials' previous and subsequent usage or further processing. On the other hand, there is no neutral, non-judgemental umbrella term for the reuse of building components with retention of form—see Annette Hillebrandt, Petra Riegler-Floors, Anja Rosen, and Johanna Seggewies, *Atlas Recycling: Gebäude als Materialressource* (Munich: Detail, 2018); Daniel Stockhammer (ed.), *Upcycling: Wieder- und Weiterverwendung als Gestaltungsprinzip in der Architektur* (Zurich: Triest, 2020).
- For the title of the German pavilion of the 13th International Architecture Exhibition in Venice 2012, the curator, Muck Petzet, borrowed the terms Reduce Reuse Recycle from the waste management industry, linking them with architectural and urban planning strategies. As a result, the buzzwords gained considerable prominence, but their meanings also shifted. Reduce was used to describe a strategy of sufficiency; reuse included all forms of conversion and additions to existing buildings; and recycling was applied as an umbrella term for the reuse of materials and components in another locality—see Muck Petzet and Florian Heilmeyer (eds.), *Reduce, Reuse, Recycle: Architecture as Resource; German Pavilion, 13th International Architecture Exhibition, La Biennale di Venezia 2012* (Ostfildern: Hatje Cantz, 2012).
- In addition to the purely material-centric ecological-economic assessment and naming of circular processes, the reuse of building materials and components has long been a focus of research in the history of art and architecture. In the German-speaking discourse, the term spolia (Lat. 'spoils' = repurposed building fragments) has come to the fore, as it is closely linked to the origin and significance of building components. Various distinctions are drawn in the technical literature, depending on the places of origin and use. The term Wiederverwendung is employed as a neutral umbrella term for the reuse of building materials. This also brings the architectural historical discourse and the current debate closer together—see Stefan Altekamp, Carmen Marcks-Jacobs, and Peter Seiler (eds.), *Perspektiven der Spolienforschung 1. Spoliierung und Transposition,* Berlin: De Gruyter, 2013; Hans-Rudolf Meier, *Spolien: Phänomene der Wiederverwendung in der Architektur* (Berlin: Jovis, 2020).

The present publication takes up this idea and uses the term Wiederverwendung in a similar way to the English term reuse (or re-use): as an umbrella term for the reuse of dismantled components, independent of changes of use, quality standards, or its implicit meaning. This establishes a name for the reuse of building components without having to make an a priori judgement, which a differentiation of context would require (parity in terms of economy, environmental impact, design, cultural significance), and, as the K 118 case study has shown, it is almost impossible in practice, as building components usually fulfil several functions. For example, the Zellweger interior doors ↖ **p. 229** are being used again as internal doors. However, at their first installation site, they had to meet fire protection requirements. Their new usage no longer requires this—so, are they still being used for the same function? On the other hand, in the case of the Orion cladding slabs ↖ **p. 225**, it is obvious that their use as balcony floors differs from their initial purpose, although this new usage is not obviously inferior. The same applies to the Eventbau marquee floor panels ↖ **p. 231**, which now function as wall cladding. And what about the windows from Werk 1 ↖ **p. 226**? While they are again used as windows, it is as parts of box-type windows, owing to their inadequate insulation values. In return, a new, non-practical function is added. The characteristic industrial windows originated in the immediate neighbourhood and help to link the new build with its local history. In practice, it is often difficult to come to a clear judgement about the parity and equivalence of functions.

Biographies

Prof. Dr. iur. Andreas Abegg is Head of the Centre for Public Commercial Law at the ZHAW School of Management and Law, associate professor at the University of Lucerne, and a practising lawyer in Zurich. Since 2018, he, together with his team, has focused on legal questions surrounding the reuse of construction elements.

Marc Angst holds a degree in urban planning. As a member of baubüro in situ, and together with Pascal Hentschel, he was co-project lead for the K.118 project and was in charge of its scientific analysis on the architects' side as part of the ZHAW Circular Construction project. Since 2020, he has also been working as a reuse expert for Zirkular GmbH.

Prof. Dr. Oya Atalay Franck is an architect and has been Director of the ZHAW's Department of Architecture, Design and Civil Engineering since 2017. She is President of the European Association for Architectural Education EAAE and works as an expert in scientific organizations, including the Swiss National Science Foundation SNSF. Her most recent publications focus on research methodologies.

Guido Brandi is an architect and has been running his firm brandiguerra with offices in Zurich and Como together with Marco Guerra since 2020. He has been researching constructive, procedural, and economic questions of component reuse since 2018 as a research associate at ZHAW's Institute of Constructive Design as part of the Circular Construction project.

Barbara Buser is an architect. Ever since she co-founded the first Swiss building components exchange in the 1980s, she has been committed to sustainable, circular construction on many different levels. As a co-founder and co-managing director of baubüro in situ and a member of the project management team at Abendrot Foundation, she played a key role in getting the K.118 project off the ground. In 2020 she was awarded the Prix Meret Oppenheim together with Eric Honegger for her work.

Dr. Michael Eidenbenz is an architect and developer. Following many years of research and teaching at the ETH Zürich in the field of planning and construction processes, in 2019/2020 he was involved as a project manager in setting up the Building Sector Platform for ZHAW's Department of Architecture, Design and Civil Engineering.

Dr. Nathanea Elte is an architect and owner of a real estate consulting agency in Zurich. She is also a board member of the Mehr als Wohnen cooperative and has been President of the Allgemeine Baugenossenschaft Zürich ABZ since 2017.

Deborah Fehlmann is an architect and has been a research associate at the ZHAW Institute of Structural Design since 2019. As an architecture journalist, she writes articles for specialist publications on current issues in architecture, including the reuse of building components.

Patric Fischli-Boson has been running a civil engineering office in Ibach and Zurich together with Christoph Büeler since 2016. At the ZHAW's Department of Architecture, Design and Civil Engineering, he researches and teaches in the field of structural theory, steel construction and hybrid lightweight construction. He has been in charge of the Building Sector Platform since 2021.

Dr. **Michaël Ghyoot** studied architecture in Brussels and in 2008 joined the Rotor collective, where he focuses on research projects surrounding reuse in the construction sector. He is also active in the fields of exhibitions, teaching, and design assistance. He has co-authored the book *Déconstruction et réemploi* (EPFL Press, 2018).

Pascal Hentschel has been working as an architect for baubüro in situ since 2014. Together with Marc Angst, he was the project manager in charge of the K.118 project. Since 2020 he has been passing on his experience in reusing building components as an expert for Zirkular GmbH.

Dr. iur. Meinrad Huser is a lawyer specializing in construction and real estate law. He is a lecturer at the ZHAW Centre for Public Commercial Law, where he focuses on public law issues regarding the reuse of components.

Christian Kohler is a consultant for real estate financing at Alternative Bank Schweiz AG, which, as an ecologically and socially oriented bank, supports various societal concerns such as future-oriented living, renewable energies, and projects relating to the circular economy.

Marc Loeliger has been running the Loeliger Strub Architektur office in Zurich together with Barbara Strub since 1999. Since 2018, he has been working as a lecturer for ZHAW's master's programme in architecture, focusing on the reuse of components in design theory. He is continuing this work in his own practice, which he founded in 2019.

Dr. Michel Massmünster's work as a cultural anthropologist is situated at the interface of urban research, journalism and cultural education. As a journalist, he has been following the work of baubüro in situ on the K.118 project since 2018 and has documented his observations for this book.

Dr. iur. Annatina Menn is a practising lawyer in Zurich. She focuses on private law issues in the art and creative industries as well as in the construction and real estate sectors. In cooperation with the ZHAW's Centre for Public Commercial Law, she focuses on contractual issues relating to the reuse of components.

Prof. em. Dr. Dr. h. c. Ákos Moravánszky is an architect, architectural theorist, and historian, and associate professor emeritus of architectural theory at the Institute for the History and Theory of Architecture at the ETH Zürich. Since 2017, he has been a visiting professor at the Universidad de Navarra in Pamplona. His book *Metabolism: Material Transformation in Architecture* (Birkhäuser, 2017) takes a closer look at the metamorphosis of materials in architecture.

Kerstin Müller is an architect and a management board member for baubüro in situ AG. She is the managing director of Zirkular GmbH that focuses on specialist planning for a circular economy and reuse in the construction sector. In 2020 she became co-president of the Cirkla association. She also represents the German Chamber of Architects both on the climate advisory board of the city of Lörrach and in the Climate Energy Sustainability strategy group.

Dr. Andreas Oefner is a trained draughtsman and historian. Since 2006 he has been working intermittently for baubüro in situ. He has also been a member of the management board of Zirkular GmbH since 2020.

Katrin Pfäffli is an architect and sustainability expert. She is the founder of the architectural office K. Pfäffli in the office partnership preisig:pfäffli in Zurich. She works as a lecturer in the architecture course at the ZHAW and is involved with the Swiss Association of Engineers and Architects in the development of the SIA Energy Efficiency Path and the information sheet on embodied energy in buildings. Their June 2020 study, 'Grey Energy and Greenhouse Gas Emissions from Reused Building Components', forms the basis for the energy evaluation found in the K.118 case study.

Michael Pöll is a mechanical engineer with a degree from the ETH Zürich and an expert on healthy and ecological building materials. Since 2005 he has been working as a project manager for the City of Zurich's Office for Sustainable Construction. He oversees the specialist group of the Plattform Ökobilanzdaten im Baubereich (LCA data platform for the construction sector).

Tina Puffert is an architect and works in the real estate department of the Abendrot Stiftung pension fund, where she works to support socially, ecologically, and economically sustainable real estate development. As the owner representative, she is a member of the project management for Lagerplatz and thus acts as the client of the K.118 project.

Prof. François Renaud is an architect with an office in Zurich. He teaches at the ZHAW, where he headed the architecture course from 2003 to 2009 and the Institute of Constructive Design from 2013 to 2015. Among other topics, his teaching focuses on special questions relating to the history of technology.

Barbara Rentsch is an architect with a postgraduate degree in real estate management. As head of portfolio management at Immobilien Basel Stadt, she represents the public sector as the owner of the ELYS project on Basel's Lysbüchel site, for which reused components and those from storage inventory were used.

Alexis Ringli has been managing the office gadolaringli architekten in Zurich together with Peter Gadola since 2006. Since 2004 he has been a lecturer in the master's degree in architecture at the ZHAW, where his teaching in design theory focuses, among other things, on constructive aspects of the reuse and reusability of components.

Andreas Sonderegger is a founding member and partner of pool architects in Zurich. In addition to his involvement in the Krokodil architects' group and the BSA, he has been co-director of the Institute of Constructive Design at the ZHAW since 2017 and in this function is also responsible for the Circular Construction project.

Eva Stricker is an architect and writer based in Zurich. Since 2017 she has been working as a research associate at ZHAW's Institute of Constructive Design, where since 2018, as project manager of the research Circular Construction project as well as the present publication, she has been working on the topic of reusing building components.

Arne Vande Capelle studied engineering and architecture and has been working for Rotor in Brussels since 2017. In addition to competitions and research projects, he also helps planners and clients in developing reuse strategies for their projects, such as the Multi Tower project in Brussels.

Cyrille Veron studied civil engineering and until 2020 was head of acquisition, renovation, and conversion for German-speaking Switzerland at the general contractor and real estate developer Losinger Marazzi AG. Today he works for the Bricks company and has been in charge of the renovation department at Complex Bau AG since 2021. He is also a co-founder of the company sumami GmbH, a member of the board of directors of the component exchange Syphon, and a board member for the associations Be Circular and Cirkla.

Barbara Zeleny is an architect with many years of experience in architecture offices worldwide. From 2015, she managed the development projects Zürich Areale West at SBB Real Estate and in this function supervised the ZHAW master studio at the Neugasse site in the autumn semester of 2019. She is currently head of the investment property development department at SBB with a focus on Switzerland-wide urban transformation areas.

Image credits

Introduction ↖p.10
Life cycle model © ZHAW Institut Konstruktives Entwerfen and baubüro in situ

Reuse! ↖p.11
[Fig.1] © Ueli Keller
[Figs.2, 3, 5, 6] © baubüro in situ, photo: Anna Buser
[Fig.4] © ZHAW IKE

Circular materiality ↖p.17
[Fig.1] Santa Costanza Church, Rome, 4th century Source: Pischel, G., Storia Universale dell'Arte, Vol. 1, Verona 1966
[Fig.2] Pilastri acritani in front of the Basilica San Marco, Venice, 6th century
[Fig.3] Wall of the Frankish Castle of Parikia, Paros 13th century © Ákos Moravánszky
[Fig.4] Lesezeichen Salbke, KARO Architekten, Magdeburg 2009 © Anja Schlamann
[Fig.5] Americana spolia in a warehouse in Bergamot Station, Santa Monica 1995
[Fig.6] Billiards room at Hearst Castle, Julia Morgan, San Simeon 1919–1945 © Ákos Moravánszky
[Fig.7] Plinth façade of the *Chicago Tribune* high-rise tower, John Mead Howells and Raymond Hood, Chicago 1923–1925 © Prof. Annabel Wahrton
[Fig.8] Marcellus Theatre, Rome, 1st century © Jensens, CC BY-SA 3.0
[Fig.9] Mosque-Cathedral of Córdoba, 8th–17th century
[Fig.10] Tempio Malatestiano, Leon Battista Alberti, Rimini 1450–1460
[Fig.11] Gehry House, Frank Gehry, first remodel, Santa Monica 1977–1978 © Ákos Moravánszky
[Fig.12] Main entrance of Stockholm City Hall, Ragnar Östberg, Stockholm 1911–1923 © Holger Ellgaard, CC BY-SA 3.0
[Figs.13, 14] Footpaths on Philopappos Hill, Dimitris Pikionis, Athens 1951–1957 © Ákos Moravánszky
[Fig.15] Exhibition building of the new city, Francesco Venezia, Gibellina Nuova 1980–1987 © alfio, Source: flickr, Link: https://www.flickr.com/photos/alfiogreen/2196211602/?
[Fig.16] Pile of debris in front of the new city hall, Leipzig 1949 SLUB/Deutsche Fotothek, Rössing, Roger & Rössing, Renate
[Fig.17] The 'Liebknecht-Portal' of the Berlin Palace, Roland Korn and Hans E. Bogatzky, Berlin 1962–1964 © Deutsches Bundesarchiv Image 183-C1009-0020-002, author: Quaschinsky, Hans-Günter, 9 Oct. 1964
[Fig.18] Cover of *Adhocism: The Case for Improvisation*, 1972 Source: Jencks, C. and Silver, N., *Adhocism: The Case for mprovisation*. London 1972
[Fig.19] Studio for Robert Motherwell, Pierre Chareau, East Hampton 1946 © Judith Turner
[Fig.20] Earthship house built following the principles of Michael E. Reynolds, USA 2011 © Biodiesel 33, CC BY-SA 3.0
[Fig.21] Cover of *Garbage Housing*, 1973 Source: *Garbage Housing, Architectural Design* vol XLIII, 12 (1973)
[Fig.22] Lucy's House, Rural Studio, Hale County, Alabama 2002 Source: momeld.wordpress.com
[Fig.23] Fondazione Prada, OMA, Milan 2015 © Ákos Moravánszky
[Fig.24] Pavilion for Vodka Ceremonies, Alexander Brodsky, Moscow region 2009 © Yuri Palmin
[Fig.25] Casa Girasole, Luigi Moretti, Rome 1947–1950 © Ákos Moravánszky
[Fig.26] City Hall, F. P. J. Peutz, Heerlen 1936–1942 © Ákos Moravánszky
[Fig.27] Put-away House, Alison and Peter Smithson, 1993–2000 © The Smithson Family Collection, London
[Fig.28] St. Michael Church, Jože Plečnik, Laibacher Moor, Slovenia, 1937–1938, interior fittings 1940 © Damjan Prelovšek
[Fig.29] Collective housing of the Seitogakushi School, Shin Takasuga, Miyake Island, Japan 1980 Source: Suzuki, H., *Modernes Bauen in Japan*, Stuttgart 1987, 108
[Fig.30] Marshall Field Wholesale Store, Henry Hobson Richardson, Chicago 1896 Source: Brube, O. W., Pran, P.C. and Schulze, F., *100 Years of Architecture in Chicago. Continuity of Structure and Form*, Chicago 1976, 18; photo of street corner façade
[Fig.31] Swiss Pavilion EXPO 2000, Peter Zumthor, Hanover 2000 © Roland Halbe
[Fig.32] Redesign of the city hall ensemble, Iván Kotsis, Székesfehérvár 1938 Source: Kotsis I., *A székesfehérvári régi városháza helyreállítása és kiépítése*, Budapest 1939, 143
[Fig.33] Rudolph Olgiati, door collection, Flims © Christian Kerez
[Fig.34] St. Anna Church, Rudolf Schwarz, Düren 1951–1956 © Ákos Moravánszky
[Fig.35] Ningbo Museum, Wang Shu, Ningbo 2008 © Siyuwj, CC BY-SA 3.0

K.118 reportage

Hunting and gathering ↖p.35
[Fig.1] Public Domain, Source: http://www.nycarchitecture.com/GON/GON013.htm
[Figs.2, 4, 5, 7] © baubüro in situ
[Figs.3, 6] © Martin Zeller

Designing and joining ↖p.39
[Figs.1, 4, 6] © Martin Zeller
[Figs.2, 3, 5] © baubüro in situ

Testing and planning ↖p.42
[Figs.1, 3, 6] © Martin Zeller
[Fig.2] © Christian Merz
[Figs.4, 5] © Saskia Widmer
[Fig.7] © baubüro in situ

Constructing and coordinating ↖p.46
[Figs.1, 5] © Matthias Niedermann/Stellwerkost
[Fig.2] © Martin Zeller
[Figs.3, 4, 6, 7] © baubüro in situ

Adapting, repairing, reinstalling ↖p.51
[Figs.1, 4] © Vanessa Püntener
[Figs.2, 3, 7, 8] © baubüro in situ
[Fig.6] © Martin Zeller
[Fig.5] © ZHAW
[Fig.9] © Jusuf Supuk / ZHAW

Essays

Reusers ↖p.59
[Figs.1–3, 27–31] © Bibliothèque Kandinsky, MNAM/CCI, Centre Pompidou. Fonds Jean Prouvé
[Fig.4] © Crovella Garelli Family
[Figs.5, 32, 33] © Marcello Mariana
[Figs.6–8, 34, 35] © Demanio italiano / Fondo archivistico Carlo Mollino
[Figs.9–11, 38–42] © A&P Smithson Hexenhaus-Archiv, Lauenförde
[Fig.12] © Nicola Lederer
[Figs.13–19, 45, 46, 48, 49] © Archiv Czech / Architekturzentrum Wien Collection
[Figs.20, 21, 44, 47] © Gabriele Kaiser
[Figs.22, 23] © Alexander Brodsky and Ilya Utkin
[Figs.24–26, 50, 51] © Yuri Palmin
[Figs.36, 37] © A&P Smithson Hexenhaus-Archiv, Lauenförde, photo: Roland Halbe
[Fig.43] © Margherita Spiluttini / Architekturzentrum Wien Collection
[Fig.52] © Alexander Brodsky
[Fig.53] © R adept, CC BY-SA 4.0

Where there's a will … ↖p.79
[Fig.1] © Stiftung Sitterwerk und Kunstgiesserei St. Gallen
[Figs.2–6, 24] © Katalin Deér / Stiftung Sitterwerk und Kunstgiesserei St. Gallen
[Fig.7] © Tierwelt AG
[Figs.8–10, 30, 32, 33] © MOKA Architekten
[Figs.11, 34–37] © N11 Architekten
[Figs.12, 13] © Thoma Holz GmbH
[Figs.14, 15, 38–40] © Corinne Cuendet
[Fig.16] © Yves Meilen
[Figs.17–23, 43, 44] © Martin Zeller
[Fig.25] © Heinrich Helfenstein; gta Archive / ETH Zürich
[Figs.26–28] © Flury+Furrer Architekten
[Figs.29, 31] © Merlin Photography Ltd
[Figs.41, 42] © Christian Jelk
[Fig.45] © baubüro in situ

Out of scarcity ↖p.95
[Fig.1] Source: http://baguenaudes.net/toitures-a-la-philibert/
[Figs.2, 3, 17] Source: De l'Orme, P., *Nouvelles inventions pour bien bastir et à petits fraiz*, Paris 1561, plate 3
[Figs.4–6, 19–22] Source: Cointeraux, F., *École d'architecture rurale …*, vol. 1, Paris 1790, plates II, IX, X, IV, V, VI, VII
[Fig.7] Source: Polonceau, C., 'Notice sur un nouveau système de charpente en bois et en fer', in: *Revue générale de l'architecture et des travaux publics* (Paris), January 1840, 27-32, plate 2.
[Figs.8, 27, 28, 30] © Victoria & Albert Museum, London
[Fig.9] © Wikimedia Commons Domain; photographer: Philip Henry Delamotte
[Fig.10] Source: Downes C. and Cowper C., *The Building Erected in Hyde Park for the Great Exhibition of the Works of Industry of all Nations*, 1851, London 1852
[Fig.11] Source: Klaus Winter and Wolfgang Rug, *Bautechnik* 69, issue 4 (1992), 86
[Fig.12] © Timothy Hursley
[Fig.13] © Håkan Sandbring / AIX Arkitekter
[Fig.14] © Natasja Jovic / AIX Arkitekter
[Fig.15] Source: Krafft, J. C., *Plans, coupes et élévations de diverses productions de l'art de la charpente exécutées …*, Paris 1805, plate 71, 272
[Figs.16, 18] Source: Maréchal, J., 1786, Bibliothèque Nationale de France, 89, 90
[Fig.23] Source: Collignon, E., *Les Travaux publics de la France …*, Paris 1883 / Bibliothèque Nationale de France, 91
[Fig.24] © Mbzt, CC BY-SA 3.0
[Fig.25] Source: de Dartein, F., Boulard, J., *Documents sur les fermes métalliques à grande ouverture*, Paris 1891, 95
[Fig.26] © AREP; photographer: Claude Le Breton
[Fig.29] Drawing by Heinz Ronner and Stephen Roethke, Source: Peters, T. F., *Building the Nineteenth Century*, London 1996

Circular load-bearing structures ↖p.111
[Figs.1, 2] © Toni Rüttimann, CC BY-SA 3.0
[Fig.3] © SRF bi de Lüt, 17 Feb. 2018
[Figs.4, 20] © Jan Brütting, Structural Xploration Lab, EPFL
[Fig.5] Source: da Vinci, L., Studies on roof structures, 1508-1510, *Codex Atlanticus*, no. 899v
[Fig.6] Source: Pieper, J., *Pienza: Der Entwurf einer humanistischen Weltsicht*, Fellbach 1997, 548
[Fig.7] Source: Thönnissen, U., *Hebelstabwerke: Tradition und Innovation*, Zurich 2015
[Fig.8] Source: Rondelet, J. B., *Traité théorique et pratique de l'art de bâtir.* Paris 1812-1814. ETH Bibliothek Zürich, Rar 8949, https://doi.org/10.3931/e-rara-45709 / Public Domain Mark
[Fig.9] Source: Müller, P., *Sternwarten in Bildern*, Berlin/Heidelberg 1992
[Fig.10] © Felipe Gabaldón, CC BY 2.0
[Fig.11] © ZHAW, Corporate Communications, Manuel Martin
[Figs.12, 14, 15] © CPC AG
[Figs.13, 32–35] © ZHAW, Dept A, IKE, Fachgruppe FVK
[Figs.16–19] © Dan Vander Zwalm
[Figs.21, 22] © Swissgrid AG
[Fig.23] © Lucas Sager / APC Architectural Pioneering Consultants Ltd.
[Figs.24–26] © Udo Thönissen
[Figs.27, 28] © Iwan Baan / ETH Zürich / Block Research Group
[Fig.29] © ETH Zürich / Block Research Group; photographer: Nick Krouwel
[Figs.30, 31] © ETH Zürich / Block Research Group

A circular approach to architecture ↖p.129
[Fig.1] © Assemble, 2019
[Fig.2] © Tony Trichanh
[Figs.3–8, 25–28] © Studio Albori
[Figs.9–11, 32, 33] © SeilerLinhart Architekten
[Fig.12] © Association Les Pierres Sauvages, in: https://www.fernandpouillon.com/marseille_banchep.html
[Figs.13, 14, 37, 38] © Atelier d'Architecture Perraudin / WYSWYG
[Fig.15] Source: Brand, S., *How Buildings Learn: What Happens After They're Built*, London 1994
[Fig.16] Source: Hyde, C., 'Assembly-Line Architecture: Albert Kahn and the Evolution of the U.S. Auto Factory, 1905-1940', in: *The Journal of the Society for Industrial Archeology*, 22, 2 (1996), 5-24 See http://www.jstor.org/stable/40968351
[Fig.17] © Dgtmedia-Simone, CC BY 3.0
[Figs.18, 41, 42] © Lacaton Vassal (edited by ZHAW)
[Figs.19, 39, 40] © Philippe Ruault
[Fig.20] Source: Semper, G., *Keramik, Tektonik, Stereotomie, Metallotechnik für sich betrachtet und in Beziehung zur Baukunst*, vol. 2. Munich 1863, 276
[Fig.21] © Fondazione Renzo Piano; photographer: Paul Vincent
[Fig.22] © Iwan Baan / Studio Anne Holtrop
[Fig.23] © gta Archiv / ETH Zürich, Fritz Haller
[Fig.24] © Ensemble Studio
[Figs.29–31] © Rasmus Norlander
[Figs.34–36] ©11h45
[Fig.43] © Zooey Braun
[Fig.44] © Roland Halbe
[Figs.45–48] © Werner Sobek

Discussion

New generalists, new specialists ↖p.151
[Fig.1] © Dirk Altenkirch
[Figs.2, 3, 5, 7–11, 13, 14] © Rotor
[Fig.4] © Vplus Architects
[Fig.6] © Mobius Réemploi
[Fig.12] © opalis.eu
[Fig.15] © Lola Pertsowsky

New paths toward net zero? ↖p.165
[Figs.1–3] © ZHAW IKE and baubüro in situ

Values and processes ↖p.177
[Figs.1, 2] © BIM Facility AG

From part to whole and back again ↖p.197
[Figs.1, 2, 4, 5, 7–17] © ZHAW IKE
[Fig.3] © Aregger AG
[Fig.6] © baubüro in situ

K.118 case study

Component catalogue ↖p.218
All photographs © Martin Zeller

Reuse in construction ↖p.283
[Fig.1] Source: Bernardo Bellotto, ruins of the Kreuzkirche in Dresden, 1765, Kunsthaus Zürich
[Fig.2] © Loeliger Strub Architekten
[Fig.3] © F.L.C. / 2022, ProLitteris, Zurich

Creating K.118 ↖p.289
[Figs.1–8, 12–28] © Martin Zeller
[Figs.9–11] © Matthias Niedermann / Stellwerkost

K.118 plan set ↖p.313
All plans and images © baubüro in situ

ZHAW IKE: Teaching ↖p.323
[Fig.1] Source: Google Maps
[Fig.2] © ETH Library Zurich, Image archive, photo: Hans-Peter Bärtschi, SIK_01-024743 /CC BY-SA 4.0
All other plans and images © ZHAW IKE

Cover
All images taken from inside this book
A]: ↖**p.41** [Fig.4], ↖**p.44** [Figs.4–5], ↖**p.67** [Fig.15], ↖**p.74** [Fig.32], ↖**p.77** [Fig.50], ↖**p.93** [Fig.43], ↖**p.107** [Fig.22], ↖**p.125** [Fig.23], ↖**p.145** [Fig.37], ↖**p.145** [Fig.35], ↖**p.155** [Fig.4]
B]: ↖**p.28** [Fig.31], ↖**p.36** [Fig.4], ↖**p.38** [Fig.6], ↖**p.46** [Fig.1], ↖**p.76** [Fig.45], ↖**p.93** [Figs.43, 44], ↖**p.104** [Fig.12], ↖**p.138** [Fig.19], ↖**p.186** [Fig.2]

Despite best efforts, we may have not been able to identify the holders of copyright and printing rights for all the illustrations. Copyright holders not mentioned in the credits are asked to substantiate their claims, and recompense will be made according to standard practice.

Imprint

Edited by
ZHAW School of Architecture, Design and
Civil Engineering; Institute of Constructive Design (IKE),
Eva Stricker, Guido Brandi, Andreas Sonderegger

baubüro in situ AG and Zirkular GmbH
Marc Angst, Barbara Buser, Michel Massmünster

Project supervision
Eva Stricker

Content editing
Marc Angst, Guido Brandi, Barbara Buser,
Michel Massmünster, Andreas Sonderegger, Eva Stricker

K.118 case study
Concept and content:
Marc Angst, Guido Brandi, Eva Stricker
Experts:
• Design and construction: Marc Loeliger, Alexis Ringli,
Alain Roserens, Andreas Sonderegger
• Construction organization: Annatina Menn (pp. 244, 245),
Michael Eidenbenz (pp. 240–243, 246, 247)
• Costs: Michael Eidenbenz, Pascal Hentschel,
Selma Nayme-Schulz, Cyrille Veron
• Greenhouse gas emissions: Harald Huth, Michael Pöll,
Katrin Pfäffli, Kerstin Müller, Dario Vittani

Text contributions
Marc Angst, Oya Atalay Franck, Guido Brandi, Barbara Buser,
Deborah Fehlmann, Patric Fischli-Boson, Marc Loeliger,
Michel Massmünster, Annatina Menn, Ákos Moravánszky,
Andreas Oefner, François Renaud, Alexis Ringli,
Andreas Sonderegger, Eva Stricker
Editorial texts: Andreas Sonderegger (pp. 322–339),
Eva Stricker (all others)

Discussion contributions
Andreas Abegg, Marc Angst, Guido Brandi, Michael
Eidenbenz, Nathanea Elte, Michaël Ghyoot, Pascal
Hentschel, Meinrad Huser, Christian Kohler,
Marc Loeliger, Kerstin Müller, Katrin Pfäffli, Michael Pöll,
Tina Puffert, Barbara Rentsch, Alexis Ringli, Andreas
Sonderegger, Eva Stricker, Arne Vande Capelle,
Cyrille Veron, Barbara Zeleny

Editorial concept
Eva Stricker with Ludovic Balland and Annina Schepping

Design and typesetting
Annina Schepping and Ludovic Balland
Typography Cabinet GmbH, Basel

Infographics concept and design (pp. 213–263)
Annina Schepping and Ludovic Balland

Font
Waldeck ©Isia Yurovsky

Plan drawings
Michèle Brand, Guido Brandi, Benjamin Poignon

Photographs K.118 (pp. 218–232, 289–294, 298–312)
Martin Zeller
All other photographs: see image credits

Translations
Horner Translations, David Koralek, Ian Pepper,
Iain Reynolds

Copy editing
Simon Cowper, Lisa Schons

Proofreading
Colette Forder

Image processing, printing, and binding
DZA Druckerei zu Altenburg GmbH, Thuringia

Paper
• Cover: Peydur lissé 135 g/m², Peyer Graphics
• Enviro Ahead 115 g/m², INAPA
• Creative Print diamant 120 g/m², IGEPA

© 2022 ZHAW Institute for Constructive Design,
baubüro in situ AG and Park Books AG, Zurich
© for the texts: the authors
© for the images: see image credits

Park Books
Niederdorfstrasse 54
8001 Zurich
Switzerland
www.park-books.com

Park Books is being supported by the Federal Office of
Culture with a general subsidy for the years 2021–2024.

All rights reserved; no part of this publication may be
reproduced, stored in a retrieval system or transmitted in
any form or by any means, electronic, mechanical,
photocopying, recording, or otherwise, without the prior
written consent of the publisher.

ISBN 978-3-03860-295-8

This book is also available in German:
ISBN 978-3-03860-259-0

Translators' note: Unless otherwise noted, all cited passages
in the texts for which no published English editions
were available have been translated from German by the
translators of this volume.

The publication of this book was initiated by Astrid Staufer
and made possible by the ZHAW School of Architecture,
Design and Civil Engineering. It was created as part of the
Circular Construction research project by the ZHAW
Institute of Constructive Design in cooperation with baubüro
in situ and Zirkular GmbH. The project was financially
supported by Stiftung Abendrot, the Federal Office for the
Environment, the Swiss Federal Railways, the Office
for Sustainable Construction of the City of Zurich's Building
Department and the Office for the Environment in Basel.

ZHAW IKE / baubüro in situ

Michel Massmünster

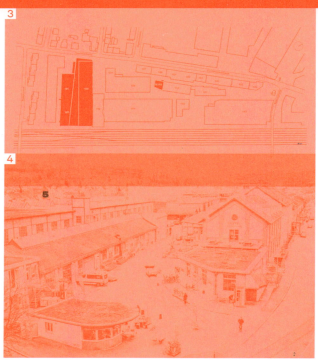

[Fig. 3] The Lagerplatz in the former Sulzer site: the location of the ZHAW School of Architecture, Design and Civil Engineering (large) and that of K.118 (small) are marked in black.
[Fig. 4] The Lagerplatz brings together provisional and existing materials.

Removal of a Belgian blue limestone block.

Playing with the available spaces: in 1990/91, the former boiler shop was the first hall of the Lagerplatz site to be repurposed and has since served the ZHAW's School of Architecture, Design and Civil Engineering as a teaching and research facility.

'How can an industrial building complex be given a different function? Experiments on this are extremely difficult, yet it's also a very exciting area of work!'